THE ADMINISTRATION
OF THE PTOLEMAIC POSSESSIONS
OUTSIDE EGYPT

COLUMBIA STUDIES IN THE CLASSICAL TRADITION

under the direction of

WILLIAM V. HARRIS (Editor) — W. T. H. JACKSON
PAUL OSKAR KRISTELLER — WALTHER LUDWIG

VOLUME IV

LEIDEN
E. J. BRILL
1976

THE ADMINISTRATION
OF THE
PTOLEMAIC POSSESSIONS
OUTSIDE EGYPT

BY

ROGER S. BAGNALL

With 3 maps

LEIDEN
E. J. BRILL
1976

Columbia Studies in the Classical Tradition *publishes monographs by members of the Columbia faculty and by former Columbia students in the following fields: Greek and Latin literature, Greek and Roman history, classical archaeology, and the influence of classical tradition on mediaeval, Renaissance and modern cultures.*

The publication of this book was aided by the Stanwood Cockey Lodge Foundation.

ISBN 90 04 04490 6

For my father and mother

CONTENTS

PREFACE

This book is a revised version of my University of Toronto dissertation, submitted in 1972, the product of graduate study supported by the Canada Council, to which I again express my thanks. Despite repeated revision, it still wears the aspect of a dissertation in the fullness of the treatment given to many problems. Much of the evidence, however, has never been collected or discussed in a systematic fashion, and this approach still seems to me the most suitable one.

Not the least of the pleasures of finishing six years of work on this book is the opportunity to renew my thanks to the institutions and people who have helped me along the way. The writing was done in Toronto and in Athens; to the staff and members of the American School of Classical Studies in 1970-1 I remain grateful for their help, above all in facing the problems of everyday life in Greece. Others were generous in their assistance to my work: Mando Caramessini-Oikonomidou, director of the National Numismatic Collection, kindly allowed me to study the collection's records and afforded me every help in doing so; and W. Kendrick Pritchett and Wallace E. McLeod took time to discuss various problems with me.

In my travels in Cyprus I was able to discuss epigraphical problems with Ino Nicolaou of the Cyprus Museum; to her and to Vassos Karageorghis, Director of Antiquities, I owe much of the pleasure and profit of that journey. In my travels in Cyprus, Egypt, Lebanon, and Turkey I was accompanied by Ian Begg, whose help was often invaluable. These journeys were made possible by travel grants from the Canada Council and the School of Graduate Studies in the University of Toronto.

A number of scholars have read and helped to improve the text of the book at various stages: G. V. Sumner, P. S. Derow, J. F. Gilliam, and John F. Oates have all made contributions. Alan E. Samuel suggested the topic, supervised the dissertation, and gave both encouragement and criticism where they were needed.

I am happy to acknowledge my very great debt to Louis Robert, whose writings have offered a stimulus and model for my study of inscriptions and who kindly read the manuscript in its final stages to its great benefit. His student Thomas Drew-Bear has, since our year in Athens, contributed much as my collaborator, critic and friend; he has read much of this book more than once and suggested numerous improvements. The faults that have survived the help and criticism of these many friends are to be laid to the charge not of their kindness but of my obstinacy.

My wife Whitney patiently bore my preoccupation with this thesis, even while she was writing her own, and has foiled the attempts of our son Alexander to prevent its completion; for this I am indeed grateful.

Columbia University   Roger S. Bagnall
New York
January, 1975

ABBREVIATIONS

1. GENERAL

BMC	*Catalogue of the Greek Coins in the British Museum*, London, 1873-
Bull. épig.	"Bulletin épigraphique" by Jeanne and Louis Robert, in *Revue des études grecques*, cited by year and item
Bull. épig. sém.	"Bulletin d'épigraphie sémitique" by Javier Teixidor, in *Syria*
FGrH	F. Jacoby, *Die Fragmente der griechischen Historiker*, Berlin, 1923-1955
LSJ	H. G. Liddell and Robert Scott, *A Greek-English Lexicon*, 9th ed. by H. S. Jones, Oxford, 1940
Pros. Ptol.	W. Peremans, E. Van 't Dack et al., *Prosopographia Ptolemaica*, 6 vols., Louvain, 1950-
RE	*Paulys Realencyclopädie der Classischen Altertumswissenschaft*, ed. G. Wissowa, W. Kroll et al.
SNG	*Sylloge Nummorum Graecorum*, cited by collection (*SNG Copenhagen*, etc.)

References to ancient authors should be self-explanatory.

2. PERIODICALS

AJA	*American Journal of Archaeology*
ANS Mus. Notes	*American Numismatic Society Museum Notes*
Annuario	*Annuario della (regia) Scuola Archeologica di Atene*
Arch. Delt.	Ἀρχαιολογικὸν Δελτίον
Ἀρχ. Ἐφ.	Ἀρχαιολογικὴ Ἐφημερίς
Archiv	*Archiv für Papyrusforschung und verwandte Gebiete*
Ath. Mitt.	*Mitteilungen des deutschen Archäologischen Instituts, Athenische Abteilung*
BCH	*Bulletin de Correspondence Hellénique*
BSA Alex.	*Bulletin de la Société Archéologique d'Alexandrie*
CRAI	*Comptes-rendus de l'Académie des Inscriptions et Belles-Lettres*
Hellenica	L. Robert, *Hellenica*
JEA	*Journal of Egyptian Archaeology*
JHS	*Journal of Hellenic Studies*
JIAN	*Journal international d'archéologie numismatique*
Op. Ath.	*Opuscula Atheniensia*
RDAC	*Report of the Department of Antiquities of Cyprus*

Rev. arch.   *Revue archéologique*
Rev. hist.   *Revue historique*
Rev. num.   *Revue numismatique*
Rev. phil.   *Revue de philologie*
Riv. Fil.   *Rivista di Filologia*
ZPE   *Zeitschrift für Papyrologie und Epigraphik*

3. INSCRIPTIONS

Asylieurkunden   R. Herzog, G. Klaffenbach, *Asylieurkunden
                                    aus Kos*, *Abh. Berlin Akad.*, Kl. f. Spr., Lit.
                                    u. Kunst, Jg. 1952, 1
CIG   A. Boeckh, *Corpus Inscriptionum Graecarum*,
                                    Berlin, 1828-1877
Durrbach, *Choix*   F. Durrbach, *Choix d'inscriptions de Délos*,
                                    Paris, 1921
I. Brit. Mus.   *Ancient Greek Inscriptions in the British
                                    Museum*, Oxford, 1874-1916
I. Cret.   M. Guarducci, *Inscriptiones Creticae*, 4 vols.,
                                    Roma, 1935-
I. Délos   *Inscriptions de Délos* (various eds.), Paris,
                                    1926-
I. Delphin.   G. Kawerau and Albert Rehm, *Das Delphi-
                                    nion in Milet* (*Milet* III), Berlin, 1914
IG   *Inscriptiones Graecae*
I. Gr. Lat. Alex.   E. Breccia, *Iscrizioni greche e latine* (Cat. gén.
                                    des antiq. égypt. du Musée d'Alexandrie),
                                    Cairo, 1911
I. Hell. Paphos   T. B. Mitford, "The Hellenistic Inscriptions
                                    of Old Paphos," *Annual of the British School
                                    at Athens* 56, 1961, pp. 1-41
I. Kourion   T. B. Mitford, *The Inscriptions of Kourion*,
                                    Philadelphia, 1971
I. Labraunda   *Labraunda: Swedish Excavations and Re-
                                    searches*, III: *The Greek Inscriptions*, by J.
                                    Crampa, Stockholm, 1969-1972
I. Lindos   Chr. Blinkenberg, *Lindos* II: *Inscriptions*,
                                    2 vols., Copenhagen, 1941
I. Magn.   O. Kern, *Die Inschriften von Magnesia am
                                    Maeander*, Berlin, 1900
I. Philae   A. Bernand, *Les inscriptions grecques de
                                    Philae* I, Paris, 1969
I. Priene   F. Hiller von Gaertringen, *Die Inschriften
                                    von Priene*, Berlin, 1906
Le Bas-Waddington,   Ph. Le Bas and W. H. Waddington, *Voyage
     Voyage arch.   archéologique en Grèce et en Asie Mineure*,
                                    Paris, 1847-1870
OGIS   W. Dittenberger, *Orientis Graecae Inscrip-
                                    tiones Selectae*, 2 vols., Leipzig, 1903-05
SEG   *Supplementum Epigraphicum Graecum*
Syll.³   W. Dittenberger, *Sylloge Inscriptionum Grae-
                                    carum*, 3rd ed., 4 vols., Leipzig, 1915-24 (2nd
                                    ed., 1898-1901)

TAM	*Tituli Asiae Minoris*
Tit. Cal.	M. Segre, *Tituli Calymnii, Annuario* 22-23, 1944-45 (1952)
Welles, *Royal Correspondence*	C. Bradford Welles, *Royal Correspondence in the Hellenistic Period*, New Haven, 1934

4. PAPYRI

Papyri are cited according to J. F. Oates, R. S. Bagnall, and W. H. Willis, "A Checklist of Editions of Greek Papyri and Ostraca," *Bulletin of the American Society of Papyrologists* 11, 1974, pp. 1-35.

5. MONOGRAPHS

Bengtson, *Die Strategie*	H. Bengtson, *Die Strategie in der hellenistischen Zeit*, 3 vols., München, 1937-52
Cohen, *De Magistratibus*	David Cohen, *De Magistratibus Aegyptiis externas Lagidarum provincias administrantibus*, The Hague, 1912
Fraser, *Ptol. Alex.*	P. M. Fraser, *Ptolemaic Alexandria*, 3 vols., Oxford, 1972
Habicht, *Gottmenschentum*[2]	C. Habicht, *Gottmenschentum und griechische Städte*, München, 1970
Holleaux, *Études*	M. Holleaux, *Études d'épigraphie et d'histoire grecques*, 6 vols., ed. L. Robert, Paris, 1938-68
IJsewijn, *De Sacerdotibus*	J. IJsewijn, *De Sacerdotibus Sacerdotiisque Alexandri Magni et Lagidarum Eponymis*, Brussel, 1961
Launey, *Armées hellénistiques*	M. Launey, *Recherches sur les armées hellénistiques*, 2 vols., Paris, 1949
Mitford, *Helenus*	T. B. Mitford, "Helenus, Governor of Cyprus," *JHS* 79, 1959, pp. 94-131
Mitford, *Seleucus*	T. B. Mitford, "Seleucus and Theodorus," *Op. Ath.* 1, 1953, pp. 130-171
Préaux, *Économie royale*	Cl. Préaux, *L'Économie royale des Lagides*, Bruxelles, 1938
Robert, *Docs. Asie Min. mérid.*	L. Robert, *Documents de l'Asie Mineure méridionale*, Genève, 1966
Robert, *Études anat.*	L. Robert, *Études anatoliennes*, Paris, 1937
Robert, *Études épigraphiques et philologiques*	L. Robert, *Études épigraphiques et philologiques*, Bibliothèque de l'École des Hautes Études, 272, Paris, 1938
Robert, *Noms indigènes*	L. Robert, *Noms indigènes dans l'Asie Mineure Gréco-Romaine* I, Paris, 1963
Rostovtzeff, *Large Estate*	M. Rostovtzeff, *A Large Estate in Egypt in the Third Century B.C.*, Madison, 1922
Rostovtzeff, *SEHHW*	M. Rostovtzeff, *The Social and Economic History of the Hellenistic World*, 3 vols., Oxford, 1941
Samuel, *Ptolemaic Chronology*	A. E. Samuel, *Ptolemaic Chronology*, München, 1962
Svoronos, *Die Münzen*	J. N. Svoronos, Τὰ Νομίσματα τοῦ κράτους τῶν Πτολεμαίων, Athens, 1904-08, 4 vols. (IV, *Die Münzen der Ptolemäer* includes a trans. of I)

Inv. Coin Hoards   M. Thompson, O. Mørkholm, C. M. Kraay,
                                   An Inventory of Greek Coin Hoards, New
                                   York, 1973
Will, *Histoire politique*   E. Will, *Histoire politique du monde hellénis-
                                   tique*, 2 vols., Nancy, 1966-67

6. COLLECTIONS

Essays Welles   *Essays in Honor of C. Bradford Welles*, New
                                   Haven, 1966
Studi Calderini-Paribeni   *Studi in onore di Aristide Calderini e Roberto
                                   Paribeni*, 3 vols., Milano, 1956-57

CHAPTER ONE

INTRODUCTION

1. Prolegomena

To students of antiquity—indeed, to the literate public—the name of the Ptolemies immediately suggests Egypt, which they ruled for nearly three centuries from the death of Alexander the Great to that of Cleopatra VII in 30 B.C. The association is not unjustified, for Egypt was the first dynastic possession to be acquired, and with its loss to Octavian the dynasty proper ended, though the line was not yet extinct. Egypt, too, is the source for the overwhelming bulk of our material for study of the Ptolemies, the thousands of papyri and ostraka in Greek and Demotic Egyptian as well as a smaller number of inscriptions. Though not themselves of Egyptian descent, the Ptolemies were, for their Egyptian subjects, kings of upper and lower Egypt, pharaohs in the traditional sense and with full religious honors.

But Ptolemy I had no sooner acquired Egypt in the division in Babylon in June, 323, than he began looking outside Egypt; in the ensuing decades he worked cautiously but energetically to create an empire that would complement Egypt. At his death in 283 he left to his son a collection of possessions including the Cyrenaica, Cyprus, Phoenicia, Palestine, Coele-Syria, and various parts of Asia Minor and the Greek islands in differing states of dependence. The next hundred and fifty years saw wide fluctuations in the external provinces controlled by the dynasty, and after the death of Ptolemy VI in 145 only Cyprus and Cyrene remained in Ptolemaic hands. The last possession, Cyprus, was annexed by Rome in 58, although Cleopatra VII later ruled for a few years over some restored possessions, sometime after 48 B.C.

The Ptolemaic empire cannot be said to have been entirely neglected by students of the Hellenistic world. The chapters that follow will make plain the many contributions on which I have been able to build in the study of the history of individual provinces and even more in the understanding of individual documents. There is no need to enumerate them here. Nor have historians of

Ptolemaic Egypt omitted to mention the role of the external possessions. M.I. Rostovtzeff's summary in the *Social and Economic History of the Hellenistic World* and Claire Préaux's discussion of the contribution of the provinces to the economy in *L'Économie royale des Lagides* are two classic passages of this type. More recently, H. Bengtson has devoted a section of Volume III of his *Die Strategie in der hellenistischen Zeit* to the *strategoi* in the empire.

None of these works, however, has been able to use as its point of departure a thorough collection and discussion of the evidence, for the only work ever devoted specifically to the empire was David Cohen's 1912 Leiden thesis *De Magistratibus Aegyptiis externas Lagidarum regni provincias administrantibus*, inadequate even when it was published and now missing mention of evidence published over the last sixty years. The contribution of Cohen and other authors will be assessed more fully in Chapter IX, but the need for something more than his thesis is obvious. If it is today possible to attempt to fill the lack of a book devoted to the administration of the empire, much of the credit belongs to Willy Peremans and E. Van 't Dack, who published the sixth volume of the *Prosopographia Ptolemaica* in 1968, gathering the vast bulk of the material on which I have drawn. The chapters that follow refer frequently to this work, which has throughout been an invaluable tool. I have been fortunate in being able to build on their labors in what is unquestionably the best-executed volume of their indispensable work.

A word about the limitations of the scope of this study is required here. I am concerned with the *administration*, with the ways and means of Ptolemaic control and operation of the empire. I have discussed other matters, such as military and political history, trade, foreign policy, and prosopography only to the extent that it has seemed necessary to do so to elucidate the problems of administration. I have not sought to exhaust the topic of the Ptolemies' dealings outside Egypt, which have many ramifications. A similar principle applies to the documentation of Chapters II through VIII, which is in the main the references to the evidence itself—inscriptions, papyri, coins, and ancient authors. Modern authors have in general been cited only insofar as they have advanced the understanding of a document, a body of evidence, or the questions arising directly from them. A broader cast of the net has been made for the general discussion of Chapter IX, but even there I have thought it neither charitable nor fruitful to record—only to oppose—the incidental remarks about the empire by those scholars who have referred to it while discussing another subject.

It has seemed to me useful to devote some pages to a brief characterization of the Ptolemaic administration in Egypt which I hope may be of help to those not already familiar with it. Later chapters require some familiarity with the terminology and basic structure of Ptolemaic administration. It hardly need be emphasized that the next few pages in no way constitute an original contribution to the subject, for I have generally recorded the common opinion of scholars about the most basic matters without reference either to the documents on which the generalizations are based or to the modern authors in whose works most of these ideas can be found. A skeleton of notes will direct the reader to basic works with fuller documentation; no one work can yet provide a satisfactory and detailed view of all facets of the administration.

2. The Ptolemaic Administration in Egypt

The essential basis of the administration of Egypt in all of antiquity was the nome, the administrative district. The entire country was divided into these nomes, whose size and number varied from time to time. In early Ptolemaic times the number stood in the low forties, divided almost equally between upper (southern) and lower (northern) Egypt. The nome division was in general of great antiquity and was fundamental to whatever administrative superstructure might be placed over it. We know little of the officials of the nomes in the country before the arrival of Ptolemy Soter as satrap, but it appears that Alexander and Ptolemy both left the essential structure unchanged. There were three branches of the nome administration, the bureaus of the nomarch, *oikonomos*, and *basilikos grammateus*. In the theoretical form of third-century Ptolemaic administration, the nomarch (with his subordinates the toparchs and komarchs at local levels) was in charge of agricultural production; the *oikonomos* and his checking-clerks (*antigrapheis*) supervised finances; and the *basilikos grammateus* (again with subordinate *topogrammateis* and *komogrammateis*) kept the necessary records, especially of the land. Other offices are mostly minor adjuncts to this system, except for the police. All of these officials reported to the *dioiketes* in Alexandria, the chief finance and interior minister of the king.

To this structure, largely traditional except perhaps for the nomarch's position as equal rather than superior to the others, the Ptolemies made one significant addition. It was necessary, in order for the king to maintain an army of Greeks and Macedonians, to provide sustenance for the troops. Rather than keep all of them constantly under arms, which was both expensive and dangerous, the king distributed them throughout the nomes on lots of land (*kleroi*) which were to provide incomes for the soldiers and their families. This practice was not new in Egyptian experience, but it was probably much the largest application of such a scheme. There developed, hence, a military structure in the country with ordinary infantry, cavalry, and their commanders of all ranks. The exact structure of the upper command is not certain, but it seems that what modern scholars call "eponymous commanders" (because the troops were designated "of the men of e.g. Nautas") bore a major responsibility for surveillance and mobilization. A more direct control over the military cleruchs fell to the highest echelon of officers, the strategoi. In the earliest times it was their responsibility to look after the interests of their subordinates and to regulate their affairs. The authority of the regular bureaucrats, which was complete over the native population, was proportionately diminished over the soldiers as the latter relied on their military commanders rather than on the civil authority. The military thus constituted a state within a state.[1]

The development of the position of the *strategos* from these beginnings is one of the most fascinating phenomena of Ptolemaic administration, one traced in some detail by Bengtson.[2] As the third century went on, the *strategoi* gained more power in nome affairs, often sharing surveillance of matters with the regular nome officials. A curious situation resulted, for the *strategos* seems to have been a direct royal appointee rather than a bureaucrat answerable to the *dioiketes*. Bengtson supposes that the reign of Euergetes saw the decisive step of creating the office of *strategos* of the nome, but I am inclined to think that a more gradual evolution

---

1. On military affairs, see J. Lesquier, *Les institutions militaires de l'Égypte sous les Lagides*, Paris, 1911; Launey, *Armées hellénistiques*; and Bengtson, *Die Strategie*.

2. H. Bengtson, *Die Strategie* III, 1952.

took place rather than change by one royal decree. For the rest of Ptolemaic rule the power of the *strategos* continued to grow at the expense of that of other chief nome officers, particularly the nomarch, who eventually disappears from sight. It is not hard to see that with the three bureaucrats each heading a department and one equal to another in authority a lack of one dominant person at the nome level would be felt; the *strategos* filled this gap. As time went on, however, this power was tempered by the fact that as the *strategos* superseded the *dioiketes'* men he too came under the all-powerful *dioiketes*. It was the Macedonian position that became dominant, but only at the price of assimilating itself to the basic pattern of Egyptian bureaucracy.

Of the central administration in Alexandria that presided over this situation we know rather less. We know that the nome officials reported to the office of the *dioiketes*, where hordes of secretaries must have taken care of central accounting and record-keeping. Beyond this, the king had his court retainers, his chancery, and his military organization. Later development added the office of ὁ πρὸς τῷ ἰδίῳ λόγῳ, the head of administering what we might call non-recurring income.[3] This post was at times combined with that of *dioiketes*. The papyri do not tell us all we would like to know about the central record offices, largely because papyri have not been found at Alexandria.

The nature of landholding in the nomes is clear only in its broadest outlines. As Rostovtzeff observed,[4] the Greeks did not have precise terminology for the classes of land tenure. The king viewed Egypt as a whole as his property, but exercised his rights directly over part of it only, the royal land. This land was cultivated by royal peasants on leases. It seems that a large portion of the land in the Arsinoite Nome (the Fayûm) was royal land; we cannot tell the proportions elsewhere. Rostovtzeff observes that the peasants were not bondsmen who could be granted with the land. They paid a rent fixed each year which depended on the condition of the land after the inundation of the year.

All other land was considered released by the king for other uses—cleruchic plots, temple lands, city land, royal "gifts", and private land. The privileges and obligations of holders of these

---

3. Most recently, P. R. Swarney, *The Ptolemaic and Roman Idios Logos* (American Studies in Papyrology 8, 1970).

4. *SEHHW*, p. 277.

classes varied widely, and no one system can be described for all. There were few if any blanket exemptions from taxes, and cleruchs paid taxes just as did private owners, perhaps even bearing some unique to them. A brief review of the taxation system may be useful here.

The larger part of government revenues from taxes came from taxes in kind: fixed rents and proportionate taxes in grain and other produce. As well as grain lands, vineyards, orchards, and other producing lands were subject to taxes. Peasants on royal land paid a rent fixed annually, while some other categories paid a percentage of the total crop; vineyards, for example, paid an *apomoira* of one-sixth (after 259, paid to the cult of Arsinoe Philadelphos). Taxes in money were also numerous. Those exercising trades were subject to a tax at a flat rate. There was a salt tax; there were taxes like the *ennomion*, pasture-tax, that fell on those using resources belonging to the king. In addition, a variety of taxes were paid to support specific state services, such as police tax, medical tax, and dike tax. The number of taxes attested is enormous and prohibits a more detailed description here.[5]

The money taxes were generally collected through a tax-farming system which differed considerably from the Greek methods that were its ancestors. The tax-farmers, wealthy men able to post a large surety bond, and often operating as a consortium, underwrote a guarantee of the revenues for a year from a specific tax. They bid for the contracts for the taxes at annual auctions. If collections fell short of the sum bid, the farmers were forced to pay the difference, but if there was a surplus the farmers retained some additional profit, though evidently not the entire surplus. It was obviously necessary for the tax farmers to be thoroughly familiar with the district for which they were bidding. The farmers supervised the various stages of tax collection in order to make sure that their position was not jeopardized by official incompetence or malfeasance, but they did not themselves collect the taxes.

The farmers also played a major role in another main source of royal revenues, the monopolies and government industries. Foremost among these was the production of oil from seeds, a business very closely regulated by the state for its own profit. Other mono-

---

5. On taxes, see Ulrich Wilcken, *Griechische Ostraka* I, Berlin, 1899, and Claire Préaux, *Économie royale*.

polies included linen, beer, and a host of less important ones.

It is difficult to speak of the role of judicial proceedings in the governing of Egypt. The bureaucrats enumerated earlier decided many things that would now require a legal decision, but it is probably more accurate to say that this reflects the extent of the administration's powers and grip on the lives of the people than to attribute to these officials "judicial powers" in the modern sense. It is true that many officials, notably the nomarch and *strategos*, heard "cases" of complaints and decided them; petitions to the king were routinely referred to the *strategoi* for action. Modern scholars have often considered this activity judicial, but to make a real distinction between administrative and judicial activities of a bureaucrat is probably to impose a modern conception on the ancient situation.

There was, however, a judicial system independent of these officials. Standing courts, *dikasteria*, are attested in the *metropoleis* of the nomes, for the needs of Greek settlers, as early as 270. The Egyptians operated under their own law where it was not superseded by royal edict and with their own native judges, the *laokritai*.[6] The most distinctive feature of the Ptolemaic judicial system was the court of the *chrematistai*, the royal judges: οἱ τὰ βασιλικὰ καὶ προσδικὰ καὶ ἰδιωτικὰ κρίνοντες χρηματισταί. Each board had three members and an *eisagogeus*; each was responsible for an administrative area. The format became gradually more systematized as time went on. At the head of it was the *archidikastes*, a prominent official resident in Alexandria. Our evidence for his functions is not extensive, but we can safely conclude that he was the king's deputy charged with overseeing the work of the entire judicial system. By the end of the Ptolemaic dynasty his control over the *chrematistai* and the other courts was explicitly spelled out in his titulature. It is not improbable that the function if not the title goes back to the third century.[7]

The nature of the civic administration of Alexandria, where the *archidikastes* had his seat, where the royal palace was located, is still very much of a question because of the paucity of source material. It was a Greek city, with a social organization of tribes

6. H. J. Wolff, *Das Justizwesen der Ptolemäer*, München, 1962, pp. 48 ff.
7. On the courts in general, see the work of Wolff (note 6) and E. Seidl, *Ptolemäische Rechtsgeschichte*, 2nd ed., Glückstadt, 1962.

and demes, with cultural institutions like the gymnasium. But the government of the city is poorly known. There was no *boule* at the end of the Ptolemaic period, but scholars have often hypothesized the earlier existence of one and the date of its disappearance. The presence of the overwhelming size and power of the royal government must have inhibited the growth of democratic institutions; such vital elements of civic life and business as the port and foreign trade were controlled by the king, not by the city.

In contrast, Ptolemais, in the Thebaid, appears to have had at least in form the typical institutions of Greek political life, such as the *boule* and *demos*. This did not hinder royal control, of course, and a royal official might hold a civic office. But in form Ptolemais acted as a Greek city. The same seems to be true for Naukratis, although we know it less well than Ptolemais.

Beyond the brief enumeration of specific institutions given above it may be well to sketch what the main characteristics of the Ptolemaic administration of Egypt were. The first is variability in time and space. The bureaucracy changed during three centuries until in many points it would have been unrecognizable to an early Ptolemaic settler. Some of these developments I have indicated above, but there were many others. This fact provides one important check in dealing with Ptolemaic documents: one may not assume that what we know about one period can be taken over without change to help to interpret another. The same is true from nome to nome: the uniformity of Egypt is a myth in both Hellenistic and Roman times. What was part of ordinary experience in the heavily Hellenized Fayûm might be rare or nonexistent in the very Egyptian Thebaid. Even the format of a contract or government document might vary widely. Our evidence often allows us to do no more than guess at these variations.

A second characteristic is tension and change in the matter of responsibility of functionaries to their superiors. The nome administration reported to the king through the *dioiketes*, but the *strategos* was originally independent of the *dioiketes*. We see thus an original principle of duality in lines of authority between military and civil-financial. With the passage of time and the assimilation of the *strategos* into the nome administration, the *strategos* in turn comes to be a subordinate of the *dioiketes*. The eternal realities of Egyptian administration thus deflected the original forms.

The Ptolemaic bureaucracy depended also on the twin principles of delegation of authority and checks and balances. The nome officials had the authority to carry out what they needed to do and a position of some self-reliance, but at the same time they were responsible for anything that went wrong—that is, that cost the crown money beyond expectation—within their jurisdiction. The bureaucrats were checked by other officials; it is partly thus that one can explain the early pattern of equal authority vested in each of three branches at the nome level. The *oikonomoi* further had their checking clerks. More important still, the tax farmers and the officials served to guard against the poor performance each of the other, for each depended on the other to avoid ruin. Only the oppression of the taxpayers was not prevented by the system. It must be pointed out that the balancing of authority at the nome level eventually broke down under the increase in the power of the *strategos*; it had proved impossible to maintain an equilibrium permanently.

The tendency to delegate the task of governing is shown in the very existence of the tax farmers, who serve to protect the government from any unforeseen variations in revenues. It is further attested by the leaving to civic institutions as much of the governance of Ptolemais and Naukratis as possible: let the cities run their own affairs so long as they satisfy whatever obligations they have to the crown. It was probably not feasible to let Alexandria have a similar degree of self-government if only because the Ptolemaic state was so closely tied to the city and made up so large a portion of its life.

One must acknowledge two overriding principles that lie behind these characteristics enumerated above. The first is a deliberate unwillingness to interfere with institutions as they existed—a desire to avoid change. The Egyptian nome structure and bureaucracy were taken over with few changes as far as dealings with the native population were concerned. Natural evolution of bureaucracy was not prevented, but formal reforms must have been exceptions. Change was usually limited to rationalization and tightening the system for the sake of higher income.

The other principle is utter flexibility in applying governmental conceptions. It was not as a matter of principle that the Ptolemies used this or that scheme of administration; it was a matter of convenience, of suiting the measures taken to the local situation. No Ptolemy would insist on a constitutional and legal view of his government or its relationship to subjects and cities. It would be absurd to suppose that two cities or two nomes should be treated alike for the sake of uniformity. We find diversity in Ptolemaic Egypt because it already existed, because it was easier to cope with it than to change it, and because government policy encouraged a lack of uniformity in new development.

The next seven chapters will examine in detail the personnel, structure, workings, and history of the Ptolemaic administration outside Egypt. It is known only in part in any one area, but I find that it is nonetheless possible to draw out patterns of administration from the evidence available. We proceed by geographical areas, roughly from Egypt outward, first through the papyri and inscriptions, together with the few useful literary sources, and then in Chapter VIII the sequence is repeated for the coinage and circulation of currency.

CHAPTER TWO

SYRIA AND PHOENICIA

1. Frontiers and Chronology

The coast between Pelusium and the northern end of the Lebanon range and the country that lies behind the coast constitute one of three areas in which Ptolemy I early showed an interest. He held the region for some five years between 320 and 315; he made another, temporarily successful, attempt in 312; and he finally gained control of the country in 301 from the spoils of Antigonus' empire, though he had not fought at Ipsos. On this ground the Seleucids were to dispute Ptolemaic possession of Syria until Antiochus III took it from Ptolemy V a century later.[1]

From the numismatic studies of Henri Seyrig it is now certain that the Ptolemies never controlled Arados or Marathos and that the northern boundary of their territory must have run on about the line of the Eleutheros river.[2] It was not until 296/5 or 287/6, however, that Ptolemy took the enclaves of Tyre and Sidon, which Demetrius had continued to hold with his fleet after the loss of the area surrounding them.[3]

During the century after Ipsos, the Seleucids and Ptolemies fought some six wars in whole or in part over possession of Syria and Phoenicia. Most of these wars are very poorly known to us, and

---

1. A full account of Ptolemy Soter's attempts to conquer Syria and his final success, with ancient sources cited, can be found in the study of F. M. Abel, *Revue Biblique* 44, 1935, pp. 559-581.

2. H. Seyrig, *Syria* 28, 1951, pp. 206-220. Arados and all of its mainland colonies used the Attic standard for their coinage. Seyrig suggests that the era of Arados (from 259) is connected with privileges granted by Antiochus II in return for support in the Second Syrian War.

3. E. T. Newell, *Tyrus Rediviva*, New York, 1923, p. 22, argues that Antigonid Alexander-type coinage continued past 290, degenerating in quality, until it disappeared with the Ptolemaic conquest. E. Manni, *Demetrio Poliorcete*, Rome, 1951, p. 57, n. 32, suggests that Ptolemy took Tyre and Sidon not long before he dispatched his fleet to the Aegean in 286. Irwin L. Merker, *Ancient Society* 5, 1974, pp. 119-126, argues that there are numismatic grounds for preferring 296 to 287/6 as the date of Demetrius' loss of Tyre; it would thus come in the same period in which Demetrius lost Cyprus to Ptolemy.

the alterations of territorial holdings that the wars may have produced are much argued. The most comprehensive modern attempt to document such fluctuations was that of Ulrich Kahrstedt in 1926.[4] Kahrstedt's argument for Arados as a northern boundary during some periods is certainly invalid. It rested solely on the fact that Arados asked Antiochus III for an alliance in 219 and that Antiochus reconciled its internal dissensions;[5] Kahrstedt interprets this to mean that the city was formerly in Ptolemaic possession. The argument was intrinsically weak, and in any case the numismatic evidence shows that Arados was certainly not in Ptolemaic hands, since it coined autonomously and not on the "Phoenician" standard imposed by the Ptolemies over their possessions in this area.[6]

Kahrstedt argued also for a more southerly boundary between the two kingdoms following the end of the Second Syrian War about 253. Again, the evidence is slight: Kahrstedt argued that Damascus was a Seleucid possession at this time, relying on (1) a passage in Eusebius indicating that at a point in the next war (242/1) Ptolemy III was besieging forces of Seleucus II in Damascus and Orthosia;[7] (2) a story of Polyaenus (4.15) according to which Antiochus son of Seleucus (that is, Antiochus I) captured Damascus from Dion, a general of king Ptolemy, by a ruse. Kahrstedt therefore claimed that Antiochus I had captured Damascus from Ptolemy II in the First Syrian War in the 270's and that he and his successors held the city until its capture by Ptolemy III in the Third Syrian War.[8] But this construction cannot hold. We have papyrological evidence that Damascus was in Ptolemaic hands in 259 and can therefore hardly have been a Seleucid prize of the 270's.[9] The literary sources on which Kahrstedt relied cannot be taken to indicate more than temporary Seleucid possession during these wars; they in no way require long-term control. There is no occasion between 270 and 259 for Ptolemaic expansion in the area; thus, whatever the fluctuations of the 270's, at their end Ptolemy II must have held Damascus. It is not possible to tell for how long the Seleucids held Damascus

---

4. *Syrische Territorien in Hellenistischer Zeit, Abhandlungen der Gesellschaft der Wissen. zu Göttingen*, Phil.-hist. Kl., N.F. 19,2, 1926, pp. 14-41.

5. Polyb. 5.68.7 ff.

6. See note 2, above.

7. Euseb. *Chron.* (Schoene) I 251 (Porphyry, *FGrH* 260 F 32.8).

8. Kahrstedt (note 4, above), p. 23. "Antiochus son of Seleucus" in Polyaenus can be only Antiochus I.

9. *P. Cair. Zen.* 59006.

before the siege of 242/1—whether it was a recent capture or a prize from the Second Syrian War. The inland border in 253 therefore cannot be placed with confidence.

Kahrstedt's other point rested on a misinterpreted papyrus, a letter of the private doctor of the Ptolemaic finance minister Apollonios to Zenon, Apollonios' estate manager in the Fayûm.[10] Artemidoros, the doctor, tells Zenon that he and Apollonios had returned to Sidon after escorting the queen to the borders (April, 252). It was assumed by Kahrstedt (following Edgar's first edition) that the sequence was otherwise; they had escorted Berenike as far as Sidon, to the border. It was thus thought that the border lay just north of Sidon. Wilcken pointed out that this interpretation was not grammatically possible.[11] There is thus no evidence for the assertion that the borders after the Second Syrian War were just north of Sidon. There is, in fact, no firm evidence for fluctuation of any kind during the third century, except for the Ptolemaic possession of Seleukia in Pieria as an enclave between 245 and 219, and for temporary shifts during the Syrian wars.[12]

Ptolemaic rule in Syria was largely interrupted for nearly three years by the Fourth Syrian War (219-217), which terminated with the battle of Raphia and complete victory for Ptolemy IV.[13] Antiochus returned after the death of Philopator, however, and in five campaigns (202-198) completely conquered the entire area, with the decisive battle being fought at Panion in 200.[14] Later Ptolemaic attempts to regain the province were unsuccessful, although Philometor might have accomplished a recovery had he not been killed in 146.[15]

---

10. *P. Cair. Zen.* 59251.

11. *Archiv* 6, 1919, p. 452.

12. *W. Chr.* 1. On Kahrstedt's constructions generally, see the critical remarks of W. Otto, *Beiträge zur Seleukidengeschichte, Abh. Bayer. Akad. Wiss.*, Philol. u. histor. Kl., 34.1, 1928, pp. 37 ff.

13. The story of Raphia is known primarily from Polyb. 5.68 ff. Various aspects of the campaign will be considered below in connection with some Ptolemaic officers.

14. The chronology of this campaign was decisively established by M. Holleaux, *Études* III, pp. 317-335.

15. M. Holleaux, *Études* III, pp. 339-340, nn. 2-3, makes it clear that Epiphanes never really received the possession of Coele-Syria promised to him by Antiochus III as a dowry for Cleopatra, whom he married in 193. In 146 the Seleucid commandant of Antioch-on-the-Orontes received Philometor and worked with him to reestablish Ptolemaic control of Syria: Diod. 32.9c.

2. MILITARY GOVERNMENT AND SETTLEMENT

There were garrisons in the main cities of Phoenicia and Syria. We know the names of one, perhaps more, of their commanders from literary sources and the names and titles of some subordinates from the papyri of the Zenon archive from the years in the early 250's when Zenon served Apollonios as a travelling representative there.

The only city commandant securely attested as such is Leontios, called by Polybius ὁ ἐπὶ τῶν ὅλων in Seleukia in Pieria in 219, who surrendered his city to Antiochus III.[16] It is possible, however, that the Theodotas whom Lucian reports as trying to seize Tyre (early in the third century) was a commandant.[17] For the other Ptolemaic military commanders attested in the area, a determination of status is not easy. From a papyrus of about 261 B.C. we know that the primary administrative unit of Syria and Phoenicia was the *hyparchia*.[18] The only official this papyrus (to be discussed in more detail below) mentions at the level of the *hyparchia*, however, is the *oikonomos*, perhaps because of the economic nature of the regulations there promulgated. Peremans and Van 't Dack have taken this provincial designation as justification for claiming that the governors of these regions were called *hyparchoi*, and have accordingly designated several men as such in the *Prosopographia Ptolemaica*. One is Keraias, whom Polybius calls a *hyparchos*, one of the many Ptolemaic officers to defect to Antiochus III in the two years before Raphia.[19] Titles conferred by historians, however, are not of the same value for ascertaining true status as those from documents; for example, Polybius immediately after seems to refer to Keraias as a *hegemon*. *Hyparchos* here must mean simply "subordinate officer", the normal meaning of the word in classical and hellenistic Greek,[20] as Keraias is called "one of the *hyparchoi* of Ptolemy." It would be difficult to assign an administrative position

---

16. *Pros. Ptol.* 15116; Polyb. 5.60.9.

17. He is called a Ptolemaic officer in *de calumn. non tem. cred.* 2. On the date, M. Launey, *Armées hellénistiques*, pp. 241-242.

18. *SB* 8008; for fuller reference, see below, note 35.

19. Polyb. 5.70.10 and 5.71.11.

20. See Walbank, *Historical Commentary on Polybius* I, 1957, p. 596: "more commonly, as here, it signifies a subordinate commander in a general sense." He cites, among other sources, Welles, *Royal Correspondence* 20.5, the only example of a technical use; see Welles' remarks, p. 371.

to Hippolochos, the commander of 400 cavalry who deserted just after Keraias, but he falls into the same category as Keraias in Polybius' account. In short, I regard Keraias' position and title as presently undemonstrated, awaiting further evidence. The same is true for Theodotas (above) whom Peremans and Van 't Dack also list as a *hyparchos*.[21] I do not see that these men should be regarded as more certainly or less certainly *hyparchoi*, or even garrison commanders, or, indeed, as permanently stationed in Syria, than other officers who appear in the accounts of the wars in Syria. Most of them may be at the head of troops sent to Syria only for the military actions in question.

It is no more possible to be precise in describing the position of the Aetolian Theodotos, called by Polybius τεταγμένος ἐπὶ Κοίλης Συρίας, the most important of the defectors to Antiochus III.[22] In the absence of evidence for the size of a *hyparchia*, we do not know whether Coele-Syria might have been such a unit, or whether indeed Polybius uses the term Coele-Syria here in a wide or a narrow sense. Theodotos' importance to Antiochus suggests that he was no mere city commandant, and he was clearly on another level than Keraias. One may be reluctant to see him as a governor of the entire area of Syria and Phoenicia if only because such a general governorship is nowhere attested in a document. It is not unlikely that a military governor existed, since an official in the financial realm, ὁ διοικῶν τὰς κατὰ Συρίαν καὶ Φοινίκην προσόδους filled a similar general supervision in his own area of competence.[23] But the question of whether

---

21. *Pros. Ptol.* 15044.

22. Full references in *Pros. Ptol.* 15045. His title, Polyb. 5.40.1, 5.46.3-4.

23. See below, note 35, for the manager of revenues. It is known that under Seleucid rule the area was governed by a *strategos* of Syria-Coele and Phoenicia, who also held the title high-priest. The first such *strategos* was Ptolemaios son of Thraseas, a former general of Ptolemy IV in 219 (Polyb. 5.65.3) usually thought to have defected during that war. An inscription of Soloi in Cilicia recording a dedication by him, *OGIS* 230, is to be dated after 197; cf. M. Holleaux, *Études* III, p. 161 and n. 6. [The text is republished in *BCH* 96, 1972, pp. 109-111, by Yves Grandjean and Georges Rougemont, with a photograph, p. 110, fig. 11. They remark, "la première édition garantit le patronymique, disparu depuis avec l'angle supérieur droit de la pierre." But they print this patronymic as Θρασέου, when the first edition and all subsequent ones give the correct form Θρασέα.] A new inscription from Skythopolis gives us some correspondence among him, King Antiochus III and his son, and various minor officials, about villages belonging to Ptolemaios; it appears that the powers of the *strategos* did not extend to many things such as military quartering. The description of part of Ptolemaios' possessions as εἰς τὸ πατρικόν suggests that he and perhaps his father had

Theodotos was such a governor must be left unresolved in the present state of our knowledge.

The forces on garrison duty—the στρατευόμενοι —swelled in time of war by additional active forces, had for the most part the same ranks and ethnic composition as Ptolemaic forces everywhere.[24] Hipparchs are particularly well-attested: one appears in Tripolis in a Zenon papyrus of 258/7;[25] another, Dorymenes, placed an inscription dedicated to Ptolemy IV on the shore opposite Tyre early in that king's reign. A third may be found in a tomb painting in Marissa in Idumaea, though the date of the painting is not certain.[26]

Several other titles appear from accounts of Zenon's journeys in Palestine, though it is generally impossible to draw any information other than name and title from the entries (which record disbursements or sales of pickled fish and other items): a *hegemon*,[27] an *akrophylax*, a *phylakarches*, a *grammateus*, and an *archyperetes*.[28]

About the rank and file it is somewhat harder to speak. Some 22 names of foreigners are preserved by painted grave stelai found in

---

held the villages in some form of grant, perhaps a *dorea*, from the Ptolemies. It does not seem to me unlikely that Ptolemaios son of Thraseas went over to Antiochus later than has been supposed and that part of his reward was retaining his old possessions and getting some new ones. But Ptolemaios' status before his defection is nowhere mentioned, and his command may have been either local, regional, or general. See Y. H. Landau in *Israel Exploration Journal* 16, 1966, pp. 54-70, and J. and L. Robert, *Bull. épigr.* 1970, 627.

24. The distinction of type of military personnel is found in *SB* 8008 (see note 35 below). Ethnic composition, see page 17.

25. *PSI* 495.

26. Dorymenes' inscription is *SEG* VII 326, where the restorations of the first editor, R. Mouterde (*Mélanges Univ. St. Joseph* 16, 1932, pp. 96-97) are printed, though they are at best possible and line 7 is very unlikely (ἐπ' ἀνδρῶν is probably attested in Cyprus before the second century, contrary to Mouterde's assertion). Dorymenes is a subordinate of Nikolaos in Polyb. 5.61.8, sent to hold a pass near Berytos in 219. M. Launey (*Armées hellénistiques* I, p. 186, n. 8) suggests that a Ptolemaios son of Dorymenes in Seleucid service somewhat later was his son. It appears to me unlikely that he is the same man as the Dorymenes in the Delphian inscription in M. Holleaux, *Études* III, pp. 141-157 (text republished as *Fouilles de Delphes* III 4.163). The hipparch of Marissa appears in a painting of which M. Rostovtzeff, *SEHHW*, p. 520, gives a photograph and discussion. I do not, however, find the reading of the title he gives certain from the photograph. Rostovtzeff takes the tombs to be third century; see note 52 below on the date of the Marissa material.

27. *P. Cair. Zen.* 59004.

28. All in *P. Cair. Zen.* 59006.

Sidon.[29] Seven come from Caria, another six from other parts of southern Asia Minor, one from Lydia, four from Greece, one from Crete, and three from uncertain places. It is unfortunately not possible to be sure whether these are Ptolemaic or Seleucid troops, for the date of the stelai cannot be precisely fixed.[30]

Besides the garrisons and the troops on active duty in the wars, the Ptolemies placed military settlers on the land. In the Vienna papyrus of 261, mentioned above, the *katoikoi* are distinguished from the soldiers on active duty, though they share with the latter an exemption from certain registration clauses of the ordinance, provided that they are living with native wives.[31] Somewhat more detail is provided by a contract from year 27 of Ptolemy II (259/8) concluded by Zenon with a resident of Birta in Ammanitis, in the Transjordan.[32] A slave girl, seven years old, is sold to Zenon for 50 drachmas. The seller and several witnesses are described in various phrases as cleruchic cavalry under the command of Toubias, τῶν Τουβίου ἱππέων κληροῦχος, with ἱππέων or κληροῦχος or both crossed out in various cases and τῶν περὶ Τουβίαν used as an alternative. In any case, these men (a Knidian, a Macedonian, two "Persians") are evidently Ptolemaic soldiers settled in and around the stronghold of Birta and under the command of Toubias, whose position evidently evoked for the Greeks resident in Egypt the nearest parallel in their experience, what modern discussions of the cleruchic system call "eponymous commanders." [33] Toubias was a member of an important local family, here taken into the service of the king and responsible for the military settlers of his area. We will encounter his family again.

---

29. Full references in *Pros. Ptol.* under the following numbers: Caria, 15320, 15448, 15468, 15470, 15509, 15510, 15627; Thyatira, 15432; south Asia Minor, 15198, 15471, 15525, 15527, 15617, 15618; Greece, 15295, 15461, 15648; Crete, 15405; uncertain, 15253, 15679, 15700.

30. L. Jalabert, *Rev. arch.* 4, 1904, p. 18, thought that the ethnic Lacedaemonian from Gythion indicated a date after 195, but M. Launey, *Armées hellénistiques* I, p. 116, has convincingly refuted the assertion, and stylistic criteria are insufficient for precision. The areas of recruiting, long under Ptolemaic control or influence for the most part, make Ptolemaic control more likely than Seleucid, but cannot rule out the latter.

31. See note 35, below.

32. *P. Cair. Zen.* 59003, reedited as *CPJud.* 1 with some slight improvement.

33. Cf. the commentary to *P. Yale* 27 and my remarks in *BASP* 6, 1969, pp. 87-90.

3. ECONOMIC AND CIVIL ADMINISTRATION

It is about the economic administration and exploitation of Syria and Phoenicia that we are best informed, in large measure because of Zenon's activity on behalf of Apollonios in the area. We have great difficulty, however, in distinguishing between the activity of Apollonios as finance minister of Ptolemy Philadelphos and that of Apollonios the wealthy entrepreneur. It is perhaps doubtful that Apollonios, Zenon, or the king himself could have drawn a clear line of demarcation. By now, however, it is reasonably clear that Zenon was an agent of Apollonios in the latter's business ventures, and that he never held a title in the royal bureaucracy. His extensive trading activities brought him into contact with many officials, some of whom appear clearly or vaguely designated in Zenon's records and letters. The organization and nature of the trade with Syria is in itself a large subject and has been repeatedly treated at length.[34] I will therefore deal with it only where it impinges on the official administration.

We may begin a survey of the economic administration in Syria and Phoenicia with the important Vienna papyrus already alluded to.[35] It contains the partial text of two *prostagmata*, royal ordinances issued by Ptolemy II to be effective in Dystros of the 25th year, and therefore probably issued late in the preceding year, in 261. We begin in the middle of the first ordinance with the requirement that within sixty days of promulgation of the *prostagma* all taxable and non-taxable livestock in each *hyparchia* are to be reported in declarations to the *oikonomos* in the *hyparchia*. Penalties are prescribed for non-compliance, in accordance with a *diagramma*.[36] A damaged passage dealt with payment of past and future taxes and again prescribed penalties.

The decree goes on to require a parallel set of declarations from

---

34. Notably by V. Tscherikover, *Mizraim* 4-5, 1937, pp. 9-90, and by G. Harper, *American Journal of Philology* 49, 1928, pp. 1-35.

35. Published by Herbert Liebesny, "Ein Erlass des Königs Ptolemaios II. Philadelphos über die Deklaration von Vieh und Sklaven in Syrien und Phönikien (PER Inv. Nr. 24.552 gr.)," *Aegyptus* 16, 1936, pp. 257-291. Text reprinted as *SB* 8008 and as *C. Ord. Ptol.* 21-22 (with bibliography). Liebesny's commentary on the legal aspects of execution is quite detailed, that on administrative aspects less so.

36. Evidently another document defining penalties and amounts; on the use of the term see C. B. Welles, *AJA* 42, 1938, pp. 245-260.

komarchs and the μεμισθωμένοι τὰς κώμας (those buying the tax contracts for the villages) for the villages for which they are responsible, and the detailed information wanted is spelled out. Every year from this time on a similar declaration is to be made and the indicated tax paid. Penalties are to be the same as those applied to those making a declaration under the name of another person. Provision for giving informers a share of penalties and confiscated properties is made.

This first decree provides us with the administrative skeleton of the province: hyparchies as the basic unit of governing, each with an *oikonomos* at the head of the financial bureaucracy. At a lower level, but perhaps not subordinate to him (they file declarations but it is not certain to whom) are the komarchs, the primary administrative officers at the village level. The tax farmers do not themselves collect taxes, although they are responsible for seeing that they are collected in the right amount. The job of collection belongs to the royal officials of the village and *hyparchia*. We will have more to say of the farmers later.

The second ordinance [37] deals with slaves. Anyone who has acquired a σῶμα λαϊκὸν ἐλεύθερον is to report it to the *oikonomos* in his *hyparchia* within 20 days of the proclamation of the ordinance, and such future acquisitions are mostly forbidden. Unreported slaves will be confiscated and the owner will be fined 6000 drachmas by the *basilikon*, which will return a part of the sum to any informer in the case. The owners may keep registered household slaves, and slaves acquired at royal auctions are to be retained without question. Soldiers and military settlers living with native wives may keep their slaves without registration. It is also forbidden to use as security the persons of natives except by explicit permission for execution on persons from the manager of the revenues of Syria and Phoenicia, in accord with the law about tax-farming. The same penalties are to be applied.

The bureaucracy here is the same, and the requirement for registration analogous. The enslavement of native persons in Syria and Phoenicia is limited in effect to crown officials and tax farmers for execution of debts to the crown. It is perhaps not a coincidence that a considerable portion of the activity of Zenon in Syria concerned the slave trade, mostly importation into Egypt. It even

---

37. Lines 33 ff.

appears at times as if Apollonios was, through Zenon, busy evading the laws that he was responsible for enforcing.[38]

We encounter the *telonai*, the tax farmers, twice in the Zenon papyri, both times in a matter of the slave trade. From a letter of 258 it appears that some of Apollonios' agents in Gaza were importing some slaves to Egypt through Gaza when the slaves escaped in the harbor there. Philotas, one of the agents, recovered the slaves and delivered them back to the person who was to take charge of the export. He also went to see Heroides the *telones*, and found there that the other agent, Apollophanes, had made a contract with the *telones* to pay a tax of 80 drachmas in the name of Apollonios. For some reason, Philotas was able to cancel this and make a new agreement in Apollophanes' own name for half the previous tax. One would like to know the basis for the reduction in tax, but in any case there was clearly a tax applicable, probably on the export of slaves.[39]

A similar transaction appears in another letter from the following year (257). Menekles, another agent of Apollonios (in Tyre), bought some slaves and brought them and some goods from Gaza to Tyre for transshipment.[40] Lacking a license for export of the slaves, he failed to make a declaration to the *telonai* in Tyre. The *telonai* learned of this and promptly confiscated the shipment. Apollophanes then intervened and said that the goods and slaves belonged to Zenon; this, evidently, saved the day. It appears that the *telonai* of the ports were concerned both with proper licensing and with taxes on the licensed goods. They may in fact have played a more direct role in the collection of taxes than tax farmers in Egypt did.

The tax-farming system on the larger scale plays a prominent role in the story of Joseph son of Tobias in book twelve of Josephus' *Jewish Antiquities*. The taxes of Judea were habitually farmed out to wealthy residents of Palestine, but Onias, the high priest in Jerusalem, was accustomed to send an additional gift to the king each year from his own resources, carrying on an ancestral custom.[41] One year he refused to do so, and Ptolemy sent an envoy, Athenion,

---

38. I cannot enter here into the long debate about the relationship of the Palestinian slave trade to the Ptolemaic attitudes about slavery in Egypt. Cf. the remarks of V. Tscherikover (note 34 above) and M. Rostovtzeff, *Large Estate*, p. 34.
39. *P. Cair. Zen.* 59804.
40. *P. Cair. Zen.* 59093.
41. *A.J.* 12.154 ff.

to complain about the missed gift. Onias refused to receive Athenion at all. Joseph, a young and ambitious nephew of the high priest, received Athenion instead, entertained him, won favor with him, and at his suggestion went to Egypt to meet the king, arriving there not long before the annual auction of the taxes for Syria. He quickly became a court favorite, and when the auction came, the men who usually bought the contracts were enraged at the favor shown Joseph. The latter proceeded to offer the king twice the usual taxes and was granted the contract for the entire province, to the consternation of the long-time tax farmers, who are said to have conspired to keep the bids low. Joseph went on to collect the taxes and make a fortune for himself over the next twenty-two years, during the second half of the third century.[42]

We know from the Vienna papyrus that tax-farming contracts were sold on as low a basis as the village unit. But it is clear from the story of Joseph, full of romance though it may be, that the business was in fact run at a far higher level, and it was in large units that the wealthy men of Syria dealt. It is not improbable that they in turn farmed out smaller units to independent operators who no doubt did much of the work.

4. The Judicial System

It appears that some sort of royal judges were placed in Syria and Palestine, but whether to judge only military settlers and garrisons or also the native population we cannot be sure. One *dikastes* appears among the witnesses to the slave sale in Birta, the others being military settlers in the area (plus some companions of Zenon travelling with him in service of Apollonios).[43] Another

---

42. A.J. 12.160-223; his son Hyrkanos eventually supplanted him. The date of Joseph's activity has been a matter of great controversy. Josephus puts him in the reign of Ptolemy V and his Seleucid wife Cleopatra, but M. Holleaux has shown that this date cannot be correct, and his conclusion—in which he followed others—has generally been accepted (*Études* III, pp. 339-340, nn. 2-3, and p. 355, n. 2 [later bibliography collected by L. Robert]). But it has proved impossible to find agreement on another date. Eusebius, *Chron.* (Schoene) II 120, gives year 1 of Ptolemy III as the beginning of Joseph's term as tax farmer of Judea, but Hyrkanos' journey to Alexandria for the celebration of the birth of a prince, as recounted by Josephus, is taken by some to point to a date about 207, shortly after the birth of Ptolemy V, as an ending date for Joseph's power, which would on this reckoning run from 229 to 207, approximately. Bibliography in H. Bengtson, *Die Strategie* II, p. 161, n. 2. None of the arguments appears to me to be conclusive.

43. *P. Cair. Zen.* 59003.

dikastes, Nossos, appears as a recipient of pickled fish on one of
Zenon's accounts.[44] Since most of the other recipients with titles
in the account are military men, it is possible that the judge was
attached in some way to a military contingent. In cases of crown
finance, of course, the king retained ultimate jurisdiction, as the
Vienna papyrus tells us.

5. The Cities

We know little about the cities of Phoenicia under Ptolemaic
rule. The old monarchy of Sidon was retained during the lifetime
of Philokles son of Apollodoros, who was king of Sidon after the
Ptolemaic capture of the city (287 ?) and at the same time a distinguished Ptolemaic admiral.[45] It is probable, however, that the
monarchy was abolished on his death, for an inscription of the mid-
third century is dated to year 14 of the people of Sidon.[46] The upper
class of Sidon and the other cities adopted Hellenic behavior in
some ways, particularly athletics: Sidonian and Byblian victors on
Delos are known from 270, and two later inscriptions, not precisely
datable, record a victory dedication to Delphian Apollo by Diotimos
son of Abdubastios, when Apollophanes son of Abduzmunos was
agonothetes, and a dedication by the *polis* of the Sidonians to
Diotimos son of Dionysios, victor in the Nemean games.[47] The
latter man is qualified by the term *dikastes*, which Bikermann
interpreted in this context to be the equivalent of the Semitic term
sofet, president of the people: in effect, a replacement of the king.[48]
Sofet itself is attested in mid-third century Tyre,[49] while Diotimos'

44. *P. Cair. Zen.* 59006.
45. Philokles has been studied most recently by Irwin L. Merker, *Historia*
19, 1970, pp. 143-150, and by J. Seibert, *Historia* 19, 1970, pp. 337-351, with
fairly full bibliography and references.
46. *Rép. ép. sém.*, Paris, 1966, III 1215, a Phoenician text whose contents
are a rendering of a typical Greek honorific decree voted by a body translated
in the Greek subscription as τὸ κοινὸν τῶν Σιδωνίων; the person honored is
in the Greek named Diopeithes, in the Phoenician Samabaal son of Mago.
The Greek character of the text is, despite language, very apparent.
47. On Delos, *IG* XI 2 203.68; at Delphi, Le Bas-Waddington, *Voyage
archéologique* III 1866c; Diotimos, E. Bikermann, *Mélanges syriens offerts
à R. Dussaud* I, Paris, 1939, pp. 91-99. The text is republished by J. Ebert,
Griechische Epigramme auf Sieger an gymnischen und hippischen Agonen,
Abh. Sächs. Akad., Ph.-hist. Kl., 63.2, 1972, no. 64; he discusses the Sidonian's participation on p. 190.
48. Bikermann, note 47 above.
49. *Rép. ép. sém.* III 1204.

victory probably comes around the end of the third century, perhaps even as late as the replacement of Ptolemaic by Seleucid rule.

A Zenon papyrus (probably from the years 260-256) records a gift of Attic honey and some myrrh from Theodotos τοῦ ἐκ Σιδῶνος ἄρχοντος.[50] Various scholars have interpreted this man as a royal official or as a civic officeholder, but without any argument for either position.[51] Two considerations seem to me to argue for the latter position: (1) *archon* is a widely known civic office in the Greek world, but nowhere occurs as a Ptolemaic term for a royal functionary; and (2) a valuable parallel is provided by an inscription from Marissa of Ptolemaic date, the funerary inscription of Apollophanes son of Sesmaios, ἄρξας τῶν ἐν Μαρίσηι Σιδωνίων ἔτη τριάκοντα καὶ τρία, who is certainly from his Semitic patronymic a lifetime president of the Sidonian community in Marissa rather than a long-immobile Ptolemaic official.[52] The question of the relationship between the terms *dikastes* and *archon* in the Sidonian city and communities I cannot resolve, for lack of evidence, but it appears to me nearly certain that *archon* is a position of the same type as the *dikastes*.

It is at the nexus between the cities and the land that our information breaks down. One may expect that the Phoenician cities, like Greek cities everywhere, had control of some land outside the

---

50. *P. Mich.* 3.

51. H. Bengtson, *Die Strategie* III, p. 171, n. 1, follows Tscherikover and Rostovtzeff in thinking the *archon* a civic magistrate, but Bikermann (note 47), p. 98, n. 6, calls him a royal official.

52. *OGIS* 593. The exact date of this text, found in a tomb at Marissa, is uncertain. It is the earliest inscription in the tomb in question. About the later ones, J. P. Peters (*Art and Archaeology* 7, 1918, p. 194) remarked, "The dated inscriptions, about ten in number, following for the most part the Seleucidan era, cover the period from 196 to 107 B.C., but the earliest of these was evidently considerably later than that of Apollophanes, and already shows deterioration." This seems to be an earlier placement of the date of Apollophanes' death than that Peters had chosen in his main publication of the tombs (J. P. Peters and H. Thiersch, *Painted Tombs of the Necropolis of Marissa*, 1905, p. 80): "the tomb itself must date from about 200 B.C., that is, quite at the end of the period in which this region was subject to the Ptolemies." In any case the Ptolemaic date of the Sidonian settlement at Marissa and the tenure of Apollophanes in office is certain. It may be noted that the reading of the earliest dated inscription is uncertain, and that it was reported by Bliss and Macalister in *CRAI* 1902, p. 500, as being ZP, year 107 Seleucid, while Peters and Thiersch support the reading of ZIP, or 117 Sel. Peters, however, raises the possibility that the correct reading is ΞP, which would be 160 B.C. Carl Watzinger (*Denkmäler Palästinas* II, 1935, p. 17) accepts the conventional dating with slight variation.

walls, which fed and supported the cities; but we lack evidence of this *chora* for Phoenicia. More significant is the fact that the bulk of the countryside in the province was dealt with directly by royal bureaucrats in hyparchies and villages, the *oikonomoi* and komarchs. The system is in essence close to what we know of Egypt, although the bureaucracy may not have been so elaborate, because the economy probably needed far less close supervision. The cities were probably less isolated from the countryside than were the cities of Egypt, which were also few in proportion to the land around them. But in both cases we find both civic and royal establishments. Wherever there is money to be made, a royal official is to be found. Thus the system of tax-farming on the basis of the royal administrative unit appears both in Syria and in Egypt.

If allowances are made for differences in the ecology and economy of Egypt and Syria, it is fair to conclude that there was a close resemblance between the two areas in administration. This is especially true in the relationship of king, city, and *chora*. Had we more evidence the similarities might be more or less striking, but it is unlikely that our basic perception of likeness will be altered.

CHAPTER THREE

CYRENAICA

I. HISTORICAL BACKGROUND

The first land outside Egypt to come under the control of Ptolemy Soter (in 322), Cyrene remained in Ptolemaic hands (though not always controlled from Alexandria) almost continuously until the death of its last Ptolemaic king in 96. Despite this long tenure and despite the extensive excavations of the Italian mission between the wars, we have nothing like the wealth of documentation in the Cyrenaica of Ptolemaic officials that we have in Cyprus. The history of the vicissitudes of Cyrene in the Ptolemaic period is complicated, and a review of its outlines must precede any attempt to understand the manner in which it was administered.

Ptolemy Soter was invited by a group of aristocratic Cyrenaeans, driven into exile during a complicated struggle which it is not necessary to recount here, to intervene in Cyrene in the year 322. The strife had centered around Thibron, a former associate of Alexander the Great's official Harpalos.[1] Ptolemy installed in power there a general named Ophellas, and he in turn seems to have placed garrison commanders in the various cities; to one of them, Epikydes in Teucheira, Ophellas handed over Thibron for execution.[2] It is certainly at this juncture that Ptolemy worked out the arrangement with the Cyrenaeans embodied in the constitution of Cyrene, which will be discussed later.

The Cyrenaeans revolted in 313, but Ophellas was rescued by forces sent from Egypt which put down the revolt. The state of affairs in the next five years is not clear, but by 308 Ophellas had adopted a certain degree of independence in his foreign policy,

---

1. The historical summary that follows will not be documented or argued in detail, for no purpose would be served by a repetition of what may be found elsewhere. The story of Thibron is to be found in Diod. 18, and Ophellas' attack and capture in Diod. 18.21.7-9. Arrian (*Diad.* F 1.17-18, Roos) and the Marmor Parium (*FGrH* 239 B 10) confirm the events and the date.

2. Epikydes (*Pros. Ptol.* 15105) handed him over to the Teucheirans for execution, with Ophellas' consent: Arrian *Diad.* 1.17 Roos (*FGrH* 156 F 9.17-18).

which led him to an alliance with Agathokles of Syracuse.[3] He
marched to aid Agathokles in an attack on Carthage but was
murdered by his ally. It appears from the Suda that Ptolemy was
able to recover Cyrene quickly.[4] It is a matter of much debate what
the relations between Ptolemy and Ophellas were after the revolt
of 313; there is no evidence of a declaration of independence on
Ophellas' part nor of his minting any coins. On the other hand,
Ptolemy's later cordial relations with Agathokles suggest that Soter
was not sorry to be rid of Ophellas.[5]

In any case, Cyrene seems to have revolted again within a few
years, and this time Ptolemy, busy elsewhere, had to wait until
after Ipsos in 301 to turn his attention to the Cyrenaica. This time,
he installed his stepson Magas as governor.[6] Magas' status, too, is
uncertain. At some point he took the royal title, and he even fought
his half-brother Ptolemy II once. We know nothing of the administration during his reign.[7] Nor is it possible to be sure when it was
that he broke with Alexandria, although it appears to have been
after the death of Soter. There is some evidence that his revolt did
not come immediately, however, but some years later.[8] Magas'

---

3. References for Ophellas' career may be found under *Pros. Ptol.* 15062,
and discussions by V. Ehrenberg, *Riv. Fil.* 66, 1938, pp. 144-151 and E. Will,
Revue des études anciennes 66, 1964, pp. 320-333. In the main I follow Will's
conclusion that Ophellas, though acting independently, probably avoided
an open break with Ptolemy, who was busy elsewhere. André Laronde has
recently (*Rev. hist.* 245, 1971, pp. 297-306) attempted to show that Ophellas'
show of independence was intended to lull the Cyrenaeans into forgetting
Ptolemaic domination in dreams of expansion to the west and that Ophellas
was acting according to Ptolemy's wishes throughout. This seems rather
overly ingenious to me, but Ptolemy may not have been sorry to see both
Ophellas and the Cyrenaeans kept busy.
4. The Suda (Adler) II, s.v. Demetrios, p. 42, recounts the fact that
Ptolemy got control of all of Libya after Ophellas' death; he places the
recovery right after Ptolemy's return from Greece in 308, after he had left
Leonides in charge.
5. On Ptolemaic connections with Agathokles, see most recently L.
Moretti, *Riv. Fil.* 93, 1965, pp. 173-179.
6. The chronology of Magas is much argued. I follow the arguments and
scheme of F. Chamoux in *Rev. hist.* 216, 1956, pp. 18 ff., which appear to
me sound despite the reservations of P. M. Fraser in *JEA* 43, 1957, p. 108,
no. 49. Chamoux gives a full bibliography and references; more recent
secondary literature is listed under *Pros. Ptol.* 14533.
7. As Chamoux points out. The coins of Magas appear to follow those
of Alexandria in the valuation of gold and silver to one another. Cf. note 27
below on the use of *eparchia* to describe Magas' kingdom.
8. The evidence is complex, and I reserve a discussion of it to another
time. A dedication evidently of the first years of Philadelphos' reign honors
that king in Cyrene and suggests that a break had not yet occurred.

death about 250 was followed by a few years of struggle which ended in the return of Cyrene to Ptolemaic control with the marriage of Magas' daughter Berenike to Ptolemy III. Euergetes, however, speaks of Libya as a possession inherited from his father, and it may well be that Philadelphos' claim to Cyrene had always been maintained at court.[9]

With the accession of Euergetes and his marriage, however, the period of agitation ended. It was not until 163 that Cyrene was again disturbed, once again to be the separate kingdom of a member of the royal family. In the agreement of this year between Philometor and the later Euergetes II, Cyrene became the kingdom of the latter, Egypt and the other possessions of the former.[10] A year later Cyrene revolted again, this time supported by the governor whom Euergetes had left in charge of the area, Ptolemaios "Sympetesis," an Egyptian.[11] This revolt was put down, but it curbed Euergetes' activities outside the Cyrenaica for some time. The separation of Cyrene lasted until Euergetes' accession to the throne in Egypt in 145. It remained in his hands until his death in 116.

In the next 15 years, Cyrene appears to have been once more a pawn in the struggle for power. I have tried to show elsewhere that it remained in the control of Ptolemy IX Soter II until sometime between 104 and 101, when his mother succeeded in dislodging him and, supposedly in accord with the wishes of Euergetes, installing the latter's illegitimate son Ptolemy Apion.[12] Apion ruled Cyrene only briefly, however, and on his death in 96 left his kingdom to Rome.[13]

2. KING, CITIES, AND LAND

The fundamental problem of Ptolemaic administration in the

9. OGIS 54 (the Adoulis inscription) records the inheriting of Libya, which is generally admitted to mean Cyrene in that context.

10. References and full discussion in Otto, Zur Geschichte der Zeit des 6. Ptolemäers, Abh. Bayer. Akad. Wiss., Phil.-hist. Abt., N.F. 11, 1934, pp. 92-95.

11. Polyb. 31.18.6-7. Ptolemy Sympetesis had been entrusted with the ἐπιμέλεια τῶν ὅλων (Polybius' phrase) by Euergetes, a post that H. Bengtson (Die Strategie III, p. 157) and H. Volkmann (RE 23, 1959, col. 1765, no. 52) regard as including both cities and chora.

12. I collect and discuss the evidence in Phoenix 26, 1972, pp. 358-368.

13. On Apion, see H. Volkmann, RE 23, 1959, col. 1737-8, no. 29, with full citation of sources. On his will, Livy ep. 70, and Otto (n. 10, above), p. 109; a list of sources and bibliography may be found in S. Oost, Classical Philology 58, 1963, p. 22, n. 3, and G. Perl, Klio 52, 1970, p. 319, n. 1.

Cyrenaica, for which we have a few key documents, is the relationship of the king, cities, and land. Much the most famous of these
documents is the so-called "Constitution of Cyrene," in which we
have considerable parts of a constitutional settlement of the affairs
of the city.[14] It will be profitable to discuss the inscription at some
length, though most of the legal issues that have produced so much
argument must be set aside. There is first a definition of who are to
be citizens of the city: children of citizen parents and Libyssai
within the borders of the Cyrenaica (Katabathmos and Authamalax)
and those from some outlying settlements, whom Ptolemy designates and the *politeuma* accepts. The *politeuma* is then defined as
the Ten Thousand, membership in which is determined largely by a
20 mina property qualification (in various forms) to be assessed by
assessors to be chosen by the elders. It is specified that the exiles
who fled to Egypt and whom Ptolemy designates are to be members
of the *politeuma*.

The council, next, is to be 500 men not younger than 50 years,
to be chosen by lot; their term of office is defined. There are to be
101 elders chosen by Ptolemy, though the *politeuma* may choose
their replacements as they die off. Of other offices, only the priests
of Apollo shall be chosen from among the elders. The others—
strategoi, nomophylakes, ephors—are to be chosen from members
of the *politeuma* of requisite age who have not previously served in
the office in question. Of the six *strategoi*, five are to be elected; the
sixth is to be Ptolemy, permanently.

The next section relates the duties of the new magistrate and
councils to the functions of their counterparts under the old constitution, and it establishes legal rules, which are to be as before
except where the old laws are superseded by the present *diagramma*.
In particular, any capital cases are to be judged by the elders,
council, and a jury of 1500 chosen from the *politeuma*, except that
for the first three years a defendant is to be allowed to appeal to
Ptolemy rather than be tried under the system here outlined. A
long and fragmentary section defines various other civic duties,
punishments, litigation, various occupational status, the garrison,

---

14. The text printed as *SEG* IX 1 (the most recent full text) is unreliable
and to be used only in conjunction with the careful rereading of many parts
by P. M. Fraser, *Berytus* 12, 1958, pp. 120-127. Very full bibliography in
SEG with recent additions in Fraser. The many legal and constitutional
issues the inscription raises must be left aside here.

and tenure of property; Ptolemy is mentioned several more times.

It appears that the entire Cyrenaica is to be under one government in this system, and that a normal set of city institutions is to be the focus of this government. Certain prerogatives are reserved to Ptolemy, however. There are some temporary ones, part of the settlement of civil strife: naming the *gerousia*, enrolling exiles in the citizen body, having appellate jurisdiction in capital cases and some voice in the admission of new citizens. The permanent ones are more significant for long-range control: placement of a garrison, permanent tenure as *strategos*, permanent control of judgments on exiles, and possibly a power of issuing decrees, the most open-ended prerogative of all, though its attestation is fragmentary.

The date of the document has been much argued, but it seems that the absence of the royal title must mean that Ptolemy was not yet king, a conclusion supported by the recently published documents from Iasos; further, A. Laronde has recently demonstrated that considerations of Cyrenaean prosopography put the date of 321 practically beyond doubt.[15] Since the mention in the inscription of the exiles to Egypt tallies exactly with what Diodorus tells us of the situation at the time of the intervention of 322-1, there can be no hesitation in accepting 321 as the correct date.

The character of Ptolemy's role appears to me to fit well with a first intervention into the affairs of Cyrene. In form, the city government is to be restored to working order, only somewhat reformed. There is no mention of resident Ptolemaic officials, no trace of a tribute. There is, however, a garrison. Most of Ptolemy's retained powers can be portrayed as an outgrowth of the function of arbitrator in the internal disputes, but the permanent post as *strategos* and the placement of the garrison—which is taken for granted rather than specifically decreed—show that Ptolemy's power went well beyond guaranteeing the settlement that he had brought about. Still, we are not entitled to assume that a Ptolemaic bureaucracy had been implanted in numbers. Ptolemy was probably unable to concern himself with more than military and diplomatic security at this time. The dynast, newly established in Egypt itself, would have had no tradition of bureaucracy to place on the city, and the evidence is that he avoided direct administration in this case.

---

15. See Chapter V. In these texts, too, Ptolemy is settling a gravely disturbed situation, acquiring some rights in return; again he lacks the royal title. See Laronde's summary, *Revue des études grecques* 85, 1972, pp. xiii-xiv.

From near the other end of Ptolemaic rule in Cyrene, more than two centuries later, comes the other document to which we owe our knowledge of the king's relationship to the city. It consists of a decree of the city of Cyrene and a letter and *prostagma* of Ptolemy IX Soter II and his wife Cleopatra Selene, dated in 108.[16] The decree deals with the establishment of a cult in Cyrene for the royal pair as the Savior Gods. The letter tells the Cyrenaeans that the sovereigns are sending them a copy of the letters sent to those set over the city (ἐπὶ τῶν πόλεων τεταγμένοις) and the ordinance thus issued. This ordinance orders those in charge of requisitions (τῶν ἐπὶ χρείαις τεταγμένων) and other officials of the crown, in carrying out confiscation of ownerless property or the belongings of defendants, not to seal up the belongings of defendants or to put them under guard without bringing warrants from the *chrematistai*. In other words, arrest and confiscation require the use of due process in the royal courts. The bureaucratic organization manifested here is quite characteristic of Ptolemaic rule in Egypt, so much so that H. J. Wolff speaks of this *prostagma* as "offenbar eine für das ganze Herrschaftsgebiet bestimmte Verordnung." [17] Cyrene was therefore at this time treated judicially as an integral part of the kingdom (although Soter's ordinances may at this time not have been of any force in Egypt, which his mother controlled).

In this text, then, we have not only the city commandants, known since the time of Ptolemy I, but also a host of vaguely defined royal officials of whom the ones in charge of requisitions and the *chrematistai* are specifically mentioned. They suggest a considerable establishment of royal financial and judicial functionaries, for whose proper behavior the city governors bore some responsibility. They had a judicial *diagramma* to guide their actions in bearing this responsibility, as the *prostagma* tells us. But despite this flowering of bureaucracy, the cities still retain a certain measure

---

16. Text and bibliography in *SEG* IX 5. There has been much discussion of the date, primarily because some scholars have maintained that in accord with Justin's (39.5.2) account of Euergetes' will, Apion's rule must date from 116 if not earlier. That this is incorrect I demonstrate elsewhere (note 12, above). The date of 108 is now nearly universally accepted. The calendaric anomalies on which Roussel based much of his argument (*REA* 41, 1949, pp. 5-18) are not helpful; cf. *P. Teb.* 105 and A. E. Samuel, *Ptolemaic Chronology*, p. 150.

17. *Das Justizwesen der Ptolemäer*, München 1962, p. 170, n. 39, where the relationship of this edict to other evidence of the situation is outlined. Cf. also his discussion of the *chrematistai*, pp. 64-89.

of autonomous action and form. Their own official structure is still flourishing: the decree mentions magistrates, priests, priestesses, *demiergoi, hierothytai*, a *prytaneion, stephanephoroi*, perhaps a *geronteion*.[18] The city makes requests, votes decrees, establishes sacrifices.

Neither the royal bureaucracy nor the civic institutions are to be dismissed as unimportant or a facade. They both had very real functions in the scheme of Ptolemaic rule. The city's subjection to the king is not in question; his ordinances are all-powerful. But he does not usurp all functions of government. The exact relationship between king and cities remains unclear; we do not know enough of the bureaucracy to say what lines of demarcation existed between royal and civic administration, as what follows will show.

The ambiguity that we cannot resolve here also appears in the royal bequests of the kingdom to Rome. In 155, before another campaign against his brother, Ptolemy VIII Euergetes II published a will of which a copy has survived on an inscription from Cyrene; another copy was sent to Rome. After a wish to get the better of his enemies, he bequeaths to the Romans, his friends from the start, the kingdom belonging to him, if he dies without heir.[19] He enjoins on them the maintenance of his property and the defense of the cities and the country from any attack. It appears reasonable to conclude from the will that Euergetes regarded the cities of the Cyrenaica as part of his kingdom and property, for it is by virtue of his alliance with Rome that he asks for this aid. The cities of the region thus enjoy the status of friend and ally of Rome by virtue not of their own act but that of Ptolemy their king.

When Ptolemy Apion died in 96 B.C., he bequeathed the Cyrenaica to Rome, which set free the cities.[20] It is not clear how this will compares with that of his father; the latter makes no special provision about the cities, and we do not know if Rome's treatment of them rests on any provision of Apion's will. The degree of civic autonomy that Cyrene enjoyed in the king's eyes is therefore not clear.

Aside from the cities (in which term I include the lands belonging

---

18. According to P. M. Fraser's reading and restoration (note 14, above), pp. 127-128.

19. Very complete publication by G. Oliverio in *Documenti Antichi dell' Africa Italiana* I.1, Bergamo, 1932, p. 14.

20. Cf. note 13, above. Otto suggested that the Roman distinction in treatment between cities and *chora* might have been in part responsible for their delay in taking up the inheritance.

to them) the Cyrenaica included a rather large amount of land inhabited mainly, it seems, by the natives of the region.[21] We know little about these peoples and their land during the Ptolemaic period, but in the period of Roman control, these lands appear in various sources which it will be useful to enumerate. Cicero[22] mentions lands belonging to the Roman people "qui Apionis fuerunt," that is to say, that had once been part of the royal lands belonging to Ptolemy Apion. That these were extensive is attested by Hyginus,[23] who describes them as "laterculi quadrati uti centuriae, per sena milia pedum limitibus inclusi," each block including 1250 iugera; such a description clearly implies lands of large extent, which need not, however, be all of the best type of farmland.[24] At least twice Roman emperors had to send representatives to halt private encroachments on the public land.[25] The lands were not limited to these large tracts outside of the cities, however; a κῆπος in Ptolemais and perhaps some land in Cyrene also were included in these public estates.

21. The boundaries are discussed by A. H. M. Jones, Cities of the Eastern Roman Provinces[2], Oxford, 1971, p. 360, with particular reference to the amount of land to be included within the non-urbanized countryside.

22. De Leg. agr., 2.18.51.

23. De Cond. agr., ed. Lachmann, I, p. 122.

24. Jones (n. 21, above), emphasizes the undoubtedly great size of the estates. S. I. Oost, CP 58, 1963, p. 13, remarks that "probably most of these large tracts were semiarid and suitable for ranching, rather than more intensive husbandry, or for the gathering of the silphium plant."

25. Both instances have long been known from ancient authors and confirmed in this century by inscriptions. Tacitus (Ann. 14.18) tells us that L. Acilius Strabo was sent by Claudius praetoria potestate to recover for the Roman people the lands of Apion which had been taken over by their neighbors; that Nero supported Strabo's actions but "se nihilo minus subvenire sociis et usurpata concedere scripsit." G. Oliverio, Documenti dell' Africa Ital. II.1, Bergamo, 1933, pp. 129-132, no. 137, published a bilingual inscription recording Nero's restoration to the Roman people through Strabo of some of these lands; Oliverio suggests that Nero's concessions may have been some minor adjustments rather than any major upsetting of Strabo's work. The second incident comes in the reign of Vespasian, and is recorded by Hyginus (n. 23, above), who notes that "lapides vero inscripti nomine divi Vespasiani sub clausula tali, OCCUPATI A PRIVATIS FINES: P.R. RESTITUIT." Oliverio published also (pp. 132-133, no. 138) a bilingual inscription indicating the restoration of a garden by Q. Paconius Agrippinos under Vespasian. Comparable is Notizie archeologiche 2, 1916, pp. 165 ff., the restoration of a Ptolemaion to public control. Views on what this was have varied, but Rostovtzeff (Social and Economic History of the Roman Empire, p. 681, n. 64) is surely right against S. Ferri, Aegyptus 4, 1923, p. 164, in asserting that this is royal land (a temenos park, perhaps) rather than a temple.

The early history of the Roman exploitation of these estates is almost as uncertain as the history of the lands under the Ptolemies, but it is at least possible that they were kept under fairly careful control from the immediate aftermath of the death of Apion in 96.[26]

3. Officials

Our knowledge of the highest echelon of administration in the Cyrenaica is very limited. Ophellas and, for a time, Magas seem to have held a post as governor of the entire province (even when he was king, Magas' kingdom was called an *eparchia*),[27] but neither title nor duties (aside from the obvious one of keeping order and control) can be discerned.

After Magas, we have no documentation of a governor until the outset of Epiphanes' reign, when Agathokles sent Philammon, supposed to be the murderer of Arsinoe III, to be what Polybius calls λιβυάρχης τῶν κατὰ Κυρήνην τόπων.[28] His term of office was brief, for he returned to Alexandria not much later only to be murdered by the mob there.[29] As is often the case in dealing with literary

---

26. The history of the Cyrenaica in the thirty years after Apion's death has been much discussed; see S. I. Oost (n. 24, above) and the bibliography cited by A. H. M. Jones (n. 21, above), p. 497, n. 12, especially the discussion by E. Badian, *Journal of Roman Studies* 55, 1965, pp. 118-121. The recent discovery of an inscription from Cyrene on a statue base of C. Clodius Ap. f. Pulcher (*cos.* 92) is of interest: se ethe publication and discussion of L. Gasperini, *Quaderni di archeologia di Libia* 5, 1967, pp. 53-57 (text reprinted in *Année épigr.* 1967, 532, which replaces the correct genitive 'Αππίω with 'Αππίου and omits Gasperini's dots, as well as indicating inaccurately "qu'il gouvernait peu de temps après cette date [92] la nouvelle province de Cyrénaique"). Gasperini suggests that Clodius, who is described by the Cyrenaeans as their patron, was responsible for freeing the cities of the Cyrenaica when Rome accepted the gift in his will; that the Cyrenaean Aiglanor may have been a sort of superintendent of Roman interests in Cyrene, nominated perhaps by Apion and accepted by Rome. In this instance one would have testimony of Rome's continuing interest in its revenues from the inheritance from Apion during the years immediately after the death of the king and long before the formal organization of the province. Gasperini argues for a peaceful and prosperous period before the tribulations of the time of the Mithridatic wars, contrary to older theories that troubles had started right after the death of Apion. The governors of Cyrene in the republican period are discussed by G. Perl, *Klio* 52, 1970, pp. 319-354, with a detailed list of Roman official figures of this time in Cyrene and Crete.

27. Term used in treaty between the Oreioi of Crete and Magas, *I. Cret.* II 17.1.10.

28. His dispatch to Cyrene, Polyb. 15.25.12; the murder of Arsinoe, 15.26a.1; of Philammon, 33.11-12.

29. See note 28.

sources, we cannot be sure of the degree of technical accuracy in Polybius' description of Philammon's title. Bengtson thought that "libyarch" was not a technical term, but that the mention of τῶν τόπων indicated that Philammon governed only the *chora* and not the cities.[30] In the absence of other attestation of such a division of administration, however, it seems risky to postulate it here. Indeed, Hippomedon *strategos* of Thrace has a similar phrase in his title, yet he was clearly involved in governing the cities of his province.[31] In any case, if libyarch is not a technical term (as seems likely) it is possible that τῶν κατὰ Κυρήνην τόπων is itself no more than a periphrasis.

The next attested governor, the only securely datable one attested by epigraphy, is Philon son of Kastor, *archisomatophylax* of the king and *strategos*, honored by the Cyrenaeans for his *arete* and *eunoia* toward Ptolemy and Cleopatra Epiphanes and their children, and the city of Cyrene.[32] The date is therefore 185-180. The same man is also known as proxenos at Delphi and Thermon in 188/7; he came of an important family, for his father was honored by Athens as a friend of Ptolemy III, and some probable descendants are to be found in the Alexandrian aristocracy.[33]

We have already encountered Ptolemy Sympetesis, entrusted with the ἐπιμέλεια τῶν ὅλων by Ptolemy VIII in Cyrene in 162.[34] He subsequently joined the Cyrenaeans in revolting against Euergetes but was ultimately defeated. His post was perhaps as much as regent (since Euergetes had no kingdom but the Cyrenaica) as it was as governor.

One further possible *strategos* appears in the fragmentary inscription for X son of . . . . nes, Cyrenaean, who has the title [ca. 15 ? σ]τρατηγὸν τῶν κατὰ | [ca. 15]ν. The dedicant is Hippis son of Hippis, bearer of a rank now lost.[35] Peremans and Van 't Dack, citing

---

30. *Die Strategie* III, p. 157.

31. Chapter VII, below.

32. Text first in *Documenti Antichi dell' Africa Italiana* II.1, Bergamo, 1933, pp. 107-108, no. 75, reprinted as *SEG* IX 55 and *SB* 9940, both of which give an incorrect date of 146.

33. On Philon's family connections, J. IJsewijn, *De Sacerdotibus*, pp. 98-99, no. 108, with references also to his career. Proxenies, *Syll.*³ 585.146 and *IG* IX² 31A. 141-2. See also H. Bengtson, *Die Strategie* III, p. 158. A. H. M. Jones' contention (n. 21, above), p. 497, n. 13, that Philon was the *strategos* nominated by the king over the city is certainly to be rejected.

34. Polyb. 31.18.6-7.

35. *Notizie Archeologiche* I, 1915, pp. 85-86, no. 1, with drawing of text, fig. 41. Text reprinted *SEG* IX 359.

Philammon's title, suggested the possibility of restoring [Κυρήνην τόπω]ν, but thought it unlikely because of the provenance of the text, which was found at Ptolemais.[36] An additional negative argument is that this restoration is shorter than any supplement for the other lines that I can think of, if a court rank is indeed lost in both men's titles. Nonetheless, one important consideration supports the restoration: the date. The lettering was described by the first editor as late second century or early first century. If this date is even approximately right, it brings us to an era in which the Ptolemies controlled no foreign possessions but Cyprus and Cyrene, and I do not see any title of the domestic administration of Egypt here. But such a phrase is not used in Cyprus, and in any case for the period 145-100 we have a fairly complete roster of *strategoi* of Cyprus, none of whom can be this man. The likelihood therefore favors his placement over Cyrene and the restoration of a title like that suggested by Peremans and Van 't Dack. We have seen enough uses of Cyrene to mean the whole province, I think, to admit its possible use here.

For the governorship of Cyrene, then, we have one and perhaps two *strategoi*, both probably of the second century, and several figures with a governing position but no title securely attested by documentary evidence.

As to city commandants (ἐπὶ τῆς πόλεως), we have the letter addressed to them by Ptolemy IX, which has already been discussed. The presence of the garrisons they commanded is attested as early as 322/1 by the mention in the constitution of Ptolemy I, and the one commander known comes from the same time: Epikydes, governor of Teucheira, the agent of Ophellas in giving over Thibron for execution.[37]

For both the *strategia* and the command of a city we have evidence of continuity of position (if not title) from the earliest to the latest days of Ptolemaic rule in Cyrene. For other official positions we have only the testimony of the decree of Cyrene and Ptolemy IX's letter and *prostagma*, with the officials mentioned there and already in the financial and judicial branches of the royal administration. They are attested only in this late document, and it is impossible to say how far back their presence went.

Other Ptolemaic officials and court figures are known in the Cyrenaica, where they either were honored or placed dedications

---

36. *Pros. Ptol.* 15090, based on Polyb. 15.25.12.
37. See note 2, above.

themselves. A few of these are lacking titles and therefore may have
been royal officials in Cyrene, though other possibilities also remain
open. A group of these statue bases from the reigns of Euergetes
and Philopator, two from the years 209-205, honor three men:
Pelops son of Pelops (the later *strategos* of Cyprus), during Euergetes'
reign; a Ptolemaios; and X son of Boiskos, both from Philopator's
reign.[38] All were probably placed by the Cyrenaeans, but none—as
presently preserved—carries an official title.[39] Similar is the situation with a statue base of one Krates, set up by his father Krates
son of Philoxenos, one of the first friends: the men were important
in the Ptolemaic court, but their role in Cyrene is unknown.[40]

Two inscriptions that surely date from after the death of Apion in
96 preserve statue dedications by the Cyrenaeans to Aiglanor son of
Damatrios, Cyrenaean, "kinsman" τῶ βασιλεύσαντος ἀμῶν Πτολεμαίω,
for his good deeds toward his fellow-citizens and (in one text) the
other cities and the κατὰ τὰν χώραν ἔθνεα.[41] It is interesting that even

---

38. Pelops son of Pelops, published by Fraser, *Berytus* 12, 1958, p. 111,
no. 4; text also in *SEG* XVIII 734 and *SB* 10081; an additional fragment is
discussed in *Ptol. Alex.* II, p. 191, n. 85. Ptolemaios, Fraser, p. 113, no. 6
(*SEG* XVIII 733); son of Boiskos, Fraser, p. 112, no. 5 (*SB* 10079, *SEG*
XVIII 732). It is possible that this last is connected with the great Samian
family of Kallikrates the admiral.

39. Mention may be made here of one Alexandros (*Pros. Ptol.* 15743)
honored by Athens (*IG* II² 891; cf. *SEG* XVI 83) ca. 188/7 for his help to
Athenians in Alexandria and Cyrene; as is usual in these decrees, his official
position is not mentioned.

40. *Annuario* n.s. 23-24, 1961-1962, p. 321, no. 182. No date is suggested,
but the text is to be placed in the second century.

41. The two texts were published in ignorance of one another and almost
simultaneously. One, published by R. M. Harrison in *Archäologischer An-
zeiger* 1962, col. 437, with plate (reprinted *SEG* XX 729, *SB* 10186), is
complete. The editor placed it correctly after the death of Apion, but *SEG*
opines that the writing is somewhat earlier. (Hauben and Van 't Dack,
ZPE 8, 1971, pp. 32 ff., cite the opinion of P. M. Fraser that the hand cannot
be so closely dated. L. Gasperini, n. 26 above, p. 54, describes the Aiglanor
text as very close in lettering to the dedication to C. Clodius, of 92 B.C.) The
mention of the former king without mention of any present king, however,
and the use of ἀμῶν seem to me to assure the date of Harrison. The second
text, of which much is lost, was published without comment by D. Morelli
in *Annuario* n.s. 23-24, 1961-1962, p. 347, no. 246. The first two lines, which
he left unrestored, should on the basis of the complete text be

Αἰγλάνωρα Δαμα[τρίω Κυρηναῖον τὸν συγγενῆ τῶ]
βασιλεύσαντος ἀ[μῶν Πτολεμαίω πολλὰς καὶ] etc.

A shorter restoration is proposed by H. Hauben (cited above), although
he also mentions the possibility of a longer restoration such as I have given.

after the end of Ptolemaic rule the former relationship to Ptolemy Apion is something of value and interest in Cyrene. But what official position, if any, Aiglanor held under Apion is not told.

This is the evidence for the Ptolemaic administration in Cyrene. It is not extensive in the upper levels, as is the case in Cyprus, nor in the lower levels, as is the situation in the Egyptian papyri. Only the outlines are discernible: a governor of the entire area (though this post might have been eliminated under a resident king limited to the Cyrenaica), city commandants in all the cities, a large number of financial and judicial officials to represent the crown. With these, there is a full apparatus of civic government, partly permeated by royal influence through the king's position as strategos, and subordinate to his commands. It is hard to give chronological depth to these observations with the scanty evidence we have; but it is not unlikely that the normal law of bureaucratic expansion operated here.

The longer restoration seems to me inevitable in the face of the parallel. Hauben and Van 't Dack are noncommittal on the historical implications of the texts and the identity of Ptolemy, for whom they review at length the various persons they deem possible. Cf. L. Gasperini, n. 26, above, pp. 56-57, who suggests that Aiglanor served as a caretaker of Roman interests in the Cyrenaica immediately after 96. Greater precision is achieved by Chr. Habicht, *Chiron* 2, 1972, pp. 127-129, who identifies the role of Aiglanor's daughter in the time of Mithridates VI.

CHAPTER FOUR

CYPRUS

Cyprus was a possession of the Ptolemaic dynasty longer than any land except Egypt; the island was the scene of Ptolemaic activity in the earliest days of Ptolemy I and in the last decade of Cleopatra VII; it had geographical position and natural resources of the first importance; and its history under the Ptolemies was less troubled than that of Cyrene, the only other foreign dominion to be held for a comparable span of time. It is, then, no cause for surprise that our documentation for Ptolemaic rule in Cyprus is more adequate than for any other part of the empire save Egypt. All the same, we do not have anything like an even distribution of evidence. Much of our epigraphical material concerns the governor of the island, the *strategos*, but little of it yields information about the nature of his administration. Most of what remains concerns his subordinates in the powerful garrison of the island. We know very little indeed about the economic administration of Cyprus.

In the pages that follow an attempt is made to give some balance to the picture; much of the detail about *strategoi* that does not directly concern their administration is relegated to Appendix A, while the roster of the rank and file is drawn up in Appendix B.

I. The Strategos

A. *The* Strategia *Before Pelops*

The centrality of the *strategos* to all discussions of Ptolemaic rule in Cyprus has generated the assumption that so central and important a figure must have been present in the Ptolemaic administration of that island from the beginning of Ptolemy I's domination. This supposition has been reinforced by the general belief that in the persons of Nikokreon, last king of Salamis, and Menelaos, brother of Ptolemy I, we have the first two holders of the position in the late fourth century. It is therefore hardly surprising that two further candidates have been advanced for the near-century between the end of Menelaos' control in 306 and the start of the tenure of

Pelops son of Pelops under Philopator (see below). Without exception it has been assumed that lack of epigraphical testimony for a *strategos* in the early and middle third century is to be attributed to the deficiency of evidence.

It is, to be sure, not impossible that these assumptions are correct. But it appears to me that they are in fact unsupported assumptions up to the present and that only new documentary evidence is likely to allow us to speak with confidence about the *strategia* before the reign of Philopator. The detailed reasons for this conclusion follow.

(1) *Nikokreon of Salamis*[1]

The last Cypriot king of Salamis, son of his predecessor Pnytagoras, had supported Alexander at Tyre, (rallying to him, like the other Cypriot kings, after Issos),[2] and after Alexander's death he was one of the Cypriot kings to league themselves with Ptolemy.[3] He had a certain renown abroad, for a statue of him was set up at Argos, and he appears as a donor in the Delian temple inventories.[4] Although the mint of Salamis was largely given over to producing Alexander coinage during the period from 332 to the end of Nikokreon's life (see Chapter VIII), Nikokreon issued a coinage of his own in the types of his father's coins, with the legend BA NI or BA NK.

In the last few years of his life, Nikokreon rose to considerable prominence. He was always Ptolemy's most powerful ally in Cyprus, and when Ptolemy became aware in 312 that a number of the other Cypriot kings were disaffected from his cause (after earlier alliance or conquest), he ousted them and turned their cities and revenues over to Nikokreon; in Diodorus' words, Ptolemy made Nikokreon *strategos* of Cyprus: τῆς μὲν Κύπρου κατέστησε στρατηγὸν Νικοκρέοντα.[5]

The Marmor Parium records for 311/0 that Nikokreon died and Ptolemy became the ruler of the island.[6] Modern scholars, led on by

---

1. *Pros. Ptol.* 15059; H. Bengtson, *Die Strategie* III, no. 132; H. Berve, *Das Alexanderreich auf prosopographischer Grundlage* II, Leipzig, 1926, no. 568.

2. Arrian 2.22.3; Plut. *Alex.* 29.2.

3. Diod. 19.59.1; 19.62.5.

4. Statue at Argos, *IG* IV 583; Delian offerings, references collected by W. Peremans and E. Van 't Dack, *Antidoron M. David* (Pap. Lugd.-Bat. 17), p. 88.

5. Diod. 19.79.5.

6. *FGrH* 239 F 17.

an ancient confusion between Nikokreon and his contemporary Nikokles of Paphos, have sometimes attributed Diodorus' account of the death of the latter to Nikokreon instead.[7] The recent thorough study of Helga Gesche[8] makes it unnecessary to rebut this argument in detail. Nikokles, it is clear, was forced by Ptolemy to commit suicide in the year after the death of Nikokreon, on suspicion of treasonable correspondence with Antigonus.[9] As to Nikokreon, a complete understanding of his position requires first an examination of the place of Menelaos, the brother of Ptolemy.

(2) *Menelaos, son of Lagos*

The brother of the first Ptolemy served him as an important lieutenant in the years after Alexander's death and was still prominent in Alexandria as the eponymous priest of Alexander in 284, near the end of Soter's reign.[10] When Ptolemy sent an expedition to Cyprus in 315, says Diodorus, he made Menelaos his brother τῶν δὲ πάντων [the troops and ships, that is] στρατηγόν.[11] Some years later at a time just before the forced death of Nikokles in 310/309, Menelaos is again called *strategos*.[12] And during the campaigning of 307, Diodorus again refers to Menelaos as τῆς νήσου στρατηγός (20.47.3) and ὁ ἐν Σαλαμῖνι στρατηγός (20.52.5). Other late literary sources call him Πτολεμαίου στρατηγός[13] or σατράπην Πτολεμαίου.[14]

---

7. Gesche (next note) gives a thorough bibliography and citation of these attempts to attribute the story in Diod. 20.21.1 ff. to Nikokreon, as well as rebuttals of these reassignments.

8. Helga Gesche, *Chiron* 4, 1974, pp. 103-125.

9. Mention may be made of the attempt of T. B. Mitford, *Op. Ath.* 3, 1960, pp. 198, 200-202, to argue that Nikokles' inscriptions, which he there collects, would have been defaced after that king's death had he been the forced suicide. V. Karageorghis, in *Salamis in Cyprus*, London, 1969, pp. 151-164, argues further that Nikokreon's supposed cenotaph at Salamis indicates that he was not buried normally. The latter argument proves nothing, and indeed directly contradicts Mitford's contention, for a cenotaph would be a signal honor indeed for a traitor. Furthermore, there is no evidence for the use of any form of *damnatio memoriae* by Ptolemy or any of the earlier Hellenistic kings. It is hard to say whether Egyptian or Roman influence is paramount in the use of erasure of inscriptions by Ptolemy Euergetes II.

10. Menelaos as priest appears in *P. Eleph.* 2 (*M. Chr.* 311) of year 40 of Soter (284/3, cf. A. E. Samuel's demonstration in *Ptolemaic Chronology*, p. 12, and not 285/4, eds., or 286/5, *Pros. Ptol.* 5196), and *P. Hib.* 84a (*M. Chr.* 131), where the reading is somewhat uncertain.

11. Diod. 19.62.4.

12. Note 7, above.

13. Polyaenus 4.7.7.

14. Pausanias 1.6.6, referring specifically to Cyprus.

It is generally assumed by modern writers that Diodorus is using the term *strategos* both for Menelaos and for Nikokreon in a technical sense; that is, they were both *strategoi* in the sense that Pelops and his successors were, holding an official position officially designated *strategos* of the island.[15] The scheme usually envisaged is the appointment of Nikokreon in 312, his death in 310, and Menelaos' subsequent tenure until the loss of the island in 306.

There are some problems here, however. (1) Menelaos is already designated *strategos* of the Ptolemaic military forces in Cyprus by Diodorus in 315. If Diodorus' terminology is accurate, one must assume either that Menelaos was replaced by Nikokreon in 312, only to regain his place on the king's death in 310, or that there were two men with the title *strategos* operating on the island at the same time.

(2) In our sole documentary evidence for these two men, they both bear the same title: king. BA appears on Nikokreon's coins in Greek letters, and on Menelaos' very similar coins BA appears in the form of the Cypriot sybllabic letter for the sound *ba* ($\neq$), following the letters MEN in alphabetic script (cf. Chapter VIII). Menelaos was therefore the king of Salamis in the years after the death of Nikokreon and asserted the fact by issuing a small amount of royal coinage in addition to the large quantities of Alexander coinage that continued to be emitted. Svoronos suggested that the use of the Cypriot syllable rather than the Greek letters on Menelaos' coins was meant to make it clear that the kingship was only local. In these years Ptolemy himself, like the rest of the successors, had not yet taken the royal title.[16] Menelaos, like Nikokreon, must have stood in much the same relationship to Soter as Philokles king of Sidon later did to Philadelphos, a vassal king ruling over a rather enlarged area, in this case most if not all of Cyprus.

(3) The attempt to extract technical terminology from Diodorus or almost any ancient historian is a difficult one. It is essential to make a distinction between official titles, which were the name of a rank or office in the royal service, and words used to describe the nature of a person's activity. The latter are descriptive and non-

---

15. Thus H. Bengtson, *Die Strategie* III, p. 139, n. 2; D. Cohen, *De Magistratibus*, p. 96: "dubium non est quin re vera Menelaus insulae strategum fuerit." H. Gesche, *Chiron* 4, 1974, p. 108, n. 19, cites various explanations of the titulature and position of Nikokreon and Menelaos.

16. J. Svoronos, *Die Münzen* I, col. 67-75.

technical. If, for example, one says that W. S. Hancock was the
commander of the Second Corps in the Union Army, one does not
mean that he was a Commander, which is a rank; he was in fact a
Major General. In the same way, it is possible to say that Menelaos
was a general, even though his title may have been king of Salamis.

In Diodorus, the term *strategos* appears frequently throughout
books 17 to 20 in a simple meaning of military commander or
general; as many as two-thirds or more of his uses of *strategos* fall
into this category. With a preponderance of this kind, one has
reasonable grounds for demanding of any claim for a more specific
or technical meaning that other evidence, internal or external, be
available to substantiate the distinction. The passages in which
Diodorus himself gives a more specific designation are clearly in the
main references to the area in which a man was to exercise his
military command; these may range from Europe down through a
particular city or small area.[17] In no instance is it possible to demonstrate that *strategos* was an administrative title attached to an area.
Rather, it is a word used to describe individual men. The very
variety of Diodorus' usage shows that his description of a man as
strategos cannot be taken without other evidence to be a technical
term describing an administrative position.

What evidence we possess, then, entitles us to assert that
Nikokreon was a king subject to Ptolemy, who extended his territory and prerogatives very considerably over much of the rest of
the island and that Menelaos succeeded to this precise position
about 310 B.C. and filled it just as Nikokreon had. The evidence
suggests that shortly after coming to power in Salamis Menelaos
acted on orders from Ptolemy to eliminate one of the few remaining
kings in Cyprus, Nikokles of Paphos. If anyone in this period is to
be designated *strategos* of Cyprus in the same sense that later
governors were, the evidence for it is yet to be found.

(3) Lysimachus

Through a curious chain of reasoning, attempts have been made to
show that Lysimachus, son of Ptolemy II and Arsinoe I, brother of

---

17. The complications of Diodorus' terminology are too great to be more
than pointed out here. Of some 153 uses that I note in books 17 through 20,
106 use *strategos* in a very broad sense to mean "general". In specific titles,
we may note three times a *strategos* of Europe (17.118.1; 18.12.1; 19.105.1),
and men in charge of various smaller areas ranging down to Argos (19.63.1).

Ptolemy III Euergetes, was *strategos* of Cyprus about 246 B.C.[18]
The stages of the argument are the following: (1) There is a much-
discussed Gurob papyrus which contains a report of actions by
Ptolemaic military forces in the Third Syrian War, the surviving
part recounting events of the early days of the war in 246 B.C. The
author was clearly an important commander, and his triumphant
welcome at Seleukia is described in some detail. He says that he
then went in to "the sister," who was Berenike, second wife of
Antiochus II and a daughter of Ptolemy II. From this situation it
is deduced by most commentators (though not all) that the author
was a brother of Berenike;[19] there is much plausibility in M.
Holleaux's argument that the welcome accorded could belong only
to royalty. The possible authors are therefore two: Ptolemy III
and his brother Lysimachus.

(2) It is then asserted that Ptolemy cannot be the author. The
reasons for the statement are two: Ptolemy is represented in the
literary sources as arriving too late, after the death of Berenike,
whereas in the papyrus she is still living; and the literary sources
again show Ptolemy coming by land, while the author of the papyrus arrived by sea. Therefore, it is argued, only Lysimachus is left.

(3) Lysimachus, as commander of the fleet, was nauarch, admiral.
From evidence later than 145 B.C. it is then argued that the fleet
was based on Cyprus, and the nauarch was the governor of Cyprus
as well.

(4) It is but a short step then to assert that Lysimachus was
governor of Cyprus; and the title of that official is well-known to
have been *strategos*. Lysimachus, therefore, was *strategos* of Cyprus.

The falsity of the argumentation under (2) was demonstrated in
detail long ago by Maurice Holleaux in a pair of classic articles.[20]
The literary sources in fact do not support either part of the argu-

---

18. The *Pros. Ptol.*, without passing judgment, lists him as a possible
strategos (14531, 15054). The listing is based on two works which present
the arguments discussed here: A. Roos, *Mnemosyne* n.s. 51, 1923, pp. 277-
278, and F. Jacoby, commentary to *FGrH* 160, p. 589, in more condensed
form.

19. Despite Ulrich Wilcken's questioning of this conclusion (commentary
to *W. Chr.* 1) it seems to me valid (cf. Holleaux's remarks, cited in note 20,
below).

20. In these two articles, *Études* III, pp. 281-310, Holleaux presents the
text, a detailed interpretation, and a refutation of many other hypotheses;
my conclusions follow his entirely.

ment, for Ptolemy is represented only as advancing with an expedition—nothing is said about its being on land. Nor does the papyrus indicate clearly that Berenike was still alive. Holleaux proceeds to outline two solutions for this problem, both possible: that the curious language and brevity of the papyrus about the meeting of brother and sister is explained by the fact that she was dead; or, that the papyrus was deliberately masking the fact that she was dead before the author's arrival, for some purpose of propaganda. In either case, it is not necessary to exclude Ptolemy from authorship. Holleaux in fact shows that it is very probable that Ptolemy was the author.

Under the circumstances, steps (3) and (4) are without foundation. They are in fact in themselves entirely without merit. There is no evidence that the fleet was based on Cyprus until the reign of Ptolemy VIII, nor that the governor of Cyprus held the post of nauarch as well until their conjunction is found in Seleukos son of Bithys in 142 (see Appendix A). Finally, there is no evidence that a governor of Cyprus at this time would have been called *strategos*. There is, then, no evidence whatsoever for the assertion that Lysimachus was *strategos* of Cyprus during his brother's reign.

(4) *Philinos*

An inscription from an unknown place in Cyprus records a dedication to Sarapis and Ptolemy and Berenike Euergetai by one Philinos son of Philoti[mos], Athenian.[21] This man has been tentatively identified by T. B. Mitford with the father of the athlophore of 197/6 and the canephore of the following year, and the father also of two women who held the same positions in the years between 187/6 and 182/1.[22] Mitford reasons from this identification and from the fact that later *strategoi* and other high officials were fathers of eponymous priestesses that Philinos should have been of high rank. He therefore suggests that Philinos was governor of Cyprus around 230 B.C.

It appears that in general women held these eponymous priesthoods at "debutante" age, in their later 'teens or early twenties. Pyrrha, the first of Philinos' daughters to be named, must therefore

---

21. *OGIS* 63.
22. On the priestesses, J. IJsewijn, *De Sacerdotibus*, p. 39, nos. 90-91; pp. 41-42, nos. 100-102, 105. Mitford's conjecture, *Op. Ath.* 1, 1953, p. 131, n. 5.

have been born about 215, her sisters a decade later. If one assumes that Philinos was no more than 60 when his last daughter was born, he must have been born after 265. In 230 he would have been at most 35 years old and even by 220 only 45, young for a *strategos* of Cyprus. If, as is more likely, Philinos was younger when his daughters were born, he might well have been under 20 years old in 230. More important than the brute statistics of theoretical age, however, is the fact that these priestesses almost invariably held their positions close to the time when their fathers were of greatest prominence and power, while Mitford's suggestion would provide a separation of at least a quarter of a century and perhaps up to nearly half a century for the younger daughter. Just such a gap caused IJsewijn to reject the identification of the *dioiketes* Athenodoros (ca. 232) with the father of priestesses of the period 193-190.[23] Philinos does not, then, seem a strong contender for governor of Cyprus, if he is the same as the father of the priestesses. If he is not their father, there is no reason to assign high rank to him. There is thus no justification for assuming that he held an office which he is not designated as holding.

B. *The* Strategoi *from 217*

The sequence of governors of Cyprus from 217 on is outlined in Appendix A, where the career and family of each man are discussed. The list given here is in many cases approximate but represents what is known with reasonable certainty or probability:

Pelops	217-203
Polykrates	203-197
Ptolemaios son of Agesarchos	196-180
Ptolemaios "Makron"	180-168
unknown	168-164
Archias	163-158
Xenophon?	158-152
Andromachos?	152-145
Seleukos	144-131
Krokos	130-124
Theodoros	123-118
Helenos	118-117
Ptolemy (IX Soter II)	117-116
Ptolemy (X Alexander)	116-114
Helenos	114-106
none (antistrategos Potamon)	105- 88
Chaereas?	88-80?

23. J. IJsewijn, *De Sacerdotibus*, p. 92, no. 94.

In 80 Cyprus passed to the bastard son of Ptolemy IX, from whom
the Romans annexed the island in 58 B.C.[24] The governors for
Cleopatra VII (during the short-lived restoration of Ptolemaic rule
to the island under Caesar and Antony) who are treated in Appendix A, do not concern us here.

The *strategoi* were men of the highest rank, for whom the governorship of Cyprus was usually the culminating point of a long career
of service to the crown. This was true especially in the second
century, when the Ptolemies had fewer overseas positions of importance to bestow. *Strategoi* are attested in later posts except in a
few instances when one returned to active life to take an emergency
position or held a sinecure like an eponymous priesthood. Pelops
was sent to Antiochus III in 204 by Agathokles to try to stave off
that king's attacks on Ptolemaic possessions. His successor Polykrates came out of retirement to help suppress an Egyptian revolt
in 185. Toward the end of the century Theodoros son of Seleukos
held a priesthood for a decade and a half after his retirement as
strategos.[25]

Many of the *strategoi* either were eponymous dynastic priests
themselves, like Theodoros and Helenos, or had children or other
relatives who served in these posts, like Pelops (father), Ptolemaios
of Megalopolis (daughter), and Seleukos and Theodoros (various
family members). From the time of Ptolemaios Makron, the *strategoi*
bore the highest rank of the Ptolemaic aulic hierarchy, "kinsman"
of the king. Much of what we know about the *strategoi* concerns
their careers elsewhere, their part in the dynastic struggles of their
times, their families, their entire position at court. For our present
purpose, we need do no more than point out this eminence. We may
mention briefly a few prominent family members: Pelops' father
Pelops, a commander of Ptolemaic forces on or visiting Samos,
and Polykrates' sons who served in important military posts on
Cyprus after their father's *strategia*.[26] It is no exaggeration to say
that in the second century, if not before, the governorship of
Cyprus was the most important post outside Egypt at the disposal
of the Ptolemies.

The most important task of the *strategos* was to keep his province

24. Details and sources in G. F. Hill, *History of Cyprus* I, Cambridge,
1940, pp. 205-209.
25. Cf. below, pp. 254 and 260, n. 52.
26. Cf. below, pp. 252-255.

under control and in Ptolemaic hands. When a *strategos* failed in this duty, it was as likely as not deliberately; Ptolemaios Makron went over to Seleucid service, and Archias was caught trying to sell the island a few years later.[27] The primacy of the military aspect of the *strategia* is evident from the choice of the title itself, but even more so from other considerations. The officers and soldiers of the garrison, whose organization is discussed below, constitute a major source of dedications to the *strategos*—usually statues of the governor and of members of his family. This tendency, evident already under Pelops and Polykrates,[28] reached a peak in the reign of Ptolemy VIII Euergetes II, when Seleukos, Krokos, and Theodoros ruled the island in times of great dynastic turmoil: of the dedications to these men and their families, fully half come from various elements in the armed forces.[29] Had we better documentation for Philometor's reign, it might well present the same picture.

More evidence of the military role of the *strategos* is found in the fact that from Seleukos (in 142) to the establishment of Ptolemy IX on the island in 106/5, the *strategoi* of Cyprus almost without exception bore the title of nauarch, admiral of the Ptolemaic fleet.[30] With the withdrawal of Ptolemaic forces from the Aegean after the death of Philometor, Cyprus became not only a military stronghold of importance but also the base for the royal fleet. It played a key part as a base in the civil wars of the reign of Euergetes II (among other times), and the *strategoi* of that reign were clearly among the foremost generals of the king.[31]

The domain of the *strategos* did not stop at the command of the garrisons placed in the island and of the fleet based on it. From the term of Pelops on, a stream of dedications by the cities of Cyprus to the *strategoi* and their families inform us that these cities, too, had an important relationship with the *strategos*.[32] The motive

---

27. Cf. below, pp. 256-257.

28. For Pelops, *JEA* 46, 1960, p. 110, no. 3; for Polykrates, *I. Hell. Paphos* 42.

29. The inscriptions are collected in Mitford's *Seleucus*.

30. Mitford, *Seleucus*, pp. 147-148, gives the evidence and a discussion.

31. Krokos, like another general of Euergetes, Lochos, bears the title of "champion of the king" (*hypermachos*). Mitford, *Seleucus*, pp. 156-163, collects the evidence for his *strategia* and its place in the campaigns of the period.

32. Paphos honored Pelops (*I. Hell. Paphos* 39) and his son Ptolemaios (*JEA* 46, 1960, p. 110); Polykrates and his entire family (*I. Hell. Paphos* 43-45); Seleukos and Theodoros (Mitford, *Seleucus*, 7, 9, 10); Krokos (*Seleu-*

formulae of these inscriptions are vague: good will toward the king, benefaction to the city. In only one respect can we be more precise, the gymnasium. Οἱ ἀπὸ γυμνασίου of Paphos honored sons of Pelops and Polykrates,[33] while Helenos was honored by the gymnasiarch of Salamis.[34] The last epigraphical monument of Ptolemaic rule on Cyprus, an inscription of 40 B.C., is a statue of a gymnasiarch of Salamis erected by Cleopatra VII's *strategos* of Cyprus and Cilicia.[35] We will see this connection between crown and gymnasium again on Cyprus and elsewhere in the Ptolemaic possessions. Aside from this, however, it is hard to discern the details of the political role that the *strategos* played in dealing with the cities.

The second *strategos*, Polykrates, added to the titulature of his office the term *archiereus*, high-priest. An inscription from the time of his successor Ptolemaios son of Agesarchos, provides some amplification.[36] Ptolemaios is called *strategos* and ἀρχιερέως 'Αρτέμι-δος δε[σποίνης ?] θεῶν καὶ τοῦ βασιλέως καὶ τ[ῶν ἄλλων] θεῶν ὧν τὰ ἱερὰ ἵδρυται ἐν τῆ[ι νήσωι]. Despite the uncertainty of the first restoration, it is made clear that the *strategos* is the chief priest of every single cult in the island, both local and dynastic.[37] It is again not spelled out anywhere just what the duties and prerogatives of the high-priest were, but their importance is manifest. Religious and corporate bodies form another important group of dedicants of inscriptions (and the statues above them) to the *strategoi* and their families, at least in the later second century. The priests of Paphian Aphrodite—probably the most prominent cult of the island—honored Seleukos once and Helenos twice (once in each *strategia*).[38] The *technitai* of Dionysos and the dynastic cult honored

---

cus 25); and Helenos (Mitford, *Helenus* 6 and 8). Salamis is represented by two dedications to Theodoros (Mitford, *Seleucus* 16 and P. Roesch, *Rev. arch.* 1967, pp. 225-238) and two to Helenos (Mitford, *Helenus* 5 and 9, the former, however, while he was not *strategos* but tutor to the strategos Ptolemy Alexander). Chytroi honored the granddaughter of Seleukos (*Seleucus* 13); Kourion, Seleukos himself (*Seleucus* 6, now *I. Kourion* 45).

33. Ptolemaios son of Pelops, *I. Lindos* 139, corrected in *JEA* 46, 1960, p. 110; Ptolemaios son of Polykrates, *I. Hell. Paphos* 46 (after Polykrates' term as *strategos*).

34. Mitford, *Helenus* 9.

35. For this inscription see below, p. 262, n. 65.

36. Mitford gives a full discussion of his text and restorations and defends them against critics in *Studi Calderini-Paribeni* II, pp. 163-176.

37. As Mitford says, *Seleucus*, pp. 144-145, n. 26.

38. Seleukos: *Seleucus* 7; Helenos: *Helenus* 3 and 8.

Seleukos, his son Theodoros, and Helenos.[39] These and other religious groups honored other Ptolemaic officials as well, as we shall see.

Of the financial competence of the *strategos* we know very little. We know that Polykrates and Ptolemaios Makron each collected the island's revenues against the *anakleteria* of his sovereign (Epiphanes in 196, Philometor in 169). The ability to do this entails a general supervision of the finances in the island, which Polybius expressly notes that Polykrates possessed; but to go beyond this would be pure speculation.[40]

It can hardly be claimed that the evidence bearing directly on the *strategos* clarifies his role within the island to any great extent, whatever it may do for prosopographical and political study of the kingdom as a whole. But the *strategos* was the supreme official in Cyprus, and all that went on there under Ptolemaic rule came within his competence. The components of this rule will emerge somewhat further from the detailed consideration of the subordinate elements of the army and administration.

2. THE MILITARY

The troops stationed on Cyprus were, to all appearances, divided into a number of garrisons placed in and around the major cities of the island. We have an inscription of a commander of a garrison in the earliest days of the Ptolemaic restoration in Cyprus after 294 who, in company with other military officers, honored Berenike I, wife of Ptolemy I.[41] He called himself *phrourarchos* over Kition and [Idalion]. The title *phrourarchos* appears once more in a fragmentary inscription of unknown provenance from the late third century, where a man whose name is lost bears the title ὁ ἐπὶ τῆς

---

39. Mitford, *Seleucus* 10, 14; *Helenus* 6.

40. Polyb. 18.55.6 (Polykrates); Mitford, *Studi Calderini-Paribeni* II, pp. 163-176 (Makron). Walbank's statement (*A Historical Commentary on Polybius* II, Oxford, 1967, p. 627) that the funds accumulated by Polykrates came "mainly, no doubt, from the rich temples," is no more than an improbable speculation. The normal revenues of Cyprus and its resources were no doubt large enough even without special levies on the temples. The administrative nature of the duties of the Seleucid high-priests is discussed by A. E. Millward in *The Ruler Cults of the Seleucids* (Diss. Toronto, 1973); Millward argues (against Mitford) that the Ptolemies, not the Seleucids, probably created the notion of a provincial high priesthood, using it first, he suggests, with Ptolemy son of Thraseas.

41. *OGIS* 20; Mitford's restoration, *AJA* 65, 1961, p. 127, n. 142.

[πόλεως] γενόμενος φρούραρχος.[42] He is thus the 'former *phrourarchos* over the city.' A similar phrase is wrongly restored at Kourion. After considerable argument about the relationship of the two offices of *phrourarchos* and ἐπὶ τῆς πόλεως, the prevailing view is that *phrourarchos* has a meaning similar to that of ἐπὶ τῆς πόλεως but harsher connotations, and that the milder term therefore came into use at the expense of the more military designation.[43] I find this explanation somewhat unconvincing. An inscription of Kition (treated below in more detail) is a dedication to a man called τὸν γενόμενον ἐπὶ τῆς πόλεως ἡγεμόνα καὶ ἱππάρχην ἐπ' ἀνδρῶν. The structure of the title appears to me parallel to that of the second *phrourarchos* inscription: the person in question has a military rank—*phrourarchos* in one, *hegemon* and hipparch ἐπ' ἀνδρῶν in the other—and a position occupied (formerly, in both cases).[44] The distinction between permanent rank and a specific post occupied seems to me an important one in both inscriptions. It is true, however, that after the end of the third century the term *phrourarchos* is not encountered in Cyprus, nor after the end of Epiphanes' reign elsewhere in the Ptolemaic empire. I suspect the reasons are to be found in expediency of military organization and the nature of our evidence, not in concessions to local sentiment. For a fuller consideration of the situation in the empire as a whole, see Chapter IX.

The importance of the commandant's position to the city under his charge will be explored further in a later section. It remains now to underline further the military importance of the position, never seen more clearly than in the case of Theodoros son of Seleukos, who during his father's *strategia* served as ἐπὶ Σαλαμῖνος καὶ ἐπὶ τῆ[ς] κατὰ τὴν νῆσον γραμματε[ί]ας τῶν πεζικῶν καὶ ἱππικῶν δυ[νάμεων].[45] The inscription in which he was so honored was placed not by Salamis, the city of which he was commandant, but by Arsinoe (Marion), quite at the other end of the island. As effective second-in-command of the entire military force under his father, he was an important man to all the island. His position was

---

42. *Archiv* 13, 1938, p. 18, no. 7.
43. For this problem, Mitford, *Seleucus*, pp. 153-154, with notes; more bibliography and discussion in W. Peremans and E. Van 't Dack, *Antidoron M. David* (Papyrologica Lugduno-Batav. 17), pp. 84-87. See Chapter IX for a broader discussion.
44. *OGIS* 134.
45. Mitford, *Seleucus* 11.

admittedly an unusual one dictated by extraordinary circumstances, but the juxtaposition of the two commands is not fortuitous.

Under the garrison commanders served the ordinary officers of the troops, the *hegemones* and hipparchs—from whose ranks, indeed, the commandants themselves were drawn on more than one occasion. We have a fair number of the *hegemones* attested, and the roster of the *hegemones* and their soldiers may help to give an idea of the military dispositions on the island.

Paphos

Hegemones: An inscription of the second century preserves a dedication by one Chairias, *hegemon*, to two daughters of Leonnatos and Olympias.[46] The complexities of prosopography and dating make it impossible to do more than mention this text here.[47] Another Paphian inscription records the placement of a statue of a man and one of his wife, during the first decades of the second century (to judge from the letter forms). He has the court rank of *diadochos*, but his title is missing: Mitford has suggested that this man, Protarchos, might have been [ἡγεμόνα ἐπ᾽ ἀνδρῶν].[48] I know of no other instance in which a *hegemon* has court rank, however, and the restoration must remain dubious.

Soldiers: Appendix B gives the roster of ordinary soldiers in this garrison known to us.

Salamis

Hegemones: The other chief city of Cyprus is even worse represented in this respect. An inscription of the *strategia* of Seleukos (142-131) or of Theodoros (after 124) honors one Diktys, who by Mitford's plausible restoration would have been [ἡγεμόνα τῶν ἐν τῆι νήσωι τασσομένων] Κρητῶ[ν], with a statue put up by Salamis.[49]

Soldiers: See Appendix B.

---

46. Mitford, *Seleucus* 22 and pp. 170-171; also *I. Hell. Paphos* 62.

47. Mitford's commentary, *Seleucus*, pp. 170-171, speculates on connections between Leonnatos (*hegemon* and son of the commandant of Karpasia under Epiphanes; cf. note 56, below), Olympias daughter of the *strategos* Seleukos, and Chaereas, admiral of Ptolemy IX in 88 B.C. The chronological gaps involved seem to me an insuperable obstacle to direct identification, but some of the family connections may be correct.

48. *I. Hell. Paphos* 49 (cf. *Pros. Ptol.* 15235).

49. Mitford, *Seleucus*, p. 151, n. 68.

Kition

Hegemones: In the inscription of the *phrourarchos* Poseidippos, of the years 294-290 (mentioned above), his co-dedicants to Berenike were Boiskos and his <σ>υνηγεμ<ό>νε[ς], according to Mitford's conjecture from the text of the copy.[50] The military officers indicated would thus be a *phrourarchos* Poseidippos over the military district of Kition and Idalion and his subordinate *hegemones*, among whom Boiskos appears most prominently.

An epitaph dated on the basis of the letter forms to the reign of Philometor records the name of Praxagoras and his rank, ἐπ' ἀνδρῶν . . . ἡγεμόνα.[51] Another more recently published inscription of this time or slightly later is a dedication by one Apollodoros, with the rank of "friend" of the king, to Boethos his son, a *hegemon*.[52]

An inscription also of this period (the exact date is problematical; see below) is a dedication by the wife of a city commandant Melankomas to her father-in-law Melankomas son of Philodamos, former city commandant with the rank of *hegemon* and hipparch ἐπ' ἀνδρῶν.[53]

Finally, a remarkable inscription of the reign of Ptolemy IX Soter II records the dedication on his behalf to Zeus and Athena by a group described as οἱ ἐν Κιτίωι [τα]σσόμενοι πρῶτοι φίλοι καὶ ἀρχισωματοφύλακες καὶ ἡγεμόνες ἐπ' ἀνδρῶν καὶ περὶ τὸ σῶμα μαχαιροφόροι.[54] The inscription probably celebrates Soter's victories in Jordan in 103; it is remarkable in juxtaposing men whom one thinks of as courtiers with aulic rank and those more overtly a part of the military; we are no doubt seeing a product of the peculiar situation common enough in those decades—in which a king resided in a Cyprus separated from Egypt.

From the locality of Ormidhia, to the east of Kition, a fragmentary inscription of the time of Epiphanes preserves the title but not the name of an [ἡγε]μόνα [ἐπ' ἀνδρῶν].[55]

Soldiers: Appendix B.

---

50. See note 41, above.

51. W. Peek, *Griechische Versinschriften*, Berlin, 1955, no. 1076.

52. Published by Ino Nicolaou in *RDAC* 1969, pp. 84-85; as published, this text presents a number of problems, which I attempt to resolve in *ZPE* 11, 1973, pp. 121-123.

53. *OGIS* 134; see the discussion of priesthoods below for the date.

54. *Archiv* 13, 1938, p. 34, no. 16. The date given is Mitford's.

55. Mitford, *Seleucus*, p. 153, n. 73; *SEG* VI 823; *Pros. Ptol.* 15255.

Karpasia

Hegemones: In the reign of Epiphanes, Leonnatos, son of the commandant of Karpasia at this time, Aristos (see below), had his statue erected; his title was ἡγεμόνα ἐπ' ἀνδρῶν.[56] Some four decades later, some residents of the same area honored Sophanes of Achaea, also as ἡγ[εμόνα] ἐπ' ἀνδρῶν.[57]

Soldiers: None attested.

Lapethos

Hegemones: An inscription dated by Mitford in the second half of the third century contains the remains of the title [ἡγεμὼν ἐ]π' ἀνδρῶν.[58] It seems to me that the title in this fragmentary text refers more probably to the dedicant than to the object of the dedication, [Aine]ias son of Kriton, whose name follows the title, and whom Peremans and Van 't Dack take to be the *hegemon*.[59]

Soldiers: Appendix B.

Kerynia

Hegemones: An interesting inscription of the mid-second century from near Akanthou, some 25 miles to the east of Kerynia along the north coast, records the dedication on behalf of Menneas the *hegemon* to the Savior Mother of the gods, of τὰ οἰκήματα τά τε ἀπὸ νότου σὺν τοῖς ἐφυπέροις καὶ τὸ ἀπὸ βορρᾶ.[60] The dedicants, Agrios, Homilos, and Hedeia, are surely, as the Roberts have suggested, the children of the man thus honored.[61]

Soldiers: Appendix B.

Any adequate study of the rank of *hegemon* would have to go far beyond the limits of this chapter and of this study as a whole. No securely attested *hegemon* on Cyprus has aulic rank, despite Mitford's restoration at Paphos; but a man of the rank of *hegemon* may hold the post of city commandant, as in the case of Melankomas son of Philodamos at Kition. At the same time, some of the

---

56. *BCH* 3, 1879, pp. 172-173, no. 23.
57. *AJA* 65, 1961, p. 122, no. 23.
58. Last seen and published by J. K. Peristianis, Γενικὴ Ἱστορία τῆς Κύπρου, Nicosia, 1910, p. 944, no. 33; the date, Mitford, *Seleucus*, p. 153, n. 73.
59. *Pros. Ptol.* 15169.
60. *RDAC* 1964, pp. 199-201, no. 12.
61. *Bull. épig.* 1966, 492.

dedications in which *hegemones* appear seem quite humble, particularly in the more remote commands in rural areas, like the
Karpas peninsula and the area of Akanthou to the east of Kerynia.
There is a spread of circumstances dimly visible: *hegemon* was a
rank, but by no means a full definition of the position a man might
find himself in at a given time. While Mitford's suggestion that
hegemon without the tag of ἐπ' ἀνδρῶν indicated a higher authority
is probably too precise (and seemingly not right in the case of
Menneas), he rightly delineates the variety possible within this
rank.[62] The *hegemon* is an officer of rank in the Ptolemaic army,
who may be used on the staff or as a subordinate commander in
a large force; he may also hold an independent command in a
place where the military importance of the command is small.
'Επ' ἀνδρῶν is probably meant to separate line from staff officers,
referring only to the former.

The details of the other aspects of the military organization of
the Ptolemaic garrison of Cyprus are relevant more to a study of
military institutions than to one of the administration. But it is
worthwhile treating the situation in outline. Mitford has argued
in detail for a four-part evolution of the organization of the Cypriot
garrison. The phases he defines are these: (1) In the earliest days
of the occupation of Ptolemy I, the troops were known as αἱ δυνάμε[ις
αἱ ἐν Κύπρωι τεταγ]μέναι, as Mitford restores one text.[63] (2) Under
Ptolemies II through V, and until the middle of Philometor's
reign, units were designated by the name of their commander,
for example [οἱ στρατιῶται οἱ ὑ]πὸ Νικάνορα [τα]σσόμενοι.[64] (3) Under
Philometor, from 163-145, the unitary aspect is again emphasized:
"During this the effective portion of his reign we hear only of αἱ
ἐν Κύπρωι τασσόμεναι πεζικαὶ καὶ ἱππικαὶ δυνάμεις or of their officers,
the ἡγεμόνες καὶ ἱππάρχαι ἐπ' ἀνδρῶν." [65] (4) In 142, shortly after
the start of the reign of Euergetes II, these united dedications
disappear, and only units based on ethnic groups are found. We
hear, therefore, of the *koinon* of each ethnic group, sometimes the

---

62. *Seleucus*, p. 153, n. 73. On the distinction between ἡγεμόνες ἐπ' ἀνδρῶν
and ἡγεμόνες τῶν ἔξω τάξεων, see M. Holleaux, *Études* III, pp. 1-14.

63. *JHS* 57, 1937, p. 29, no. 3. The discussion that follows here is largely
based on Mitford's remarks in *Seleucus*, pp. 149-153.

64. *JHS* 57, 1937, p. 35, no. 9; Mitford's date is mid-third century.
Nikanor is perhaps the same as the eponymous commander known in Egypt
from 254 to 236 (*Pros. Ptol.* 1961). Cf. also *I. Kourion*, pp. 121-122.

65. *Seleucus*, p. 150.

officers of these groups as well.[66] Mitford speculates that this division of the garrison into ethnically homogeneous groups represents an attempt to prevent the garrison from developing sufficient cohesion to threaten the safety of Euergetes' power.

It does not appear to me nearly so certain for the first three of these phases that the divisions are real rather than accidents of evidence. For (1) there is only one text, whose exact date is uncertain, though Mitford takes it that the king honored by the troops is Soter. It does not seem impossible to me that the subdivisions of the garrison, identified by the name of their commanders, could have co-existed with an overall term for the entire garrison of "the troops stationed in Cyprus." Phases 1 and 2, therefore, may be only two aspects of the same type of military organization.[67]

Phase 3, in Philometor's reign, is open to much the same criticism. The general designation of the troops stationed in Cyprus is reminiscent of phase 1, and one may prefer to think that such designations had never gone out of use. The *hegemones* and hipparchs, too, are not new in the second half of Philometor's reign; they cannot be counted as an element of military reorganization.

For the period down to 142, then, it appears to me that we have insufficient evidence to take the chronological distribution of the documents at hand as conclusive evidence for a sequence of military organizations. We cannot say that Mitford's scheme fits reality as well as it does the inscriptions now known. Mitford is, of course, right to point to the large number of inscriptions involving the army and its more technical divisions under Philometor, but that may indicate as much the tense dynastic situation, the need for affirmation of loyalty, as it does a change in the nature of the garrison.

Mitford's fourth phase, under Ptolemy VIII, is more pronounced, and its general outlines are clear from a comparatively large number of documents, which Mitford has assembled.[68] The *koina* of the Cretans, Lycians, Cilicians, and others sponsor statues honoring the *strategoi* and members of their families. The officers of the *koinon* may appear, but never the soldiers separate from their union. No two *koina* ever act together. Mitford sees in this change

---

66. The material is collected by Mitford (note 63, above), pp. 150-152.
67. *Seleucus*, pp. 149-150.
68. Cf. note 66.

a move by Euergetes to weaken the fighting force which after years of development by Philometor remained hostile to Euergetes after his accession.

I see no way, however, of determining that the creation of more homogeneous 'regiments' was in fact detrimental to the effectiveness of the army. Nor am I persuaded by Mitford's notion that this reorganization is to be attributed to evil motives. Given the difficulties of controlling a mercenary garrison—with which the Ptolemies were all too familiar—a reduction in the ability of the entire garrison to set itself up to act independently without direction from the crown would by no means be a foolish thing for a king to do, nor would it weaken the usefulness of the troops for fighting external enemies. The generous grants in Euergetes' letter to the garrison in 145/4 show how much he owed his troops and how dependent on their good will he (like other monarchs) was.[69] If he subsequently tried to reduce the power of this military force to serve divisive dynastic interests, it is scarcely to be wondered at or to be condemned. Sympathy with the vigor of Philometor's reign and character need not blind us to the skill of many of Euergetes' moves. For the remainder of his reign, in fact, he had no trouble that we know of with his garrison, and it served him as a base in the civil war of 131-126.

The bulk of this evidence about the garrison appears to concern those who were on active duty as soldiers, for the terms δυνάμεις and στρατιῶται are words for active military forces, not for settlers.[70] The *hegemones* and hipparchs ἐπ' ἀνδρῶν are also generally accepted to have been commanders of troops on active duty.[71]

That these men were also mercenaries is also reasonably certain. One inscription of the reign of Epiphanes says specifically that the soldiers responsible for the dedication were hired as mercenaries by a certain person.[72] In the earliest days of Ptolemaic intervention in Cyprus there were large numbers of mercenaries under the command of Myrmidon, a subordinate of Menelaos.[73] The *thiasos* of the ἀποσκευή which appears at Chytroi suggests the baggage train of goods and family that followed a mercenary unit in its

69. For the Larnaca amnesty and letter, see below, section 4.
70. On δυνάμεις see below, Chapter V, note 20; on στρατιῶται, G. T. Griffith, *Mercenaries of the Hellenistic World*, Cambridge, 1935, p. 126.
71. Mitford, *Seleucus*, p. 153.
72. *CIG* 2623; cf. *I. Hell. Paphos* 46.
73. Myrmidon: *Pros. Ptol.* 15223; Diod. 19.62.4.

campaigns or settled around it when it was on garrison duty.[74] The soldiers themselves, as the list in Appendix B shows, come from much the same areas from which the *koina* of Euergetes' reign are drawn: Asia Minor, particularly Lycia and Cilicia, and less prominently Greece, but with better representation from the north, the Chalcidic peninsula, Thrace, and the islands than from other areas. Indeed, it is difficult to think of any way except by being hired that these men could come into Ptolemaic service.

There is some hint, however, of something more than the garrisons on active duty. Mitford goes so far as to say that "in early Ptolemaic times the island was held, it would seem, in much the same manner as was the χώρα of Egypt itself: there is some hint of military settlement on the land."[75] The strongest piece of evidence to this effect is the presence of thiasoi in the *chora*, particularly in the Mesaoria plain. In particular, an inscription from modern Morphou (probably part of the *chora* of Soloi) is a dedication, probably of the later third century, by a *thiasos* of the *epigonoi* to a Ptolemaic officer in Cilicia.[76] The presence of the *epigonoi*, characteristic of a system of military settlement in which the sons follow their fathers in service, ensures that the garrison of Cyprus was not composed only of the troops on active duty in the cities. But the exact workings of this system in Egypt are not necessarily applicable in Cyprus.[77]

The garrison of Cyprus, then, appears to have consisted of standing forces in many if not all of the cities, varying in size according to the military importance of the place, together with the families of these men and perhaps retired soldiers themselves living on land in the *chora* of the cities. To provide the scene for this distribution, we turn next to the cities themselves.

3. THE CITIES

For long it was assumed that city institutions were relatively undeveloped in Cyprus during the Hellenistic period. Rostovtzeff, for example, wrote that Cyprus, with its "semi-Phoenician and semi-Greek" cities, was one of "the provinces in which city life

---

74. *Ath. Mitt.* 9, 1884, p. 137, no. 8.

75. Mitford, *Seleucus*, p. 149.

76. *AJA* 65, 1961, pp. 134-135, no. 35, and p. 142, where Mitford collects and discusses the evidence for *thiasoi* in Cyprus.

77. In particular, the problem of land tenure is insoluble without specific evidence now lacking.

was undeveloped, or developed on Oriental lines." [78] But in 1953
Mitford suggested on the basis of a partial collection of evidence,
particularly the unpublished Kourion material, that this assumption was mistaken. More evidence has accumulated since Mitford
wrote, and it has brought confirmation to his thesis.[79] It seems
to me worthwhile to collect the material now available in some
detail here, with both the civic institutions and the city commandant taken into consideration, in order to give an idea of the thorough permeation of Hellenic political forms through Cypriot cities.

Salamis

Our presently available evidence shows characteristic Greek civic
institutions from the early second century: a gymnasium with its
gymnasiarch, ephebes (by restoration), and alumni; an *agonothetes*,
a *grammateus*, a college of *chreophylakes* and its officers; and a city
strategos. The royal posts of commandant and judge are also attested.
It will be of interest to see some details of this city's flourishing
Greek forms of educational and political organization.

Two dedications to the king from the first decade of Epiphanes'
reign have recently been published, one by Themias son of
Aristagoras, gymnasiarch, the other by Philokrates son of Naukra-
tos, former *agonothetes* (who honors the king in the gymnasium).[80]
The gymnasium continues to be the center of our Salaminian
documentation, in part a result of the recent excavations there.[81]

A long-known but recently revised inscription of the time of
Philometor honors a city commandant (below); its dedicants were
οἱ [ἔφηβοι καὶ] οἱ ἐκ γυμνασίου.[82] Another gymnasiarch, Simalos
son of Timarchos, honored the *strategos* Helenos in 107/6.[83] The last
known inscription of Ptolemaic Cyprus, from the revival in the

---

78. Rostovtzeff, *SEHHW*, p. 339.
79. Mitford, *Aegyptus* 33, 1953, pp. 80-90.
80. T. B. Mitford and I. Nicolaou, *The Greek and Latin Inscriptions from
Salamis (Salamis,* v. 6), Nicosia, 1974, nos. 3 and 4.
81. J. Pouilloux publishes in *BCH* 95, 1971, pp. 569-572, a fragmentary
statue base of Ptolemy II dedicated by [οἱ ἀλειφόμενοι] ἐν γυμνασίωι.
82. Le Bas-Waddington, *Voyage archéol.* 2756, now revised and re-inter-
preted by J. Pouilloux, *Rev. arch.* 1966, pp. 337-340, where the old belief
in three gymnasia at Salamis (based on misinterpretation) is laid to rest.
On the restoration of this line, J. and L. Robert, *Bull. épig.* 1968, 571; see
for the survival of the mistaken interpretation in *I. Kourion* the remarks
of Bagnall and Drew-Bear, *Chronique d'Égypte* 49, 1974, pp. 183-185.
83. Mitford, *Helenus* 9.

reign of Cleopatra VII (40 B.C.), was a statue of Stasikrates son of Stasikrates, gymnasiarch for the year 41-40.[84] The same man is known in a fragmentary inscription also dedicating a statue of him.[85]

An inscription probably dated to 150/149 gives us some officers of the city government: a *grammateus*, a college of χρεοφύλακες, and a πρὸς τῆι διαλογῆι of the records in the office of the χρεοφύλακες.[86] It is to be expected that a full range of other magistrates accompanied these men, and further excavations may yet provide evidence of them.

Two commandants of Salamis are known. The first, Trit[ ], was former ἐπὶ τῆς πόλεως in the dedication of the ephebes and alumni of the gymnasium mentioned above, in the reign of Philometor.[87] Under the next king, Theodoros son of Seleukos, the future *strategos*, served as ἐπὶ Σαλαμῖνος between 142 and 131, during his father's *strategia*, holding the rank of first friend and the additional position of head of the secretariat of the armed forces of Cyprus.[88]

A final inscription of Salamis poses a number of problems. The person honored, [Dion]ysios son of Aigibios, has the titles τῶν φίλων καὶ [βασ]ιλικὸν δικαστὴν τὸν γενόμενον πολιτικὸν στρατηγὸν τοῦ λδ L καὶ λε L.[89] Those honoring Dionysios describe themselves as

[ca. 8]ιων οἱ κωμῆται καὶ
[ca. 7]. οὖντες στρατιωτικοὶ καὶ πολιτικοὶ

The restoration of the lacuna in line 2 is uncertain.[90] The inscription does not come from Salamis itself, but from a field near Sinda, in what was certainly the hinterland of Salamis; the fact that the

---

84. Appendix A, note 65.

85. *Opuscula Archaeologica* 6, 1950, p. 2, no. 1, dated by Mitford to the first century A.D. The name Stasikrates can now be restored there with certainty. The connection, drawn by J. Pouilloux, is made in the article cited on p. 262, note 65.

86. *AJA* 65, 1961, pp. 140-141, no. 6.

87. Note 82, above.

88. Mitford, *Seleucus* 9 and 11.

89. I. Nicolaou, *Berytus* 14, 1961-1963, pp. 133 ff., where Philometor's reign was preferred to that of Euergetes II. In the reprinting of the text as *SEG* XXIII 617 the date is given as 135/4 without discussion.

90. In place of Ino Nicolaou's [οἱ ὑπηρε]τοῦντες, J. and L. Robert (*Bull. épig.* 1965, 453) suggested [οἱ κατοι]κοῦντες. An examination of a cast of the stone in the Cyprus Museum has convinced me that this reading is not possible; but the Roberts are almost certainly correct about the sense required.

dedicants are villagers provides confirmation of its character as a
rural dedication.

The office of political *strategos*, known elsewhere on Cyprus,
appears to be a locally elected position rather than another term
for city commandant; the description of the years in which Dionysios served in the office as thirty-fourth and thirty-fifth (148-146
or 137-135, probably the former) [91] indicates that it was an annual
magistracy, for the terminology is paralleled in Cyprus only in the
case of the office of gymnasiarch.[92] There is, therefore, every likelihood that Dionysios was himself a Salaminian, the earliest
Cypriot known to have attained court rank under the Ptolemies.
His rank is not high in the hierarchy, but any rank is of considerable
importance.

But Dionysios' competence did not stop at his city *strategia*;
he was βασιλικὸς δικαστής, royal judge. The term is in this form
not common, but one example at some distance in space and time
from our text affords a striking parallel. It is a papyrus contract
at Dura-Europos, from A.D. 88/9, in which three of the witnesses
describe themselves as βασιλικοὶ δι[κ]αϲταὶ [καὶ] τῶν πρώτων καὶ
προτιμωμένων φίλων καὶ τῶν σωματ[οφυλάκων].[93] Welles comments
"All the officials of the court bear Parthian court titles, but it is
probable that the court went back to Seleucid times, especially
since its members were local people, bearing typical Dura names." [94]
Another local man held the title of *strategos* and *epistates* of the
city.[95] One may conclude from this parallel, nearly exact, that
Dionysios was a local man holding royal title and court rank in
addition to a locally elected office. His position marks an interesting bridge between the royal authority and the civic government.

One also sees the dependence of the *chora* of the great cities
upon the officials of those cities. The villages, though they had
sufficient local government or self-organization to act as a unit
here and in other cases, were certainly responsible to the officials
of Salamis, and through them to the crown. It is also interesting
that military settlers find cause to honor this Salaminian.

---

91. Cf. note 89 on this problem.
92. Cf. *I. Hell. Paphos* 98. For the local character of the magistracy,
cf. p. 65 below and n. 117 and my remarks about other Cypriot cities.
93. *P. Dura* 19.18.
94. *P. Dura*, p. 11, and n. 1.
95. *P. Dura* 17 and 25.

Paphos

At Paphos, as at Salamis, there was a gymnasium. We know that the government rested on a *boule* and the *demos*, and that the *boule* and city had secretaries. Here, too, there was a city *strategos*, and typically Hellenic religious offices appear. The close relationship of the royal governor and the city meant that there was no commandant, making Paphos unique among important Cypriot cities.

The alumni of the gymnasium of Paphos appear as early as 209-204, when they erected a statue of the son of the strategos Pelops.[96] Our next evidence for the civic institutions of the city comes under Philometor (probably in 154) when the master of tactics, Kallikles, was honored at Old Paphos by the college of the *strategoi* and former *strategoi* of Paphos.[97] The office is presumably similar to that held by Dionysios son of Aigibios at Salamis, but we have here definite evidence that Paphos had a college of them, indeed that the alumni of the college maintained some association.

A group of inscriptions from the reign of Ptolemy IX, again from Old Paphos, helps to fill out the picture. In 105, the city of Paphos erected a statue of its citizen Kalippos son of Kalippos, whose distinguished career is recounted: twice *grammateus* of the *boule* and *demos*, ἠρχευκότα τῆς πόλεως and of the *technitai* of Dionysos, *grammateus* of the city, and successful gymnasiarch in the twelfth year (that of the return of Soter to power in Cyprus).[98] Likewise, Potamon son of Aigyptos, Soter's *antistrategos* and head of the mines, served Paphos as gymnasiarch and was honored twice by the κοινὸν τὸ Κυπρίων for his services.[99]

No city commandant is known for Paphos, which is generally accepted to have been the seat of the *strategos*. But during the civil war of 131-126, the then *strategos*, Krokos, added the title of *epistates* to his titulature. Mitford suggests that the reason lay in a desire to make explicit his military authority in his base for the duration of the crisis; this explanation is not unreasonable.[100] But it would appear that Paphos lacked a commandant in normal times, for none is yet known from this best documented of the

---

96. *JEA* 46, 1960, p. 110.
97. *I. Hell. Paphos* 59.
98. *I. Hell. Paphos* 98.
99. *I. Hell. Paphos* 99 and 107.
100. Mitford, *Seleucus*, p. 162, n. 105.

Hellenistic Cypriot cities. It is to be presumed that the *strategos* filled the necessary functions for himself. Unfortunately, the entry for Paphos in the Delphian list of *theorodokoi* is lost, so that we do not know whether a local man—as at Salamis—or a Ptolemaic official (as at several cities, below) served in this position.

Kition

Besides a political *strategos* and gymnasium, Kition had vestiges of older Phoenician offices. It included in its *chora*, as it had in its kingdom before the Hellenistic period, the area of Idalion, as far north as Kafizin, a few miles from modern Nicosia, then the small city of Ledroi. It calculated dates not only by regnal years but also by an era of the city beginning in 311/10, in use at least in the third century.[101] Its gymnasium is attested as early as the reign of Euergetes I, who is honored by its alumni as their προστάτης with a statue.[102] Some 150 years or more later, a statue base of a woman Herois informs us that her paternal and maternal grandfathers both served as gymnasiarchs, the latter at the time when the inscription was set up by his daughter, the mother of Herois.[103] The lateness of the inscription is suggested by the names of the girl's grandfather (Nauarchos, surely given later than 142, when the *strategos* of the island acquired this title) and mother (Strategis).

Here too there was a city *strategos*, twice attested in the second century. The title appears in full in the inscription of Apollodoros son of Dionysios, honored by the city of Kition;[104] in the case of the somewhat earlier Zenon, the fragmentary condition of the stone prevents our knowing whether this dedication (probably of the earlier second century) also contained the word πολιτικός.[105]

An undated and fragmentary Phoenician inscription of Kition is a dedication to a man styled son of a "quaestor" (in the editors' translation), evidently a financial official.[106] Identification of his office with a Greek title would be speculative and fruitless.

---

101. *RDAC* 1969, p. 89; O. Masson, *BCH* 92, 1968, p. 398, a better text. For dates on the era of Kition at Kafizin, only 4 miles from modern Nicosia, cf. Mitford, *Classical Quarterly* 44, 1950, pp. 100-101.

102. *RDAC* 1969, p. 86, with bibliography.

103. *RDAC* 1969, p. 86; Mitford, *AJA* 65, 1961, p. 113, n. 79.

104. Le Bas-Waddington, *Voyage archéol.* 2729; republished *RDAC* 1969, p. 87, no. 15.

105. Le Bas-Waddington, *Voyage archéol.* 2732.

106. *Corpus Inscriptionum Semiticarum*, Paris, 1881, I 74.

The commandant is well known at Kition. Poseidippos served as *phrourarchos* of Kition [and Idalion] in the reign of Ptolemy I (in the years 294-290), and honored that sovereign's queen Berenike.[107] More than a century later, in the years 163-145, Agias son of Damothetos, a Cretan with the rank of *archisomatophylax*, was honored by the city as ἐπὶ τῆς πόλεως for his good-will towards the sovereigns and benefaction to the city.[108] Probably in the next reign (see below under priesthoods) Melankomas son of Philodamos, Aetolian, and his son Melankomas, both served as ἐπὶ τῆς πόλεως of Kition, the former in addition being priests of the Theoi Euergetai.[109]

Kourion

The inscriptions found at Kourion in the University of Pennsylvania excavations have recently been published by T. B. Mitford.[110] The *boule* appears here in the middle of the third century, in connection with one of the civic decrees of which fragments were found. An *archon* and *grammateus* appear in the latter part of the century. The civic *strategos* and the *agoranomos* are also attested here.[111] On the basis of these texts the development of the political institutions of the city is attested earlier in Kourion than anywhere else on Cyprus, though the fact of excavation surely accounts in large measure for this situation.

Two inscriptions also reveal the presence of a city commandant at Kourion; two holders of this post are known from statue bases of the early second century: Demetrios of Thessaly and X son of .... ippos, of Demetrias. Both had the rank of *archisomatophylax*.[112]

Amathous

One inscription of Amathous gives us evidence of the civic offices of *strategos*, *archon*, and gymnasiarch. It is a decree placed

---

107. *OGIS* 20; cf. Mitford's restoration, *AJA* 65, 1961, p. 127, n. 142.
108. *OGIS* 113.
109. *OGIS* 134.
110. *Inscriptions of Kourion*, 1971. For remarks on many of the Hellenistic inscriptions, see my review of this volume (with Thomas Drew-Bear) in *Phoenix* 27, 1973, 99-117, 213-244.
111. *I. Kourion* 32 (*boule*); 34 (college of former archons); 46-48 (city secretary); 35 and 46 (college of former *strategoi*); 34 (*agoranomos*).
112. *I. Kourion* 42 (Demetrios, to be discussed in the Guarducci *Festschrift* by Chr. Habicht) and 43 (the man from Demetrias). Mitford restores no. 32 as honoring a Sidonian commandant, but this is refuted by Th. Drew-Bear and me in *Chronique d'Égypte* 49, 1974, pp. 181-182.

by Mitford in the reign of Philometor on the basis of the letter forms and bearing a date by the priesthood of Cyprian Aphrodite of Charinos son of Charinos, who has the titles former *strategos*, former gymnasiarch, former *archon*, and is proposed by a man holding those titles and that of *hegetor*.[113] The offices thus indicated are typical of the other cities we have examined so far.

The city also had an ἐπὶ τῆς πόλεως, a son of Ammonios, a Samian, bearing the rank of *archisomatophylax*. His wife, an Alexandrian, is the daughter of Karpion, a "friend" of the king; their sons, also honored, have the rank τῶν διαδόχων.[114] The letter forms seem to be late third century, according to the recent republication by Ino Nicolaou, but the use of court ranks in the inscription makes her dating untenable; it must be lowered to the early second century at the earliest.

Arsinoe (Marion)

Arsinoe, the foundation of Ptolemy II, replaced the ancient city of Marion destroyed by Soter's orders in 312. It probably had full civic status from the beginning; in the reign of Euergetes I an inscription refers to a former gymnasiarch whose term of office seems to serve as a means of referring to a year.[115] There is no evidence for the presence of a commandant of the city, but the paucity of the evidence forbids us to treat this absence as an established fact. It honored Theodoros as commandant of Salamis in the years 142-131 (see above).

Soloi

No evidence has come to light about the institutions of Soloi under the Ptolemies; nor is a city commandant attested. Its civic status, however, is established by the mention of it in the Delphic list of *theorodokoi* of the early second century as a city in which the Delphian *theoroi* were received. Accident of preservation and lack of excavation (which one hopes will soon be remedied by the excavations of the Université Laval) are no doubt responsible for the paucity of our information.

---

113. *I. Brit. Mus.* 975; cf. Mitford, *JHS* 66, 1948, p. 40, n. 46.

114. M. Strack, *Die Dynastie der Ptolemäer*, Berlin, 1897, 171, now republished by Ino Nicolaou, Κυπριακαὶ Σπουδαί 32, 1968, p. 30, no. 14.

115. M. Strack (preceding note), 47, restored by Mitford, *Archiv* 13, 1938, p. 29.

Lapethos

A civic *strategos* is attested at Lapethos, apparently in the middle of the third century.[116] Since his name is Cypriot and in fact local to Lapethos (as Mitford has established), it is quite certain that here, too, we are dealing with the local elective officer and not a royal bureaucrat.[117]

There was a commandant at Lapethos. Aristokles son of Polianthes, Gortynian, the *theorodokos* at Lapethos in the Delphic list of the early second century, is undoubtedly the commandant of the city which he represented in this way (like the *theorodokos* at Karpasia; cf. below). A restoration by Mitford of an inscription of 193-184 makes Euximbrotos, an *archisomatophylax*, the ἐπὶ τῆς πόλεως of Lapethos.[118]

Kerynia

Our only evidence for the civic status of Kerynia in the Hellenistic period is its appearance in the Delphic list of *theorodokoi* as a city receiving the *theoroi*.

Karpasia

We lack evidence for the institutions of Karpasia as well. But it appears in the Delphic list. The *theorodokos* there is one Aristos son of Timodemos, a Chian, who is also known from a dedication to him by some villagers of the area in the years 193-184 to have held the position of ἐπὶ τῆς πόλεως.[119] His son, we have seen above, was a *hegemon* in the same area during Aristos' time in office. Thus, while the city had civic status, its autonomy was limited by the enforced choice of a royal official to represent it in receiving representatives from Delphi. What forms of civic government were in use here we do not know.

---

116. Le Bas-Waddington, *Voyage archéol.* 2789.
117. Mitford, *Archiv* 13, 1938, p. 14, no. 4.
118. *Archiv* 13, 1938, p. 23, no. 11.
119. On the Delphic list (*BCH* 45, 1921, p. 4, Col. 1) cf. the remarks of L. Robert, *Rev. Phil.* 65, 1939, pp. 154-156, where the man was identified on the basis of Mitford's remarks in *Archiv* 13, 1938, p. 22, n. 1. The text in question is now published by Ino Nicolaou, Κυπριακαὶ Σπουδαί 32, 1968, p. 31, no. 17 without critical care; brackets omitted can be placed by the reader from the photograph.

Tamassos

Tamassos, too, appears in the Delphic list of *theorodokoi*, also with a foreigner as *theorodokos*: Thraseas son of Thraseas, an Aspendian. That here, too, a native was not allowed to be *theorodokos* indicates limits on civic autonomy similar to those at Karpasia. Thraseas was no doubt the highest-ranking royal official in the city, probably the ἐπὶ τῆς πόλεως.[120] No other evidence survives about Tamassos and its civic institutions during this period.

Chytroi

The institutions of Chytroi are attested only for athletics. There survives the dedication, not dated by its editor, of a statue base of Iason son of Aristokreon, gymnasiarch, by the παλαιστρῖται.[121] Athletic offices also appear in an inscription of the reign of Philometor (163-145), a dedication by a man describing himself as παισὶ λαμπαδαρχῶ[ν] to the sovereigns, Hermes, Herakles, and the [τυχ]ῆι Χυτρίων.[122] The same office appears in another dedication of year 35 (probably of Philometor, 147/6) to Hermes and Herakles by Alexandros son of Mnestheus, γενεθλίοις παισὶ [λαμπα]δαρχῶν.[123] The city of Chytroi was also probably responsible for a dedication of a statue of Ptolemy II [124] and one of a granddaughter of the *strategos* Seleukos (142-131).[125] The institutions of the city are thus fairly well established in the realm of games and festivals, but are not otherwise clear. No evidence of a commandant survives.

Ledroi

Ledroi probably appears in the Delphic list of *theorodokoi*, and it seems assured that it enjoyed civic status in the Hellenistic period, but nothing else can be said.[126]

Insofar as the extant evidence allows us to judge, thirteen of the ancient towns of Cyprus enjoyed civic status in the Ptolemaic period, including some that had been subject to one of their neigh-

---

120. As L. Robert (note 119) remarks.
121. *JHS* 57, 1937, p. 34, improved text of *CIG* 2627.
122. *JHS* 57, 1937, p. 33, no. 8; for the restoration of [τυχ]ῆι rather than [βουλ]ῆι (Mitford), see L. Robert, *Études anatoliennes*, p. 175, n. 6.
123. *AJA* 65, 1961, p. 129, no. 29.
124. *AJA* 65, 1961, p. 127, no. 27.
125. Mitford, *Seleucus* 13.
126. *Theorodokoi*, note 119 above. Civic status, Mitford, *AJA* 65, 1961, p. 136.

bors in the preceding centuries, such as Ledroi, Chytroi, Tamassos, and Karpasia. We have as yet little documentation of the working of these governments.[127] With our present evidence it is impossible to delineate any local variations on the basic model of the Hellenistic city, but we can give a composite sketch that is in all probability a very close approximation to the picture in any Cypriot city. The fundamental democratic structure of the *boule* and *demos* was present, and there was a secretary both to the *boule* and to the city as a whole. The political process was presided over by the chief magistrates, of whom the *archon* and city *strategos* are attested. The *strategia* may have been filled by more than one person at a time in many cities, if the college of "*strategoi* and former *strategoi*" at Paphos is any indication.

In the financial part of city administration we can cite the Salaminian college of *chreophylakes* and the chief auditor of records for that college. We have no doubt to deal with a financial official in the Phoenician inscription of Kition mentioned above.

Among the most characteristic institutions of Greek cities in all periods are the educational and athletic facilities and officers. The gymnasium is attested for several cities and was no doubt universal. It had ephebes (if a restoration is correct) and an alumni association as well as the annually chosen gymnasiarch. The *palaistra* was another prominent feature, and the *palaistritai* are attested at Chytroi. The *agonothetes* is known at Salamis, and the lampadarch is twice attested at Chytroi in connection with games honoring the royal family. It is clear that the athletic education of the young played an important part in the Cypriot cities and that the significance of these institutions was not limited to a few cities or to any one age group.

The activities of the city officials and bodies that we have described are not well-attested, except for their involvement in dedications, but a few fragments of decrees survive to assure us

---

127. The destruction of marbles in lime-kilns is in part responsible, but so too is the absence of systematic excavations on most sites. One may hope that more inscriptions like one of unknown provenance in the Cyprus Museum will appear in excavations. This stone preserves the remains of the last four lines of an honorary decree couched in language familiar throughout the Greek world; its letter forms go back to the second half of the third century. (Published by Mitford, *Archiv* 13, 1938, p. 18, no. 6; recognized and further restored by J. and L. Robert, *Bull. épig.* 1939, 528, and, better, G. Klaffenbach, *Archiv* 13, 1939, pp. 212-213.) Kourion has already yielded some such inscriptions, as we have seen.

that a normal range of activities is likely. Naturally not all cities enjoyed equal autonomy or had equally flourishing institutions. Most but not all were able to receive the Delphic *theoroi* and entertain them at their own expense, but in Karpasia and Tamassos the resident royal official assumed this duty.

In their internal workings and structure, then, the Cypriot cities display a full range and genuine depth of Hellenic institutions. The contrast with the occasional veneer of Hellenism in the Phoenician cities of the coast opposite is striking. We are not, however, to conclude that the royal presence meant little in the cities. The *phrourarchos* and the men he commanded were very influential, perhaps more so in the less wealthy and prominent cities. It is perhaps unnecessary to insist further on the importance of the city commandant, whose pervasiveness is by now evident. An example of the role of the common soldiers, however, is of some interest. We have one and perhaps two lists of soldiers, foreign mercenaries, who contributed from their pay to help ensure the supply of oil for a gymnasium.[128] We have already seen the numerous appearances of the gymnasia, their alumni, and their gymnasiarchs in honoring the various Ptolemaic officials on the island, especially the *strategoi*, and the oil contribution lists are proof of the depth of the involvement of the representatives of the crown in the gymnasium.

A special aspect of civic life in Cyprus is the dynastic cult of the Ptolemies. A number of inscriptions call one or another person a priest of some royal cult; the *Prosopographia Ptolemaica* groups all these people together as one category, overseas priesthoods of the royal family.[129] A number of these inscriptions, however, do not appear to be entirely relevant to the problem of Cypriot civic cults. It will be necessary first to justify the exclusion from my conclusions of texts that others have used.

In the years 142-131, Artemo, daughter of the strategos Seleukos, is called priestess of Cleopatra Euergetis in an inscription of Paphos.[130] She is not attested in Alexandria in any papyrus protocol as holding this priesthood; but she was the eponymous priestess

128. *I. Hell. Paphos* 8 (224/3) and (less certainly) 9 (c. 150). A photograph of no. 8 in I. Nicolaou, *Cypriot Inscribed Stones*, Nicosia, 1971, pl. XXII, shows clearly that the list was originally much longer.

129. Under nos. 15014-15030.

130. Mitford, *Seleucus* 12. On the priesthood, cf. Mitford's *Helenus*, pp. 112-113.

of Arsinoe Philopator in the years 141-115.[131] Artemo was, I imagine, resident in Alexandria, not in Cyprus; it is likely that her priesthood during this period is to be ascribed to Alexandria, not to Cyprus.

An interesting inscription of Kition, to which we have referred several times above, is a statue base of Melankomas son of Philodamos, Aetolian, placed by the wife of his son Melankomas.[132] Both men had been ἐπὶ τῆς πόλεως of Kition, the son holding the post at the time of the dedication. The father is also called priest of the Theoi Euergetai. The wife's name is Aristo daughter of Dion; IJsewijn has suggested a connection between her and Eutychos son of Dion, the eponymous priest sometime between 165 and 149 (the precise date is not fixed).[133] Connection with a man who was prominent under Philometor would suggest that our inscription dates to his reign rather than to the succeeding one, as would a second link: in *P. Teb.* 811 of 166/5, the eponymous priest is named Melankomas, according to Glanville and Skeat's emendation.[134] Either Φιλοδάμου or Μελαγκόμα could be restored in the following line as patronymic. Glanville and Skeat suggested Μελαγκόμα τοῦ Μελαγκόμα, the son of our inscription. If this prosopographical connection is made, it becomes necessary to place the inscription in which the father is priest yet earlier. And yet the very nature of the priesthood poses problems; one would *a priori* expect that a priesthood of the second Theoi Euergetai would date to after 145 rather than two decades or more earlier; and it would be curious, if this pair is not the second Euergetai, to find a cult of Euergetes I and Berenike attested apart from the rest of the royal cult in a second-century text. There remain a number of problems here which do not seem to me soluble at present; but I incline to place the inscription in the reign of Euergetes II, given the un-

131. J. IJsewijn, *De Sacerdotibus*, pp. 112-113, no. 146.
132. *OGIS* 134.
133. *De Sacerdotibus*, p. 105, no. 121. IJsewijn suggests that Aristo was a sister of Eutychos.
134. They make the correction tacitly, *JEA* 40, 1954, p. 52; IJsewijn, similarly without comment, suggests Philodamos, again restored. The preserved portion of the name appears to be Μελαγκόμα τοῦ, which is visible on the plate of *P. Teb.* 811. I am indebted to James G. Keenan for examining the original papyrus in Berkeley; he remarks that what is taken as the *tau* of τοῦ in reality appears to be a *nu*, but I cannot see that the sense will allow this reading (the name Melankomanos is not attested), which is admittedly palaeographically preferable.

certain nature of the prosopographical connections drawn. If one is to give any credit to these family links at all, however—be they more or less direct—it becomes clear that these people are Alexandrians of some importance, from the higher levels of the aristocracy. It is likely in this case that the priesthood is Alexandrian rather than a local cult of Kition.

An inscription of the *strategia* of Helenos records a dedication to Soter by that governor.[135] In addition to his ordinary titulature, Helenos, according to Mitford's restoration, calls himself [ὁ κατὰ τὴν] νῆσον ἱε[ρεὺς ...]. Mitford himself, however, shows little confidence in his restoration, characterizing this naming of a specific priesthood on the island after Helenos has called himself archiereus as "thoroughly anomalous," "superfluous," and "without parallel." His misgivings are shared by the Roberts,[136] and it seems best in the fragmentary state of the text not to use this highly dubious restoration as evidence.

It appears that all of these examples deal with priesthoods in Alexandria mentioned by the Cypriots in honoring the persons in question. The same is in part true of a statue base of Onesandros son of Nausikrates of Paphos, "kinsman" of Ptolemy Soter II, secretary of the city of Paphos, and after Soter's return to Egypt the head of the great library in Alexandria.[137] Onesandros is called priest for life of the king—certainly the royal cult in Alexandria— and of the Ptolemaieion founded by him—certainly on the island. An unpublished Demotic papyrus of 84/3 mentions a priest for life of the king, Unsjm, 's son of [Nu]sjkrts (Onesitimos son of Nausikrates), according to information received by IJsewijn.[138] IJsewijn thought this man a brother of Onesandros; I suspect rather a scribal error or a mistaken reading of the papyrus; the correct word is surely Onesandros.

Onesandros' exercising a priesthood in Alexandria, however, does not obviate the fact that he had founded a Ptolemaieion and was priest of it. At this time, shortly after his move to Alexandria,

---

135. Mitford, *Helenus* 4 (pp. 98-99). The inscription comes from 118-117, when Helenos served as *strategos* while Soter was resident on Cyprus.

136. *Bull. épig.* 1961, 824.

137. *I. Hell. Paphos* 110.

138. *De Sacerdotibus*, p. 59, no. 199a. Mitford's restoration of a Cypriot inscription would make a daughter of Onesandros a priestess for life of Cleopatra III, though the restoration is somewhat uncertain: *Archiv* 13, 1938, p. 37, no. 18.

this foundation can hardly have been anywhere except at Paphos itself. A similar situation seems to have obtained in the case of Asklepiades, whose statue base bore the legend [ἱερ]έα τοῦ ἰδ[ρυμένου ὑπ' αὐτοῦ ...]; [139] Mitford suggests a date in the late second or early first century.

We learn thus that there were local cults of the sovereigns on Cyprus, in sanctuaries founded and maintained by Cypriots; we are not dealing with a dynastic cult organized by the crown from above, but with local initiative. As indicators of general Ptolemaic practice, these testimonia may be somewhat suspect, coming as they do under the remarkable and in some ways revolutionary reign of Ptolemy IX on the island. But evidence is available from the previous century, and even from the third century, to show that this development is not late but very early.

In an important article in 1956, Hans Volkmann used two Phoenician inscriptions from Cyprus to explore another aspect of the situation. We have seen that in some cases, at least, it was possible for Cypriots to found independent centers of the royal cult on the island. Volkmann stressed precisely this point—that local initiative and not centralized directives marked the Ptolemaic royal cult; neither one priest in Alexandria for the whole empire nor (on the Seleucid model) a priest appointed in each province appears in the Ptolemaic empire.

Volkmann relied on three texts. The first comes from the area of Lapethos, and is dated to year 11 of Ptolemy son of Ptolemy, year 33 of the city of Lapethos, thus 273/2.[140] It contains a dedication by Yatonbaal son of Gerastart, who uses as a third element of dating the priesthood of the lord of kings of Abdastart son of Gerasart—his brother. Both men are called *rab'eres*, whose Greek equivalent is not certain; Volkmann took *toparches* or *chorarches* to be the nearest translation, and those to be royal offices. Van den Branden calls them "chef du quartier" and like other Semiticists considers the term an office of the local civic government.[141] The

139. *JHS* 9, 1888, p. 254, no. 120; cf. Mitford, *Seleucus*, pp. 166-167, n. 119, for the restoration and date.

140. H. Donner, W. Röllig, *Kanaanäische und Aramäische Inschriften*, Wiesbaden, 1962, I 43. Volkmann's treatment, *Historia* 5, 1956, pp. 448-455.

141. Van den Branden's treatment of the inscription in *Oriens Antiquus* 3, 1964, pp. 245-261, is the fullest recent discussion, with text, translation, and notes. His citations of previous studies of this text obviate the need of giving them here. For further discussion and criticism, J. Teixidor, *Bull. épig. sém.* 1967, 43.

"lord of kings" whose cult is celebrated is probably (as Van den Branden argues) Ptolemy I, not (as Volkmann claims) Ptolemy II, for whose cult at this date there is no other evidence. It is worth noting that the father and grandfather of the brothers are also called *rab'eres*; it is not likely, in the early days of the third century, that a royal office would go back two generations in a family. The definitive organization of the royal bureaucracy can have gone back no farther than 294, when the island was recovered.

The second inscription is from Idalion. It too has a triple date: year 31 of Ptolemy son of Ptolemy, year 57 of the era of Kition, and in the canephorate of Arsinoe Philadelphos of Amatosir daughter of M[   ] son of Absas son of Gidath.[142] The canephore is not the Alexandrian one, who was Berenike daughter of Nikanor in this year. Here, too, therefore, we are dealing with local people— Semites speaking Phoenician, not Greeks—serving in what can only be local priesthoods of the royal cult.

A third piece of evidence is an inscription, to be dated by the letter shapes to the first half of the second century, placed by Onesitimos son of Aristion, priest of Arsinoe Philadelphos, gymnasiarch.[143] Its provenance is unknown, but Mitford points out that Aristion is in Cyprus a name of the south coast, found most commonly at Amathous, less so at Kition, and occasionally at Paphos or Salamis. He, too, must be a local man.

All of these cults are to be seen as manifestations of the normal prerogative of any *polis* to establish a cult to any god it chose. It is not necessarily a mark of a Ptolemaic subject to have such a dynastic cult. If Eresos, Methymna, and Joppa, all Ptolemaic dependants or subjects, had cults of the royal family, so also did Athens and Rhodes, neither a subject of Alexandria, though both on good terms throughout most of Ptolemaic history.[144] Here on

---

142. Donner-Röllig (n. 140, above) I 33; *Corpus Inscriptionum Semiticarum* (n. 106, above) I 93.

143. *Archiv* 13, 1938, p. 28, no. 13.

144. For Eresos (Philopator), *Pros. Ptol.* 15015; Methymna (209-205; cf. below, p. 162), 15020; Rhodes (Philopator), 15028 and 15029; Athens (Euergetes), 15022, 15024. Joppa (Philopator), 15017. The Arsinoe Philadelphos plaques are also manifestations of private participation in the civic cults in many places in the Ptolemaic dominions and some outside it: L. Robert, *Essays Welles*, pp. 202-210. C. Habicht, *Gottmenschentum*[2], p. 110, n. 7 and (more fully) pp. 158-159, n. 83, argues that the use of the official cult titles in inscriptions indicates that the city where the titles are so used was under the control of the sovereign thus worshipped. This is at least

Cyprus we have one more witness, if one were needed, to the civic status and character of the cities of Cyprus, even those where a Semitic heritage still flourished amid Hellenic institutions.

But the local autonomy in religious matters to which Volkmann points was not so complete as he seems to make it. One must remember that the *strategos* was after 203 the high priest of every cult on the island. No civic cult or sanctuary was dedicated without his scrutiny and participation. In 273, in 255, this was, apparently, not the case, though our scanty documentation for the period does not allow us to be certain what authority royal officials had at that time. But after Pelops, every *strategos* held this immensely powerful position, by which the local autonomy of the cities of Cyprus was thoroughly curbed. In this domain as in others, the cities functioned and acted as Greek *poleis*, but always with a royal official placed in a position of supervision and overall control. The cities were too significant not to be allowed a measure of self-government, but also too important not to be kept in check.

4. ECONOMIC LIFE AND ADMINISTRATION

Cyprus was, by virtue of its metals, its forests, and its agricultural wealth, an important part of the Ptolemaic economy; it is then particularly unfortunate that we have so little evidence of how the Ptolemies exploited the resources of the island. Cyprus served as a granary for the empire when the flood of the Nile failed to provide a sufficient crop in Egypt; the Canopus decree of 238 tells us that Ptolemy III spent large sums to import wheat from Cyprus and Syria to avert famine in Egypt.[145]

It is very probable that there was an *oikonomos* of Cyprus. A letter of 257 in the archives of Zenon, estate manager of the great *dioiketes* Apollonios (finance minister of Ptolemy II) speaks of Satyrion, τοῦ ἐκ Κύπρου οἰκονόμου.[146] A man of that name has now appeared in an inscription of Salamis with the patronymic Eumelos and ethnic Amphipolitan, dedicating a statue of Ptolemy II.[147]

---

dubious: *I. Cret.* II 19.2 is a dedication at Phalasarna, for Ptolemaic rule of which there is no evidence, on behalf of βασιλέως Πτολεμαίου καὶ βασιλίσσης Βερενίκης Θεῶν Εὐεργετῶν. Cf. Habicht's remarks on Rhodes, pp. 257-258.

145. *OGIS* 56.16-18.

146. *PSI* 505.5-6, completed by *P. Lond.* 1951.

147. *BCH* 95, 1971, pp. 567-569, where J. Pouilloux provides a prosopographical and historical commentary.

It is therefore more likely that Satyrion was a royal official than that he was only an employee of Apollonios in the latter's private business dealings.[148]

Only one other royal financial official is unequivocally attested in Cyprus, the ἐπὶ τῶν μετάλλων. Our one specimen of this official is Potamon son of Aigyptos, the *antistrategos* who served Ptolemy IX during that king's reign in Cyprus between 105 and 88. Potamon held the position of ἐπὶ τῶν μετάλλων at the same time as the *antistrategia*.[149] The office was important enough to be joined with that of *antistrategos*; yet it does not appear in the titulature of any of the known *strategoi*. It was no doubt delegated to a high-ranking subordinate in previous reigns.

The question of the organization of the *chora* of Cyprus must now be considered. One estate, on the Karpas peninsula, appears to be attested in an inscription from the area of Karpasia.[150] It is a dedication of a statue of Sophanes the *hegemon* by Zaton ὁ τ[αμίας καὶ οἱ παν]οίκιοι γεω[ργοί]. The restoration by Mitford of Zaton's title is uncertain, though not implausible. But what is of interest here is the designation of the farmers, who are like the residents of Pannoukome in Asia Minor in being attached to the land they live on: not slaves, but not free to move. If the land were sold, the residents and all their belongings would go with it.[151] The system was previously known elsewhere in Asia Minor; this is the first evidence for it in Cyprus. It would be interesting to know who the owner of the estate was—Cypriot or foreign.

It has been suggested that the *dioiketes* Apollonios had an estate in the area of Paphos, but it appears that the textual emendation on the basis of which the suggestion was made is incorrect.[152] It

---

148. Whether the same is true of a *grammateus* in Cyprus, who appears in a letter of 259 travelling on business in Tyre and Berytos (buying for Apollonios) is uncertain (*P. Cair. Zen.* 59016.1; verso 8-10). His title is not sufficiently specific to allow decision.

149. *OGIS* 165.

150. *AJA* 65, 1961, pp. 122-123, no. 23.

151. Mitford (n. 150) cites for the institution C. B. Welles, *Royal Correspondence* 18 (commentary, p. 94), where the term is explained with citation of other examples.

152. The alleged mention of goods sent to Apollonios from Paphos in *PSI* 428.56 was extracted by C. C. Edgar (commentary to *P. Cair. Zen.* 59016) from the original reading ἐκ τῆς Τετταφου. But Manfredo Manfredi of the Istituto Papirologico "G. Vitelli" of the Università degli Studi di Firenze

is still possible, however, that the estate on which Zaton served was owned by an Alexandrian notable; but this conclusion is far from necessary.

Kafizin is a hill some four miles southeast of modern Nicosia, seven miles north of Dhali, ancient Idalion, to the territory of which (and hence to Kition) the site apparently belonged in antiquity. Over the years, illicit digging had produced a certain number of inscribed pots and sherds, dedications in a sanctuary there of a nymph. A number of these made their way to the University Museum in Philadelphia.[153] The existence of these and other finds prompted an excavation by the Cypriot authorities with the assistance of T. B. Mitford. The results of the excavation have not yet been published in full, but an article by Mitford two decades ago offers some of the primary results.[154] After Mitford's article made the importance of the Kafizin material evident, K. Friis Johansen published some further material located in Danish museums.[155] In the absence of Mitford's promised corpus, any remarks and conclusions here are inevitably tentative and based only on the publications cited.

The inscriptions on the pots are found in both Cypriot syllabic script and Greek alphabet, with the latter largely in the majority. Many of them bear regnal years, and Mitford has been able to demonstrate that they form a sequence from the later years of Euergetes to the first years of Philopator, that is, 225-217. The dedicant of most of the material is a man whose full designation (which appears mostly in various shortened forms) is Ὀνησαγόρας Φιλουνίου Κουρεὺς ἀπὸ Ἀνδρόκλου οἴκου τῆς Ἰδαλιακῆς ὁ δεκατηφόρος. A number of problems are raised by this name and title.

We may begin with Κουρεύς. Mitford identified it in his article as a demotic designation within Idalion. But in 1971 he listed κουρεύς, barber, as an occupation attested on Cyprus, giving Kafizin

has kindly checked a microfilm of this papyrus for me and writes that "Se non è da leggere come nell' ed. princ., leggerei εκτηστεσγυταφου, che mi sembra l'unica incertezza nella linea" (letter of 25.3.1971), and further that in Vitelli's copy of *PSI* another conjecture in the line, but not Edgar's, is noted: "Evidentemente aveva controllato anche l'altra congettura escludendola."

153. Texts in *SEG* VI 838-860.

154. *Classical Quarterly* 44, 1950, pp. 97-106, where Mitford's primary interest is in the persistence of the Cypriot syllabary.

155. *Weihinschriften*, Dansk Arkaeol. Kunsthist. Medd. 4.1, 1953.

as the source. Latte, on the other hand, has argued that it was a variant form of Κουριεύς, the ethnic of Kourion.[156] But the ethnic of Kourion is well-attested, and the gratuitous creation of this consistent misspelling appears to me to be both unnecessary and unwarranted. The common noun κουρεύς, now seemingly embraced by Mitford, can hardly be correct, as it comes before the completion of the man's personal self-designation. As an occupation it would belong at the end, where *dekatephoros* already fills that place. A solution along the lines originally proposed by Mitford seems indicated, though the demotic may belong more precisely to the city of Kition and within that territory to Idalion.

The succeeding phrase also presents a problem. Latte, following his choice of a misspelled ethnic of Kourion, argued that ἀπ' Ἀνδρόκλου οἴκου referred to a phratry and τῆς Ἰδαλιακῆς to the phyle to which that phratry belonged. But Androkles is a person, while the οἶκος Δεκελείων of Latte's parallel is quite a different sort of phrase.[157] It is also difficult to understand an Idalian tribe in the territory of Kourion, when Idalion belonged to Kition and the dedications fell exactly within the area of Idalion. Whether Ἰδαλιακῆς refers to a tribe or to some other word, I think it likely that it means a subdivision of the domain of Kition, and Κουρεύς a demotic within this subdivision.

In keeping with this interpretation, οἶκος ought to mean household or, more broadly, estate. Onesagoras would then belong to this estate in some capacity, a position defined by δεκατηφόρος. It is possible that Androkles was former owner of the land in question, and that it retained the tag after his death, much as *kleroi* in Egypt might retain the name of a third-century B.C. Ptolemaic settler well into the third century of Roman rule, but this possibility is no more than speculative. Since Onesagoras is "from" the estate of Androkles, it seems that the estate was an entity if not in possession of Androkles and that the question of whether Androkles was alive in 225-217 is not important.

What, then, is a δεκατηφόρος? Mitford has suggested two possibilities: that Onesagoras was *oikonomos* of Cyprus; or that he was a wealthy native who had contracted for the taxes of the island—alternatively, that Androkles had done this, and that

---

156. Mitford's new opinion, *I. Kourion*, p. 260, n. 1. Latte, *Glotta* 34, 1955, pp. 194-195.
157. He cites *Syll.*[3] 921.

Onesagoras was representing him. Latte, on the other hand, explains the term as meaning that Onesagoras, a potter, dedicated a tenth of his production in the shrine. Mitford's first suggestion seems to me untenable; we know of no high-ranking Cypriot in the Ptolemaic administration at this time, and the entire form of designation speaks of a purely local importance for our dedicant. For the second suggestion there is more to be said, if it is restricted to a more local area than the whole of Cyprus, for this is a small local shrine, and Onesagoras' self-designation is meant for understanding locally, within the territory of Kition and Idalion. A larger audience would demand an ethnic, not a demotic. In the absence of any word indicating that Onesagoras was a potter, I think we must reject Latte's thesis.

The word δεκατηφόρος is not common. It is known primarily as an epithet of Apollo at Megara, Argos, and Hierapytna on Crete, meaning "tithe-receiving." [158] Aside from these occurrences, I know of only one appearance, the ἀπαρχαὶ δεκατηφόροι which Callimachus says come to Delos—tithe-bearing first-fruits.[159] Used as a noun as it is by Onesagoras, the word seems otherwise unknown.[160] The tithe, δεκάτη, is itself known from Seleucid, Attalid, and Ptolemaic Asia Minor, where it was a royal tax on produce of land not belonging directly to the king.[161] It was a *pars quota*, a percentage of the yield of the land, to be distinguished from the *ekphorion*, a fixed rent (*pars quanta*) on royal land.[162]

It is the meaning of "receiving" rather than "paying" that is most commonly encountered in the examples of δεκατηφόρος cited above, and it is this meaning that we are to look for here. A farmer would probably not use a word descriptive of his tax-burden to describe himself, while a tax-collector would use precisely that word to designate his occupation. Onesagoras, then, was a collector of tithes, probably from the many tenants or land-holders on the

---

158. The evidence is collected by M. Guarducci in *I. Cret.* III 3.9 (pp. 57-58).

159. *Del.* 278.

160. *LSJ* Suppl., 1968, refers to the Kafizin material as follows: (s.v. δεκατηφόρος): "I. [meaning of tithe-paying] add. '; κουρεὺς *AJA* 30.249 (Cyprus).' " The suggestion that the dedicant was a tithing barber is peculiar especially in view of the word-order; but the editors of *LSJ* Suppl. are apparently unaware of any problem or controversy.

161. References in M. Rostovtzeff, *SEHHW*, pp. 337, 444-445, 464-470, 562, 1434, 1450, 1526.

162. A distinction made in Ps.-Arist. *Oikon.* 2.

estate of Androkles. If his post was limited to this estate, it is the more comprehensible that he himself and not merely his appointment is designated as "from the estate of Androkles." His life and work lay within the limits of that estate, as indeed the local character of his dedications indicates.

Our evidence therefore points to the existence of large estates with a settled and legally attached peasantry, who paid a fixed percentage of their produce, probably to an agent of the owner, who would in turn have been responsible for the royal taxes imposed on the land. We are far from seeing details, but the outline is clear.

A small amount of additional information comes from a fragment of what is probably a royal letter to the Cypriot city of Arsinoe, although the alternative suggested by Mitford, a letter from the *dioiketes*, is not quite impossible.[163] Only the last ten to twelve letters survive in each line, scarcely enough to support adequately any attempt at restoration. There is mention of καρποί, crops; of the payment of an ἀπόμοιρα; of the tax on each *metretes* of wine; of various amounts of money; of pasture tax; of a release from some obligation to the crown. The provisions appear to be reminiscent of those mentioned in the decree of Telmessos for Ptolemy son of Lysimachus, but one cannot tell whether the actual structure was similar. Nor is there any indication of the scope of the letter. It is likely to be directed to a specific recipient (whether Arsinoe or other cities in Cyprus as well) because the remission is not stated in the general and impersonal terms familiar from Ptolemaic amnesties.

The one example of this latter genre known from Cyprus is indeed directed at the entire Ptolemaic kingdom and seems to form at least part of a general amnesty issued by Ptolemy VIII in 145/4 on his accession to power in Egypt.[164] Its general character forbids its use for specific remarks about the administration of Cyprus. All crimes up to Ptolemy VIII's accession are forgiven, and stringent penalties are envisaged for any who prosecute or try offenders for such offenses. Those who have fled from their homes are ordered to return to their work and to such of their property as has not yet

---

163. Le Bas-Waddington, *Voyage archéol.* 2783. The fullest recent treatment is that of M. Segre, *Annuario* n.s. 11-13, 1948-1951, pp. 319-330, who restores extensively and without sure foundation; cf. *Bull. épig.* 1954, 262. Mitford, *Aegyptus* 33, 1953, p. 88, thinks the *dioiketes* an alternative author.

164. The extensive literature on this document is discussed in M.-T. Lenger's re-edition of the text in *BCH* 80, 1956, pp. 437-461.

been sold. Accompanying the amnesty is an extract from a letter to the troops stationed on Cyprus, granting them various privileges.

It is impossible to draw many general conclusions from the narrow range of evidence on the economy that we have at our disposal. It is clear that the cities had control over an area of land around themselves and that this land must have included all or nearly all of the island. Kition, Salamis, and Paphos, in particular, extended their influence over large tracts, while the smaller cities like Chytroi, Ledroi, Tamassos, and Karpasia served as centers for their own areas. The royal administration was concentrated on control of the cities, which had garrisons and in most cases at least commandants. Their local autonomy was nonetheless considerable. One may surmise that the economic life of the countryside as of the city was largely in the hands of the civic authorities, rather than directly ruled by royal bureaucrats. Had we other evidence, like papyri, the picture might be altered somewhat, but the basic organization around and through the cities appears to be certain and distinctly different from the system in use in most of Egypt.

Details within this general outline are even less clear. There were certain large estates within the *chora* of the cities, but we do not know who their owners were; some may have been prominent men in the Ptolemaic kingdom who received royal grants. But we do not know how much land the king considered to be at his disposal and whether this land was included in the land attached to the cities or was separate from it. It seems certain that there was military settlement on the land attached to cities, though its extent is uncertain.

Of the larger aspects of economic exploitation, we know only that the mines were of importance and that a major official was in charge of them. There was probably an *oikonomos* who served as the representative of the *basilikon* on Cyprus, but what his relationship to the *strategos* was, what minor officials served under him, how his business was carried out, all remain unknown to us.

CHAPTER FIVE

ASIA MINOR: THE SOUTH COAST

1. SAMOS

Samos, which before 281 had been a possession of Lysimachus, came into the hands of the Ptolemies not long after that king's death. In or about 280 it was the scene of the meeting of the synedroi of the league of the islanders called by Philokles king of Sidon to deal with Philadelphos' establishment of a festival in honor of his parents.[1] There is, however, no evidence to tell us whether Samos itself was a member of the league.[2]

From the same period comes a decree of Samos honoring two Myndians, Theokles son of Theogenes and Herophantos son of Artemidoros, sent to Samos as *dikastai* by Myndos at the direction of Philokles.[3] Philokles' action is analogous to Ptolemaic interference in this way in other islands in the Aegean (cf. Chapter VI, below) and, taken with the summoning of the meeting in Samos, demonstrates that the island was without any doubt not only an ally but a possession of the Ptolemies.

That control was terminated twenty years later. A passage of Frontinus tells us that Timarchos, the tyrant of Miletos, killed Charmades, general of king Ptolemy, and, dressing in his clothes, slipped into and took the harbor of the *Saniorum*.[4] It has often been supposed that *Sanii* is a corrupt form of some word not now recoverable and probably referred to Miletos.[5] It appears to me,

---

1. The decree of this meeting is *Syll.*³ 390.

2. Both views have been advanced with no firm evidence. W. König, *Der Bund der Nesioten* (Diss. Halle, 1910) p. 49 rejected the arguments of Delamarre and Dittenberger that Samos was a possession and hence would not be a free league member, preferring to think that its status as possession was not material to the question; he cites Beloch for his view. Irwin Merker, *Historia* 19, 1970, pp. 148 and 158, follows Dittenberger against König. Only new evidence can settle the question, but the negative argument seems to me excessively dependent on an insecure and legalistic argument.

3. Published by M. Schede, *Ath. Mitt.* 44, 1919, p. 21, no. 9, and reprinted as *SEG* I 363.

4. *Strat.* 3.2.11.

5. So Bengtson, *Die Strategie* III, pp. 177-178, n. 4; cf. also *RE* 15, 1932, col. 1606 (s.v. Miletos, by Hiller); *RE* 6A, 1936, cols. 1236-1237, no. 4, s.v. Timarchos (4), by K. Ziegler.

however, that Habicht is correct in thinking that Frontinus means that after he was installed in Miletos, Timarchos took Samos as well, and *Samiorum* is the original reading.[6] It is not insignificant in this respect that Miletos appears to have been ungarrisoned, while Samos, as we shall see, was almost certainly at least a Ptolemaic naval base.

Timarchos' tyranny lasted no longer in Samos than in Miletos, for Antiochus II came into the area and gained control of the coastal territories of Samos; it appears that Timarchos was no longer in power at this time. The Samian decree for Boulagoras reveals that Antiochus' officials on the mainland (none on the island are mentioned) deprived Samians of their lands but that Boulagoras, on a long embassy at court, finally won them back.[7]

The period of Seleucid dominance in the area lasted until the beginning of the reign of Ptolemy III, about 246, although there is no evidence that Samos itself was subjected or occupied by Antiochus. Not long after the beginning of the reign of Euergetes, Boulagoras was sent as one of a group of *theoroi* to Alexandria to deliver honors and sacrifices to Ptolemy and Berenike, for some of which he himself paid.

From this time to the end of the third century, Ptolemaic control in Samos seems to have been undisturbed. Polybius tells us that Samos was inherited by Philopator, and that it was at that time (221) a major naval base.[8] But in 201 Philip V took Samos—apparently without much, if any resistance—and used some of the ships he found there in the battle of Chios that year, though he had not had time to arm all of them. Some of the sailors, too, served him in the battle.[9] The island returned to Ptolemaic control before long, however. Holleaux thought that Philip relinquished it voluntarily, but a recently published inscription from Samos

6. *Ath. Mitt.* 72, 1957, p. 220 and n. 74. The corruption thus assumed is very minor. "Saniorum" appears once more in Frontinus, at 3.3.5, where it seems to refer to a Thracian town attacked by Philip II and thus to have nothing to do with the present case.

7. The Boulagoras inscription, *SEG* I 366. Its importance for Samian finance and grain trade is discussed by E. Ziebarth, *Zeitschrift für Numismatik* 34, 1924, pp. 356-364.

8. Polyb. 5.35.11. For the reign of Euergetes, cf. the Samian decree about asylum rights in the sanctuary of Hera, *Ath. Mitt.* 72, 1957, pp. 226 ff., no. 59, where the king is honored.

9. The best discussion of the campaign is still that of M. Holleaux, *Études* IV, pp. 211-335; for Samos and its sailors and ships, see pp. 233-241, where the scattered testimonia are collected.

makes it clear that this was not the case.[10] This text, a decree of
Samos, honors Diodoros son of Dioskourides, the public doctor in
Samos for many years, whose meritorious services are praised in
general and in three specific instances: (1) assistance at the time
of some σεισμοί, (2) saving the lives of some *dikastai* who had come
to the island, (3) incessant ministering to the needs of those wounded
during the ἀποκατάστασις εἰς τὰ τοῦ βασιλέως Πτολεμαίου πράγματα,
which took the form of attacks on the acropolis and hand-to-hand
fighting during the days.[11] The use of the word πράγματα is of
interest, confirming the view that Samos was in fact a possession
and not merely an ally of the Ptolemies. As Welles remarked,
"In the Hellenistic kingdoms, the πράγματα of the ruler were the
'affairs of state,' just as his own personality constituted the state."
Samos thus formed part of the king's business, the civil administration.[12]

The restoration must have been short-lived. In 197 the Rhodians
helped to defend the island from the attacks of Antiochus III.[13]
At some time during the next decade the island passed from Ptolemaic control along with their other remaining possessions in the
area. We know nothing of the exact date or circumstances.[14]

From the evidence thus far adduced, we know that Samos was
a Ptolemaic possession and naval base in the years 280-260 and
245-195, approximately. It was the home base for a substantial
fleet, was considered part of the civil administration of the empire,
and was important enough to persuade Ptolemy V's ministers to
mount a military expedition sufficient to recapture it about 200,
when demands on their resources were great.[15] The king interfered

10. *Ath. Mitt.* 72, 1957, pp. 233 ff., no. 64, with a good commentary by
C. Habicht.

11. This detail may suggest that the Ptolemies had previously had a
garrison in the acropolis, but it is also possible that Philip had installed one
where the Ptolemies previously had not had one.

12. Welles, *Royal Correspondence*, p. 182.

13. Livy 33.20. Samos is listed with Myndos, Kaunos, and Halikarnassos
as Ptolemaic possessions (*civitates sociae Ptolomaei*).

14. No traces of Ptolemaic occupation are found after 197, and Rhodian
"protection" from 197 on no doubt meant the end of any real Ptolemaic
control. Rome and Rhodes used Samos as a naval base in 190 (Livy 37.10.6-
18.10; 22.1-2; 26.2-27.1; Polyb. 21.8, cited by J. P. Barron in *The Silver
Coins of Samos*, London, 1966, p. 153, who assumes that 197 was the effective
end of Ptolemaic control).

15. The date can fall between Philip's capture (mid 201) and Livy's
mention of Samos as a Ptolemaic ally in late 197 (Livy 33.20.12). Cf. C.
Habicht, *Ath. Mitt.* 72, 1957, p. 238.

freely in the internal affairs of the island through his admiral
Philokles and the *dikastai* appointed by Philokles, and the latter
thought Samos a suitable place for the league of the islanders to
meet. Samos took its part in the dynastic cult and its celebrations
in Alexandria.

Given this state of affairs, we might expect to find Ptolemaic
officials on the island. We do; but they and their role on Samos are
rather ambiguous. From the first period of Ptolemaic control we
have several officials mentioned in our sources. First, a Samian
decree from the decade 270-260 honors Aristolaos, son of Ameinias,
Macedonian, στρατηγὸς ἐπὶ Καρίας, for his good works toward the
Samians, which are worthy of the attitude of the king. Nothing
more specific is said about these benefactions.[16] It is noteworthy
that ambassadors are chosen to take the decree to him; he is not
resident on Samos. We do not know what his good works were,
and hence in what capacity he performed, or what his relationship
with Samos was. We cannot tell whether the island fell under his
authority or whether it had perhaps appealed to him for help in
some circumstance. In any case, the inscription establishes a connection between Samos, the sole known Ptolemaic base in the
Ionian area at this time, and Caria, where the king had much
wider interests. It is not impossible that Samos fell within Aristolaos'
jurisdiction.

A second decree from the period honors Pelops son of Alexandros,
Macedonian, friend of the king and τεταγμένος ἐπὶ δυνάμεως.[17]
L. Robert's conclusion,[18] that Pelops was commander of a garrison
on Samos,[19] is generally accepted. I think this conclusion not
supportable with our present evidence. First, the phrase τεταγμένος
ἐπὶ δυνάμεως is used nowhere else in the Ptolemaic empire to denote
the commander of a permanently installed garrison. Holleaux noted
long ago that δύναμις in Hellenistic documents tends to refer to
an armed force on active duty in time of war, especially in the
phrase "the king and his forces are well."[20] A garrison commander,
on the other hand, may bear any of a number of other titles:
epistates, ἐπὶ τῆς πόλεως, ἐπὶ + the name of a city, *phrourarchos*.

---

16. *Ath. Mitt.* 72, 1957, pp. 218 ff., no. 57; cf. also L. Robert's comments
in *Hellenica* 11-12, 1960, pp. 126 ff., on some provisions about sacrifices.

17. *SEG* I 364.

18. *Études épigraphiques et philologiques*, pp. 113 ff.

19. He is so listed by *Pros. Ptol.* 14618.

20. *BCH* 29, 1905, pp. 319 ff.

It is not difficult to find an occasion when Pelops would have commanded forces active in the Aegean. The absence of Arsinoe from the inscription (the king is mentioned alone) suggests a date after 270—the Chremonidean War, in fact, a date supported by two other pieces of evidence: (a) Pelops' career is otherwise attested by his tenure of the eponymous priesthood of Alexander and the Theoi Adelphoi in Philadelphos' twenty-second year (264/3); [21] (b) there is a group of small islands off the Peloponnesos called the νησῖδες Πέλοπος.[22] It is possible that the point of this name, which contrasts with that of the Peloponnesos itself, Πέλοπος νῆσος, is a joke referring to our Pelops. If this is so, the Chremonidean War would have been a logical time for the name to have been coined; we know that the Ptolemies were active in the Saronic Gulf under Patroklos and that he, too, gave his name to a small off-shore island, Patroklou nesos off Attica. Methana was probably a Ptolemaic base at this time (see Chapter VI below, section B.2).

Secondly, one expects that an eponymous priest will be a man of some importance. When the holders of the post are identifiable in another role, it is usually an important one: Kallikrates the admiral, Patroklos, the supreme commander in the Chremonidean War, Menelaos the brother of Ptolemy I, are only three examples. Pelops himself was an important man. His son Pelops married the daughter (Myrsine) of another prominent man, Hyperbassas (see below), and became *strategos* of Cyprus under Philopator.[23]

In sum, it appears to me likely that Pelops was the commander of an important part of the Ptolemaic military forces during the decade 270-260, and that he served in the Chremonidean War in a high command capacity that we cannot otherwise define. He may have commanded a fleet based on Samos or have been a more temporary visitor there. Nothing, however, entitles us to see in him the commander of a garrison on Samos. He may have held that post at some time, but it remains for other evidence to be found to demonstrate the fact.

The statue raised by the Samians to Hyperbassas son of Eteoneus

21. *P. Hib.* 92. On the family, the commentary of C. Habicht, *Ath. Mitt.* 72, 1957, p. 210, is useful.

22. References in *RE* 19, 1937, cols. 392-393. On Patroklos' island, see J. R. McCredie, *Fortified Military Camps in Attica, Hesperia* Suppl. 11, 1966, pp. 18-25, 109-119.

23. C. Habicht (note 21) gives the references. On Pelops, see above, p. 46, and below, p. 252.

probably belongs to the same period.[24] As we saw above, one of his daughters married Pelops' son. Another daughter was canephore of Arsinoe Philadelphos in 242/1.[25] It is not impossible that Hyperbassas' statue dates to that period rather than to the earlier Ptolemaic occupation of Samos. He is unfortunately given no title by the Samians, a fact which may suggest that his relationship to them was not a simple administrative post. It is obviously impossible at present to say more about his status.

Two other inscriptions add little to the picture. In one, the Samians honor two Lampsakenes who are friends of the king. The first editor, M. Schede, thought that the text was to be placed in the reign of Philadelphos, but certainty is impossible, and we know nothing of the mission of these men.[26] Another decree honors one Nausistratos and orders the decree to be taken to him.[27] On the basis of this instruction, L. Robert has suggested that Nausistratos was a high Ptolemaic official.[28] If this is correct, he was in any case not resident on Samos, and his position is thus analogous to that of Aristolaos, as Habicht pointed out. Once again it is uncertain what role he played in the administration.

The last Ptolemaic official to come into question is Straton son of Straton, honored in a Samian decree.[29] His mission on the island is described as ἀποστ[αλε]ὶς ὑπὸ τοῦ βασιλέως | Πτολεμαίου ἐπὶ ‹τὸ› τὰς παραβολὰς τῶν [. . .]ων λαμβάνειν. He is thus a royal official who has come to the island to collect some kind of money for the king. The question of what he is to collect, however, is difficult and has been much argued. In a classic article, Holleaux proposed the restoration παραβολὰς τῶν [δικ]ῶν and amassed a body of parallel material to support the phrase.[30] His point of departure was the Athenian use of παρακαταβολή to denote a deposit put down by the prosecutor of a lawsuit, which is returned to him if he wins, but forfeit if he loses. The Aristotelian *Oikonomika* (1348b.13) mentions παραβολ-- πολλῶν δικῶν as a source of revenue, but the

---

24. *Ath. Mitt.* 75, 1960, p. 133, no. 6, with a commentary on the family by C. Habicht.

25. *PSI* 389.

26. *SEG* I 365; see Habicht's comments, *Ath. Mitt.* 72, 1957, p. 205.

27. Habicht (note 26), p. 231, no. 60.

28. *Hellenica* 11-12, 1960, p. 131.

29. *OGIS* 41.

30. *Études* III, pp. 39-42, with supplementary notes by L. Robert bringing the 1897 article up to date.

operative word varies in the manuscripts among παράβολον, παραβό-
λου, παραβολή, and παραβολήν. Pollux (8.63), however, remarks
that what some call παραβόλιον, Aristotle called παράβολον, so that
this reading may be preferable in the *Oikonomika*. Support comes
from instances of πάρβολον in some inscriptions with the same
meaning.[31] It is thus apparent that παρακαταβολή, παραβόλιον, and
παράβολον can all refer to judicial deposits, and that παραβολή may
well have the same possible meaning.

For παραβόλιον and παραβολή the papyri give two instances each
that are pertinent to the inquiry. The meaning of "judicial deposit"
appears for παραβόλιον in a papyrus of A.D. 99 or 100, unpublished
at the time when Holleaux wrote.[32] Two Zenon papyri, duplicates
save for the addressee, are letters of 261/0 B.C. from the *dioiketes*
Apollonios to his agents, ordering that those exporting wheat from
Syria are to pay either the price of the wheat or a παραβόλιον, and
are to be given a receipt for it.[33] The word appears to have a more
general meaning of deposit, perhaps official deposit, in these
papyri, but without any judicial implication.

For παραβολή itself the situation is less clear. One of its attesta-
tions comes in a Ptolemaic account in a fragmentary context and
is followed by an amount in drachmas; it does not further the
inquiry.[34] The other attestation is more promising, as Robert has
noted in his additional comments to Holleaux's article. It is a
petition to the king dated to year 4 of Philopator, concerning some
wool that the petitioner had bought (for the account of?) Amyntas,
ὥστε . [. . . . .] . . . ειαν ἀπὸ τῆς βα[σι]λικῆς παραβολῆς.[35] O. Guéraud,
the editor, thought the *parabole* involved a payment to the crown
in connection with some sort of royal control of an aspect of trade,
perhaps a monopoly. The petitioner points out that only if the

---

31. *IG* XII 3 254.25 and B. Haussoullier, *Traité entre Delphes et Pellanes*,
Paris, 1917, index s.v.

32. *P. Stras.* 227 Col. 1.24.

33. *PSI* 324 and 325. The agents in question, Apollodotos and Hikesios,
both appear in Zenon documents referring to Caria (see below) as crown
financial officials. G. Harper (*American Journal of Philology* 44, 1928, pp.
5 ff.) thought that the wheat in question belonged to Apollonios, but there
is no evidence on this point. Harper's contention that these letters were
prompted by earlier fraudulent exports is only a hypothesis, without ground-
ing in evidence.

34. *P. Petr.* III 93.

35. *P. Enteux.* 2.4. Robert, following Guéraud's interpretation, underlines
the potential importance of this text for the problem in Holleaux, *Études*
III, p. 41, n. 1.

complaint about non-delivery of goods is solved will Amyntas be able to pay the proper amount of taxes in Alexandria. Amyntas' presence in Alexandria makes it possible that he was active in foreign trade.

In sum, these words are attested as meaning more than one type of deposit, and the most nearly contemporary evidence that we have for them in the Ptolemaic realm suggests a connection with trade rather than the judicial system.[36] It is neither impossible nor unparalleled, however, that the word could have a judicial meaning in the Samian inscription. The existence of a decree for Straton suggests that his mission involved discretion in managing financial affairs, since he is praised for his fair handling of the matter. Trade, perhaps the grain trade, appears to me to offer more scope for the use of discretionary power than the collection of judicial deposits already forfeit. But it is evident that in the present state of the evidence, prudence dictates refraining from a final judgment.

Straton's date, regrettably, is no more certain than the nature of his mission. It has been suggested that he is to be identified with one or more of the Stratons appearing (without patronymic) in various Zenon papyri from the years 259 to 257.[37] Most of these Stratons appear with too little context for us to be sure; they are generally agents of Zenon for some purpose. One of them, however, is of greater interest, a *gazophylax* in Halikarnassos who must have been a royal treasurer there.[38] It is by no means improbable that this official might have been on a mission to Samos to collect funds due the crown there; the connection between Caria and Samos would be reminiscent of the appearance of Aristolaos the *strategos* of Caria in a Samian decree. Here, once again, judgment must be suspended for the present, but the identification has some plausibility.

When Louis Robert collected the evidence for Ptolemaic relations with Samos 35 years ago, he began with an inscription bearing the

---

36. The recent attempt of G. Dunst, *ZPE* 4, 1969, pp. 197-199, to restore [νε]ῶν in this decree and to understand Straton's function as setting up a naval base in 280, is to be rejected as distorting the Greek beyond recognition; cf. J. and L. Robert, *Bull. épig.* 1970, 448.

37. *P. Cairo Zen.* 59015 verso; 59018; 59036; *P. Lond.* 1930.

38. *P. Cairo Zen.* 59036, which will be discussed below in more detail. He received some tax proceeds and later paid them out on order from Apollodotos (note 33).

names and ethnics of fifteen men, whom he took to be members of the garrison.[39] Their ethnics are generally regional rather than those of specific cities, and there are no patronymics; the form thus suggests that these are not *proxenoi*. While the men may have been sailors in the fleet rather than members of the garrison, they were in all probability mercenaries in Ptolemaic employ. Their geographical origins are interesting in that the preponderance of natives of central Greece is quite unlike the composition of the Ptolemaic armies as we know them from other sources.[40]

Samos, then, was a Ptolemaic naval base, but there is no unequivocal evidence of a land force garrisoning the city. It is possible that the list of names is made up of garrison soldiers, but we have no reason to think that this was the case. No official is securely attested by our present evidence as resident on Samos, although many visited it, helped it, taxed it, and directed its life in various ways. This situation, too, future finds may change. The island was probably under some form of financial control and taxation, though the form and details escape us. There appears to have been a close connection between the Ptolemaic officials resident in Caria and the city of Samos, though its extent and nature are unclear. In sum, the Ptolemies controlled Samos and used it as a port for their navy; their cultural influence was strong (as Robert has made clear); but so far as we now can tell they did not keep a resident bureaucracy on the island.[41]

---

39. *Études épigraphiques et philologiques*, pp. 113 ff.

40. It is not possible to discuss the matter in detail here. The tables of Launey, *Armées hellénistiques*, pp. 67-87, show a heavy representation of Asia Minor and the islands, particularly Crete, but much less for continental Greece; a tabulation of private soldiers listed in *Pros. Ptol.* gives similar results, as does a perusal of Heichelheim's list in *Die Auswärtige Bevölkerung im Ptolemäerreich*, 2 ed., Aalen, 1963. The Samian text, on the contrary, yields 60 per cent for central Greece, smaller amounts elsewhere, and one Egyptian—reminiscent of the Egyptian sailors taken into Philip's fleet (note 9, above).

41. In leaving Samos, we may mention that it was the home of the renowned Ptolemaic admiral Kallikrates son of Boiskos, who was responsible for many dedications on Samos and elsewhere in the reign of Ptolemy II. For a recent collection and discussion of the evidence, see H. Hauben, *Callicrates of Samos*, Studia Hellenistica 18, 1970. It is possible also that the Ptolemies furthered Samian aggrandizement at the expense of neighboring Amorgos and other islands; cf. L. Robert's study of Samians on Amorgos in *REG* 46, 1933, pp. 421-442.

2. NORTHERN CARIA

In the part of Caria north of the peninsula of Halikarnassos we have testimony of Ptolemaic influence in three areas, each at a different point of history. The first of them is Iasos, for which some recently published texts give us an entirely new view of the Ptolemaic role in the area. These documents were inscribed together in a long text from Iasos, and include the provisions of a three-way treaty between Ptolemy, Iasos, and three mercenary captains and their soldiers, as well as the oaths of all three parties and some later correspondence between royal officials and Iasos. The importance of the inscription demands that its contents be set forth in detail.[42]

The beginning of the inscription is lost, but it must have set forth many provisions for the agreement of the three parties as well as a recapitulation of the history of the presence of the troops in Iasos. The scraps that constitute lines 1-15 mention Polemaios son of Polemaios, whom the editor takes to have been the well-known general of Antigonus Monophthalmos, who went over to Ptolemy in 309 and was later put to death on Kos. It appears that he may have been responsible for the installation of the soldiers, either as general of Antigonus or on his own responsibility.

The next section contains the provisions for completing the agreement: the Iasians shall pay the soldiers their back pay within 15 days of the arrival of the ambassadors sent to Ptolemy, and on paying shall receive from Machaon, Hieron, and Sopolis, the commanders, the acropolis and its contents and the city itself. The soldiers are to be allowed to evacuate the city without molestation and leave where they will by land or sea; they also have the opportunity to remain as resident non-citizens of the city if they wish. Some incompletely preserved provisions about mutual charges and complaints follow.

There follow the oaths to be sworn: first, the Iasians and their residents to Ptolemy, that the city will be a free, autonomous, ungarrisoned, and untaxed ally of Ptolemy and his descendants; second, the soldiers and their captains to the Iasians and the Iasians to them, that they will abide by the agreement and that the

---

42. G. Pugliese-Carratelli, "Supplemento Epigrafico di Iasos," *Annuario* 29-30, 1967-1968, pp. 437-445, no. 1. For amelioration of the text and interpretation see *Bull. épig.* 1971, 620, and Y. Garlan, *ZPE* 9, 1972, pp. 223-224.

captains will not receive new soldiers without the Iasians' consent; third, Ptolemy, that he will protect the agreement between the other two parties; fourth, the Iasians and Ptolemy to one another, the Iasian oath being essentially the same as the first oath and Ptolemy's (fragmentary) that he will preserve the city in that same status. Provisions for publication follow.

It appears that this part of the inscription is to be placed after 309, after which Polemaios was no longer a factor, but before 305, when Ptolemy took the title of king, which he nowhere bears in the parts of the inscription so far described. Ptolemy undertakes a type of protectorate over the city but renounces any direct control, taxation, or placement of a garrison. The terms are clear and establish Iasos as an ally but not a subject, though Ptolemaic hegemony is clearly accepted.

The second part of the inscription contains two letters and two oaths. First there is a letter from Aristoboulos to Iasos, written in response to an embassy from the city asking recognition of the city's free and autonomous but allied status. Aristoboulos grants this request. The next request was that the city should pay (something lost) for the guarding of the country, but should remain masters of their own harbor and other revenues. The latter request was granted, but the establishment of the amount of Iasos' contribution to the royal treasury is referred to the king, so that no disagreement between Aristoboulos and his king will interfere with the proper carrying out of other decisions. Aristoboulos then swears an oath to the Iasians to protect their freedom and autonomy and to grant them their own revenues, but to refer to the king the decision about the amount of the city's contribution. He swears to protect the city from attack and to benefit it in any way within his power.

A second letter is written by one Asklepiodotos, agreeing to an Iasian embassy's request to swear the same oath that Aristoboulos had sworn and giving the text of the oath again.

The exact date of these letters is unclear. Ptolemy is now the king, so that we have passed the year 305.[43] On the other hand, Aristoboulos is to be identified with some confidence, as the editor points out, with the Ptolemaic envoy to Antigonus of that name mentioned in Antigonus' letter to Skepsis after the making of

---

43. See the discussion of the date in A. E. Samuel, *Ptolemaic Chronology*, pp. 4-11.

peace in 311.[44] We are therefore probably justified in accepting a date in the last five years of the fourth century or not long after for the two letters, almost certainly for the first letter.

The relationship between the city and the king has changed. The city is still to be αὐτόνομος and ἐλεύθερος, but there is no longer any mention of ἀφρούρητος (though there is also no sign of any Ptolemaic garrison), and in place of ἀφορολόγητος we find a discussion of finances in which the king has the final say. He grants to the city, through his representatives, the right to keep its own revenues. There is to be no direct royal taxation of the citizens. The exemption is a privilege conferred, however, not a right of the city. And in return for the exemption, the king exacts a contribution (σύνταξις) in an amount that he himself decides. The city's independence is thus not absolute in the financial realm. We lack the intermediate steps by which Ptolemy asserted his claim to a contribution from the city, a right renounced expressly in the earlier oaths, but the transition is clear enough as it is.

The status of Aristoboulos and Asklepiodotos is not certain. Pugliese-Carratelli took the former to be a temporary representative-extraordinary of the king in the area and the latter to be a permanent governor of the region. This interpretation is possible, but it seems to me at least as likely that Aristoboulos was governor (of Caria?) and was followed by Asklepiodotos in the same position; hence we find the request to the latter (not elsewhere attested) to renew the oath of his predecessor. Both men acknowledged responsibility for the protection of the city, but neither indicated the existence of any subordinates located in Iasos. We may conclude, then, that Iasos was subject to a regional or provincial governor imposed by the king, who had a wide competence and responsibility over military and financial affairs, but who did not place a garrison in the city. In some matters, however, the governor left a decision to the king.

From a later period comes an Iasian inscription accepting a crown given by Kalymna for Iasian judges and recording the decree of Kalymna in honor of these judges.[45] The date established by Segre is the reign of Ptolemy II. The text gains its importance for us from the fact that Philadelphos not only ordered the *dikastai*

44. Welles, *Royal Correspondence* 1.
45. *Tit. Cal.* test. xvi. It is possible that *Tit. Cal.* 17 is to be connected with the same incident.

to be sent but provided a *diagramma* to guide the settlement of disputes. The inscription is discussed in greater detail below, under Kalymna, but it is noteworthy here that the Iasian judges, by operating under rules laid down by king Ptolemy, in effect acknowledge his sovereignty, and we may therefore be justified in thinking that Philadelphos exercised his rule over Iasos for some time.

For subsequent periods, we have no datable testimony to Ptolemaic rule in Iasos. The city had a gymnasium called the Ptolemaion; it also had an Antiocheion.[46] The foundation of neither can be dated. It is certain that the city was in Seleucid hands after 197, but we do not know how far back the shift went nor whether many changes of alliance intervened.[47]

In the reign of Philadelphos we have some evidence of Ptolemaic rule in inland areas of Caria, the areas of Mylasa and the future Stratonikeia. From the site of Stratonikeia comes an inscription of a contract for the sale of a vineyard, bearing a formula dating it to the ninth year of Ptolemy son of Ptolemy.[48] The year is therefore 274. It is noteworthy that Caria figures in Theocritus' list of Ptolemy II's possessions and in the list in the Adoulis inscription of countries inherited by Ptolemy III from his father. These general references, however, do not preclude considerable variation in what was actually controlled from reign to reign, and we find no later indication of Ptolemaic control from this region of Caria.

For the area of Mylasa, we have now an indication of Ptolemaic control in year 19 of Philadelphos (June, 267).[49] The text is a decree of a meeting of the Chrysaoreis at the shrine of Zeus Labraundios at Labraunda near Mylasa. Apollonios son of Diodotos

---

46. For the gymnasia of Iasos, see L. Robert, *Études anatoliennes*, pp. 450 ff.

47. E. Meyer, *Die Grenzen der hellenistischen Staaten in Kleinasien*, Zurich, 1925, pp. 72-73 and 141, thought considerable frequency of change of alliance probable, though he had no evidence for it. A letter of Laodike III demonstrates, with other documents, Seleucid power at that time: "Supplemento Epigrafico di Iasos," (note 42), pp. 445-453, no. 2. For the date see *Bull. épig.* 1971, 621, and studies of F. Sokolowski, *Greek, Roman and Byzantine Studies* 13 (1972) 171-176 and Y. Garlan, *ZPE* 9 (1972) 224.

48. Published by J. and L. Robert, *Mélanges Isidore Levy*, in *Annuaire de l'institut de philologie et d'histoire Orientales et Slaves* 13, 1953, pp. 553 ff. Text reprinted in *SEG* XV 652. For the date of the ninth year of Ptolemy II, cf. the discussion of A. E. Samuel, *Ptolemaic Chronology*, pp. 25-28.

49. *I. Labraunda* II 43; cf. discussion in *I. Labraunda* I, p. 34. Crampa suggests that Apollonios may be the future *dioiketes*, surely useless speculation.

(?), appointed *oikonomos* by King Ptolemy, is praised for incorruptibility and other good qualities in administering justice and in according the Chrysaoreis their due. The editor's conclusion (partly based on restoration) that Ptolemy had made grants to the Chrysaoreis is very likely; this corresponds with Philadelphos' tendency to favor local leagues that would in turn support Ptolemaic power, as in Pamphylia and the Aegean islands. Later Seleucid and Antigonid monarchs, by contrast, supported Mylasa against the priests.[50]

We therefore know that Ptolemy II ruled this area as he did the neighboring districts, and we know that one of the key officials representing the king was an *oikonomos*. We know already of *strategoi* of Caria before this period (cf. below on Amyzon); it is therefore likely that the joint jurisdiction of the *strategos* and *oikonomos* visible in the Zenon papyri goes back to the early years of the reign of Philadelphos. Labraunda and Mylasa appear to have been controlled by the Seleucids at the time of the Laodikean war, and perhaps earlier. It may be that Ptolemaic rule was terminated as early as 259.[51]

For another isolated inland city of Caria we have only two indications of a Ptolemaic alliance. A letter of Antiochus III, dated in May, 203, promises to grant to Amyzon all of the privileges that it had had while it was in the Ptolemaic alliance.[52] It appears that the transfer from Ptolemaic to Seleucid allegiance was recent. L. Robert's study of the sanctuary of Artemis at Amyzon has yielded a third-century decree for "un gouverneur ptolémaïque, Margos." [53] Robert has kindly informed me that this decree for Μάργος ὁ στρατηγός, which is dated to year 9 of Philadelphos, is of a banal formula which tells us nothing of his activities and

---

50. *I. Labraunda* II 44-45 and 57 seem to refer, at a later date, to decisions of Apollonios, after the end of Ptolemaic control; see Crampa's historical discussions *ad* 43 and in volume I, cited in n. 49, above. The Ptolemaic second-century *archidikastes* Dionysios son of Timonax of Mylasa appears to be honored in no. 48, long after the end of Ptolemaic rule; for his position see below, p. 000.

51. Cf. *I. Labraunda* 3 for Seleucid rule.

52. Welles, *Royal Correspondence* 38.

53. The inscription is mentioned in *CRAI* 1948, p. 4 (*Opera Minora Selecta*, p. 1458). On the subsequent excavations of Amyzon and the character of the site, see L. Robert, *CRAI* 1953, pp. 403-415 (*Op. Min. Sel.*, pp. 1525-1537). More recently, Robert has cited a phrase from an inscription of Margos in *Nouvelles inscriptions de Sardes*, Paris, 1964, p. 15, n. 5, where he calls Margos a "stratège lagide."

residence. Amyzon is quite isolated from the other parts of Caria controlled by the Ptolemies in this period, and the inscription demonstrates the dangers of generalizing about the relations of a dynasty with a city on the basis of supposed control of its sur-roundings. It is clear that the conquests of the early part of the reign of Philadelphos in Caria were very widespread.

3. THE PENINSULA OF HALIKARNASSOS

The history of Halikarnassian relations with the Ptolemies is long and in a few places well-documented.[54] The earliest testimony is the sending of *dikastai* to Samos from Halikarnassos (as well as Miletos and Myndos) by Philokles king of Sidon not long after 280.[55] From the decree preserved for the Myndian judges, it is clear that Phi-lokles directed the cities to send the *dikastai*, and that a measure of Ptolemaic sovereignty at this time can be assumed. Two papyri to be discussed in detail below show that the Ptolemies still controlled the city in 257. We have also a dedication to Philopator and Arsinoe from Halikarnassos,[56] and in 197 the city was still in Ptolemaic hands; the Rhodians helped defend it in that year against Antiochus III.[57] The date of its final loss is uncertain; it fell, like that of Samos, during the next decade.

There was, then, continuous control from 280 to about 195. Within this period falls an otherwise undatable inscription of Halikarnassos dealing with the establishment of a new gymna-sium for the youth of the city. It is mentioned that king Ptolemy has sent the city by ambassador his permission to construct the gymnasium.[58] The text has been taken by some as evidence for harsh Ptolemaic treatment of the city—the city had to ask permis-sion to build, yet Ptolemy did not contribute. But the latter state-

---

54. Diodorus (20.27.2) does not mention Halikarnassos as an object of Ptolemy's offensive of 309 in Lycia and Caria, but it is generally thought that Demetrius' repulse of such a Ptolemaic siege (Plut. *Dem.* 7) belongs to 309. Between that date and Lysimachus' control after Ipsos we have no evidence, though it is assumed that Antigonus ruled the city.

55. *SEG* I 363.

56. *I. Brit. Mus.* 907. The text would fall between 217 and 209.

57. Livy 33.20.

58. Improved text with bibliography in A. Wilhelm, *Jahresh. Österr. Arch. Inst.* 11, 1908, pp. 53 ff. Perhaps in connection with this gymnasium, the Halikarnassians built a stoa to Apollo and king Ptolemy (again it is uncertain which one): *OGIS* 46.

ment assumes that this one fragmentary inscription tells all there
is to know about the gymnasium. We will see, indeed, that a close
supervision of municipal finance is typical of Ptolemaic administration in Caria, but I fail to see that anything more than this is
indicated.

Two papyri from the archives of Zenon, general agent and later
estate manager in the Fayûm for the *dioiketes* Apollonios, provide
useful information about the Ptolemaic presence in Halikarnassos.
Zenon was himself a Kaunian, and he retained wide contacts in the
area when he was in Egypt; to these contacts we owe much of
what we know of administration in this area.

The first text is a group of letters concerned with the advancing
of funds to the royal navy.[59] Apollodotos, a royal agent in Halikarnassos, advanced some 5465 drachmas to Antipatros, who was
commanding a ship in the Ptolemaic navy in the absence of its
regular commander. The funds came from three sources, and were
accordingly disbursed through three channels: (1) a sum of 2000
drachmas raised from the *iatrika* was disbursed by Straton, ὁ ἐν
Ἁλικαρνάσσωι γαζοφύλαξ, on orders of Apollodotos, to Perigenes,
who was to pass them on to Antipatros; (2) Apollodotos himself
advanced from an unnamed source 465 drachmas and some small
change via Hekatonymos to the same Antipatros; (3) 3000 drachmas
which had been given to the king as a crown by the Halikarnassians
and had been paid into the bank of Sopatros by the city *tamiai*
(and therefore receipted by Apollonios the *dioiketes* to the city
official Epikydes) were paid by Apollodotos to Antipatros through
the bank of Sopatros where the funds were on deposit. All of these
sums are to be repaid by Xanthippos, the *trierarchos* of the ship,
either to Apollonios or back to Apollodotos.

Some salient facts emerge from the proceedings. Two types of
royal revenue appear in the text, an extraordinary contribution
of money by the city to the king (the crown), no doubt voted on
some specific occasion, and *iatrika*, which would appear to be direct
royal taxes on the city for medical services. Since the money is to

---

59. *P. Cair. Zen.* 59036. I cannot discuss here the many problems raised
by this text. The trierarchy I consider in my "The Ptolemaic Trierarchs"
(*Chronique d'Égypte* 46, 1971, pp. 356-362), where I reject the universally
accepted view first presented by Wilcken that the trierarch is a Halikarnassian performing a liturgy.

return to the crown, it does not constitute city revenue.[60] The city, in fact, plays no part in the entire transaction; it is mentioned only as the source of the funds—it was important to the bureaucracy to know the proper category into which a sum of money was to be placed. It appears that the city dealt primarily with the resident financial official (Apollodotos) but might also deal in important matters (like a 3000 drachma crown) directly with the highest financial official in Alexandria, Apollonios.

It is also of interest to note that Apollodotos, here and elsewhere a crown financial agent, is in this text involved in a military matter. There is no absolute separation of the two areas visible, but rather a large degree of intermeshing of work.[61]

Another papyrus document concerning Halikarnassos merits discussion; once again it is a Zenon papyrus, and once again Apollodotos appears as an important participant.[62] The transactions appear to have taken place as follows: Danaos of Halikarnassos, involved in some large-scale financial dealings with the crown, defaulted on his obligations, also implicating a banker Iason. Danaos subsequently disappeared from sight (he presumably died), as his son Kratinos was currently carrying on his affairs. Kratinos worked out a settlement with Apollodotos involving the payment of 20 talents to the *basilikon* to settle the debt. Kratinos sent Hedylos to Alexandria, bearing letters from himself and Apollodotos to the *dioiketes* Apollonios. The date of these actions was 258/7; the actions of Danaos may go back several years. In the letters Kratinos asks Apollonios to approve the agreed-upon settlement.

On arriving in Alexandria, Hedylos not only failed to carry out his mission, but took up quarters in the house of Aristoboulos, plotting against Apollonios. Back in Halikarnassos, in the meanwhile, a former associate of Danaos, one Pankris, tried to use the influence of Epikydes, a city official whom we met in the naval loans case, to get himself the civic office of *nomophylax*. Epikydes

---

60. The fullest collection of documents on *iatrika* is to be found in the article of O. Nanetti, *Aegyptus* 24, 1944, pp. 119-125, but the basic conclusion of that article has been vitiated by *P. Hamb.* 171, where the nature of the tax is made clear: the sums collected were credited in the bank to the *iatrikos logos*, from which doctors were paid.

61. For Apollodotos' other appearances, see the references collected under *Pros. Ptol.* 16346.

62. *P. Cair. Zen.* 59037.

passed the matter on to the *dioiketes* (perhaps trying to avoid a decision). Pankris, annoyed at the delay, started rumors around Halikarnassos that Apollonios was responsible for the scandal about Danaos, obviously an affair of importance in the city. Iason, too, wrote to Apollonios, evidently seeking forgiveness of his past complicity.

All of this is narrated to Zenon by a correspondent whose name is lost. His object in writing is to persuade Zenon to influence Apollonios to write to Apollodotos and two other officials speaking well of him, and to Iason forgiving him and crediting Zenon's correspondent with the forgiveness. Zenon is also to warn Apollonios against Pankris, and presumably, though it is not said explicitly, to try to break up the logjam in settling the whole affair.[63]

The document shows clearly the close daily interconnections between crown financial officials and those important in civic financial life, be they entrepreneurs or bureaucrats. Civic political factions are interwoven with Alexandrian court factions, with Apollonios insidiously opposed and strongly disliked by certain groups in both Halikarnassos and Alexandria. It is interesting that Epikydes can refer the matter of the appointment of a *nomophylax* to Apollonios. I doubt that this referral was a necessary and routine action. Epikydes was probably using a discretionary authority to refer any dubious action to the crown. The crown involvement in the Danaos case is quite in line, since the debt was owed to the crown. Apollodotos was clearly the person of first resort, but his autonomy in handling major matters was limited by the ever vigilant eye of Apollonios. Twenty talents was a lot of money, perhaps the proceeds of a major tax-farming contract, and would be of key interest to Apollonios.

The nearby city of Myndos appears to have been under Ptolemaic control during the same period of 280-195. It appears in the Samian decree already mentioned, in which two Myndian *dikastai* are honored for their services in Samos, performed at the direction of Philokles king of Sidon.[64] At the other end of the period, Myndos was one of the cities in Ptolemaic possession that Rhodes helped to defend from Antiochus III in 197.[65] The date of final Ptolemaic

---

63. For Apollodotos and Hikesios in connection with Syrian wheat, see note 33, above.
64. *SEG* I 363.
65. Livy 33.20.

loss of the city is unknown, but it must fall not long after this date. The administrative framework in use at Myndos is entirely unknown to us.

4. SOUTHEASTERN CARIA

A survey of southeastern Caria will show some further aspects of the royal role in city finance. It is certain that Knidos had some links with the Ptolemies but far from clear what they were. In editing the text of a Milesian decree about a large sum of money borrowed by Miletos from Knidos, A. Rehm hypothesized that the presence of a Halikarnassian and a Cyrenaean in this text of 283/2 indicated a Ptolemaic connection to the loan, and hence Ptolemaic control of Knidos.[66] This suggestion appears to me exceedingly fragile, and not only because Ptolemaic control of both Halikarnassos and Cyrene in these years is a matter of doubt. There is no reason why the action of an individual citizen need reflect the official policy of the city where he was born.

More directly interesting is the mention in a Zenon papyrus of a Knidian who wanted to set up a Serapeion in an unknown coastal city under Ptolemaic domination,[67] but who did not accomplish his aim. Once again, it is difficult to ascribe to civic policy an act of individual piety, and judgment must be suspended.

Finally, during the reign of Philopator (or perhaps that of Euergetes) a statue was dedicated in Knidos by an Alexandrian, Agathoboulos son of Neon, of the famous minister Sosibios son of Dioskourides.[68] The placement of the dedication may suggest a strong Ptolemaic influence in Knidos, but it is far from proving direct rule.

From Knidos we turn to Kaunos, home city of Apollonios' agent Zenon. His papers, unfortunately, have given us no direct testimony of the administration of his city, but he retained many friends in Caria and brought many fellow-countrymen to Egypt to serve in lucrative positions. Kaunos, captured first in 309 by Ptolemy I (Diod. 20.27.2), remained long in Ptolemaic possession and was

---

66. *I. Delphin.* 138.298.

67. *P. Cair. Zen.* 59034 (text improved from *PSI* 435). The city appears to have Greek and non-Greek quarters, but no identification has been proposed with any certainty.

68. *OGIS* 79. Similar statues are known in Boeotia.

defended against Antiochus III in 197 by the Rhodians.[69] The next year, however, Rhodes bought the city from Ptolemy's generals for some 200 talents.[70] It would therefore appear that Kaunos, like Halikarnassos (where ships from the royal navy put in) had some military importance.

Two inscriptions of Kaunos discovered by G. E. Bean show the existence in the Hellenistic period (and probably its earlier part) of the demotic Πτολεμαιεύς at this city.[71]

For a third city in this area, Kalynda, we again have the evidence of a Zenon papyrus.[72] The first part of the papyrus is occupied by a long letter giving the details of a rather involved transaction. In year 38 of Ptolemy II (248/7), Theron, a farmer of Theopropos (the author of the letter), bought the contract for supplying wine for the yearly festival held by Kalynda at nearby Kypranda. Theopropos supplied Theron, who in turn supplied the festival, with 84 metretai of wine, at 10 drachmas per metretes, giving a total of 850 drachmas (Theopropos was weak in multiplication). Theopropos added, then deleted, the remark that he had borrowed money to buy the wine. Of the 850 drachmas, Theron (and thus presumably Theopropos) was paid 600 drachmas by the *tamiai* of the city, but they refused the remainder on the excuse that the συμβολαί (contributions) to the festival had not yet all been paid. Theron would have to wait.

Theopropos, becoming impatient for his money, brought the *tamiai* before the *strategos* Motes and the *oikonomos* Diodotos. The *tamiai* replied that they lacked authority to pay the sum out of regular city funds until they had received full payment of the special contributions. A decree would be necessary, and it appears that the officials told them to get one. The *prytaneis* and *gram-*

---

69. Livy 33.20. See P. M. Fraser, *Ptol. Alex.* II, p. 151, n. 216, with a reference to *Rhodian Peraea and Islands*, London, 1954, pp. 105-107, and I, p. 67.

70. Polyb. 30.31.6. For the date, see M. Holleaux, *Études* IV, p. 304, n. 3—perhaps even later in 197 itself.

71. Published by G. E. Bean, *JHS* 73, 1953, pp. 21 and 26-27 (cf. also the reflections in his second article on Kaunos, *JHS* 74, 1954, pp. 85-110). Bean accepts the assertion of L. Robert, *Hellenica* VII, 1949, pp. 189-190, that this Carian Ptolemais (for both assume that the Ptolemaieis are residents of a town Ptolemais) is the same as the independent city of that name attested in *I. Magn.* 59.29-30, and notes that its status as a deme of Kaunos must have changed before about 205 B.C. (*JHS* 73, 1953, p. 23).

72. *P. Cair. Zen.* 59341. Part (a) deals with the problems of Theopropos.

mateus of the city delayed, however, and no decree was passed. At this juncture Theopropos was appointed *theoros* to Alexandria (together with Diophantos, one of the *tamiai*). Being in Alexandria, Theopropos therefore takes the opportunity to seek redress from Apollonios, whom he wants to write to the city, *strategos*, and *oikonomos* about the matter. Another claim for interest on the borrowed money was stricken out on second thought.

The key point of the appeal to royal officials to settle an internal dispute has aroused a great deal of interest.[73] Rostovtzeff is certainly right in ascribing it to a royal desire to keep the finances of a subject city in proper order,[74] but more than this must be involved. The jurisdiction of the *strategos* and the *oikonomos* is not part of their day-to-day administrative routine, nor do they issue a direct order for release of the funds. Rather, they instruct the city officials to take the proper steps. Apollonios, similarly, is asked to write to the city to tell it to take steps to solve the problem and to write to his subordinates to spur them on to vigilance in the matter. Motes and Diodotos, who seem to be viewed as a college rather than a hierarchy, hold a supervisory position over the city but do not directly administer the city finances.

The second and third sections of the same papyrus reveal Diodotos' role somewhat further.[75] A relative of Zenon's writes that his father had enjoyed freedom from quartering soldiers and providing supplies to the army, but that he, Neon, had since his father's death not been accorded this privilege. He therefore asked Zenon to write to Apollonios, asking him to write to Diodotos and the *boule* and *demos* to request that Neon be freed from the obligation. The bottom of the papyrus contains a draft of a memorandum from Zenon to Apollonios complying with Neon's request.

Several aspects of this document are important. Diodotos has a connection with the supplying and financing of the army, reminiscent of the *oikonomos* Eirenaios in the next century, with his concurrent post of secretary of soldiers and *machimoi* in Thera, Crete, and Methana. Here again the persistent interweaving of financial and military jurisdictions is attested. Diodotos does not,

---

73. For various opinions, see C. C. Edgar's original commentary to the papyrus as *P. Edgar* 54, *Annales du Service des Antiquités d'Égypte* 20, 1920, pp. 32-38; U. Wilcken's comments in *Archiv* 7, 1924, pp. 75-76, and H. Bengtson, *Die Strategie* III, pp. 175-177.

74. *Large Estate*, p. 172.

75. *P. Cair. Zen.* 59341 (b) and (c).

however, have unique control over the problem; it appears that the city government too had a role in determining the obligations of its citizens to the crown; it could at least influence the distribution of the city's burdens. Apollonios appears primarily as the chief of the financial bureau and determiner of its interests, but the extent to which his influence in the matter might have been informal—as Zenon's was—cannot be ascertained. It is clear that Ptolemaic bureaucracy worked through means other than official channels to accomplish its ends, and that the citizens of the subject cities knew it.

5. THE ADMINISTRATION OF CARIA

The fortuitous preservation of a few papyri enables us to see details of the workings of Ptolemaic administration in Caria that are hidden from us elsewhere. The area was headed by a *strategos*, of whom we know a certain amount. Margos, attested at Amyzon in 278, is the first known; Motes was one; another appears in an inscription of Samos from the decade 270-260, where he is honored for his good deeds toward that city.[76] This man, Aristolaos son of Ameinias, Macedonian, dedicated a statue of Ptolemy II at Olympia.[77] It is not improbable that Aristoboulos and Asklepiodotos, high officials with jurisdiction over Iasos in the fourth century, held the position if not the title of the later *strategoi*. The *strategos* was responsible in general for the defense of the Ptolemaic possessions in the area and for exercising general administrative care over them. We do not know where he resided. Motes was appealed to in a case involving Kalynda, but he may have been elsewhere when he held a hearing or may have visited the city on one of his periodic rounds. The *strategos* also exercised a role in financial transactions, acting as an associate of the *oikonomos*. He was in direct touch with Apollonios and presumably with the king as well.

The *oikonomos*, who appears to have been as much a colleague as a subordinate of the *strategos*, held a similarly bifurcated position. He was obviously chief financial officer for the *basilikon*, certainly

---

76. *Ath. Mitt.* 72, 1957, p. 218, no. 57 (Habicht); see also the remarks of L. Robert on the provision of a sacrificial animal for Aristolaos, *Hellenica* 11-12, 1960, pp. 126-131.

77. The inscription of Samos thus confirms F. M. Heichelheim's conjecture in 1940 (*RE* Suppl. 7, col. 49, no. 2) that Aristolaos would be found someday in a document as a high Ptolemaic official. Pausanias 6.17.3 records the dedication at Olympia.

a subordinate of the *dioiketes*. At the same time, he played a role in certain aspects of military administration, in particular those connected with logistics.

There may have been other royal officials, too, but we cannot define their posts or competence with any confidence. For example, one would like to know the title of Apollodotos, so prominent in Ptolemaic administration in Caria around 260. We cannot exclude either *strategos* or *oikonomos* from his possible titles, for his interests were wide and his connection to Apollonios very close. On the whole, the connection of financial activities with military supply and maintenance inclines me to think that he was an *oikonomos*. His associate Hikesios, too, recipient of an identical letter in 261/0 about exportation of Syrian wheat—what post would he have held? Apollodotos' greater prominence in the Danaos dispute may reflect less his relative importance than the relevance of the problem to the respective jurisdictions of the different officials.

All of these officials exercised their occupations in constant touch with the cities of Caria. They did not run the city governments nor usurp their normal functions. City bureaucrats appear at the same time as the Ptolemaic functionaries, and the city governments are anything but inactive. Even when the royal officials direct the city's actions, they do not take over the routine management of the city's finances. All is done in a supervisory capacity, and orders were probably always given as advice. And yet the interference of the royal officials might fall on problems of almost any scope, ranging down to minor problems of contract farming in local festivals. Much of the interference was accomplished through informal channels of influence—it might take a letter to an estate manager in the Fayûm to resolve a controversy in Kalynda. It may well be that Ptolemaic bureaucrats acted habitually as much by their personal authority as by the definition of the jobs they held.

It is very probable that in some respects the Carian cities were directly taxed—the *iatrika* of *P. Cair. Zen.* 59036 and the twenty talent obligation of Danaos to the crown suggest taxes farmed by the *basilikon* to local citizens of importance who could provide surety. At the same time, contributions by the city (rather than its citizens) also appear, like the crown given to Ptolemy II by Halikarnassos.

6. Kos and Kalymna

Ptolemaic relations with Kos continued long after the end of any possible control of the island by the kings; Kos, moreover, had in the sanctuary of Asklepios one of the major Hellenistic shrines in the Aegean and by virtue of this engaged in extensive diplomatic relations with various kings; these relations reflect no control of Kos by the kings. For this reason, evidence from Kos must be used with considerable caution.

Ptolemy Philadelphos was born on Kos in 309/8, as the Marmor Parium tells us; [78] Theocritus confirms the fact.[79] It is possible that Soter controlled the island in these years, as he seems to have exercised power elsewhere in the area for a short period. On the other hand, he may simply have seen the island as a sanctuary safe for the keeping of his family.

In any case, Philadelphos himself maintained cordial relations with Kos from early in his reign. A Naxian inscription from not long after 280 informs us that the nesiarch Bacchon had sought Koan *dikastai* to settle affairs on Naxos and that they were successful in their mission.[80] In another situation, this text might be conclusive evidence for Ptolemaic control of Kos, but that island acted as arbiter in many disputes having nothing to do with the Ptolemies; its prestige may have been as important a factor here as its current political stance.

A fragmentary inscription from Kos appears to concern the establishment, on advice from an oracle, of a *temenos* of Arsinoe Philadelphos on the island.[81] Another fragment appears to record a gift or sale of wheat (from Cyprus, perhaps) by a Ptolemy to Kos; the mutilation of the text prevents our grasping a connected sense, but the editor, A. Maiuri, suggested a date in the reign of Philadelphos.[82] We have also a small portion of a letter of Ptolemy II to Kos about the sanctuary of Asklepios.[83]

Another inscription evidently concerning the early third century

---

78. *FGrH* 239 B 19.

79. *Id.* 17.58 ff.

80. The two relevant texts in Holleaux, *Études* III, pp. 27-37. Cf. Chapter VI, note 117, below, for further bibliography.

81. M. Segre, *BSA Alex.* 30-31, 1937, pp. 286 ff.

82. A. Maiuri, *Nuova silloge epigrafica di Rodi e Cos*, Firenze, 1925, 433.

83. Published in full for the first time by G. Klaffenbach from notes of R. Herzog as *Asylieurkunden* 1, where a bibliography of earlier partial publications can be found.

remains unpublished today more than 70 years after its discovery and 40 after its first mention in print.[84] It is a decree of Kos for one Diokles son of Damarchos, Akarnanian, τεταγμένος παρὰ βασιλεῖ Πτολεμαίωι. We have, unfortunately, no way of assessing his role in Ptolemaic relations with Kos. When this inscription, together with the rest of the Koan material, is finally published, we will be in a better position to know whether Kos was a Ptolemaic possession or, perhaps more likely, merely on close and friendly terms with Ptolemy II.

Two other documents concern Ptolemaic relations with the sanctuary, one a letter of Ptolemy III recognizing the sanctuary and its asylum,[85] the other a Koan decree for one of their own citizens who served on a *theoria* to a king Ptolemy and returned with a royal letter and sacrifices.[86] The latter document does not seem to be precisely datable.

Before turning to the last topic about Kos, the Koan *sympoliteia* with Kalymna, it will be useful to review the earlier evidence from the latter island. Two inscriptions from Kalymna and Iasos indicate that Ptolemy II sent *dikastai* once and perhaps twice to Kalymna to settle affairs.[87] The Iasian text is of particular importance. It records the Iasians' acceptance of a crown for judges sent to Kalymna, and gives the text of the Kalymnian decree conferring the crown. Those problems that the judges could not settle by amicable reconciliations were decided by reference to the *diagramma* of the king. The scope of the *diagramma* is not made clear, whether it referred to the situation at hand only or was part of a wider scheme of restoring order to various Ptolemaic dominions. It may have contained general principles for settlement of disputes or more specific decisions on aspects of the Kalymnian disorder. In any case, both the Iasians and the Kalymnians felt bound to accept it as a source for the final decision in disputed cases. We may therefore conclude that Kalymna was under Ptolemaic sovereignty at

---

84. Mentioned by R. Herzog in *Abhand. Berlin. Akad.* 1928, 6 Abh., p. 42, with some of the phraseology of the decree, but not the clauses about Diokles; also in L. Robert, *Hellenica* 5, 1948, p. 11.

85. Welles, *Royal Correspondence* 27.

86. *OGIS* 42.

87. Decree of Kalymna, *Tit. Cal.* 17. Inscription from Iasos, *Tit. Cal.* test. xvi. Segre's establishment of the date in the reign of Philadelphos was accepted by G. Klaffenbach, *Gnomon* 25, 1953, pp. 456-457.

some time in the reign of Ptolemy II.[88] It is not impossible that Kos and Kalymna, distinct entities at this time, had somewhat different relations with Philadelphos, the larger island being on more nearly a relationship of equality. It is also possible, however, that Ptolemy II exerted a much stronger influence or even control over Kos than did his son.

In an agreement of the late third century, probably imposed by Kos, Kalymna became a part of Kos and lost its independence.[89] This agreement, called a ὁμοπολιτεία, included provisions of φιλία and συμμαχία toward king Ptolemy. Klaffenbach has shown that the Koan decree containing the agreement and oaths must date to the end of the third century, and the Ptolemy mentioned be Philopator.[90] The extent of political control indicated by this clause is not certain, but it must have been substantial to cause the phrase to be included in this document.[91]

There is no evidence, then, for any Ptolemaic officials resident on either Kos or Kalymna, but the inscriptions point distinctly in favor of long cordial relations between the kings and these islands, with Ptolemaic hegemony particularly in evidence in the reigns of Ptolemy II and Ptolemy IV. It is to be hoped that the publication of the inscriptions of Kos will make possible considerable improvement in the precision of this picture.

7. LYCIA

We have a fair amount of information about the extent of Ptolemaic holdings in Lycia and two documents of capital im-

---

88. A number of extant Kalymnian decrees for Cyrenaeans and Alexandrians arise from benefits conferred on Kalymnians in Ptolemaic service in Egypt or the Cyrenaica rather than from the actions of any Ptolemaic official on Kalymna: *Tit. Cal.* 18, 57, 58, 59.

89. *Tit. Cal.* test. xii.

90. *Gnomon* 25, 1953, pp. 455-457, showing the impossibility of Segre's earlier dating and complicated political history derived from it.

91. M. Holleaux, *Études* IV, p. 333, n. 2, quotes a letter of R. Herzog saying that in the unpublished inscriptions of Kos there was no trace of Ptolemaic domination in the reigns of Philopator and Epiphanes. That statement seems somewhat extreme in the light of this inscription. An inscription from Kos published by P. M. Fraser, *BSA Alex.* 40, 1953, p. 61, is interpreted there as revealing the making of a joint will by two persons, a type of will known otherwise only from Egypt; Fraser thinks that direct interference by the Ptolemies in Koan law is unlikely. He also gives a list of documents illustrating Ptolemaic relations with Kos, which continued to the days of Euergetes II (*OGIS* 141) and even Auletes (*OGIS* 192, if this stone is not a "pierre errante" of non-Koan origin).

portance for the nature of the administration of those possessions. We may begin with a survey from west to east of the cities for which Ptolemaic control is attested.

For Lissa, first, there are two inscriptions from the early years of Ptolemy II, both decrees, one for a Rhodian, one for a Lissan, bearing dating formulae of the reign of Philadelphos, years 8 and 11.[92] Both thus come from the middle 270's. A third document, dated only by a local priest, has been restored as mentioning [Π]τολε[μ]αίο[υ Σ]ω[τῆρ]ος, and thus might date from the first few years of Philadelphos' reign. The text contains no other relevant information. We may conclude with some confidence that Lissa was under Ptolemaic control in the 270's. Another decree of the same city, of year 2 of Ptolemy III, shows continuance or resumption of Ptolemaic control of Lissa.[93]

A decree of the inland city of Araxa bears a date year 8, Gorpiaios, with no sovereign's name.[94] The editor, A. Maiuri, suggested that the reigns of Ptolemy II and III were the most likely time, though we cannot be sure that the date is even that of a Ptolemaic reign.[95] If it is, and the probabilities favor the supposition, it would on analogy to the decrees of Lissa be more attractive to choose year 8 of Ptolemy II. Most interesting in either case is the inland reach of Ptolemaic power, which in southern Asia Minor is in general coastal.

The case of the city of Telmessos is rather more complicated and interesting. It first appears as subject to the Ptolemies between 265 and 256 (the date is not completely preserved) in a decree dated to the reign of Philadelphos by a regnal formula.[96] The decree honors Leimon son of Antipatros, who being a friend of Ptolemy son of L[ysimachus] has shown his good will toward the city.

This Ptolemy, the son of Lysimachus (the king, as is now generally admitted) was still in Telmessos in 240, when he was honored by the famous decree of that city.[97] The document begins with a

92. *TAM* II 158 and 159.
93. *TAM* II 161 and 160.
94. *Annuario* 8-9, 1925-1926, p. 315.
95. A. Maiuri (note 94). The man honored is a Rhodian who has assisted Araxians in Rhodes. The date of regnal year and Macedonian month is a close parallel to the Ptolemaic documents of Lissa.
96. First published by M. Segre in *Clara Rhodos* 9, 1938, pp. 185-186 and fig. 1; improved edition in L. Robert, *Docs. Asie Min. mérid.*, p. 55.
97. *TAM* II 1 = *OGIS* 55. The bibliography of this text is enormous, particularly on the end of line 18. It is discussed by M. Segre with the other

date to year 7 of Ptolemy III, thus assuring that the city still recognized the authority of the king in Alexandria at this time. Ptolemy son of Lysimachus is honored because of his good care of the city since the time he received it from king Ptolemy son of Ptolemy. It is generally believed that the king in question is Euergetes and that the grant dates from the end of the Laodikean War. It is possible, however, that Philadelphos is the king meant, for Euergetes is generally referred to, here and elsewhere, as the son of the Theoi Philadelphoi, rather than the son of Ptolemy, whereas Philadelphos is often called son of Ptolemy. The fact that Ptolemy son of Lysimachus was already at Telmessos in the reign of Philadelphos may lend support to this supposition.

In any case, the primary interest of the document is its information on taxation, to which we will return later. Ptolemy had a son named Lysimachus, who probably succeeded him not long after the time of the Telmessian decree for Ptolemy. A decree of the city gave privileges to a Macedonian friend of Lysimachus in accordance with a request made by Lysimachus in a letter.[98] The dating formula is not preserved, so that we have no way of knowing what were the relations between Alexandria and Telmessos at this time. Segre put the date at about 220, and that is probably near the truth.

Between this decree and the end of the century we have no information, and when we next have a document, in 193, Ptolemy son of Lysimachus, the next generation, is spoken of as a relative of Antiochus III, and Ptolemy's daughter Berenike is appointed the chief-priestess for Laodike in the satrapy.[99] By this time at the latest the local dynasts had broken away from Ptolemaic influence, and the subsequent history of Ptolemy son of Lysimachus does not concern us here.[100]

documents pertaining to the family in *Clara Rhodos* 9, 1938, pp. 181-208. Segre did not succeed in solving the problem of line 18; see *Bull. épig.* 1954, 230. The most recent attempt is H. Bengtson's in *Kokalos* 10-11, 1964-1965, p. 325, n. 15, but I find this, too, unconvincing.

98. Segre (note 97) gives references to his earlier treatments of this text and a commentary in light of the other documents.

99. The letter of Antiochus and covering letter of Anaximbrotos are best consulted in Welles, *Royal Correspondence* 36 and 37. Since Welles wrote, two other examples of the letter have been found in Iran (with different priestesses), giving the correct date, which is not entirely preserved in the Eriza stone: L. Robert, *Hellenica* 7, 1949, pp. 5 ff. (esp. p. 17 for the family of Ptolemy) and *CRAI* 1967, pp. 281-296.

100. The references are collected in Segre's article (note 97, above).

From Hieronymus' description of Antiochus III's conquests in
197, we gain four more names for Ptolemaic possessions, Xanthos,
Patara, Andriake, and Limyra.[101] Patara is also known as a Ptolemaic
dependency from two Zenon papyri in which it figures as a way-
station for travellers,[102] and from an anecdote in Strabo, who tells
us that Philadelphos tried to rename Patara after Arsinoe, but that
the name failed to stick.[103] Xanthos dated a decree of 257/6 by
the regnal year of Ptolemy II.[104] Between these indications for the
latter two decades of Philadelphos' reign and its loss in 197, we
have no published information. For Xanthos, however, an unpublished inscription contains a decree of that city for a *phrourarchos* named by Ptolemy II; a garrison is thus certain.[105]

Our information thus confirms Theocritus' statement that Lycia
was under Philadelphos' control and Euergetes' claim in the Adoulis
inscription that it was an inherited possession. Our documentation
between the early part of Euergetes' reign and the loss of the area
to Antiochus in 197 is weak, but one document of importance not
only confirms possession but gives us considerable information on
the ways of taxation in the area; this is *P. Teb.* 8, which contains
much abbreviated drafts of letters about foreign revenues, written
probably in the office of the *dioiketes*.

Three of the letter drafts in this papyrus, which I date to about
219,[106] mention Lycia. One, a letter to one Nikostratos, tells how
much money has been brought in by the sale of the contract for
the ἀργυ(ρικῶν) προσόδων in Lycia for the fourth year. A second
letter to the same official (nowhere given a title) reveals that the
contract for the διαπύλιον, the customs toll, was short by over two
talents. The writer, naturally concerned, requests the records of
wine imports since the sixteenth year. A third letter tells us that

---

101. Hieron. *in Dan.* 11.15-16 = *FGrH* 260 F 46.
102. *P. Mich.* 1 and 10.
103. Strabo 14, p. 666.
104. *TAM* II 262, which is a Roman copy (lettering of the second or
third century) of the text, of which only part survives. It granted tax-
exemption among other privileges.
105. Indication of H. Metzger, *Rev. arch.* 1970, p. 307. Metzger also (p.
317) indicates that a decree of Xanthos is dated to 116 Sel. (196/5 B.C.),
confirming that Antiochus III kept the city after dislodging it from Ptolemaic
control in 197.
106. The date has been disputed between the reigns of Philopator and
Epiphanes; I argue in *JEA* 61, 1975, that the material in the unpublished
second column of the papyrus supports an earlier date.

Zethos and a partner have taken the πορφυρικόν in Lycia for a period of five years, at an annual payment of one talent 1800 drachmas.

From these texts several facts of importance emerge. The *dioiketes* in Alexandria, the probable author of the letters, dealt with one or more subordinate crown officials in Lycia whose titles are not preserved. All of the letter drafts here involve the letting of contracts for royal taxes or monopolies (if the purple industry is the actual working concession and not a tax), all payable in cash. No revenues in produce are under consideration here. There is, significantly, no direct collection of any of these taxes, either the revenues within the areas or the customs tolls. All are farmed out to entrepreneurs, whether for collection or underwriting we do not know.

It is time now to return to the decree for Ptolemy son of Lysimachus.[107] An important passage of the decree deals with the main reason for the honors given him, a sweeping change in the method of taxation levied on produce. He released them (perhaps only for a limited time) from taxes on orchard crops and from pasture tax (ἐννόμια). As for the *apomoira* on grain, millet, pulse, and sesame, formerly collected strictly according to the law, he remitted all but the collection of a tenth of the produce. Rostovtzeff is no doubt right in thinking that the reforms marked a shift from a complicated system of taxation and rents imposed by the Ptolemies to a tithing scheme analogous to that known elsewhere in Asia Minor.[108]

It is clear that the situation in Telmessos was out of the ordinary. Ptolemy had acted with a great deal of independent authority in dealing with the taxation problem, making changes that would in all probability have come normally from the king or at least the *dioiketes*. Unfortunately, we cannot compare the system of treating taxes in money in *P. Teb.* 8 with the taxation in kind that Ptolemy son of Lysimachus dealt with in Telmessos. Nor can we tell to what extent he took his orders from Alexandria, or how far the crown might have extended such changes around other cities in Lycia or elsewhere.

It is certain, however, that in both documents we are dealing with a situation in which the crown levies taxes itself, either through

---

107. Note 97, above.
108. *SEHHW*, pp. 336-337.

tax-farmers or through its own agents. The taxes themselves are reminiscent of those known in Egypt. There is nowhere any sign of city responsibility for taxation and thence a contribution to the crown. And yet the various cities exhibit normal institutions of the *polis* in their decrees. It may be that *P. Teb.* 8 is somewhat misleading in this respect, however, and that the cities did play some role that we cannot see.

Ptolemaic influence in Lycia did not end with the loss of the cities to Antiochus. A dedication at Xanthos tells us that one Euphrainetos, a *hegemon*, dedicated a temenos, temple, and statue of Artemis on behalf of Ptolemy V and Cleopatra and the city of Xanthos.[109] Euphrainetos was an Aetolian on his father's side, but not on his mother's; she was quite possibly Xanthian.[110] From the same reign but slightly later a decree of the *koinon* of the Lycians honored Ptolemaios son of Ptolemaios, both men having the title of ἀρχικυνηγός, both with court rank, for the father's good-will towards the sovereigns and their children and the *koinon*.[111] These inscriptions are interesting testimonies of an active connection between Lycia and Alexandria past any date at which we can assert Ptolemaic hegemony in Lycia.

8. Pamphylia and Pisidia

Theocritus gives Pamphylia to Philadelphos along with Lycia, but Euergetes (in the Adoulis inscription) claims it as a conquest

---

109. *TAM* II 263 = *OGIS* 91.

110. The mother's ethnic is lost, but editors have generally restored it as Xanthian to account for the placing of the dedication, probably rightly. M. Launey is right, however, in asserting that we have insufficient information to find Euphrainetos' motivation; he offers the possibility that his father was a Ptolemaic soldier stationed in Xanthos (*Armées hellénistiques*, pp. 193-194, 921).

111. *OGIS* 99; text most recently in *SB* 8274. Discussion of this text and the *koinon* in Oskar Treuber, *Geschichte der Lykier*, Stuttgart, 1887, pp. 149 ff., esp. p. 150, n. 1; Gustave Fougères, *De Lyciorum Commune*, Diss. Paris, 1898, p. 15; J. A. O. Larsen, *Classical Philology* 51, 1956, pp. 151-169. These two Ptolemaic officers also appear in *I. Philae* 9, a dedication recently published by A. Bernand which must be slightly earlier in date than the Lycian one (cf. Bernand's commentary, *I. Philae* I, pp. 110-111). P. M. Fraser, *Ptol. Alex.* II, p. 183, n. 59, reports with approval the opinion of T. B. Mitford that this inscription was originally erected on Cyprus, "where the κοινὸν τῶν Λυκίων is regularly attested"; but the Cypriot *koinon* is always τὸ κοινὸν τῶν ἐν τῆι νήσωι τασσομένων Λυκίων, and the same phrase is always found with the *koina* of other ethnics: cf. *Op. Ath.* 1, 1953, p. 151 (Mitford). I do not see that it can be such a *koinon* here; rather it is, as has traditionally been thought, the Lycian league.

of his own. It does not seem possible to find other evidence for these shifts of control from epigraphical documents, but there is no conflicting testimony and probably some supporting numismatic evidence. It is possible, moreover, to add some information about various cities, moving again along the coast from west to east.

The earliest securely datable testimony for the Ptolemies comes from Termessos, in a decree of that city dated to the reign of Ptolemy II, year 5 (late 278), honoring Philippos son of Alexandros, Macedonian, ὑπὸ βασιλέως Πτολεμ[αίου] χατασταθεὶς Παμφυλι[.[112] The end of the phrase is restored, no doubt correctly, by L. Robert as Παμφυλι[άρχης].[113] The remainder of the stone is lost, and we do not know what the services of this Pamphyliarch were. His discovery is, however, valuable evidence that Ptolemy II had one official appointed to govern the entire area of Pamphylia, and that Termessos, on the border between Pamphylia and Pisidia, came within his competence.

We come next to Aspendos and one of the most complex problems of this chapter. The city was an important source of Ptolemaic mercenaries even in the second century,[114] but it has yielded only one trace of the connection in its inscriptions. This text is a decree for some soldiers who came with two commanders to help Aspendos:[115] ὅσοι μετὰ [. .] λοκλέους κ[αὶ] Λεωνίδου παραγενόμενοι ἐβοή[θη]-σαν τῆι πόλει. Their places of origin are listed: Pamphylia, Lycia, Crete, Greece, Pisidia. There is mention of king Ptolemy, and at the end an almost entirely lost list of names. The outlines of the action are clear: Ptolemy sent two commanders with their mercenary troops to protect Aspendos. The protection may have served against another king, or another city, or was perhaps preventive in nature: the installation of a garrison.

Although the outlines are clear, two questions have remained subjects of debate from the first publication: the date of the text and the name to be restored as Leonides' associate. The first editors read the word as [Δη]μοκλέους, but Roussel suggested [Φι]λοκλέους

---

112. L. Robert, *Docs. Asie Min. mérid.*, pp. 53-58.

113. J. and L. Robert, *Bull. épig.* 1967, 601, show the incorrectness of the text and the impossibility of the restoration Παμφυλι[ας] proposed by C. Brixhe (and mentioned by Brixhe and E. Will).

114. Cf. the discussion of Thera in Chapter VI.

115. First published by P. Romanelli and R. Paribeni, *Monumenti Antichi* 23, pp. 116 ff. Text also in the studies cited in the following notes and most recently reprinted in *SEG* XVII 639.

instead, and his restoration and proposed identification of this man with Philokles king of the Sidonians have been generally accepted, not without some exceptions.[116] The restoration of the name appears to me sound, but the validity of the interpretation depends on the dating.

The first editors left the question of dating the text open, but pointed out that Leonides was probably the general of Ptolemy I known in Greece and Cilicia during the last decade of the fourth century.[117] A broad dating to this period is therefore probable, and the date is further placed after 305 by Ptolemy's having the title king. Segre, in the fullest study of this inscription that has been made, tried to narrow the limits by a variety of arguments to the years 301-298.[118] For the date 301, the justification lies in Antigonus' control of the area until the battle of Ipsos, and if this text represents more than a brief raid, it is unlikely that it falls before Ipsos. The upper limit thus seems relatively secure.

The lower limit is, however, a different matter. Segre argued that Pamphylia, as a possession mentioned in Theocritus, should have become Ptolemaic by about 279, and the Termessian decree mentioned would now tend to confirm this date. It is not, however, clear whether the Aspendos decree concerns the capture by Philadelphos near this time, or rather an earlier and probably more ephemeral period of control. Segre argued that in later times Philokles king of Sidon was, as Ptolemaic admiral, too important to be sent to Aspendos on this kind of mission; but without knowing the context of the arrival of the soldiers, I do not think this by any means certain.

In any event, Segre's argument turns on the identity of the enemy against whom Aspendos is to be defended. Segre thinks it can only have been Demetrius and that Demetrius himself was threatening the city; he therefore suggested 298, when Demetrius was coasting along to Cilicia. If, however, we do not grant that the enemy must be Demetrius in person, a number of occasions become possible for the capture of Aspendos, and indeed any time after

---

116. *REG* 29, 1916, p. 454.
117. In Cilicia in 310, Diod. 20.19.4. In Corinth and Sikyon in 308, Suda s.v. Demetrios and Plut. *Dem.* 15.1, where he is mistakenly called Kleonides. An undatable offering at Delos, *IG* XI 2 161 B 77.
118. *Aegyptus* 14, 1934, pp. 253-268.

294 (Ptolemy's recapture of Cyprus) appears to me possible.[119]

In sum, the date of the inscription does not appear certainly determinable; nor does it appear to me that a certain identification of Philokles can be made. We know yet too little of the history of Pamphylia in this period to assign this incident to its place.

Two Ptolemaic city foundations are known to us in Pamphylia. Between Kibyra and Augai lay a Ptolemais known only from a remark of Strabo.[120] An Arsinoe somewhat further east is better known. Strabo, again, tells us that after Korakesion, known from Hieronymus to have been taken by Antiochus III in 197 from Ptolemy V,[121] lay an Arsinoe.[122] A native of the city was buried in an urn in Alexandria dated to year 8 of an unknown king.[123] A Zenon papyrus dated in 257 tells us that some travellers from Egypt, driven off course by storms to Patara, there found a boat to take them back along the coast to Arsinoe, which is most likely the city in Pamphylia.[124] More recently a Cypriot inscription, whose letter forms Mitford dates to the later third century, has attested a commandant of Charadros in Cilicia who bore the ethnic Arsinoeus from the city in Pamphylia.[125] G. E. Bean and T. B.

---

119. J. Seibert, *Historia* 19, 1970, pp. 344-351, has argued that neither the name nor the date is secure. One may agree with him on the date; indeed, Rostovtzeff long ago demurred at Segre's precision (*SEHHW*, p. 1315). Seibert's discussion of the name is, however, a ruin. The photograph given by Romanelli and Paribeni (note 115) shows clearly that *mu* in this inscription is not formed like two *lambdas*, but has a different angle. Seibert suggested 14 possible names depending on whether the letter in question was *alpha*, *delta*, *lambda*, or *mu*. *Mu* is excluded, however, and Seibert himself recognizes that Naokles and Laokles do not fill the lacuna. Seibert's remaining suggestions are taken from Dornseiff-Hansen's reverse name index without any of the critical care of which the necessity was underlined by J. and L. Robert in *Bull. épig.* 1959, 89. Had Seibert examined any indices to epigraphical corpora (or even Dornseiff-Hansen's source, Pape-Bensseler), he would have seen that Rhadokles, Kydokles, and Telokles are very rare, and that Philokles is in fact vastly more common than Rhodokles. One would need compelling reasons to substitute an uncommon name for Philokles, and we have no such reasons here.

120. Strabo 14.4.2 (p. 667).

121. Note 101, above.

122. Strabo 14.5.3 (p. 669); for a summary of the evidence to 1938, see L. Robert, *Études épigraphiques et philologiques*, p. 255.

123. E. Breccia, *I. Gr. Lat. Alex.* 191.

124. *P. Mich.* 10, for which Robert's interpretation (note 122) is to be preferred to C. C. Edgar's *ad loc.*

125. T. B. Mitford, *AJA* 65, 1961, p. 134, no. 35.

Mitford have argued [126] that Strabo is confused and that Arsinoe was a refoundation of Korakesion. L. Robert points out that this identification gains much probability from the very great fortress qualities of Alanya, such as are typical of cities renamed for Arsinoe in the reign of Ptolemy II (cf. the remarks on Koresia on Keos, p. 142).

It cannot be said that we know much about the Ptolemaic rule of Pamphylia. Its conquest appears to go back to the early part of Philadelphos' reign, with perhaps temporary or even permanent control already in the previous reign. Ptolemy II placed a Pamphyliarch over the area, and the crown appears to have controlled a number of points at various times: Termessos, Aspendos, Ptolemais, Korakesion, Arsinoe. Neither the length of his control nor its geographical extent can be determined, but in various cities it goes back as far as 278 and lasts as long as 257 and perhaps later. It may be that Philadelphos lost control over much or all of the area before his death, so that Euergetes could call it his own conquest. Some coin series of the area also suggest this sequence of events (cf. Chapter VIII). At least one point in the area, Korakesion, remained Ptolemaic in 197.

About the nature of the administration little can be said. The Pamphyliarch, a regional governor, is the most significant indication we have. It is not improbable that he had some city commandants and garrisons under him, but they have left no record. One has the impression of a series of strongholds along the coast, rather than a pacified countryside, but Termessos shows that this situation need not have been the case. New finds may yet greatly expand this limited picture.

9. CILICIA

Our information for Cilicia is still less plentiful. Ptolemy I sent Leonides to the area in 310, but Demetrius soon regained it for his father.[127] Theocritus lists Cilicia as one of Philadelphos' possessions, but Euergetes claims it as his own conquest. In this Hieronymus supports him, including it among his conquests in the Third Syrian War and stating that on returning to Egypt Ptolemy gave

---

126. *Anat. Stud.* 12, 1962, pp. 195-196 and n. 22.
127. Diod. 20.19.4.

Cilicia to his friend Antiochos to govern; it figures with Mesopotamia in this respect.[128]

Euergetes' conquests seem to have lasted, at least in Rough Cilicia, for Hieronymus lists seven places taken by Antiochus III in 197 from Ptolemy V: Selinus, Anemurion, Zephyrion, Aphrodisias, Korykos, Soloi, and Mallos, the last being in the plain, the rest (from west to east) in Rough Cilicia along the coast.[129] We have no information about the Ptolemaic control of these points from other sources, with the exception of Soloi. An inscription found there is a letter probably from a Ptolemy to one of his functionaries, of which a copy was erected by the city.[130] It reproves the official for permitting abuses of billeting by soldiers in the city. The date is late third century (on grounds of letter forms) and hence probably in the reign of Philopator.

A few places may be added to Hieronymus' list. An inscription of Cyprus honors a Theodoros son of Demetrios from Arsinoe in Pamphylia, ἡγεμόνα τὸν τεταγμένον ἐπὶ Χαράδρου and his wife, a Samian, and their sons. There was, therefore, a garrison in Charadros at the time of the inscription, probably in the reign of Euergetes.[131]

Between Anemurion and Zephyrion in Hieronymus' list an Arsinoe and a Berenike may be added. The former is described by Strabo as πρόσορμον ἔχουσα and is placed between Nagidos and Kelenderis.[132] The second is mentioned by Stephanus of Byzantium and in the Stadiasmus, the latter telling us that it had a κόλπος.[133] No further information is forthcoming about these places.

Mention may be made, finally, of a Cypriot text honoring Nikandros, τὸν καθεσ[τηκότα ὑ]πὸ τοῦ βασιλέως [ἐπιστάτ]ην τῆς περὶ [. . . . . . N]εαπό‹λ›εως. This inscription, coming from the area of Salamis, was reedited by Mitford, who suggested that Neapolis was probably a city in Rough Cilicia with a garrison like Charadros; the date of this text is approximately the same as the one honoring the commandant of Charadros.[134] The suggestion is not unattrac-

---

128. Hieron. *in Dan.* 11.6-9 = *FGrH* 260 F 43.
129. Note 101, above.
130. Welles, *Royal Correspondence* 30.
131. Note 125, above.
132. Strabo 14.5.3 (p. 670).
133. Steph. Byz. s.v. Berenike, fifth entry. Stadiasmus 190, in Müller, *Geog. Graec. Min.* I, Paris, 1855, p. 485.
134. *AJA* 65, 1961, p. 136 (Mitford); text reprinted as *SB* 10155 and *SEG* XX 315.

tive, but we have no way of deciding its merits at present.[135]

For Cilicia, then, we can discern a long string of strongholds along the coast of Rough Cilicia, most or all garrisoned, in probability. There is also a possibility that these garrison commanders were subject to the overall control of an area commander.

---

135. Mitford speculates, in G. E. Bean and T. B. Mitford, *Journeys in Rough Cilicia 1964-1968* (*Denkschr. Oesterr. Akad. Wiss.* 102, 1970), p. 209, that Neapolis was located at the modern Gargara, which was formerly called Nemetli, a name Mitford thinks to be derived from Neapolis. Bean registers his dissent, and the association must be judged purely speculative.

CHAPTER SIX

THE AEGEAN

A. Crete

The Hellenistic history of Crete is a complex affair, at times brightly illumined by documents or authors, usually lost in darkness. The role played by the Ptolemies, as has often been remarked, was considerable and touched nearly every part of the island and all periods of the Hellenistic age, even after the Ptolemies had long lost any Aegean possessions. In particular, the Ptolemies like other Hellenistic rulers drew a substantial part of their manpower needs from the mercenaries of Crete; the evidence for recruiting and use of Cretan mercenaries in Ptolemaic service has often been more or less completely collected and analyzed, most adequately by Marcel Launey in 1949.[1] There is no need to repeat Launey's work here, the less so as Ptolemaic recruiting in an area is no indication that they controlled it.[2]

From the many other contacts the Ptolemies had in Crete, we must exclude most from the area of administration. Ptolemy III and Berenike were honored at Phalasarna;[3] an unknown Ptolemy in Eleutherna;[4] and another unknown Ptolemy at Lappa.[5] These texts reinforce our impression of widespread Ptolemaic activity in the island, but do nothing to clarify the nature of that activity.

For Gortyn, more evidence is available. The earliest text is the testimony of Strabo (9.4.11, p. 478) that Ptolemy IV began the walling of Gortyn. This has been seen by some [6] as an indication

---

1. M. Launey, *Armées hellénistiques*, pp. 248-286 (discussion) and 1152-1169 (prosopography). More recent evidence only supplements Launey's work without significantly altering his conclusions.

2. Ptolemaic recruiting was very heavy in their spheres of influence, but they used sparingly some of the areas that they actually governed (notably Cyprus) and continued to draw in later years from possessions they no longer held in Asia Minor.

3. *I. Cret.* II 19.2, a dedication to the Great Gods on their behalf.

4. *I. Cret.* II 12.25, a statue base for which several restorations are possible, belonging evidently to the reign of Euergetes or Philopator.

5. *I. Cret.* II 16.11.

6. P. M. Fraser, *Op. Ath.* 3, 1960, p. 31, n. 1, in taking this position cites earlier views for and against.

that Philopator controlled Gortyn at the time; it certainly demonstrates close relations and a substantial degree of military aid;
but in the lack of corroborating evidence, it seems to me best to
refrain from concluding that Philopator was in fact master of
Gortyn.

Several other texts show Ptolemaic intervention on Gortyn's
behalf in the reign of Philometor, perhaps a half-century later.
Ptolemy VI was chosen by Gortyn to arbitrate any disputes arising
from a peace treaty it made with Knossos, and it appears that his
ambassadors were instrumental in bringing about the agreement.[7]
It is possible that Ptolemy V had also played this role in an earlier
agreement between the two cities, if Guarducci's dating is correct.[8]
Another Gortynian decree honors some soldiers, all of whom bear
Egyptian names, sent by Ptolemy (Philometor) to aid Gortyn
against its enemies (Knossos?).[9] While the chronology of these
texts is not certain, it is clear that Philometor played an active
part in defending Gortyn and assisting it diplomatically. At the
same time, we see that there was almost certainly no Egyptian
force regularly stationed in Gortyn at the time help was sent.

Close though relations were, then, there is no decisive evidence
to show that Ptolemaic relations with Gortyn ever went further
than a close diplomatic and military alliance, such as existed at
various times between different kings and Cretan cities. Philometor
was perhaps more active than others in fulfilling his pacts.

For Olous, again, we have some evidence pointing to a diplomatic
entente. In the proxeny lists of the city there is one year a large
contingent of men who seem to be Ptolemaic military officers.[10]
The list is headed by Patroklos son of Patron, Macedonian, well-
known as the commander of the Ptolemaic forces engaged in the
Chremonidean War; it is generally agreed that the group honored

---

7. *I. Cret.* IV 181. Guarducci's date of 168-165 seems to me unlikely, but
I cannot discuss the point here.

8. *I. Cret.* IV 176. The date is by no means certain.

9. *I. Cret.* IV 195, containing a decree followed by a list of names. Part
(c) appears to me to have been restored wrongly to an excessive width,
a problem I discuss in *ZPE* 11, 1973, pp. 124-127. On the other side, a
Gortynian named Pyroos who had served the Ptolemies and returned to
Gortyn about this time has left two dedications in the Iseum, *I. Cret.* IV
243 and 244; the fuller of these, in verse, is mutilated and frustrates the hopes
it raises.

10. *I. Cret.* I 22.4.A.35 ff., in the midst of Rhodians and others honored in
various years.

here was en route to Greece.[11] It may well be that Olous was the fleet's last stop on Crete before departing for Thera. Once again, it appears that a Cretan contact was limited to military and diplomatic operations.[12]

Georges Le Rider has recently established from numismatic evidence that the city of Rithymna on the north coast of Crete was refounded at some point in the third century under the name Arsinoe.[13] The dating of the change of name is less sure, though Le Rider places it in the reign of Philopator. It may be that this is the same Arsinoe that appears as a Cretan city in a Magnesian inscription of about 200,[14] but in any case Rithymna had its original name again by the time of the Delphic *theorodokoi* lists in the early second century.[15] The possibility also exists that there was another Arsinoe on Crete, but for it we have no independent testimony aside from the reference in Stephanus of Byzantium.[16] In the case of Rithymna, at least, we must reckon with the possibility that the Ptolemies administered it directly for a space of time (which need not have been long), but no evidence yet found provides any indication of the nature of this administration.

A final testimony that is worth mentioning before we pass on to Itanos is a pair of inscriptions found on Delos, recording dedications by Cretan σύμμαχοι. From Holleaux's discussion [17] it appears

---

11. For Patroklos' route, see M. Launey, *REA* 47, 1945, pp. 33-45. The list of those honored, of the greatest prosopographical interest, includes several persons otherwise known in Ptolemaic service.

12. It is not necessary to review here in detail all possible Ptolemaic-Cretan connections in proxeny decrees. See notably the Apteran decree *I. Cret.* II 3.12c.6 and L. Robert, *Noms indigènes*, p. 416.

13. "Les Arsinoéens de Crète," *Essays in Greek Coinage presented to Stanley Robinson*, Oxford, 1968, pp. 229-240. Le Rider's evidence is a series of coins struck by a city named Arsinoe, all small bronzes identical in design (and once apparently in die) to a series of Rithymna; the coins of Arsinoe are, furthermore, found until now only in the region of Rethymnon.

14. *I. Magn.* 21.8.

15. Le Rider would place the beginning of the series of Rithymna about 250, and the Arsinoe series after at least the beginning of the Rithymnian series. Time slots in which Rithymna is not otherwise attested are about 265-235 and 220-190, making the latter more probable; but the argument seems to me inconclusive.

16. Bibliography and the many emendations suggested will be found in Le Rider's article (note 13).

17. Publication with full discussion by M. Holleaux, *Études* III, pp. 7 ff. Republished as *I. Délos* 1517 (also F. Durrbach, *Choix* 92) and 1518. One dedication honors Philometor, the other Aglaos of Kos who had helped the soldiers in Alexandria.

quite certain that these were allies sent by the Cretans (by the *koinon*, perhaps) rather than mercenaries hired directly by royal recruiters or their captains, who served under Ptolemy VI on Cyprus in the struggle against his brother (Ptolemy VIII Euergetes II) that ended in about 154 with the capture of the latter at Lapethos. We may infer from these texts a treaty of mutual assistance between Philometor and a number of Cretan cities, which now repaid his aid of previous years.

The task of fitting all this information into the Hellenistic history of Crete, of giving it life, has been attempted by many in whole or in part, and it is not my purpose here to add to this work. Rather, the main conclusion we are to draw from this evidence is negative. Of all these cities, only Arsinoe-Rithymna appears to have been certainly under Ptolemaic control at any time, and for it we have as yet no details about the manner of its administration. For the rest we see abundant testimony to expenditure of Ptolemaic energy and money in Crete and to the long-lasting and widespread effect it had. Of control, however, we see no trace in the Ptolemaic relations with these cities.

The one city in Crete of which this statement is not true is to be found at the extreme eastern end of Crete, not far from the cape that forms the northeastern tip of the island. Itanos, like the other cities, took a significant part in the politics of the island, a part recently discussed at some length by Stylianos Spyridakis, who has had some success in placing Itanos within the power struggles of Crete and in particular its eastern third.[18]

Our first view of the Ptolemies in Itanos comes at the time of the visit of Patroklos, the admiral of the Chremonidean War, who seems to have made Itanos one of his way-stations in 266 on his way to Attica. The Itanian description of his actions is worth quoting: πολλὰ συνήργησε τοῖς Ἰτανίοις ὅπως τά τε κατὰ τὰν πόλιν ἀσφαλέως ἔχηι πολιτευομένων τῶν Ἰτανίων κατὰ τοὺς νόμους καὶ τὰν χώραν μετὰ πάσας ἀσφαλείας νέμωνται.[19] It would appear, as Spyridakis rightly says,[20] that Patroklos' role included both stabilizing

18. *Ptolemaic Itanos and Hellenistic Crete*, Berkeley, 1970.

19. Two copies of this text survive, *I. Cret.* III 4.2 and 3.

20. Spyridakis (note 18), pp. 71-77. The real value of Spyridakis' work here and elsewhere in the book in reconstructing the political history is unfortunately in considerable part vitiated by his slovenly methodology; cf. *Phoenix* 25, 1971, p. 405.

internal conditions in Itanos and creating peaceful conditions between it and its neighbors so that it could manage the land it claimed in peace. His role thus combines the attributes of *dikastes* and ambassador, though he is called *strategos* sent to Crete by king Ptolemy in the decree that conferred on him Itanian citizenship. Though there is no specific evidence to that effect in the document, it is generally thought that Patroklos implanted a garrison to ensure the safety of Itanos and the lasting effect of his intervention. As we shall see later in this chapter, such an action would be consistent with Patroklos' subsequent actions; it also fits the later presence of a garrison. As long as we cannot be sure of the meaning of the later Itanian reference to Ptolemy III as παραλαβών Itanos from his father and his *progonoi*, however, we cannot be sure what the state of Ptolemaic relations with Itanos was prior to the visit of Patroklos or whether Ptolemy I might have planted a garrison. The title of *strategos* given to Patroklos here represents his military command, as Launey pointed out; [21] the phrase ἐς Κρήταν represents perhaps an egocentric view of Patroklos' mission by the Itanians, who were concerned only with the fact that creating a line of bases and regulating the security of his rear was part of Patroklos' mission.

The garrison left behind by Patroklos—if such there was—must have remained long after his departure. One text, probably early in the reign of Ptolemy III, records the dedication of a *temenos* to him and Berenike by the Itanians, together with yearly sacrifices.[22] Ptolemy is thanked for gloriously benefiting and protecting the city in its laws. It is very likely that he maintained the garrison that guaranteed the security of Itanos.

For the reign of Philopator, we have continued evidence of the existence of the garrison in the form of a dedication to Philopator and Arsinoe by Lucius son of Gaius, Roman, *phrourarchos*.[23] We may place the text in the period 217-209 on the basis of the presence of Arsinoe but the absence of any mention of their child Epiphanes. Two other inscriptions may be dated approximately to Philopator's reign (on the basis of the letter forms); [24] in them king Ptolemy

---

21. Cf. M. Launey's article, note 11, above.

22. *I.Cret.* III 4.4. On the date, probably 246, see C. Habicht, *Gottmenschentum²*, p. 122, following M. Guarducci and F. Hiller von Gaertringen.

23. *I. Cret.* III 4.18.

24. *I. Cret.* III 4.5 and 6. Spyridakis (note 18), however, pp. 45-47, seems to place these treaties earlier in the third century.

plays a role in regulating relations between Hierapytna and Itanos, though the fragmentary character of the reference to him makes it impossible to know just what Ptolemy had done.

The garrison appears to have been maintained into the reign of Epiphanes, if Guarducci is right in dating to the reign of that king (on the basis of the letter forms) a dedication to Zeus Soter and Tyche Protogeneia by Philotas son of Genthios, Epidamnian, *chiliarchos* and *phrourarchos*, one of the "first friends." [25] The presence of the court title appears to confirm the date given on the basis of the letters insofar as it shows that the text can be no earlier than Epiphanes.

Ptolemaic troops figure on Crete again during the reign of Philometor. A Magnesian arbitration settlement of the late second century, reviewing the history of the conflict between Itanos and Hierapytna over various territories, refers several times to Ptolemy, identifying him once as Philometor.[26] He had been asked for help by Itanos, had sent troops to garrison Itanos and the island of Leuke, and perhaps other areas too. On his death these troops were brought back to Egypt by his successor. One may not unreasonably see in these soldiers the soldiers and *machimoi* in Crete of whom Eirenaios (discussed in more detail later in this chapter) was *grammateus*, according to his inscription on Thera.[27] He was at the same time *oikonomos* of Crete, which is in both of his offices joined to Arsinoe (Methana) and Thera. From the remarks in the Magnesian settlement, it appears that the soldiers had been sent by Philometor on request from Itanos; there is present a clear implication that Itanos was not garrisoned at the time of the request. If this conclusion is correct, we must postulate a withdrawal of the troops sometime between the middle of Epiphanes' reign and the middle of Philometor's rule, say between 195 and 165, roughly. The period was unquestionably a difficult one for the dynasty, and the return of the garrison may be a part of what seems to be a general reassertion of the royal power abroad after Philometor's return to Egypt in 163. In any case, the activity ended with his death, and Egyptian troops were not to be seen again in the Aegean.

---

25. *I. Cret.* III 4.14. P. M. Fraser, *Ptol. Alex.* II, p. 169, n. 343, dates Philotas (without discussion) to the reign of Philometor.

26. *I. Cret.* III 4.9. The Ptolemaic role is mentioned in lines 40-45, 96-101, and 119-121.

27. See below on Thera and Arsinoe-Methana.

If we summarize what we know of the administration of Ptolemaic Itanos, it is not very much. There was a garrison, commanded by a *phrourarchos*. Of this official's competence outside military matters we know nothing. In the time of Philometor, the troops there were viewed by the crown as part of a general command including the other two bases in the Aegean then left to the Ptolemies, Thera and Methana, and one *grammateus* served the three bases. If he had a superior who commanded all three places, we know nothing of him. The same man served as *oikonomos* of the three places, the manager of the royal fiscal interests. We have no knowledge, however, of what these interests were in Crete. The king reserved to himself and his highest officers the role of arbitrator of quarrels and keeper of the peace; it was evidently not to the Ptolemies' liking to have the peace disturbed in eastern Crete or elsewhere on the island.[28] Ptolemaic activity elsewhere on the island appears to have reflected the same interest in stability and protection of Ptolemaic interests. But in dealing with the other cities the king relied in general on military aid and diplomatic intervention to effect his wishes rather than assuming responsibility for direct administration of the areas involved.

B. The Central Aegean

In this section will be included not only the Cyclades but also Thera and the Ptolemaic base at Methana on the coast of the Peloponnesos. We will take first Thera and Methana, the long-controlled military bases that frame the area of the islands and then the other islands of the area, first as a whole—the league of the islanders—and then individually.

1. *Thera*

Our epigraphical evidence for the Ptolemaic rule of Thera is perhaps better than that of any other of the possessions outside Egypt except Cyprus. We owe this comparative plenty to the long Ptolemaic presence on the island, at least a century and a quarter, and to the energetic exploration of Thera by Hiller von Gaertringen, which formed the basis of his monumental volume of inscriptions

---

28. The Ptolemies' role as supporters of peace in Crete is delineated by Van Effenterre, *Crète et le monde grec*, Paris, 1968, pp. 212 ff., in opposition to views of Ormerod, Tarn, and now Spyridakis.

from the island in *IG* XII 3 and of his general report on the island in the four volumes of *Thera*.

We may begin with the garrison of the island. It was commanded by an officer appointed by the king. The first such commandant is Apollodotos, attested at the time of the Chremonidean War (ca. 265). He had been sent to Thera by Patroklos, the Ptolemaic commander in that war, and brought with him five *dikastai* from Ioulis on Keos who were to help settle disturbed affairs on Thera.[29] It may well be that Apollodotos was not only the first commandant attested but the first in fact. The similarity between the situations of Thera and Keos (below) suggests that the *epistatai* were sent to both places at the same period by the same man, probably for the first time in both places.

After Apollodotos, the next commander attested falls in the reign of Philometor, nearly a century later. There are, in fact, three such commandants known from this reign. We may surmise, from his position as addressee of the royal letter in *IG* XII 3 327 that Apollonios (son of Koiranos) was the commander of the garrison in 163 and from his position heading the list of contributors to the oil supply of the gymnasium later in the same inscription, that he still held his post in 159. He appears to have been an active man, advancing Ptolemaic interests outside of his command on Thera. He is named as a proxenos of the Cretan cities Aptera and Lappa; in the decree of Aptera his fellow *proxenoi* may be fellow members of the Theraean garrison.[30]

Another commandant of Thera was Aristippos son of Theoxenos, Alexandrian. He was responsible for a dedication to king Ptolemy, queen Cleopatra, and their son Ptolemy, in which he bears the titles τῶν διαδόχων and ὁ τεταγμένος ἐπὶ Θήρας. Another inscription presents a more complicated situation. It was first a dedication to the same three members of the royal family, placed by an official whose name has usually been restored as Aristippos and by the oikonomos Eirenaios.[31] At some later time it was partially erased

---

29. *IG* XII 3 320 = *OGIS* 44.

30. For Apollonios, see L. Robert, *Noms indigènes*, pp. 382-398. The decree of Aptera, *I. Cret.* II 3 12C; the decree of Lappa, *I. Cret.* II 16 6A. Ios also gave proxeny to a son of Koiranos from Aspendos; see p. 148.

31. The unchanged dedication by Aristippos alone, *IG* XII 3 467 (use as 1391, a revised text) = *OGIS* 110. The inscription that was altered, *IG* XII 3 466 and 1390, is most conveniently consulted as *SEG* I 343 for the original form, but in *IG* for the altered version.

and re-engraved, so as to be a dedication to king Ptolemy "and the other gods" by Eirenaios on behalf of Aristippos for his nobility toward the soldiers, city and possessions of the king.

The original text cannot be dated with precision. E. Van 't Dack has recently suggested, following a discarded suggestion of Hiller von Gaertringen, that the erased name was that not of Aristippos but of Apollonios son of Koiranos, ἐπὶ τῆς πόλεως ca. 163-159.[32] The restoration of the royal titulature, if correct, does not help very much. The son of Philometor, evidently Eupator, mentioned in the first dedication, was not the first child born to Ptolemy and Cleopatra, and his mention without the other children does not, therefore, indicate that there were no other children. It may, rather, come from some time at which Eupator was more prominent in the public eye than the other children—perhaps at his birth as the first male heir or nearer the time of his elevation to the throne in about 152.[33] Either time would be possible; the former would require either an extended term for Apollonios (if it is he) beginning earlier than has been known, or a rather short tenure of office by Aristippos before being replaced by Apollonios, in order to allow Apollonios to be commandant by 163. The later date would allow a more ample margin of time in which to set these events, but the later the date the less likely it is that Apollonios is involved. In fact, Eirenaios' presence in the periods of both Apollonios and Aristippos is necessitated by Van 't Dack's theory, and this in turn requires for someone a very long tenure of office, especially in view of Van 't Dack's hypothesis about the occasion for the erasure and re-engraving of the text.

On the latter question, Van 't Dack argues that we have here a case of *damnatio memoriae* in which Eirenaios has, after the death of Philometor and the coming of Euergetes II to power, erased the name of the appointee and partisan of Philometor, Apollonios, in favor of Aristippos, who had chosen to support Euergetes; the change in the royal formula from the family of Philometor to

---

32. *Ancient Society* 4, 1973, pp. 71-90, esp. p. 86. His full discussion and bibliography need not be repeated here.

33. M. Launey discusses this and other issues of the dating of these inscriptions in publishing Eirenaios' inscription from Methana, *Rev. arch.* 31-32, 1949, pp. 572-578. The Cypriot inscriptions suggest that if the dedication fell after his elevation the title of Eupator would appear: *BSA* 56, 1961, nos. 56 and 57.

"king Ptolemy and the other gods" would be of the same significance.

The problems are, however, formidable. (1) On Van 't Dack's view, the first text belongs in or before 163, the second ca. 145, thus producing a very long and stagnant career for Eirenaios; (2) Aristippos, in the second version, is honored for τῆς εἶχεν καλο[καγ]αθίας εἰς τοὺς στρατιώτας κα[ὶ τ]ὴν πόλιν καὶ τὰ τοῦ βασιλέως [πρ]άγματα καὶ εἰς τοὺς θεοὺς εὐσ[ε]βείας. The εἶχεν is an embarrassment; that it honors the "commandant de Théra qui allait évacuer ou venait d'évacuer définitivement les lieux" is no solution. If the evacuation is still to take place, why the tense? Or if it has taken place, why is Eirenaios still present? (3) Van 't Dack remarks "Après la mort de Philométor et l'élimination de Néos Philopator, on jugea bon de faire disparaître toute dédicace vexatoire ou compromettante." But one may observe that only this, of the numerous inscriptions honoring Philometor or his functionaries on Thera, was changed; that the evidence of *damnatio memoriae* in the empire comes only from Cyprus, where Ptolemaic rule continued; and that there would have been no real motive for such an action on Thera, soon to be evacuated entirely, where in the absence of any Aegean policy at all such texts could neither embarrass nor compromise anyone. In sum, neither the dating of these inscriptions seems to me secure, nor the occasion, nor the restoration of the earlier version.

The third commandant attested is Ladamos son of Dionysophanes, honored by the Bacchistai of Thera, also probably in the reign of Philometor.[34] His titles are τῶν περὶ αὐλὴν δια[δόχων] and ἐξαποσταλεὶς ὑπὸ τῶν βασιλ[έων] καὶ ταγεὶς ἐπί τε τῆς πόλεως καὶ ἡμῶν.

---

34. *IG* XII 3 1296 = *OGIS* 735. Cf. Hiller von Gaertringen, *Festschrift zu Otto Hirschfeld*, Berlin, 1903, pp. 88 ff. Hiller's restoration of Ladamos' ethnic as Ἀλεξανδρεύς is challenged as pure conjecture by P. M. Fraser, *Ptol. Alex.* II, p. 150, n. 211, with reason. The career of Ladamos is discussed at length by E. Van 't Dack (n. 32, above), pp. 77-80. He returns to the old view that "sovereigns" in the plural refers to the reign of Ptolemies VI and VIII together between 170 and 164. Despite his admission that this dating is open to objection on the grounds of Ladamos' seeming appearance in *IG* XII 3 327.20 (163-159) as an ordinary soldier, and despite his own conclusion that the use of οἱ βασιλεῖς proves nothing, he prefers 170-164—largely on the basis of the presence of an *alpha* with rectilinear cross-bar in the text. Within a matter of a few decades, however, such a criterion is not of much value. None of Van 't Dack's arguments in fact provides any support at all for 170-164, and some tell against it; his conclusion is little more than leap of faith. I see no possibility of certainty here.

He, his wife, and their descendants are made *thiasitai* with full rights. Hiller thought that the date of the inscription should be placed near the end of Philometor's reign, but there is in this matter as in the case of Aristippos no certainty.

We do not get much information about the activities of the commandant from these inscriptions. He was the chief officer of the garrison and its spokesman before the king, by whom he was directly appointed, although Apollodotos was sent by Patroklos. He was responsible for keeping order on the island and for protecting it. It appears that Apollodotos was the escort and general supervisor for the *dikastai* sent with him. He also was active in the same areas of life on the island that the garrison as a whole took part in, as we will see—support of the gymnasium, patronage of cults (like the Bacchistai), and in particular the royal cult. He did not have responsibility for financial affairs, as we will see; that function belonged to the *oikonomos*. Finally, in the case of Apollonios, we apparently see the elements of a role for the commandant as Ptolemaic representative at large in the Aegean, particularly in the reign of Philometor, when the Ptolemaic bases for such diplomacy were few.

We turn next to the rank and file of the garrison. From the reign of Philometor, and specifically for the years 163-159, we have lists of a great many names of soldiers. Only rarely does a soldier on these lists have an abbreviated patronymic, and never an ethnic.[35] It is nonetheless possible to learn a considerable amount about the composition of the garrison from the study of the names. Many of these, of course, are far too widespread in the Greek world to provide geographical precision about their bearer. Some, however, are less common, and for a number of these L. Robert has shown their Aspendian origin. The names (Eumelos, Koiranos, and Anaxion are examples) are not limited to Pamphylia, but singly and particularly as a group they are characteristic of the area.[36] The possibility of identifying three members of the garrison with Aspendians honored by Aptera in Crete lends further strength to the thesis that there was a sizeable Pamphylian contingent in the garrison.[37]

---

35. *IG* XII 3 327.

36. L. Robert has demonstrated this in detail in a series of studies of Aspendian names in *Noms indigènes*, pp. 382-416, especially pp. 411 ff.

37. Besides the commander Apollonios son of Koiranos, (*Noms indigènes*,

Some grave *stelai* found in the island also confirm the Pamphyl-ian—and more broadly, south Asian—character of the troops. It is, of course, not always certain that a *stele* bearing a non-Theraean ethnic is to be taken as that of a soldier, but where the evidence coincides with that of other indications, the likelihood is strong that the person was indeed a member of the garrison. For example, among the persons attested in this manner are Hephaistion son of Eumelos, Aspendian,[38] Noumenios son of Artemidoros, from Side,[39] and Prepelaos son of Ortoundios, Lycian.[40] Another stele records Epitimidas son of Pythagoras, of Soloi, who may well be the same man as his namesake in the list of soldiers.[41]

The first duty of the garrison was to preserve Ptolemaic control. The second was to protect the island itself from any damage. An interesting inscription mentions that eternal scourge, pirates, and a raid they had made on the island.[42] The pirates appear to have captured soldiers on this particular visit. Defense against such attacks must have been one of the most important roles of the garrisons. The damaged condition of the inscription, however, prevents us from more specific conclusions about the incident.

Beyond these primary functions, the garrison seems to have played an active role in the life of the island. The support of the gymnasium was of primary concern. The large list of soldiers discussed above lists in part those soldiers who contributed to the supply of oil for the gymnasium of Thera from the eighteenth to the twenty-second years (of Philometor).[43] Some further informa-tion may be provided by a decree of the alumni of the gymnasium, honoring Baton son of Philon, who had served as gymnasiarch for

pp. 382-398), Robert suggests that Eumelos and Anaxion sons of Eumelos in *I. Cret.* II 3 12C may be identical with members of the garrison with those names (though their patronymics are lacking in the Theraean inscription), *Noms indigènes*, pp. 398-411.

38. *IG* XII 3 831. A Zoilos from Aspendos is similarly attested by a stele, *IG* XII 3 1619.

39. *IG* XII 3 834.

40. *IG* XII 3 833.

41. The stele, *IG* XII 3 835; the mention in the list, *IG* XII 3 327.134. Cf. L. Robert, *Noms indigènes*, pp. 411-413.

42. The pirates were Cretan Allariotes. The soldiers seem to have joined the pirates in raids before being ransomed. *IG* XII 3 328 and Suppl., p. 283 = *Syll.*² 921. E. Ziebarth, (n. 61, below) pp. 23 ff., discusses the piratical aspects of the inscription. M. Rostovtzeff, *SEHHW*, p. 1361, thought ca. 260 to be the correct date.

43. *IG* XII 3 327.

five years consecutively, and who is asked to continue in office for another year.[44] During his tenure he had held gymnastic contests on behalf of the king. The date of the inscription is in the latter part of year 28 or the early part of year 29 of an unnamed king, who can be only Philometor; the writing is too late in style for Philadelphos, the only other king who could have been ruling Thera in his twenty-ninth year.[45] The date must be 153, then. A particular interest attaches to the inscription because the Baton honored is quite possibly the same Baton who appears (without patronymic) in the long list of soldiers, less than a decade before.[46]

The religious life of the soldiers accounts for a considerable part of the extant documentation. A treasury was dedicated to Sarapis, Isis, and Anoubis by one Diokles, associated with some *basilistai*.[47] The latter appear to have been a feature of the royal cult habitually found in connection with army establishments.[48] Another indication comes from the letter of Philometor to the commander of the garrison, which is found at the head of the great list of names, *IG* XII 3 327. In this letter, the soldiers are granted the revenues from some lands on Thera to pay the expenses of sacrifices.

Two members of the garrison set up an altar to Dionysos Thrakios.[49] Their titles reveal something of the more formal structure of military religious life on Thera. One of them is called Attalos son of Charmokles, λειτορεύσας [τὸ δ]ε‹ύ›τερον, the other Onesimos son of Aristion (surely a Cypriot), ἀρχεύσας [τῶν ἐν] ‹Θ›ή‹ρ›αι μ[α]χίμων. That the verb ἀρχεύω referred here to a religious post, was made clear by Dittenberger in his commentary to the text. Similarly, λειτορεύω is essentially a synonym for ἱερεύω.[50] It is

---

44. Best consulted in L. Robert, *Coll. Froehner* I, Paris, 1936, 95; also *IG* XII 3 331. Discussed by Hiller von Gaertringen in *Festschrift zu Otto Hirschfeld*, Berlin, 1903, pp. 87-99.

45. Cf. Hiller's article cited, preceding note.

46. *IG* XII 3 327.50.

47. *IG* XII 3 443. The date is apparently early in the Ptolemaic period on Thera. Cf. P. M. Fraser. *Op. Ath.* 3, 1960, p. 24, nn. 3 and 5. There are still traces of the treasury: Hiller von Gaertringen, *Thera* I, Berlin, 1899, p. 260; III, 1904, p. 86, n. 1.

48. For their function and milieu, see M. Launey, *Armées hellénistiques*, pp. 1026 ff. and J. Lesquier, *Les Institutions militaires de l'Égypte sous les Lagides*, Paris, 1911, pp. 159-160.

49. *SEG* VIII 714; cf. addenda for provenance. The Ptolemaic interest in Dionysos is manifested at this time by a dedication to him on behalf of Philometor and Cleopatra by the demos of the Theraeans, *OGIS* 112 = *IG* XII 3 468. On the date, Hiller von Gaertringen, *Klio* 17, 1921, pp. 97 ff.

50. See the commentary to *OGIS* 166 for the former, *LSJ* s.v. for the latter.

interesting to note that Attalos may well be the same as the Attalos Cha(   ) of the great list.[51] Both of these men evidently exercised religious offices in Thera, evidently during the reign of Philometor.[52] It is particularly interesting to find the *machimoi* constituting a religious unit, evidently distinct from the *stratiotai* whom we know to have been there at the same time.[53] The distinction between Egyptian and Greek was thus maintained in the religious sphere, even though they served as parts of the same garrison.

Ptolemaic soldiers on Thera, then, are revealed to have been active in more areas than their official capacity. They contributed to the maintenance of the gymnasium and helped fill the positions of responsibility in that institution. In this and other ways they played an important role in the social and religious life of the island, reinforcing the crown's ties to the city.

We turn now to the economic administration of Thera. The office of *oikonomos*, the second prominent member of the administration of Thera, is of great interest. For Thera it is attested only in the reign of Philometor, though this fact may be due as much to the personal prominence of Eirenaios as to anything else. We have already mentioned him in connection with his joint dedication with Aristippos. He was the son of Nikias, and an Alexandrian. He is known, outside of the island, in Arsinoe in the Peloponnesos (Methana). The documentation for his role there will be discussed in the next section. He is described in the inscription of Thera as "*oikonomos* of Crete, Arsinoe in the Peloponnesos, and Thera, and *grammateus* of the soldiers and *machimoi* in those places," while at Methana only his court rank (τῶν φίλων) is given.[54]

The second mention of an *oikonomos* comes in the letter that heads *IG* XII 3 327. The revenues that are granted to the soldiers had been confiscated by the crown. More precisely, the *oikonomos* had confiscated from four men the lands that yielded the revenues: τὰ ἀνειλημμένα ὑπὸ τοῦ οἰκονόμου εἰς τὸ βασιλικὸν χωρία. Their annual

---

51. *IG* XII 3 327.130.

52. The evidence is the identification of Attalos with his namesake (but note that his name is partly restored in *SEG* VIII 714) in *IG* XII 3 327, the interest in Dionysos under Philometor (cf. n. 49, above), and more generally the letter forms.

53. *OGIS* 102.

54. Best consulted in M. Launey's article with the restorations, n. 33, above.

yield was 111 Ptolemaic drachmas. The king promises these funds to the soldiers for support of sacrifices and says that he will give the order to the *oikonomos* to release the funds, through the *dioiketes* Diogenes.[55] It is not possible to be certain whether this *oikonomos* was Eirenaios, as long as we do not know whether the tenure of office by Eirenaios' comrade Aristippos is to be placed just before the time of this inscription or a decade or more later.

The *oikonomos* is thus clearly revealed as having the primacy in financial matters that the epistates or ἐπὶ τῆς πόλεως had in military and general administrative affairs. He is answerable to the king through the general finance minister, the *dioiketes*, and not through the commandant. He also appears to exercise authority over a wider geographical area than the commandant. Eirenaios was *oikonomos* of the entire surviving Aegean possessions of Philometor, Itanos (which must be the meaning of the rather grandiose term "Crete" here), Methana, and Thera, and exercised his secretariat of the soldiers and *machimoi* over the same area. Aristippos shows no signs of such a broad jurisdiction. Eirenaios is not a subordinate of Aristippos; indeed, in the inscription of Methana he is τῶν φίλων, a court rank higher than that of Aristippos. He is a representative of another area of the crown interests.

Aside from these two offices we see little of the actual administration on Thera. We have already mentioned the *dikastai* sent by Patroklos from Ioulis on Keos to settle affairs on Thera. They are temporary magistrates of a type well-known in the period, perhaps to be viewed more as judges formally requested by Thera (whether at Patroklos' instigation or not) and dealing directly with the city and honored by it. They are, however, clearly in close relations with the royal administration, and form part of the same effort to restore order to Thera and make it a useful base. Ioulis, their home city, was certainly located on an island controlled by the Ptolemies; its natural port, Koresia, was a major Ptolemaic base (see below, section 4).

Thera, besides being garrisoned by Ptolemaic troops and administered by Ptolemaic officials, played the role of an independent city in maintaining diplomatic relations directly with Alexandria during the period of Ptolemaic control. A recently published inscription shows us that the patterns of such contact were the ones

---

55. *IG* XII 3 327.

normal to relations between a sovereign and a city with whom he was on good terms, even though it was not under his control.[56] Thera honors Aristokrates and Ptolemaios, sons of Iason, of Alexandria, who being friends of the king have been of use to Theraeans who have visited Alexandria to see the king. The editor assigned the text on palaeographical grounds to the late third or early second century.

We may mention briefly here an inscription from Delos, a dedication by the *demos* of Thera to Dionysios son of Timonax, Mylasian, one of the first friends of king Ptolemy and queen Cleopatra, and *archidikastes* (*IG* XI 4 1131). The date is not clear, and the man is not otherwise known. From the concentration of other evidence in the reign of Philometor, one is tempted to associate the text with his reign, but the placement can scarcely be more than a guess. The office of *archidikastes*, found both in Ptolemaic and in Roman Egypt, has never been adequately studied, but it appears that this official was the head of the entire Ptolemaic legal system rather than a local magistrate in Alexandria, as Jouguet rightly maintains.[57] Our inscription appears to suggest a competence extending over the overseas possessions as well, analogous to that of the *dioiketes*. The details, unfortunately, escape us.

Before we leave Thera, there are two problems to be considered. The first is the meaning of an inscription that names a Ptolemaic official; the second, related to the first, is the problem of the continuity of Ptolemaic occupation of the island.

A much damaged decree of Thera, dated on rather vague palaeographical grounds to the reign of Ptolemy III, honors one . . . . οπαφιλος son of Philostratos, Rhaukian of Crete, described as ἀποσταλεὶς ὑπὸ τοῦ βασιλέως Πτολεμαίου [ναύαρ]χος καὶ στραταγὸς τᾶς πόλιος.[58] His services to the city consisted in sending one Hephaistios, a Kalyndian given neither patronymic nor title, to drive off some λαισταί threatening Thera, thereby affording safety to the island. There is a great deal about this inscription that is unclear. First, the titulature of . . . opaphilos: if the restoration [ναύαρ]χος

56. Published by P. M. Fraser, *JEA* 44, 1958, pp. 99-100. For essential corrections, L. Robert, *Hellenica* 11-12, 1960, pp. 111-115.

57. *La vie municipale dans l'Égypte romaine*, Paris, 1911, pp. 167-170.

58. *IG* XII 3 1291. The reading of the name was advanced by P. M. Fraser, *Ptol. Alex.* II, p. 150, n. 211.

is correct (and I can see no plausible alternative),[59] the man is too important for the phrase *"strategos* of the city" to mean that he was the commandant of Thera. It is likely that the position thus described is analogous to that of Patroklos, rather self-centeredly described by Itanos in Crete as having been sent as *"strategos* to Crete."[60] The city would thus fall within his military competence but by no means circumscribe it.

The second problem is the location of this person. He was himself in Thera at the time of the attack by the brigands,[61] but if he were only the resident commandant of Thera, of the level of an ἐπὶ τῆς πόλεως, it is scarcely to be imagined that he would have sent a subordinate to deal with the attack or that this subordinate would have been of sufficient importance to warrant an inscriptional mention of his actions. The "admiral" cannot, therefore, be an official of local rank, for neither his delegation of authority nor his titles allow this.[62] But neither can he be an important commander based elsewhere, for he was on the spot. One may most reasonably conclude, therefore, that —opaphilos was the chief commander of Ptolemaic naval forces in the Aegean, that he was resident on Thera, but his command was not limited to Thera or even defined in terms of Thera.

From this conclusion we pass to the question of the continuity of Ptolemaic control. Besides the inscription just discussed, some other evidence may be adduced for the reign of Euergetes (assuming that the dating of the admiral to that reign is accepted). This evidence does not directly concern administration, but it is nonetheless of great importance; it comes from a long series of inscrip-

---

59. E. Van 't Dack, *Ancient Society* 4, 1973, pp. 74-77, argues for [φρούρ-αρ]χος, on the grounds (1) that there is no evidence of naval action in the inscription; (2) στραταγὸς τᾶς πόλιος must be a city commandant and the combination of this with the *nauarchia* is unexampled; (3) *phrourarchos* does work in this context. Of these, (1) seems to me irrelevant if the attack did not require a response by sea, and (2) to be incorrect (see below); (3) depends on (2). And the restoration of Van 't Dack is probably too long.

60. See the discussion of him in section 1 of this chapter.

61. See E. Ziebarth, *Beiträge zur Geschichte des Seeraubs*, Hamburg, 1929, p. 24, and Van 't Dack (n. 59, above), p. 74.

62. Van 't Dack (n. 59, above), p. 76, offers only the third-century date as a justification for the claim that στραταγὸς τᾶς πόλιος could be the title of a commandant. It is true that titulature is less fixed at this epoch than later, but even irregular titulature elsewhere has its parallels; this has only one (loosely) in the case of Patroklos (n. 60, above), where the person in question is demonstrably *not* a city commandant.

tions from Thera, found in the *temenos* of a sanctuary established by one Artemidoros son of Apollonios, from Perge, but at some point also made a citizen of Thera.[63]

Artemidoros' early career is unknown. He settled in Thera, apparently a wealthy man, and placed his series of religious dedications. He is not attested as holding any official position. His dedications include the sovereigns and other gods and fall roughly in the reign of Euergetes. He seems to have died and been buried on the island.[64]

For the reign of Euergetes, then, we have evidence of a Ptolemaic admiral and general almost certainly a permanent resident in Thera and actively providing for its defense. Thera was thus the headquarters of the Ptolemaic Aegean fleet after the reign of Philadelphos, a position that probably remained unchanged until 145, when at the death of Philometor Euergetes II drew back from the Aegean. We also find a man retired from a life perhaps in the service of the Ptolemies settled in the island and honored by it with citizenship.

There remains a period of perhaps a half-century for which we have little evidence, the reigns of Philopator and Epiphanes. The continuance of close relations is demonstrated under Philopator by the decree for two Alexandrians, discussed above. Despite the lack of specific evidence, however, the weight of probability seems to me to be strongly on the side of continuity, if only because of the great unlikelihood that Philometor would have been responsible for expansion into the Aegean at this late date. Philometor was an active king, and the large number of inscriptions from his reign in Thera testify to his energy. But Ptolemaic expansion into the Aegean in these troubled years is not probable. The garrison of the island is known to have been already established in 163, together with an *oikonomos*; it is hard to see expansion on Philometor's part in the years before this time when the throne in Egypt itself was at issue.

---

63. *IG* XII 3 421, 422, 863, 1333-1350, 1388.
64. *OGIS* 70 has long been thought to be a dedication by him at the Paneion of El-Kanaïs, but A. Bernand, *Le Paneion d'El-Kanaïs: les inscriptions grecques*, Leiden, 1972, no. 43, has replaced Artemidoros' name in the text in question with a certain Melanias. For some aspects of his dedications, Hiller, *Thera* III, Berlin, 1904, pp. 89-102; Wilamowitz, *Glaube der Hellenen*[3] II, Basel, 1959, pp. 382-384.

2. Arsinoe-Methana

Aside from Methana, the Ptolemies never controlled any significant part of the Greek mainland for a period of time. Their
armed forces more than once waged campaigns in Greece, occupying
territory temporarily in the process. From 308-303, for example,
Sikyon and Corinth were held by Ptolemaic garrisons. One of the
commanders in this war, Leonides, has already been seen active in
Pamphylia and Cilicia; the second, Philippos, is documented as
Pros. Ptol. 15129. We may pass over these brief occupations as
affording no significant material for our subject.

The one Ptolemaic base in Greece was chosen for its strategic
position near Attica, probably during the Chremonidean War, and
for its excellent port facilities. Methana, a peninsula projecting
out from the Peloponnesos, was renamed Arsinoe, most likely by
Patroklos. Methana formed a logical part of Patroklos' ring around
Attica in this war, and the renaming of it as Arsinoe comes almost
certainly (like other such refoundations) from the period soon after
the death of Arsinoe II in 270. Philopator and Arsinoe III are the
only other possibilities, but it is hard to imagine that he engaged
in expansionistic activities in these waters.

Some half-century ago Hiller von Gaertringen summed up the
evidence then known for the Peloponnesian Arsinoe, and concluded
that it could be only Methana.[65] Such a place was known to have
existed from Eirenaios' inscription on Thera, and two other inscriptions from Epidauros confirmed its existence. One was a
decision of the Achaean cities in a dispute between Epidauros and
Arsinoe, inscribed in third century lettering.[66] Hiller pointed out
that all other possible neighbors of Epidauros were known under
their normal names at this time, leaving only Methana as a possibility.[67] Confirmation came from an inscription in lettering of
the second century, which contained an agreement of Troizen and
Arsinoe.[68] The agreement had been settled after intervention of
ambassadors and judges (κριταί) from king Ptolemy. It concerned
a wide variety of disputes: the boundaries between the two states,
cutting of wood and stone, common use of certain areas and fa-

---

65. 'Αρχ. 'Εφ. 1925-1926, pp. 68 ff.
66. Published in 'Αρχ. 'Εφ. 1921, pp. 152-153.
67. 'Αρχ. 'Εφ. 1925-1926, p. 71.
68. Hiller von Gaertringen (n. 65, above), pp. 72 ff.

cilities, beaching, launching, and portage of ships. The extensive references to the last aspects point up the importance of the shipping facilities at Methana for the Ptolemies.

Hiller's conclusion was further confirmed by an inscription found at Methana and restored by Launey as mentioning a dedicant Eirenaios, the *oikonomos* under Philometor known from Thera.[69] Eirenaios has here the court rank of τῶν φίλων and was accompanied from Alexandria by the ἡγεμ[όν]ες ἐπ' ἀ[νδρῶν καὶ ἔξω] τάξεω[ν καὶ στρατιῶται καὶ μάχιμοι]. The recipients of this dedication on behalf of king Ptolemy and his wife and children were the "great gods", probably the Dioskouroi. Once again, the dating is not secure. Eirenaios did not use court rank in his inscription on Thera, but it is not therefore entirely certain that he did not then have it. If the Methana text is a dedication on the occasion of his first arrival from Alexandria, it must be earlier; but it could be a later return.

Eirenaios appears alone here as the mover of the dedication. No commandant is mentioned, though this may mean that one was already at Arsinoe. In keeping with the military duties that he exercised as *grammateus* (as he is called in the Theraean inscription), he is accompanied by officers and troops, which are designated as "sent with him", not stationed under him. There may have been a higher military official in Arsinoe who would be the actual commander.

3. *The League of the Islanders*

Before considering the evidence for the relations between the Ptolemies and the various islands of the area of the Cyclades, we may consider the league of the islanders. The role of the nesiarchs, exemplified primarily by Bacchon son of Niketas, will be illumined on a number of occasions and will be summarized in the conclusions to this chapter. The situation of Delos, to be discussed later, will also be considered to a considerable degree in terms of its relationship with the league of the islanders (τὸ κοινὸν τῶν νησιωτῶν).

A goodly amount has been written about the league.[70] With its

---

69. M. Launey, *Rev. arch.* 6 ser. 31-32, 1949, pp. 572-578, republishes, restores, and discusses the inscription, adducing also a Delian inscription from the period before 170 in honor of an Eirenaios; he considers the problems of chronology.

70. In particular, the dissertations of A. T. Guggenmos, *Geschichte des Nesiotenbundes bis zur Mitte des 3. Jahrhunderts v. Chr.*, Diss. Würzburg, 1929, and König, *Der Bund der Nesioten*, Diss. Halle, 1910. The most recent

history before the Ptolemies we are not concerned. Despite all that has been said, it does not seem to me possible to date the beginning of its Ptolemaic period. We know that the nesiarch Bacchon, who is known to have been a Ptolemaic appointee, was active sometime before 280. The inscription of Ios discussed below (section 7) is generally taken as the first text to illustrate Ptolemaic control of the league.[71] Since Bacchon bears the title nesiarch in the text, it is reasonably certain that the Ptolemies did control the league at this time. The date of the inscription is taken to be ca. 286 because Zenon, the person honored, is attested in Athens at that time, precisely as a commander of undecked ships, as he is in the Ietan text. The year 286 is therefore generally taken to be the year in which Ptolemy Soter won the league away from Demetrius Poliorcetes.

Before this conclusion is accepted, some reservations may be in order. A nesiarch prior to Bacchon is attested, named Apollodoros son of Apollonios, of Kyzikos. He appears in various Delian accounts as a donor and as a debtor of the temple, paying 10 drachmas interest a year on a loan until 279, after which he is carried as an unpaying debtor.[72] He is called the nesiarch in an inscription of Kyzikos recording that the Parians set up a statue to him in Kyzikos, his home city.[73] No king is mentioned in this inscription. He was also honored in Delos in a decree proposed by Hierarchos son of Prokles, who, as we note below, also proposed a decree for the Naukratite Dionysios son of Potamon, known from a dedication to Philadelphos and Arsinoe in lower Egypt.[74] There is therefore a strong possibility that Apollodoros was a Ptolemaic official. His period of activity must date before 280; until that date he maintained interest payments to Delian Apollo on his loans from the god, but after 280 these payments stop. An active and prominent Ptolemaic official in this region would scarcely cease his payments while he remained in his official position. And if Bacchon is taken to be nesiarch from 286 to after 280, Apollodoros can have held the

---

study, with up-to-date bibliography, in particular of many much-argued questions, is that of Irwin L. Merker, in *Historia* 19, 1970, pp. 141-160. I have not cited the differing opinions of these authors for all points here.

71. See note 106, below.

72. References in commentary to F. Durrbach, *Choix* 20 and *Pros. Ptol.* 15035.

73. Michel, *Recueil* 534.

74. *IG* XI 4 562; *OGIS* 724.

post only before 286.[75] It is possible, of course, that Bacchon's
first appearance is to be put later than 286, but it does not appear
to me that without a firm date for Apollodoros we can in any case
have a secure date for the initial Ptolemaic capture of control in
the Cyclades.

The lower limits for control of the league are equally uncertain.
Bacchon was succeeded, with or without intermediate nesiarchs,
by one Hermias, recorded in 267 as giver of a foundation in honor
of Arsinoe.[76] It is likely that he is the Hermias son of D . . . ,
Halikarnassian, honored in a vague decree by the Delians.[77] Since,
however, it is universally admitted that the Ptolemies lost no
ground in the Aegean until the Chremonidean War of 266-261 or
even later, Hermias scarcely extends our chronological perspective
on the league.

Dates claimed for the end of Ptolemaic hegemony over the league
vary by as much as 35 years, and I do not think precision or certainty is possible in the present state of our documentation. So far
as the league in itself goes, there is very little evidence. The Nesiotai
set up a statue on Delos of Agathostratos son of Polyaratos, the
Rhodian, who is known to have been the victorious admiral in
the battle of Ephesos against a Ptolemaic fleet.[78] The dedication is
not dated, but when taken in conjunction with the decree of Delos
in the mid-third century in honor of another Rhodian admiral,
for his protection of the islands and the Greeks with the fleet, it
suggests a dramatic lessening of the importance of the Ptolemaic
fleet after this battle.[79] It does not seem to me that we are justified

---

75. F. Durrbach, *Choix*, pp. 29-30, suggested the possibility that Apollodoros might have been an Antigonid official; he is followed more confidently
by Merker (note 70), pp. 152-153. Neither of them, however, appears to
have considered the relationships of the proposer.

76. References in commentary to *IG* XI 4 565 and *Pros. Ptol.* 15042.

77. *IG* XI 4 565.

78. The statue, *IG* XI 4 1128, where other references are collected.

79. *IG* XI 4 596. The literature on the battles of Kos, Andros, and Ephesos
and the shifting political situation in the Aegean in the middle to later third
century is enormous. Most recently, J. Crampa has discussed the battles in
a study of Ptolemy the son, *I. Labraunda* I, pp. 100-120, where he places
both Kos and Andros in the Chremonidean War and Ephesos about 258.
Crampa's full discussion of earlier work on the subject makes further bibliography here superfluous, though his conclusions do not rest on very secure
foundations. The evidence then known for the Antigonid influence in the
Cyclades was collected by P. Delamarre in *Rev. Phil.* 26, 1902, pp. 301-325;
he concluded that the reigns of Demetrius II and especially of Antigonus

in thinking that the Ptolemaic fleet was destroyed in the battle. We are in no position to assess the degree to which a conscious decision that the Cyclades were not worth the trouble of keeping them may have influenced Philadelphos. It does not appear that the Rhodians thought the league worth running themselves, if they had the ability to do so, for no documents of the league appear after this date until its later revival. An effective life span for the league under the Ptolemies of some 30 years is therefore not unreasonable.

The functions of the league are only somewhat clearer. They are known primarily from a series of its decrees found on Delos. These in general confer proxeny and other honors on various benefactors of the league. Some of the persons honored are identifiable; some mean nothing to us. In one decree, Sostratos son of Dexiphanes, Knidian, otherwise renowned as the builder of the Pharos of Alexandria, is honored for the help he has given in Alexandria to those islanders who have come to see the king. He receives citizenship from all the member cities.[80]

Another honors one Theon son of Philiskos, τεταγμένος under king Ptolemy in Alexandria, for his good works toward the king and the islanders, much as for Sostratos.[81] Similarly, a Thrasykles is honored by a decree which is said to be his second.[82] This Thrasykles may be the *oikonomos* of the islands recorded on Ios (see section 7 below). Various other honored persons are not otherwise sig-

---

Doson were the periods in which Macedon was the most powerful state in the area. M. Holleaux's study of a monument for the battle of Sellasia, *Études* III, pp. 55-73, also led him to 228 as an effective *terminus ante quem* for the end of Ptolemaic control. On the festivals, E. Bikermann's remarks in *REA* 40, 1938, pp. 369-383, are worth reading. It appears to me that the thirty years after the battle of Ephesos (for which I accept the commonly proposed date of 258) were a time of competition more than of the domination of any one power. Euergetes' assertion in the Adoulis inscription (*OGIS* 54) that he inherited the βασιλεία of the Cyclades from his father is probably to be received with the same skepticism warranted by his claims to vast areas of the Near East in the same inscription. He did inherit several good bases and a competitive position.

80. *IG* XI 4 1038. Sostratos, obviously an important figure, was also honored by Delos (*IG* XI 4 563), the city of Kaunos (*IG* XI 4 1130), and a Cyrenaean (*IG* XI 4 1190). Sostratos is usually described as the architect of the Pharos, but P. M. Fraser, *Ptol. Alex.* I, pp. 18-20, and II, pp. 49-54, nn. 105, 111-121, argues that he was the dedicant and probably donor instead, which may be right.

81. *IG* XI 4 1042.

82. *IG* XI 4 1043.

nificant to us.[83] In these decrees the league behaves much as an individual city might in carrying on diplomacy.

A major portion of the activity of the Nesiotai appears to have been the sending of *theoroi* to festivals and otherwise honoring major occasions. The best known and best preserved of the inscriptions of the islanders, the Nikouria decree (ca. 280), deals with precisely this function.[84] Philokles and Bacchon had written to the member cities to send the *synedroi*, the representatives of the cities who formed the council of the league, to Samos to deliberate on sending *theoroi* to the sacrifices and games to be held by Ptolemy to his father in Alexandria. The *synedroi* declared that since both Ptolemies had done good to their ancestors and other Greeks, freeing cities, restoring laws and ancestral constitutions, lifting the εἰσφορά, and in general doing many good things, the *koinon* would recognize the games as equal to the Olympic ones and send *theoroi*. It was also voted to crown the king, and for the member cities to pay to Bacchon their contributions to this crown, through whatever agent Bacchon designated. A crown or some other contribution of this sort may have been at stake in another league decree found on Amorgos.[85] Another decree refers to sending *theoroi* to Alexandria.[86]

It would appear, in sum, that the league acted as a means for the islanders to pool their actions in the standard areas of city dealings with monarchs. The league sent ambassadors and *theoroi*, decreed proxeny and citizenship (in member cities), collected contributions for the king, and took care of regulating and perhaps

---

83. *IG* XI 4 1040 (where one of the Thebans honored is also honored at Delphi ca. 274/3), 1041, 1046-1048. Nos. 1044-1045 tell us little, but one of the three Samothracians honored may also be the honorand of 1023, where the proposer was Sosimenes son of Antigonos, a brother perhaps of the Sosidemos son of Antigonos who proposed the decree (565) in honor of the nesiarch Hermes.

84. *Syll.*³ 390. Its date must be ca. 280. A parallel text from Delphi, published by P. M. Fraser in *BCH* 78, 1954, p. 52, records the Amphictyonic acceptance of the festival in terms like those of the Nikouria decree (for doubts on Fraser's text, cf. *Bull. épig.* 1955, 122). But the Delphic acceptance is now known to date from 265; a more complete text is given by J. Bousquet, *BCH* 82, 1958, pp. 77-82, who speculates on a later date for the Nikouria decree and the institution of the Ptolemaieia. Fraser's attempt at a precise date based on the Delphic text must thus be abandoned, but he successfully defends the earlier approximate date of 280 for the Nikouria decree in *Harvard Theological Review* 54, 1961, pp. 141-145. Cf. the cautious discussion of C. Habicht, *Gottmenschentum*², pp. 258-259.

85. *IG* XII 7 13.

86. *IG* XI 4 1037.

collecting debts. It might send judges to help quell internal dissension in one of the member cities. The king in turn used it for his side of these transactions. The nesiarch appears in a good many transactions in which the *koinon* is never mentioned, and the king must often have found it more convenient to use this representative to deal swiftly and effectively with a problem than to use the cumbersome machinery of the *synedroi*. For something requiring the cooperation of all of the islands, however, the *koinon* was of great utility, and no doubt saved Bacchon and the other nesiarchs much time in dealing with common affairs. There is no extant evidence that the *koinon* either was taxed directly or served as a vehicle for the collection of taxes from the individual cities. It did, however, offer the king crowns of considerable value, and it apparently possessed the authority to extract the requisite contributions from the member cities. Since Bacchon was to designate someone to receive the crown money, it seems that he did not have a regular tax collector who would automatically be expected to perform this task.

To see the details of the league's actions, we turn to a summary, island by island, of Ptolemaic dealings with the islands that made up the league.

4. *Keos*

Keos, site of the third major Ptolemaic base in the Aegean, makes a suitable starting point for a survey of the remaining islands. Keos had in this period four cities, Ioulis, Karthaia, Koresia, Poiessa. Of these, three have provided evidence of relations with the Ptolemies; only Poiessa, the least important, has not. These Ptolemaic relations extend from the end of Soter's reign to the end of the century, from regulation of unsettled affairs on the island by high Ptolemaic officials to a naval base at Koresia, which changed its name to Arsinoe.

It has long been known from its inclusion among other island cities in a Magnesian inscription, that there was, ca. 205, a city named Arsinoe among the states of the islands.[87] The discovery of *IG* XII 5 1061, a decree of Karthaia mentioning an *epistates* in Arsinoe who had aided Karthaia, made it clear that the city was to be found on Keos. P. Graindor, followed by Launey, argued for

---

87. *Syll.*[3] 562.

Koresia as the logical candidate, with its excellent port; Poiessa too found its adherents. The question was taken up again in 1960 by Louis Robert, who brought to bear extensive topographical evidence, showing the value of the port of Koresia to a naval power.[88] After his demonstration, there can hardly be any question that Koresia was renamed Arsinoe, probably by Patroklos during the Chremonidean War.[89]

Robert also discusses the Delphic *theorodokoi* list, showing that at the date of its composition Koresia had resumed its original name.[90] The date of this document remains disputed, but it may be placed in the early part of the second century.[91] By this time, then, Ptolemaic control must have lapsed in Koresia.

The *epistates* in Arsinoe has already been mentioned. He was named Hieron, son of Timokrates, Syracusan, designated in general terms τεταγμένος ὑπὸ τὸμ βασιλέα Πτολεμαῖον. He came to the island with the *strategos* Patroklos and by him was named καθεστηκὼς ἐπιστάτης ἐν Ἀρσινόῃ.[92] In the decree he is honored by Karthaia for his goodwill in general and his help to an afflicted Karthaian in particular. The terminology of Hieron's appointment, like that of Apollodotos on Thera, suggests that he was the first resident commandant to be placed in Arsinoe, and that the creation of this base, like that on Thera, may be a part of Patroklos' activities in the Chremonidean War.[93]

Aside from Hieron, only one other Ptolemaic official is attested here, and he only by inference. An epigram of Callimachus contains the dedication of a shell to Arsinoe Zephyritis in a shrine near

---

88. L. Robert's discussion in *Hellenica* 11-12, 1960, pp. 146-160, summarizes previous discussion and provides a full conspectus of the evidence.

89. *Grosser Historischer Weltatlas* I, ed. H. Bengtson and V. Milojcic still showed (4 ed., 1963) Poiessa as Arsinoe, but the fifth edition (1973) corrects the error.

90. Robert's discussion (note 88) of the port is followed (pp. 161-175) by one in which he restores the name of Koresia on the list, rebutting G. Daux's suggestion of Arsinoe in that place; Robert discusses also the dating of the list. Daux continues to contest Robert's thesis; cf. Robert's remarks in *Essays Welles*, p. 200, n. 155. Cf. also *Bull. épig.* 1969, 85, where in reviewing G. Longega, *Arsinoe* II, J. and L. Robert point out that the continued citation of Wilamowitz in favor of Poiessa is erroneous, that scholar having in 1922 accepted Graindor's argument for Koresia.

91. For Robert's discussion of the date, note 90; his placement of the list in the 190's is confirmed on Cyprus by a prosopographical link (p. 65, n. 119).

92. *IG* XII 5 1061. Hieron: *Pros. Ptol.* 15148.

93. *IG* XII 3 320 (Apollodotos).

Alexandria. The dedicant is one Selenaia, daughter of Kleinias.[94] The shell is said to have come from near Ioulis. Hiller von Gaertringen suggested that it was likely that the commissioner of this epigram had considerable standing at court and that the most likely person to have had both high rank and a past stay on Keos was an official at Arsinoe. The suggestion was taken up and defended by Robert in his discussion of Arsinoe.[95] Kleinias is therefore a probable addition to the list of Ptolemaic officials in Koresia.

For Ioulis, whose natural port Koresia was, we have only the evidence of the sending of judges from the city with Apollodotos to Thera, evidently also at the time of Patroklos' visit.[96]

It is for Karthaia that our information is best. We have already seen that it was the source of our knowledge of the *epistates* in Koresia. The text in which he is attested, *IG* XII 5 1061, suggests several aspects of the Ptolemaic domination of the island: (1) there was no official resident in Karthaia, or he would have given assistance himself; (2) Hieron's responsibility was not formal, that of a governor; (3) he was nonetheless expected to be of help to the other cities of the island.

Another decree of Karthaia honors Philotheros son of Antiphanes, a Malian, τεταγμένος ὑπὸ τὸν βασιλέα Πτολεμαῖον, who had come to Karthaia for the κομιδή of [   ]των, variously restored as [δανεισμά]των and [χρημά]των and interpreted variously as taxes or debts, according to the author's views. The frequent discussions in other inscriptions about other debts owed by islanders suggest that "debts" is the more likely interpretation. The character of mercy that the decree attributes to Philotheros also seems somewhat more in accord with a position as creditor's agent.[97]

---

94. Most recently published in A. S. F. Gow and D. Page, *The Greek Anthology, Hellenistic Epigrams* I, London, 1965, lines 1109-1110, epigram 14. L. Robert's discussion in *Hellenica* 11-12, 1960, pp. 153-155, was unknown to Gow and Page; cf. Robert's remarks in *Essays Welles*, p. 200, n. 155.

95. Cf. note 94.

96. *IG* XII 3 320.

97. *IG* XII 5 1066. Merker, *Historia* 19, 1970, p. 151, n. 46, refers to him as a "tax-gatherer" without any qualifying remarks. But *LSJ* s.v. II.2 defines the word κομιδή as "carrying away for oneself, rescue, recovery ... esp. recovery of a debt." It cites among others the Aristotelian *Oikonomika* and *P. Hal.* 1. And the Polybian uses cited by A. Mauersberger, *Polybios-Lexikon*, Berlin, 1956-66, s.v., show sufficient variety to preclude a determination that κομιδή must have one or the other meaning in the inscription. In Welles, *Royal Correspondence* 4.10, the word clearly means "repayment."

There are two further inscriptions that indicate Ptolemaic intervention in Karthaian affairs, consisting in both cases of sending in judges to settle internal disputes. The first goes back perhaps to the 280's or 270's.[98] Karthaia, finding itself beset by internal strife, appealed to Bacchon (as the nesiarch of the league of the islanders) for help. He sent some kind of document outlining the basis for a settlement, but it was evidently not entirely success-ful. When Philokles arrived in the islands later, Karthaia asked him to confirm the οἰκονομίαι of the earlier orders of Bacchon. Philokles responded by sending some judges to effect a final settlement. They evidently met with success, which led to the decree. It is evident that the initiative lay throughout with the Karthaians, but that the Ptolemaic officials were intent on pre-serving order. And that the Karthaians did not have complete power over the situation seems to be indicated by the implicit acknowledgement of Philokles' right to accept or reject earlier dispositions.

The second text is much more fragmentary, despite its rereading and great amplification in 1954.[99] It is a decree crowning an Athe-nian (deme of Halai), whose name is lost, ... ὑπ]ὸ τὸμ βασιλέα Πτολεμαῖον and, it seems, δικαστὴς ἐν τῶι στρατηγ[... Α κριτήριον is mentioned later in the inscription. It is by no means clear what the details of this transaction were. It may be that Ptolemy re-quested the intervention of a judge and that the phrase mentioning the king refers to this request and not to the man honored. The editors' supplement ἐν τῶι στρατηγ[ίωι] seems to have no alternative. The term is not used to refer to the command of a strategos in any Ptolemaic context; perhaps it indicates a municipal building in which the dikastes exercised his functions.[100] The date of the

98. IG XII 5 1065. The date is indicated by the references to Bacchon and Philokles, who will be discussed in detail in their other appearances.

99. The only useful edition is that of Chr. Dumont and J. Thomopoulos in BCH 78, 1954, pp. 336-338, no. 13. Text reprinted in SEG XIV 543. An earlier and less useful transcription appeared as IG XII 5 541. Merker (note 97), pp. 147-148, n. 32, wrongly ascribes the assignment of a date during the Chremonidean War to the editors, who do not offer so specific a date (p. 338: "Nous ne pouvons savoir à quelle occasion on avait fait appel à son jugement, ni préciser la date de son intervention").

100. Cf. LSJ s.v. on strategion as the office of the strategoi (as in Athens) or strategos (of the nome, in third century Egypt: P. Petr. II, p. 26). In this case, however, there is still a question of what strategos (or strategoi) are meant, local officials or a Ptolemaic commander in the area.

inscription is approximately the middle of the third century.

For the fourth city on the island, Poiessa, we have no direct evidence of Ptolemaic control, nor any evidence at all of relations between the king and the city. A decree of the city indicates that a king Demetrius interfered in the city's affairs; it appears that this Antigonid was Demetrius II (239-229) rather than Poliorcetes. One may conclude from this text, then, that Ptolemaic power on Keos was not able or perhaps not interested by the 230's in keeping out Antigonid interference.[101]

For the island as a whole, then, the following picture may be drawn. The Ptolemies first appear on Keos in the latest years of Soter's reign or the first decade of Philadelphos', regulating through the nesiarch and their admiral the unsettled affairs on Keos as on so many other islands. Karthaia in particular is attested as closely linked with the Ptolemaic officials. At the time of the Chremonidean War, this influence was extended here as elsewhere to the establishment of a naval base in the best port of the island, indeed the best in the area, and a first-rate base for operations in Attica. With the establishment of this base the city of Koresia was renamed Arsinoe after the late queen, and a resident governor was installed, with the charge not only of the base but of overseeing the rest of the island and taking care of any needed Ptolemaic intervention. The island was also used as a source of *dikastai* to regulate affairs elsewhere. At some indeterminable point Ptolemaic power declined and no longer extended over the whole of the island. But the name Arsinoe, and perhaps the base there, remained to the end of the third century, reverting back to the name Koresia not long after. For the administration, the *epistates* in the base and the absence of resident officials elsewhere are the salient features.

5. *Kythnos*

No direct evidence has survived from Kythnos to indicate any Ptolemaic connections. There is, however, one inscription that indicates Kythnian membership in the league of the islanders, the Nikouria inscription of ca. 280.[102] At the end of this decree by the *synedroi* of the Nesiotai, the *theoroi* to be sent to Alexandria are named; one of them is a Kythnian.

---

101. *IG* XII 5 570.
102. *Syll.*³ 390.

6. *Siphnos*

One inscription from this island testifies to its relations with the Ptolemies.[103] It is a decree of Siphnos stating that their ambassador to the king reports that the king and queen and his δυνάμεις are well and keep their friendly attitude toward the Siphnians; further, that when the ambassador made his report, Perigenes, son of Leontiskos, Alexandrian, being present offered to provide entertainment for the city in celebration. The date and significance of the text have been much argued, being put ca. 217 by its editors and ca. 274-270 by Holleaux, followed by Robert. Holleaux has shown that the mention of δυνάμεις being well in the decree indicates a state of war.[104] Since the queen mentioned is Arsinoe, only Philadelphos and Philopator can be possibilities and only the Syrian War of 274-270 and the war of Raphia are possible. Holleaux argues that the islands would have been too poor in 217 to vote a crown of 2000 drachmas, while it would be natural in the reign of Philadelphos; at the same time he stresses that there was no other evidence from the reign of Philopator to indicate a comparable Ptolemaic power in the Aegean, while the evidence for the reign of Philadelphos is abundant. These arguments seem to me, in the absence of any indications to the contrary, to be conclusive. Siphnos thus formed part of the Ptolemaic circle in the Aegean but evidently carried on its relationship by normal diplomatic means rather than through any resident bureaucrats.

7. *Ios*

A mutilated inscription of Ios provides a tantalizing glance at the administration of the islands. It is a decree in honor of a man whose name is almost entirely cut off, but may have begun in Thrasy-.[105] His title is lost, but it ended in βασιλ]έως Πτολεμαίου;

---

103. First published in *Archiv* 2, 1903, p. 545, no. 23, whence *IG* XII 5 481. The best text is that of *IG* XII Suppl., p. 111, established by a re-reading of the stone by G. Klaffenbach. The essential articles are those of M. Holleaux, *BCH* 29, 1905, pp. 319 ff. and L. Robert, *BCH* 60, pp. 184-189; cf. Robert's comments in Holleaux, *Études* VI, pp. 25-26, n. 74, on later work. On the inutility of M. Vandoni's recent reprinting of the older text, *Bull. épig.* 1965, 6, p. 75.

104. Holleaux (cited, note 103) gives a series of passages in which the term is used, always in time of war when the term refers to troops on active service.

105. *IG* XII Suppl. 169.

his virtues were διετέλει εὔνους ὢν καὶ πράσσων ἀγαθὸν[. One phrase
provides concrete information about his benefactions: ἀ]ποσυνιστὰς
οἰκονόμον τῶν νήσων Θρασυκλῆ Ἱππα[, who has in turn done the good
in his power for the city. It appears that the man honored, Thrasy-,
is the subject of the participle, and that he is not the same as
Thrasykles son of Hippa-. The title of Thrasykles is of great interest:
oikonomos of the islands. The first editor, W. Peek,[106] understood
the title to mean that Thrasykles was appointed by the Nesiotai,
and was purely a league official; Hiller, in *IG*, expressed his doubts
about this interpretation. It seems to me quite unacceptable,
since Thrasy- is clearly a Ptolemaic official (with a title ending in
βασιλ]έως Πτολεμαίου). Since he has appointed Thrasykles, the
latter is essentially a royal appointee. He is *oikonomos* of the islands,
not of the islanders. He can scarcely be other than the chief administrator of royal financial affairs in the islands. It is a pity that
we do not know more about the position of the man who appointed
him.

One of the two, more probably the *oikonomos*, was quite possibly
honored on Delos at least twice.[107] The Delian decree was passed
by the Nesiotai, but is unfortunately as vague as these decrees
usually are, and we learn nothing of Thrasykles' actions from it.

The inscription commonly cited as the evidence for the date of
the earliest Ptolemaic control of the Cyclades is also an inscription
from Ios.[108] Its script, according to the editor, is of more nearly
a fourth-century style than third. It honors one Zenon, a subordinate of Bacchon the nesiarch. Some undecked ships (ἄφρακτα
πλοῖα) under Zenon's command had visited Ios, and a number of
ἀνδράποδα belonging to citizens of Ios had escaped on the ships
when they left. The Ietans sent ambassadors to Zenon, and the
commander summoned his trierarchs and ordered an investigation,
which apparently yielded results.

Zenon is known also from an Athenian decree honoring him for
overseeing a shipment of grain from Soter to Athens in the archonship of Diokles (286/5). He was commander of ἄφρακτα at this time
also; the identification with the man honored by Ios thus seems

---

106. *Ath. Mitt.* 59, 1934, p. 57, no. 16.
107. In *IG* XI 4 1043, a previous decree is mentioned. The honors were to
be announced at the Ptolemaia.
108. *IG* XII 5 1004 (*OGIS* 773). Zenon, *Pros. Ptol.* 15043.

certain.[109] It is therefore generally assumed that the date of the Ietan inscription is the same as that of the Athenian, and not without reason. In any case the date must be approximately correct. It is difficult to extract much information about Zenon's relations with the Ietans, as we do not know why he stopped in Ios.

A third inscription from Ios, in very mutilated condition, appears to refer to *dikastai* sent to Ios to regulate affairs.[110] There is also a mention of *theoroi*, and also the king's father, making a date in Philadelphos' reign likely.

We may mention here, finally, the Ietan proxeny decree for [. . . . .]ς Κοιράνου.[111] The man honored was an Aspendian. We have noted above the possibility that this man may be the Apollonios son of Koiranos who was commandant of Thera and proxenos of two Cretan cities during the reign of Philometor.[112] The lettering, however, if in fact of the third century (as the editor stated), appears to rule out this possibility, as Robert has said.[113]

Ios, then, appears to have been a member of the league and to have engaged in diplomatic relations with the Ptolemies during the reign of Philadelphos.

8. *Amorgos*

There is a limited amount of evidence showing Ptolemaic influence on Amorgos. First, the Nikouria decree (*Syll.*[3] 390) of the *synedroi* of the islanders was found on the small island of Nikouria just off the coast of Amorgos. It is likely that it was originally erected on Amorgos and much later moved to be used as building material on the smaller island.

Another inscription from Arkesine, one of the three cities on the island, appears to be a decree of the league of the islanders, though all of the key terms that would put this attribution beyond doubt are lost from the much damaged stone.[114] There is mention of inscribing yearly the expenses to each city for something and an account of debts owed by the islanders and each city for something else. This latter expense appears to be connected with something

---

109. *Syll.*[3] 367.
110. *IG* XII 5 7 and Suppl., p. 96.
111. Cf. note 30 above. In Ios, *IG* XII Suppl. 171.
112. See note 30.
113. *Noms indigènes*, p. 391, n. 4.
114. *IG* XII 7 13, discussed by P. Delamarre, *Rev. Phil.* 28, 1904, pp. 98-102.

decreed to king Ptolemy by the *koinon*, but the word telling what was decreed is lost; perhaps it was στέφανος. Finally, there are provisions for judges to be sent, apparently by the *koinon* to individual cities, in the event of disagreements, and for the maintenance of these judges. The decree was to be inscribed on Delos and in each city, according to P. Delamarre's restorations. One may surmise from this document that Arkesine was a member of the league of the islanders.

Two other inscriptions may have originally testified to the Ptolemaic period of the history of Amorgos, but they are no longer in sufficiently complete condition to allow any conclusions to be drawn.[115] Both seem to concern foreign judges in Arkesine.

9. *Astypalaia*

The small island of Astypalaia has yielded one trace of friendly relations with the Ptolemies, a statue base of Ptolemy Euergetes.[116] No conclusions about control and sovereignty can be drawn from such a document.

10. *Naxos*

For Naxian relations with the Ptolemies, we have knowledge of one incident involving foreign judges. Two inscriptions tell about the incident, both found on Kos, the home city of the judges.[117] One of them announces that Bacchon the nesiarch (whose name is lost at the beginning but restored by Holleaux from a later mention) came to Kos and carried out the wishes of the king by asking for judges to settle affairs on Naxos. The second is the decree of Naxos honoring the judges themselves, four Koans. The Naxians also crowned the *demos* of Kos and decreed sacrifices to Ptolemy Soter. This mention of Ptolemy I without the term θεός dates the text to the early part of Philadelphos' reign, and the mention of Bacchon provides confirmation. The provision of foreign judges

---

115. *IG* XII 7 14 (cf. *IG* XII Suppl., p. 142; mention of a *diagramma*) and 15.

116. *IG* XI 3 204.

117. Both texts are to be found in M. Holleaux, *Études* III, pp. 27-37, with extensive editorial additions and added commentary, particularly to the decree for the judges, by L. Robert. The text referring to Bacchon has been published before as *OGIS* 43 + II, p. 539, and W. R. Paton and E. L. Hicks, *The Inscriptions of Cos*, Oxford, 1891, p. 31, no. 16.

through intervention of the royal officials is in accord with incidents seen elsewhere, and belongs to the earlier part of Philadelphos' hegemony.

11. *Paros*

Although Paros has been far more productive of inscriptions than any island in the area except Delos and Thera, it has not produced any direct testimony to Ptolemaic involvement in the third century except for the Ἀρσινόης Φιλαδέλφου plaques from altars of the private cult of that queen.[118] Paros did, however, honor a nesiarch named Apollodoros with a statue in his home city, Kyzikos.[119] I have argued above that Apollodoros was a Ptolemaic nesiarch, and if this conclusion is correct, it is likely that it was some act in Ptolemaic service that caused Apollodoros to be honored *qua* nesiarch by Paros. We would then be justified in suggesting that Paros was a member of the league.

From the reign of Ptolemy VI comes an inscription of Paros honoring Aglaos son of Theokles, a Koan in Ptolemaic service attested elsewhere.[120] He is described as διοίκησιν [ποι]ούμενος for the king and queen, a phrase which led the editor to argue that he was *dioiketes* in Alexandria; J. and L. Robert have questioned whether the arguments for this conclusion are valid.[121] Part of the considerations is damaged, and the editor's restorations are doubtful (as the Roberts point out), but Aglaos had presented a crown of gold to Hestia of Paros; in return he receives a golden crown and a marble statue. It is not surprising, given Philometor's active Aegean politics, to find the Ptolemaic court and Paros in correspondence in this time (154-150, according to the editor), but the vagueness of the description of Aglaos' duties makes it difficult to know what his administrative position was. Since we have no other evidence for Ptolemaic direct intervention in Paros at this time, the assumption that Aglaos was active in Alexandria is probably correct.

---

118. On these plaques, see L. Robert, *Essays Welles*, p. 202, where he summarizes the known plaques. In the area of the islands they appear also on Ios, Amorgos, Thera, and Delos.

119. C. Michel, *Recueil d'inscriptions grecques*, Bruxelles, 1900, 534.

120. G. I. Despinis, *Arch. Delt.* 20A, 1965, pp. 119-133, with a lengthy commentary. Cf. above, p. 119.

121. *Bull. épig.* 1967, 441.

12. *Mykonos*

As the home city of an epimeletes of the league of the islanders attested in two Delian publications of league decrees,[122] Mykonos may be presumed to have been a member of the league.

13. *Tenos*

Only two traces of any connection with the Ptolemies have survived from Tenos, both decrees honoring citizens of Alexandria for good works and good will towards the people of Tenos. One,[123] in which the person's name is lost, is not datable. The other,[124] for which a date of ca. 200 B.C. was suggested by P. Graindor on the basis of the letter forms and accepted in *IG* by Hiller von Gaertringen, honors a Basileides son of Basileides. In the absence of more precise dating or information about the persons honored in these two documents, it would be unwise to draw any conclusions about the relations between Tenos and the Ptolemies.

14. *Andros*

Andros is like Kythnos attested as a member of the league of the islanders by the presence of an Andrian among the *theoroi* chosen by the league to go to Alexandria ca. 280.[125]

15. *Delos*

By virtue of its extensive yield of inscriptions, Delos has long been a favorite source for those seeking to reconstruct the political history of the Aegean islands; for no period is this more true than the third century B.C. And yet much of the epigraphical testimony of the island must be ruled out of consideration for the particular question of control and administration of Delos. It is clear, for one thing, that the sanctuary was open to all to make dedications, both during the period of independence from the late fourth century to 166 and after 166, under Athenian control. The temple accounts of properties, payments, and loans, therefore, however useful for a host of other questions—including often the Ptolemaic officials with whom we are concerned—fail to tell us if anyone was exercising

---

122. *IG* XI 4 1040 and 1041.
123. *IG* XII 5 811.
124. *IG* XII Suppl. 306.
125. *Syll.*[3] 390.

any protectorate or control over Delos. Thus the large body of evidence of this sort must be set aside for the present.

Similarly, actual dedications by foreign rulers and their subordinates or subjects are not of probative value for the question of rule. The presence of several Attalid dedications (*IG* XI 2 1105-1110) does not indicate any control exercised from Pergamon over Delos. By this token a considerable mass of material is removed from consideration. If dedications to and by the Ptolemaic kings and queens of the late second century (*I. Délos* 1531-1537, for example) do not indicate that they ruled Delos, neither do dedications of 150 years before indicate that their ancestors had done so.

Two important classes of documents remain: decrees of Delos and decrees of the league of the islanders. To begin with the latter, the fact that the league placed its decrees in Delos is not in itself an indication that Delos belonged to the league; the placement of a city's decrees in a foreign city and instructions to that effect in the decree are very common. The decrees erected by the islanders on Delos often had no importance to Delos itself: no Delian need be honored, nor the people of Delos, nor need the cause of the honors have anything to do with Delos.[126] Delos was not, in other words, a party to the transactions. This status is not unique to Delos nor is the league the only issuer of decrees to have a copy of a decree placed on the island. But the league did this not on special occasions but regularly; Delos was, in a sense, the central records depository of the league, the common place of public notice. That this indicates membership in the league is by no means certain. No league ambassadors or functionaries are Delians. The formal relationship of the two—if any existed—is not clear. A certain closeness of relations, but not necessarily dependence, is demonstrated.

The situation of the Delian decrees is yet more complex. The number of Delian proxeny decrees is quite large; the vast majority have no specific benefactions alleged, only vague terms. Their geographical range is enormous, and the presence of persons resident within the Ptolemaic possessions is thus of very limited value even for a consideration of diplomatic relations. Heliodoros of Kition and X the Alexandrian, therefore, are no more than names to us.[127]

---

126. The decrees of the league published on Delos appear as *IG* XI 4 1036-1048.

127. Heliodoros: *IG* XI 4 512. A number of Alexandrians are known: *IG* XI 4 650, 670, 674, 742 (late third century). A Cyrenaean: *IG* XI 4 657.

A better indication of close relations is provided by an inscription in honor of one Demetrios, said to be a friend of king Ptolemy and of Bacchon the nesiarch.[128] Further confirmation is given by the identity of the proposer of the decree, Aristolochos son of Nikodromos, also known to have proposed honors for Gorgion son of Demaratos, a Spartan important in the eyes of king Lysimachus and queen Arsinoe.[129] The nexus between Lysimachus and Ptolemy is not unexpected. But Aristolochos was also the proposer of another eight decrees for men of whom we know nothing but their names.[130] It would be pushing things too far to designate him simply as a member of the Ptolemaic party, but friendship with these monarchs was at least an important part of the stance of this prominent Delian.

Another connection of interest may be traced through the proposer of the decrees in question. Hierarchos son of Prokles, a Delian known from about 301 to 281,[131] proposed a decree honoring Dionysios son of Potamon, of Naukratis.[132] Dionysios is known also from *OGIS* 724, a dedication to Ptolemy and Arsinoe Philadelphos found in lower Egypt. Since he has a patronymic in the Egyptian inscription also, the identity of the man is quite certain. The same proposer is found in a decree for Apollodoros son of Apollonios of Kyzikos, the nesiarch, who was discussed above.[133] Another nesiarch, Hermias, was honored by Delos at a later time.[134]

The same kind of honors continued to be paid during the reign of Euergetes. Sosibios, the well-known minister of Euergetes and Philopator, was honored for his good will toward the king and Delos.[135] P. Roussel, in editing this text, argued from the lettering and the absence of the name of the president of the meeting that the date must be before 230. A fragment of another decree refers to Ptolemy and Berenike, who are according to the letter forms taken to be the Euergetai.[136]

Another text of uncertain date honors Dikaios son of Diokles,

---

128. *IG* XI 4 551.
129. *IG* XI 4 542.
130. *IG* XI 4 543-550. The man honored in 545 was honored at Delphi in the archonship of Archelas (275/4?).
131. References in commentary to *IG* XI 4 561.
132. *IG* XI 4 561.
133. *IG* XI 4 562 = F. Durrbach, *Choix* 20.
134. *IG* XI 4 565.
135. *IG* XI 4 649.
136. *IG* XI 4 677.

Cyrenaean, who bears the familiar title of τεταγμένο[ς ὑπὸ τὸν] βασιλέα Πτολεμαῖον.[137] Nothing is indicated of his province of action or the nature of the help that he has given to Delos. These inscriptions all taken together demonstrate close and long-lasting relationships between Delos and the Ptolemaic court, in which high-ranking Ptolemaic officials played an important part. But we cannot speak from these texts either of control or of administration.

Of rather more decisive interest is a decree in honor of Philokles king of Sidon, the Ptolemaic admiral, whose service is fortunately spelled out in more specific detail: he has assisted Delos in recovering debts from the islanders.[138] It was an important matter: Delos sent an embassy to Philokles requesting his help in recovering monies owed by the Nesiotai to the sanctuary; the king instructed him to act on their request; Bacchon the nesiarch was somehow involved (the portion preceding his name is lost). The Delians gave Philokles the usual honors and in addition a considerable series of sacrifices on his behalf to various deities. The mention of the Nesiotai as an entity distinct from Delos leaves an impression that Delos was not a member of the group, even though it acted as banker and recordkeeper for it.

All in all, it is a fairly impressive group of documents testifying to Delian connections with the Ptolemies; in particular the decree for Philokles shows a state of dependence in the period of Bacchon and Philokles—the early part of the reign of Philadelphos. During the early part of these close relations there is no other foreign power rewarded with such a group of honors, and a true hegemony involving a protectorate over Delos may be inferred.[139] But after the Chremonidean and Second Syrian Wars the situation is not at all clear, in part because the dates that can be assigned to many documents are too vague. For the period after 255, it is worth considering some of the evidence for other influences at Delos.

The question of the battle of Ephesos and the honors paid in

---

137. *IG* XI 4 631.

138. *IG* XI 4 559. On Philokles see most recently the studies of Merker (note 70) and Seibert, *Historia* 19, 1970, pp. 337-351.

139. For the period 285-260, when Ptolemaic domination was at its peak, there are no documents conferring any significant honors on other kings or their officials, except for the honors to a friend of Lysimachus already mentioned, and Lysimachus was a Ptolemaic ally. Nor do the other kings dedicate major monuments on Delos during this period.

Delos by the islanders to the Rhodian admiral victorious there
have been discussed in section 3. Another Rhodian admiral, however, is an important factor. Delos honored, at some time not too
far from the middle of the third century, Antigenes son of Theoros,
nauarch of the Rhodians, for the devotion that he and his trierarchs
showed in the guarding of the islands and the keeping of the safety
of the Greeks.[140] Whatever the situation was in other respects, at
the time of this dedication the Ptolemies were no longer providing
a naval force for the policing of the Aegean.

The Antigonids provided a number of offerings and foundations
for royal cults on Delos in the years after 260; they founded a
number of festivals: the Stratonikeia (253), Soteria and Paneia
(245), Demetrieia (238) and Philippeia (ca. 221-216). The Ptolemies
ended their period of foundations in 246. Philippe Bruneau, in his
recent study of cults on Delos,[141] remarks on the longer career
of the Antigonids in foundations on Delos. Ptolemaic activity was
intense but short-lived; it diminished with the death of Philadelphos
and after Euergetes there was little contact for more than a century.

The reign of Demetrius II has left some testimony of his relations
with Delos other than the foundation of the Demetrieia. One
decree, sponsored by a man otherwise attested in 250 and 240,
honors Autokles of Chalkis;[142] another honors Aristoboulos of
Thessalonike, sent to Delos by Demetrius as *sitones*, for his actions
to the advantage of the king and temple and *demos*.[143] There is no
evidence that the Antigonids ever exercised any real control over
Delos at any time after the reign of Demetrius Poliorcetes,[144] but
their role in contrast to that of the Ptolemies appears to enlarge in
the period after 240.

It is difficult to be precise about chronological limits of influence.
It would appear that for the first half or somewhat more of his

---

140. *IG* XI 4 596.

141. *Recherches sur les cultes de Délos à l'époque hellénistique*, Bibliothèque
des écoles françaises d'Athènes et de Rome 217, 1970, pp. 516-580. Bruneau
points out that private royal cults on Delos died quickly after a political
occasion passed, while Delos itself avoided decreeing official cults to kings.

142. *IG* XI 4 680.

143. *IG* XI 4 666.

144. The Delian evidence for the time of Poliorcetes includes *IG* XI 4
514 and 566, the first honoring a sculptor for making a statue of Stratonike,
his daughter, the second a very mutilated fragment mentioning kings
Antigonus and Demetrius, both apparently alive, and hence between 306
and 301, while the first dates after 300.

reign Philadelphos was very prominent at Delos as elsewhere in the islands, but that at some point the situation changed from a Ptolemaic protectorate to a situation best described as competition for favor and advantage, in which the Ptolemies continued to play a part, particularly in the reign of Euergetes. At no time is there any indication that the Ptolemies placed any resident official on Delos. The Delians dealt with the officials generally responsible for Ptolemaic interests in the Aegean.

16. *Summary*

We find in the Cyclades and on their fringes two rather different aspects of Ptolemaic administration. The crown dealt with most islands either through the league or individually, but in any case through mechanisms that were essentially a normal part of international diplomacy. Ambassadors were sent and received, proxeny granted, crowns decreed, judges requested, sent, and honored. These forms did not mask the royal power that dominated the Cyclades for 30 years and remained rather less active in them for another century and more; they were not intended to. For dealing with a large number of small states, direct administration would scarcely have been a profitable venture, even had it been feasible. We have seen that the league performed various functions most conveniently carried out by the islands in unison, while the islands dealt individually with the king on matters of particular interest, including, generally, internal unrest. The king protected the area militarily, tried to keep order in it domestically, and expected the islands to support his efforts in both secular and religious areas. The financial aspect of the relationship is not clear, but two elements are well attested, crowns voted to the king by the islanders and money lent by the king or by another party (Delos) to the islands and for whose eventual repayment the king was concerned. The functionaries who carry on this extensive diplomatic protectorate are in general designated vaguely, with two exceptions.

These two are the *oikonomos* of the islands and the nesiarch. The nesiarch appears in a number of contexts where he is clearly a royal agent, but where the league over which he was the head does not play a part. From this pattern it may be inferred that he was a royal appointee and served as governor of the islands in a broader sense than merely as agent of the *koinon*.[145] His competence extended over all areas, it seems; he was in general a surrogate for the king. That he was subordinate to the nauarch and the other high military officials who had dealings with the islanders, as is sometimes alleged, does not seem to me apparent. Bacchon worked closely with Philokles king of Sidon in several situations, but their jurisdiction always appears to be more concurrent than conflicting or hierarchical. The military commanders and the nesiarchs had different functions although, as we have seen, a military appointee like Patroklos, Philokles, or Kallikrates might take a leading role in the diplomatic governance of the islands and give orders to subordinate officials, acting in effect *in loco regis*.

Of the functions of the *oikonomos* of the islands in the period of the efflorescence of the league, we know almost nothing. We have too little of the documentation pertaining to Thrasykles to define his role exactly. It would appear, on the analogy of Eirenaios' role in the next century, that he was the general agent of the *basilikon* in the Aegean, responsible for the varied activities relative to royal finance that might be taking place in the area.

The other aspect of administration demonstrated, both in the third and the second centuries, is the direct control of a few strategic places; these were Thera, Methana, and Koresia on Keos. Two of these were renamed Arsinoe to emphasize their character as naval bases of the Ptolemies. Here a very different situation prevailed. The patterns of civic life and international diplomacy and democracy were not eliminated in any of these places. Instead, another set of officials was placed above the regular government.

The main part of this superimposed rule was, of course, the military force left to hold the base—its soldiers, officers, and commander, who was responsible to the central government for the place in question, in the case of Keos for the well-being of the island as a whole, not merely for the garrisoned city. Their competence was perhaps not strictly defined, but a commandant was no doubt

---

145. In support of the thesis that Bacchon and the other nesiarchs were royal appointees, one may note (1) that the contemporary Pamphyliarch (p. 111) is expressly stated to have been appointed by Ptolemy in the inscription honoring him, and (2) Zenon in the Ietan inscription (*IG* XII 5 1004) is stated to have been left behind in command of ships by Bacchon, who therefore must have commanded a significant part of the Ptolemaic naval forces in the Aegean. It is hard to see that Ptolemy would have entrusted this command to someone not of his own choice.

expected to maintain the royal presence in its manifold aspects.

The commandant was not alone, however, in representing the crown. An *oikonomos* was also present. As he was in the third century the *oikonomos* of the islands, in the second he was *oikonomos* of Thera, Crete, and Methana, all the remaining possessions in the area. His jurisdiction was wider than that of a commandant, extending to the interests of the *basilikon* over the entire area. The case of Eirenaios and the evidence of the royal disposition of confiscated lands and their revenues on Thera show that the *oikonomos* was answerable directly to the *dioiketes* in Alexandria and through him to the king. A balance of power and distribution of functions was thus achieved. After the passing of the period of hegemony in the early part of Philadelphos' reign and the great admirals and nesiarchs who dominated it, we cannot be sure if there was a military commander responsible for the whole of the Ptolemaic interests in the Aegean; . . . aphilos on Thera may have been one such.

The bifurcated administration that we have outlined served two quite different purposes with its two aspects. The earlier one, however much it might reflect complete hegemony, faded quickly, and served the needs of a short-term foreign policy in the area. Administration could be indirect in areas that the king did not intend to occupy but only to dominate. Different needs were served by the forces and officials put in cities that were meant to be controlled permanently.

CHAPTER SEVEN

THE NORTH AEGEAN AND IONIA

A. The North Aegean

Under this heading we will consider Thrace, the Hellespont, Samothrace, and Lesbos. The rationale for this grouping is administrative as well as geographical and will become apparent as the evidence is presented. The somewhat peculiar nature of the information that we possess, however, makes it difficult to use the geographical method of Chapter VI, and a topical one has been employed instead.

1. *Chronology*

One document attests to a possible Ptolemaic presence in the northern Aegean before the reign of Ptolemy III.[1] It is an Ἀρσινόης Φιλαδέλφου plaque from Methymna.[2] If the royal cult thus attested was accompanied by more substantive relations between Methymna and the kings, or if any Ptolemaic functionaries had control over the island, we do not know. It is possible that Ptolemaic control over the island might have existed in the 260's only to be lost in 259 or thereabouts, as part of the territorial losses the Ptolemies sustained in Asia Minor at that time.

After this document our next intimation of a Ptolemaic presence in the north comes with the claim in the Adoulis inscription (*OGIS* 54) that Ptolemy III Euergetes conquered Thrace and the Hellespontine area during the Third Syrian War (246-241). This testimony is by itself not conclusive evidence, for that inscription is full of extravagant claims for the conquests of Euergetes in the east. Nonetheless, it does show that Euergetes did not inherit any interests in the area from his father.

---

1. The friendly relations of Ptolemy II with Byzantium do not come into question here, since there is no indication that any control or administration was involved. See for a good summary C. Habicht, *Gottmenschentum*[2], pp. 116-121, and G. Le Rider, *Rev. num.* 6 sér. 13, 1971, p. 152. On Ptolemaic activity in this area a general summary may be found by C. Habicht in *RE* s.v. Ziaelas, col. 393.

2. *IG* XII 2 513. On this class of monument, see L. Robert's definitive study in *Essays Welles*, pp. 202-208.

There is, moreover, corroborating evidence for the conquests. A decree of the Thracian city of Ainos recognizing requests of the sanctuary of Kos, apparently from the year 242, mentions Ptolemy, Berenike, and their children and a priest of their cult.[3] It thus appears that Ainos' foreign policy, though independently carried out, coincided with the wishes and attitudes of Ptolemy III.

Some further evidence is provided by an incident that fell within the reign of Euergetes but is not more closely datable than 241-221. It is known to us through two very similar inscriptions, one for Hippomedon son of Agesilaos, a Spartan, *strategos* of Thrace and the areas on the Hellespont, the other for Epinikos, governor of the Thracian city Maroneia.[4] Both men had taken thought for the safety of the mainland territory of Samothrace by providing troops, weapons, and money to pay the mercenaries hired by Samothrace. The specific contents will be discussed below, but the date in the reign of Euergetes is reasonably secure, particularly taken with the testimony of Teles that Hippomedon was appointed *strategos* of Thrace by Euergetes.[5]

For the reign of Philopator there is again some evidence to be brought to bear. Polybius notes in general terms that the Ptolemies held, at Philopator's accession, various points to the Hellespont and the τόποι around Lysimacheia, as well as Ainos, Maroneia, and πορρώτερον ἔτι πόλεων.[6] Hippomedon was still alive in 219, according

---

3. *Asylieurkunden* 8. The date is established by the editors on the basis of the known presence of Koan ambassadors that year in the area seeking similar decrees. C. Habicht, *Gottmenschentum*[2], p. 122, argues that the priest in this document is one of the dynastic cult.

4. The Hippomedon decree most recently revised on the stone: P. M. Fraser, *Samothrace: Inscriptions*, pp. 39-40, where earlier bibliography is cited. The Epinikos decree is nowhere satisfactorily published, but references to the original publications and subsequent corrections may be found in Bengtson, *Die Strategie* III, p. 183, n. 1; more recently D. Pippidi has restored another passage in *Studii Clasice* 9, 1967, pp. 223-224. In *Bull. épig.* 1968, 403, a better restoration by L. Robert is promised (to appear in *Studii Clasice* 16, 1974). Cf. also L. Robert in *Gnomon* 35, 1963, pp. 78-79, for bibliography of the stone and an important emendation.

5. Teles, *De Fuga*, ed. Hense[2], p. 23.

6. Polybius (5.34.7-8) does not indicate a date of acquisition for any of these territories. Walbank, *A Historical Commentary on Polybius*, Oxford, 1957, I, p. 565, accepts Beloch's contention (*Griechische Gesch.* IV.2, Berlin-Leipzig, 1927, pp. 346-347) that Lysimacheia, Sestos, and Kypsela on the Hebros also came under Ptolemaic rule. Beloch has inferred Lysimacheia from Polybius' periphrasis; the claim to Sestos (also accepted by C. Habicht, *RE* s.v. Ziaelas, col. 393) rests on *OGIS* 88, a dedication to Ptolemy IV,

to Polybius (4.35.13), and that he was still active in the north Aegean is shown by his presence in the second column of *P. Teb.* 8, a collection of letter drafts to Ptolemaic functionaries which I date to 219. The financial interest of this document will be considered below; what matters here is that 219 is the earliest possible date for the papyrus, and Hippomedon was still active then.

For Lesbos, where no trace of Euergetes' reign is found, the situation is otherwise under Philopator. Since not all of the dating of these documents is based on solid evidence, we can only be approximate. For Eresos, first, a decree is preserved honoring Damon son of Polyarchos for his services to the *demos*.[7] These services include recovering spoils taken from Eresos by an undefined adversary and going on other embassies to Ptolemy περὶ ἐπιστατείας. He is spoken of as [ὁρ]μάμενος κρίσιός τε ἐ[πι]στατείας καὶ [φ]ιλί[ας]. He had, in sum, made himself useful to the city and to the king (the latter restored). He is to be crowned in the games held by the city for Ptolemy and Herakles. The letter forms, according to Hiller, date the text to the reign of Philopator. Of the other Eresian texts of the period, only one appears to be securely datable: a decree for the gymnasiarch of the Ptolemaion, which mentions the king and queen and their son; in a late third century context (the date suggested by Hiller on the basis of the letter forms) the date can be only 209-205, the trio Philopator, Arsinoe, and the future Epiphanes.[8]

For Methymna we have a decree of the *koinon* of the Proteoi dated by the reign of Philopator (without mention of a specific

---

Arsinoe, and their son (hence 209-205) of a sort not restricted to Ptolemaic dependencies (cf. on Crete, p. 117 and chapter IV, n. 144); and Kypsela was ruled by the dynast Adaios. Sestos and Lysimacheia may indeed have been Ptolemaic possessions, but present evidence does not establish it.

7. *IG* XII 2 527 and *IG* XII Suppl., p. 33.

8. *IG* XII Suppl. 122. The proposer of this decree, Bacchios son of Hermodikos, also appears in *IG* XII Suppl. 125 as a proposer, where there is again mention of honors to be announced during the Ptolemaia. He was sent to Paros as a judge (*IG* XII Suppl. 121). A mention of the Ptolemaia is also restored in *IG* XII Suppl., p. 36 (*ad* XII 2 528), honors for an *agoranomos* whose past services include going to Lampsakos and receiving Chian ambassadors and a Roman (Cn. Junius, whom I do not find in any other source). The palaeographical date of this text was put in the second century. It is likely that the decree for the gymnasiarch demonstrates real Ptolemaic control, and that the gymnasium (Ptolemaion) and the festival (Ptolemaia) were established during this control, but the festival may well have outlived the Ptolemaic control of the island. On the Ptolemaion of Eresos, cf. L. Robert, *Études anatoliennes*, pp. 174, 452.

year).[9] It is thus certain that Methymna was a direct Ptolemaic dependency during the reign of Philopator. There is also a decree of Methymna for a citizen of that city who had served as priest of a royal cult; his title is read and restored as ἱερατεύσαντ[α βασιλέος Πτολεμαίω τῶ Πτ]ολεμαίω καὶ Πτολεμα[ίω τῶ υἱῶ αὐτῶ.[10] Hiller, following Wilcken, took the son to be Ptolemy "the son", the co-regent with Philadelphos in the years 267-259. But to this it may be objected (1) that no cult of this man is elsewhere attested, and (2) the presence of an *alpha* with broken bar among the forms reproduced by Hiller makes a date before 250 unlikely. The son, therefore, is Epiphanes, as an infant added to the royal protocols; the date is 209-205.[11]

For Lesbos as a whole, finally, one may cite the fact that in *P. Teb.* 8 there is question of royal revenues from Lesbos in at least one letter. For the reign of Philopator, then, we have evidence in Thrace and Lesbos, mostly but not entirely from his early years and the close of his reign. For the reign of Epiphanes, however, things are less well documented. We know that Philip took over the remaining Ptolemaic possessions in Thrace in 200. The Ptolemaic commandant who surrendered Ainos, Kallimedes, is specifically mentioned in Livy.[12] If *P. Teb.* 8 is placed in the reign of Philopator,[13] there is no other testimony for the reign of Epiphanes.

In sum, aside from a barely possible and brief Ptolemaic presence on Lesbos before 259, we are probably entitled to assume that parts of Thrace and the Hellespont came under Ptolemaic control in the 240's, together with Lesbos and Samothrace, and that this control lasted at least in some areas until the year 200, when it was terminated and not resumed.

2. *Military and Civil Government*

Garrisons are known to have been placed in two Thracian cities, Ainos and Maroneia. We know of both from Livy's description of Philip V's conquests in 200, and a commander of Maroneia, Epini-

---

9. *IG* XII 2 498 (*OGIS* 78).

10. *IG* XII Suppl. 115.

11. This date is asserted by C. Habicht, *Gottmenschentum*[2], p. 109, n. 1 ("wie ich anderwärts zu zeigen hoffe").

12. Livy 31.16.4.

13. I give this document the detailed study that is not possible here in an article, *JEA* 61, 1975.

kos, appears in a Samothracian inscription mentioned above.[14] We know nothing of the relationship of these men to the cities whose commandants they were, but for Epinikos we may consider his connection with Samothrace. He took an active role in providing money, men, and weapons to Samothrace to help defend the ἐν Χωρίωι μερῶν, the mainland possessions belonging to the islanders, which had come under attack from barbarians. His actions in the matter paralleled those of Hippomedon, the *strategos* of the entire area.[15] Epinikos' competence, in his own eyes as in those of his superiors, extended beyond his command in Maroneia to the defense and aid of any area under Ptolemaic control or domination in his region. His responsibilities were thus wide; of his power to impose his will outside Maroneia, however, we know nothing.

The question of a garrison in Lesbos is less clear. We have already mentioned an inscription of Eresos honoring one of its citizens, Damon son of Polyarchos, for his eagerness for Ptolemaic κρίσις, ἐπιστατεία and friendship.[16] There is, unfortunately, no other evidence to explain this mention of ἐπιστατεία. We do not know whether Damon was discussing something that the Eresians had and wanted removed, or lacked and wanted, or had but wanted to alter in some way. It is quite possible that Damon was trying to limit Ptolemaic control to "friendship." Judgment must be suspended.

Another inscription which has sometimes been adduced on this question does not seem helpful to me.[17] It is a list of names from Eresos, headed by the following:

----α(ρ)χος ἐπὶ ῎Ερε[σον]
----αρ]χος ἐπὶ ῎Ερε[σ]ον

Hiller von Gaertringen suggested restoration of the damaged word as φρούραρχος.[18] There are problems with the suggestion. First, Eresos is in the accusative, while ἐπὶ in a commandant's title always takes the genitive. Second, there is no likelihood that there were two commandants at the same time in the way that this text

---

14. Livy, cf. note 12; Epinikos' inscription, note 4.
15. Cf. note 4 for Hippomedon's inscription praising his actions.
16. See note 8.
17. *IG* XII 2 533 and *IG* XII Suppl., p. 38.
18. In *IG* XII Suppl., p. 38.

would then indicate. Third, the reading is highly uncertain. The facsimile was read as follows:

ΑΙΧΟΣΕΠΙΕΡΕ
ΧΟΣΕΠΙΕΡΕ ΟΝ

It can be seen that no *rho* is certain, the amount to be restored is conjectural, while four other lines in the inscription indicate a maximum loss of four letters to the left. For these reasons I do not think Hiller's restoration and its consequences can be accepted.

Whether there was a garrison on Lesbos thus must for the present remain uncertain. It is, however, clear that the decision to place one rested with the king. There was no question of the power, only of the form.

We may next turn to Hippomedon himself, in particular to his role in dealing with Samothrace. The inscription that honors him [19] tells us that he had been initiated into the mysteries in the sanctuary of the great gods. He had then sent cavalry, infantry, catapults, and missiles to help defend the *chorion* when it was under attack. Further, he advanced funds to pay Tralian mercenaries hired by Samothrace and for whom the island found itself without funds for pay. The second part of the inscription, more fragmentary, deals with some requests to be made to Hippomedon by the city through its ambassadors. They ask the *strategos* to grant to them σίτου ἐξαγωγὴν καὶ ἀτέλειαν δοῦν[αι τ]ῆι πόλει Χερρονήσου καὶ ἄλλοθεν ὅθεν αὐτῶι εὔκαιρον φα[ί]νηται εἶναι. They also ask him to assist in the re-establishment of Samothracian cleruchs and farmers on the mainland together with their fortress so that the land may yield revenues for sacrifices to the royal family.

Although Hippomedon bears the title of *strategos* of the places in Thrace and the Hellespont, he appears here with clear authority over Samothrace. He has the responsibility that Epinikos had to advance aid to Samothrace in time of trouble. But he also has direct governing power. He stands in the place of the king as the recipient of a petition asking for exemption from what must have been the rules of royal finance in the area (to be considered below). Samothrace itself was probably not garrisoned, or we would find mention somewhere of its commandant at the time of this incident. It was no doubt easier for public relations not to garrison a city

---

19. Note 4, above.

whose sanctuary was of wide renown. But Hippomedon's power extended over the island nonetheless.

For the political organization of the northern Aegean under the Ptolemies, then, we may present the following picture. The Greek cities of the area—Ainos, Maroneia, Samothrace, the cities of Lesbos—carried on their civic institutions and foreign relations and diplomacy as they had in previous periods. Their actions, however, were carefully guided so as to be in accord with the royal will. In the Thracian cities, perhaps also on Lesbos, were garrisons with commanders who in time of need extended their resources to defend areas in Ptolemaic control but outside their immediate jurisdiction; their governing authority, however, did not extend that far. The *strategos*, however, exercised wide powers in the place of the king, over both garrisoned and ungarrisoned cities. His authority was supreme in matters of military affairs, civil government, and perhaps in financial dealings, though the complicated picture in this realm deserves more consideration.

3. *Economic Administration*

Even from the brief description already given of the documents for the north Aegean, it must be evident that their primary interest lies in their economic aspects. To take Hippomedon first, the passage quoted above gives us the request of the city of Samothrace to him: to allow import of wheat from the Chersonese into Samothrace; to allow it from another area if he thinks it better; to exempt the import from taxation. The primary conclusions to be drawn from the request are straightforward and have been made before.[20] The king controlled the sources of supply of grain for his possessions, to his own profit. The control took the form of not allowing import except from certain specified places, and even that was subject to a customs charge. It is not necessarily certain that the same rules applied to other territories as to Samothrace or that we should imagine this rule in force in all periods. If the Chersonese was under Ptolemaic control, it presumably did not have a need to import grain. But it is quite possible that the same rules applied in other wheat-short areas. Hippomedon, as *strategos*, had the power to waive such rules in an individual case; were it

---

20. As by M. Rostovtzeff, *Studien zur Geschichte des Römischen Kolonates*, Leipzig, 1910, p. 264, n. 1.

otherwise, we would see the Samothracians applying to the king to direct Hippomedon to grant these privileges.

The second part of the request to Hippomedon asks that he cooperate with the city to complete the re-establishment of Samothracian cleruchs on the mainland, around the stronghold that he had helped defend earlier from the barbarians and in whose restoration he is now asked to help. From the labor of these cleruchs should come revenues to support sacrifices to the royal family. It is uncertain for how long the land in question, be it all or part of the Samothracian enclave on the mainland, had been previously settled, and whether the basis of the Samothracian possession was a grant, probably from the king or Hippomedon himself, or whether the land was an ancestral possession. It is noteworthy that the reason given to Hippomedon for the crown to interest itself in the resettlement is that some revenues from this land should go to maintenance of the royal cult. It is likely that this refers to a cult carried on by the Samothracians. One is reminded of the royal grant of confiscated lands to soldiers on Thera so that the revenues may support sacrifices.[21] It is regrettable that in this instance we do not know the original source of this land for the Samothracians.

We turn now to Lesbos and *P. Teb.* 8. Lines 6-11 of this enigmatic papyrus, probably from 219 B.C.,[22] are the draft of a letter to one Aphrodisios. The author is generally agreed to be the *dioiketes* or some very high subordinate of his, since the other letters on the papyrus deal with Lycia and perhaps other areas. Aphrodisios, like other addressees in the papyrus, is distinguished by no title, so that his post is quite uncertain.[23] Rostovtzeff suggested that he was an *oikonomos*, but we have no real evidence for that. All that we know is that he is an official with a financial competence and a subordinate of the *dioiketes*, who gives him orders in the letter.

I reproduce here the text of the letter:[24]

> ᾿Αφροδισίωι. χρημάτων καὶ σίτου
> καὶ τῶν ἄλλων φό(ρων) τῶν ὑπαρξάντων
> 8   ἐν τοῖς κατὰ Λέσβον καὶ Θράικην
> τόποις διασαφῆ(σαι) εἰ μετείληφεν
> καὶ τοῦ ʽΗρακλείτου καὶ τῶν γρα(φῶν)
> ἀποσ(τεῖλαι) ὅπως διεξαχθῆι.

---

21. Cf. above, p. 131.
22. Cf. note 13.
23. Rostovtzeff's view, *SEHHW*, p. 335.
24. According to my text (cf. note 13).

An approximate translation is "About the money and grain and other revenues in the places in Lesbos and Thrace, to let me know if he [Aphrodisios] has received part of them; and about Herakleitos and the accounts, send so that it may be settled (?)." It can be seen that the form is cryptic in the extreme, and it is difficult if not impossible to find connected sense. Aphrodisios is asked, it seems, to let the *dioiketes* know what the state of his receipts of revenues in money, grain, and other (produce) in Lesbos and Thrace is. His competence, therefore, extends over both places, though it is not necessarily limited to them, and he may not himself be in that area. Aside from this conclusion about the geographical competence of Aphrodisios, however, few conclusions can be drawn. We do not know whether the *phoroi* in question were private royal revenues from crown property or rather taxes paid by the citizens of the cities in the areas in question.[25] From one source or another, however, the Ptolemies had revenues from these areas, paid in diverse forms, but handled by an agent of the *dioiketes*, who evidently himself had a number of subordinates. It is worth noting that the extremely brief and cryptic nature of the notes requires the assumption that such correspondence was frequent and intensive and that the *dioiketes* maintained a very close watch over affairs in the province. The parallels of the structure of administration and taxation with Egypt are significant and will play a part in Chapter IX.

In the second column of the same papyrus (lines 47 and 54) [26] appears the name of Hippomedon. Its case is unfortunately not certain. The contents are completely lost, and speculation would be fruitless. Without them, however, we cannot solve the question of the relative positions of the *strategos* and *dioiketes*. The one dealt with the other; we have already seen Hippomedon's high competence in financial affairs. But we do not know whether Hippomedon took his orders in these matters from the *dioiketes* or from the king.

The overall picture for the area remains cloudy. Thrace and

---

25. Rostovtzeff (note 23) took the revenues to be taxes paid to the crown by the inhabitants, while D. Magie, *Roman Rule in Asia Minor*, Princeton, 1950, pp. 936-937, n. 1, thought they came from private possessions of the king.

26. Not published in *P. Teb.* I. I publish it in my study of the papyrus (above, n. 13).

Lesbos were grouped for purposes of economic administration, and it may be that Samothrace should be included in the group, on the basis of Hippomedon's apparent financial competence. There were crown revenues, probably a host of crown officials; their relative positions we cannot define.

B. Ionia

The west coast of Asia Minor was long the scene of Ptolemaic activity, both on the coast and on the islands off-shore. The extent and duration of Ptolemaic influence and possessions have been the subject of much controversy, generally on the basis of little evidence. I have tried to outline the evidence and to draw conclusions somewhat conservatively from it; new conclusions may come from new evidence, but it is best at present not to go beyond what we now have. For a few places in the area the documents tell us something.

1. Chios

We have one text for Ptolemaic influence in Chios, a decree of the third century, probably of the period 278-270, of the city of Chios, honoring Apollophanes son of Apollodoros for his services as mediator and *dikastes* on the island.[27] He had been sent by king Ptolemy; the motive formula speaks of his good will toward the city and the βασιλεῖς and of the fact that he has carried out the mission for which the king sent him.

It would appear that Apollophanes had undertaken his mission at least as much by royal order as by request of the city and that we must therefore understand the royal interference to mean royal control. The fact that the king sent a man who was evidently a royal functionary rather than a citizen of an impartial city underlines this fact. There is no sign of resident bureaucracy or of military forces, and Chios would thus appear to belong to a category of ungarrisoned cities acknowledging Ptolemaic control. But it is hard to say how conclusive the silence of other inscriptions may be.

Unlike many other islands, such as Samos, Chios was not near any part of the mainland controlled by the Ptolemies, so far as

---

27. A. P. Stephanou in Εἰς Μνημὴν Κ. Ι. Ἀμάντου, 1960, pp. 140-145 (text reprinted from revision on a squeeze by W. G. Forrest as *SEG* XIX 569). Cf. the remarks of J. and L. Robert, *Bull. épig.* 1961, 466, and a further restoration by G. Klaffenbach in *SEG* XX 787.

present evidence reveals. This fact, coupled with the mention of the sovereigns in the plural, which could refer to Ptolemy II and Arsinoe II, suggests that the 270's may well be the chronological setting of the inscription, in the brightest days of Ptolemaic sea power and hegemony in the islands. The character of the writing belongs definitely to the earlier third century, and another occasion for mention of βασιλεῖς in this period does not readily present itself.

2. *The Ionian Coast*

The picture given us by Theocritus (17.86-90) of Philadelphos' possessions (in the 270's) and the claims of Ptolemy III in the Adoulis inscription (*OGIS* 54) combine to suggest a pattern of Ptolemaic control in Ionia not entirely in accord with our other evidence. Theocritus does not mention Ionia,[28] while Euergetes claims it as one of his conquests, along with the Hellespont and Thrace. From our other evidence, it appears that only seven mainland cities can at present come under consideration as possible possessions of either king: Lebedos, Ephesos, Kolophon, Magnesia, Priene, Miletos, and perhaps Teos.

We know from a Magnesian inscription of the late third century that at that time there was a city whose inhabitants were called Πτολεμαιεῖς οἱ πρότερον καλούμενοι Λεβέδιοι.[29] That Lebedos was refounded as Ptolemais was first discovered from numismatic evidence, coins of a certainly Lebedian type with the legend ΠΤΟΛ.[30] There is, unfortunately, no evidence as yet for dating the refoundation. It does not necessarily indicate continued Ptolemaic control that the city retained the name at the end of the century; in fact we cannot determine with any certainty Lebedos' political stance at this time.[31] We know that Ptolemaic sovereignty was at one time very real, but we do not know when. It may be noted that Lebedians appear as part of the *koinon* of the Ionians in a decree for Antiochus I in 266 or shortly after.[32] This would seem

---

28. On the other hand, he makes no mention of Cyprus, certainly a possession.

29. *I. Magn.* 53.79-80.

30. The most recent useful discussion of the coins and the problem of Lebedos generally is that of L. Robert, *BCH* 70, 1946, pp. 516-519, where a full summary of the numismatic studies is given.

31. As H. Schmitt, *Untersuchungen zur Geschichte Antiochos' des Grossen*, Wiesbaden, 1964, p. 282, points out. Lebedos had resumed its old name by the time of the Delphic *theorodokoi* list (cf. Robert, note 30).

32. *OGIS* 222.

to make the reign of Euergetes more likely than that of Philadelphos, whose power in the area collapsed not much after 266.

This decree is also our starting point for considering Ephesos, which appears in it as a Seleucid dependency. Sometime after 266, we cannot tell when, Ptolemy II gained control of the city for a brief period attested by the combined Rhodian and Seleucid attack that ended it about 259 or 258.[33] It is clear that in these few years the Ptolemies saw it as a key base.

The date of the Ptolemaic recovery of Ephesos is not precisely known. The city was Seleucid in 254/3, and a Seleucid garrison still held it in 246.[34] The date of its subsequent recovery by Ptolemy III is a part of the complicated and much controverted problem of Ptolemy "the son," recently discussed by Jonas Crampa with some new evidence from an inscription from Labraunda (near Mylasa) in Caria. It has long been known that a Ptolemy who was a son of Philadelphos deserted his father's side while the son was in Asia Minor, and that some time thereafter he was killed in Ephesos by Thracian mercenaries evidently forming part of the garrison with which Ptolemy was holding that city.[35] The new text from Labraunda shows a Ptolemy acting as an administrator, wrongly believed by Crampa to have been in Seleucid service, who on one occasion gave an opinion in a protracted city-priests controversy over the temple at Labraunda and its property. This Ptolemy is also identified with the "son" who appears as co-regent with Philadelphos in documents from Egypt in the years 267-259; in 259 his name drops from the protocols.[36]

Crampa took the appearance of Ptolemy as giver of a past

---

33. I follow here the dating of J. Crampa, *I. Labraunda*, I, pp. 114-120, who gives full references and bibliography. Crampa's date for this event varies only slightly from most other estimates.

34. In 254/3, Welles, *Royal Correspondence* 18. The Seleucid governor in 246 was Sophron, mentioned in a story from Phylarchos (*FGrH* 81 F 24) given in Athenaeus 13.593b-d.

35. J. Crampa, *I. Labraunda* I, pp. 114-120, discusses the problem in great detail, if sometimes with more ingenuity than plausibility. I may refer to his work for the ancient sources and modern bibliography, alike exhaustively set out. That his reconstruction is in certain points followed here does not mean that his conclusions are to be followed in other respects. On various problems in the texts of *I. Labraunda* I, cf. J. and L. Robert, *Bull. épig.* 1970, 542-553. C. Habicht, *Gnomon* 44, 1972, pp. 162-170, calls much of Crampa's reconstruction into question, with much reason. See esp. pp. 168-170.

36. On this question, cf. Welles, *Royal Correspondence*, pp. 75 ff.

administrative decision, cited next to Sophron, as evidence that Ptolemy and Sophron had both been Seleucid administrators in the area, but there is no reason to assume that this is correct, as C. Habicht has shown.[37] Habicht, in turn, argues that Sophron was a *strategos* in the service of Ptolemy II before the time of Ptolemy the son's coming to the area, and that this Sophron thus is not to be identified with the Seleucid commandant of Ephesos in 246. H. Bengtson, on the other hand, while rejecting Crampa's interpretation, thinks that Ptolemy the son became an independent dynast until 246 or even after, while he takes Sophron to have been a Seleucid functionary in the years before 246.[38] Habicht seems to me correct in thinking that the reference to Ptolemy the son comes from the period before 259, but I see no way of demonstrating the identity and date of Sophron.

Whatever the exact date—and I do not see that it can be fixed at present—of Ptolemy's death and the subsequent (and connected, Crampa thinks) reacquisition of Ephesos by Euergetes, by the beginning of Philopator's reign Ephesos was certainly a Ptolemaic base with a large garrison, as Polybius tells us.[39] During that reign Athens honored Ephesos for its goodwill to Philopator, and the city evidently remained in Ptolemaic control until it was taken in 197 by Antiochus III.[40]

As dates for Ptolemaic control of Ephesos, then, we have approximately (or after) 265 to 259, and ca. 230(?)-197. We know that the city was garrisoned, probably in both periods, and that in Polybius' account it was a military base corresponding to the position of Samos as a naval base. Aside from the Ephesian *theoroi* sent to the Athenian Ptolemaia in the late 220's, who appear in the Athenian decree for Ephesos, however, we have not a trace of the way in which Ephesos was affected. There was, no doubt, a garrison commander, but we do not know to whom he was answerable, or what sort of garrison he commanded.

If Crampa's attribution of the fragment of Porphyry mentioning a Ptolemy who sent troops to Magnesia to help Hierax to the son

---

37. Habicht (n. 35, above); cf. the summary in *Bull. épig.* 1972, 422.
38. H. Bengtson, *Sitzb. München*, Phil.-hist. Kl., 71, 3, 1972; cf. *Bull. épig.* 1972, 421.
39. Polyb. 5.35.11.
40. Decree of Athens published *Hesperia* 6, 1937, p. 448, no. 3, discussed and amended by L. Robert, *Études épigraphiques et philologiques*, pp. 62 ff. For Antiochus in 197, Hieron. *in Dan.* 11.15-16.

rather than to Euergetes is correct, we would have only one piece of evidence alleged to show a period of Ptolemaic control of Magnesia.[41] Polyaenus tells that a Kallikratides, a Cyrenaean, captured Magnesia.[42] No mention of his employer is made, but it has often been thought that a Cyrenaean would probably have been in Ptolemaic service and that his exploit would therefore be an indication of a period of Ptolemaic rule.[43] It is not impossible that this is correct, but it scarcely seems that this passage is sufficient evidence for the hypothesis. We must leave Magnesia in the realm of uncertainty for now.

A possibility of Ptolemaic influence in Priene is raised by a reference in a Prienian inscription, the well-known decision of Rhodian judges in a dispute between Priene and Samos over land around a fortress on the mainland.[44] In the Rhodian summary of the arguments of the two sides, after a mention of a Samian complaint to Priene in the time of Antiochus (II), the inscription becomes fragmentary and refers to the Laodikean War, then to an *epistates* named Simon sent to Priene, then to Philip V. At this point it appears that the judges began speaking again of the late fourth century, referring to a judgment of Antigonus Monophthalmos. There follows mention of an Antiochus (it is uncertain which one) and a line mentioning Ἀν]τίοχον τὸν ὑπὸ βασιλέως Πτολεμαίου τεταγμένον ἐπὶ [. It appears that he, like the others mentioned, had given an opinion on the matter or had at least been referred to by one of the parties to the dispute. We know neither over what he held a command nor by whom he was approached in the matter. It is not even certain that he was acknowledged by both sides as an authority of importance.

The possibility remains open, therefore, that Antiochus was a Ptolemaic official in Priene, or that he was stationed on Samos; or, indeed, that he held a wider command in the area. It is also conceivable that the *epistates* Simon mentioned not long before him was a Ptolemaic official. But nothing allows us yet to draw firm conclusions or to put any date (except to the third century) on the careers of these men.

---

41. E. Will, *Histoire politique* I, p. 232, thought that the Ptolemies controlled Magnesia at this time (during the war of the brothers).

42. Polyaenus 2.27.1-2.

43. So F. Heichelheim, *RE* Suppl. 5, col. 386, no. 3, and M. Launey, *Armées hellénistiques*, p. 591.

44. *I. Priene* 37.

In a letter dating to about 262/1 written to Miletos, Ptolemy II spoke of his father's goodwill toward Miletos, manifested in particular by his removal of harsh *phoroi* and *paragogia* placed on the city by other kings.[45] Welles has argued that this period of Ptolemaic alliance with Miletos in the reign of Soter can be only the years 314-313; if so, the rapport did not last long, for the Milesian list of stephanephores shows that in 313/2 the city was liberated by Antigonus and the democracy restored.[46] Antigonid influence, still strong when Demetrius was stephanephore in 295/4,[47] gave way by 289/8 to the rule of Lysimachus. By 280, after the death of Lysimachus, Antiochus I held the city, being named as stephanephore for 280/279. The following year, however, the Milesian list records that a grant of land was given to the city by king Ptolemy, and it would appear that Philadelphos had taken advantage of the confusion at the beginning of Antiochus' reign to draw Miletos away into his own alliance.

The next 18 years were not quiet—Apollo held the stephanephorate in six of them—but there is no reason to suppose, as some

45. Welles, *Royal Correspondence* 14, with full discussion of the date, which has now been generally accepted to be 262/1, as Rehm thought.

46. *I. Delphin.* 123. C. Habicht, *Gottmenschentum*[2], p. 115, argues that 294-288 are more likely dates for a first Ptolemaic hegemony over Miletos in which he follows Rehm, Beloch, and Roussel. He argues (1) that τινὲς τῶν βασιλέων must refer to Seleucus I and Demetrius Poliorcetes in alliance, rather than to Antigonus I alone; (2) that the royal title in any case indicates a date after 306; (3) that in 314/3 Miletos was in Asander's control, not that of Ptolemy (Asander was stephanephore in 314/3); (4) that Antigonus is called liberator of Miletos in *I. Delphin.* 123.1-4. In response, however, one may observe (1) that it is too much to expect technical accuracy or specificity in reference to rulers some 50 years before the time of *Royal Correspondence* 14; the kings (as Welles observed) did not like to refer to an opponent by name; (2) the use of the royal title would come automatically in 262, and a distinction between Antigonus before and after 306 is hardly to be expected; (3) Asander was a Ptolemaic ally (Diod. 19.62.2); (4) the honors paid to a king might well be viewed with less enthusiasm in retrospect, and shifts of control over Miletos were too frequent for the city to have avoided honoring any of the kings at one time or another. The use by Miletos of τὸν θεὸν καὶ σωτῆρ[α] Πτολεμαῖον (*I. Delphin.* 139.24-25) to refer to Ptolemy I testifies only to what he was called in 262 by Miletos, and does not (*pace* Habicht) indicate the establishment of a cult to him in 314/3 or 294-288, for the statue of him set up in the sanctuary of Apollo (line 53) need not have borne the designation "god and savior" at the time of dedication, though it is called that in 262. J. Seibert, *Chiron* 1, 1971, pp. 159-166, supporting Welles' date, suggests that the taxes of "some of the kings" date to 313-309, their removal to 309/8.

47. Cf. note 46. Lysimachus in 289/8, *Syll.*[3] 368.

have done, an interruption of the Ptolemaic alliance, though it is not impossible that this happened. At all events, by the time of Philadelphos' letter to Miletos and the accompanying decree in 262, the alliance was still in existence, though Miletos was threatened, as the decree tells us, both by sea and by land.[48] Ptolemy sent an embassy composed of Kallikrates (the admiral), his son Ptolemy (who later defected), and other friends, to help confirm Miletos in its alliance, which is always referred to as *philia* and *symmachia*. All of the Ptolemaic ambassadors mentioned were visitors to the city, not resident officials. For the latter, we have no firm evidence.

About 260, an Aetolian named Timarchos usurped tyrannical power in Miletos. The date and circumstances are obscure, and Timarchos' background is unknown, though it is often assumed that he was a Ptolemaic officer.[49] Timarchos has already been discussed under Samos (above, p. 80), and may be left aside here. It is not certain when Timarchos was ousted, but his reign may have been as brief as a year or two.[50]

From the evidence cited, it appears that Miletos stood as an ally, perhaps a dependency, but probably not a possession to the Ptolemies. We have no evidence for resident officials. On the contrary, it appears that Ptolemy II made every effort to conciliate the city by benefactions and to confirm it in its alliance with him, just as his father had a half-century before.

It has generally been thought that Miletos returned to the Ptolemaic alliance in the reign of Ptolemy III. The only evidence that Rehm could cite for this thesis, however, was Euergetes' own vague claim in the Adoulis inscription (*OGIS* 54) to have conquered Ionia.[51] In fact, however, there is absolutely no evidence for Miletos specifically indicating Ptolemaic influence after 260.[52] Our evidence

---

48. *I. Delphin.* 139; the letter also in Welles (note 43). Crampa (note 33) discusses the circumstances in great detail with interesting suggestions and full bibliography.

49. E.g. by Crampa (note 33) and Welles (note 39).

50. It is possible that the beginning of a new list of stephanephores in *I. Delphin.* 139 in 259/8 reflects the liberation of the city by Antiochus II; or that act may come several years later.

51. *I. Delphin.*, p. 267, citing B. Haussoullier's defense of Euergetes' accuracy in *OGIS* 54 (*Études sur l'histoire de Milet et du Didymeion*, Paris, 1902, chapters 7 and 8).

52. M. Holleaux, *Rome, la Grèce et les monarchies hellénistiques au IIIe siècle*, Paris, 1921, p. 91, n. 1, summarizes in words still true today: "Milet, qu'on

for Miletos as a Ptolemaic ally, therefore, must for lack of other evidence be taken to be limited to 314/3 (or perhaps 294-288) and 279/8 to 260.

On the basis of unpublished material from his excavations at Klaros, Louis Robert has stated that Kolophon and its dependent territory were under Ptolemaic control in part of the third century: "Un décret intact du IIIe siècle avec un formulaire très banal, mais rendu en l'honneur d'un officier de Ptolémée (sans doute Evergète), ce qui atteste, contrairement à ce qu'on admettait, une occupation lagide à Colophon, comme à Lebedos, et à Ephèse, et aussi, à notre avis, à Téos." [53]

If Theocritus did not consider Ionia one of Philadelphos' possessions, it may be that he recognized the relatively independent status of Miletos as that of a free state and not a possession, or that alliance with even several other cities did not warrant description of Ionia as a possession. But it is still unclear what cities in Ionia were held by Philadelphos and what by Euergetes. The conquests of the latter may have included Ephesos, Kolophon, Lebedos, and Teos, as well as the recapture of Samos. Whether Priene belongs in his list or in Ptolemaic control at all is uncertain.

---

range volontiers, à la même époque, parmi les villes 'ptolémaiques' . . . semble, en réalité, avoir été indépendante . . . si les Lagides exercent sur elle quelque autorité, cette autorité n'est guère que nominale. La ville pourrait donc prendre place parmi les cités 'autonomes'."

53. This report may be found both in *Türk Arkeoloji Dergisi* 10, 1960, p. 59, and in *Annuaire du Collège de France* 60, 1960, pp. 328-329, in identical form; now in *Opera Minora Selecta* IV, pp. 183-184. Robert informs me that the inscription tells us nothing about this τεταγμένος except his existence.

CHAPTER EIGHT

COINAGE AND CIRCULATION

Every student of Ptolemaic Egypt knows that the Ptolemies coined silver money on a weight standard peculiar to the dynasty and considerably lighter than the Attic standard prevalent in much of the rest of the Greek world, including the Seleucid kingdom. The date of the adoption of this lighter standard has been much argued, but it probably came about 310 B.C. for silver, with gold of new weights coming perhaps at the time of Ptolemy Soter's assumption of the royal title in 305.[1] Under Philadelphos, if not before, it was policy to allow only Ptolemaic coinage to circulate in Egypt; all foreign money was to be handed over to the crown to be replaced with the coin of the kingdom. The gold and silver issues of the royal mints were supplemented by substantial issues of a probably fiduciary bronze currency, often of strikingly larger size than the small bronzes minted elsewhere in the Hellenistic world. As time went on, and silver for minting became harder for the Ptolemies to get, the bronze coinage became almost the sole coinage in common circulation in Egypt.[2] The value of these bronze coins relative to silver was reduced greatly over the years by a considerable inflation.

It has generally been assumed, explicitly or tacitly, that the entire Ptolemaic empire was included in the zone of monetary isolation produced by the peculiar standard and the later prevalence of bronze. Thus Rostovtzeff wrote thirty years ago:[3]

> Like Athens in the past, they endeavoured to make their own currency the exclusive currency for the whole of their vast empire,

1. For the dating of the early issues of Ptolemy I, I follow G. K. Jenkins, *ANS Mus. Notes* 9, 1960, pp. 17-37 and O. H. Zervos, *ANS Mus. Notes* 13, 1967, pp. 1-16, who give careful analyses of these series and particularly of die-links. They also take account of the overstrike evidence assembled by B. Emmons, *ANS Mus. Notes* 6, 1954, pp. 69-84. The implications of the standard for the main currents of Ptolemaic policy are discussed most recently by E. Will, *Histoire politique* I, pp. 155-158.

2. A good discussion of money within Egypt is given by Claire Préaux, *Économie royale*, pp. 267-280. The policy of prohibiting circulation of foreign coins is known from *P. Cair. Zen.* 59021.

3. *SEHHW*, p. 401.

in this respect differing from their neighbours the Seleucids. The first step which they took to achieve this aim was to force their own monetary system and their own coins on their foreign dominions. As a rule, the Greek cities under their control were not allowed to retain their own currency or, in the rare cases where this was permitted, they were obliged to convert it to the Phoenician standard.

But Rostovtzeff offered no evidence for this sweeping remark, and it indeed would seem that the complex problem of circulation of currency in the Ptolemaic empire has not been adequately treated in the light of excavations, hoards, and find-spot evidence.

It is no easy matter to remedy this lack, and I cannot pretend that the survey that I give here offers any final conclusions. I have given a survey of the empire in the same geographical order as in Chapters II-VII, synthesizing the situation in each part. For the question of minting in the empire the outlines have been clear since the publication of Svoronos' corpus of Ptolemaic coinage in the first decade of the century.[4] Some problems remain, largely those of Svoronos' more dubious attributions, particularly to minor Ptolemaic mints supposed to have existed in various parts of Asia Minor, Thrace, and Greece. I do not treat in detail the problems of the attribution of many bronze issues to Cyprus which do not seriously affect the general conclusions; their place of minting will in any case probably be determined during the next decade or two by the large-scale excavations in progress at Salamis, Kition, Paphos and other Cypriot sites.

Circulation has been a more difficult problem than minting. The pattern for Syria, Cyrene, and Cyprus has been more or less clear; elsewhere it is much less so. The evidence comes in several forms: (1) excavation of sites known to have been Ptolemaic possessions and full publication of the coins found—an all too rare phenomenon, for briefer notices or none tend to be the fate of excavation coins, which are rarely of precious metals and usually badly worn; (2) hoards of coins found in an area. Different areas have had varying productivity of hoards, but there are in aggregate large numbers known from all over the ancient world. Arguments from absence of a coin type from a hoard or hoards do not have the same force as absence from an excavated site, but in view of the

---

4. Svoronos, *Die Münzen*. As we shall see, his dates are not always to be trusted.

large number of hoards known, the argument from silence can be a powerful one in many instances. (3) Individual finds on a site which are reported in a publication. When these finds are made over a span of time and represent a large body of material, they may be of value almost comparable to that of excavation. (4) Collections formed in the area of an ancient site or region and containing a largely local variety of coin-types. These are of varying utility, because there is often limited information about the method and aims of a collector. A collection formed in a major city like Athens or Istanbul will have very little value for the question of what has been found locally. A smaller town may provide much better information. In this category I have relied primarily upon the records of the National Numismatic Collection in Athens for accessions of 1892-1924, which it may be well to describe in some detail.[5]

When J. N. Svoronos became director of the National Numismatic Museum of Athens at the age of 26, in 1889, the collection contained some 40,000 coins; no systematic records of the sources of these coins survive. Svoronos instituted in 1892 a system of recording each accession to the collection in a yearly volume, a system he maintained until his premature death in 1922. His method survived his death only two years. For a period of a few years just before the First World War, Svoronos published a list of these acquisitions in the *Journal international d'archéologie numismatique*; for the other years the records survive, unpublished, in Athens. In these volumes are recorded the receipt of some 180,000 coins in more or less detail.[6]

This prodigious total of coins came largely from gifts and bequests from Greeks living all over the Mediterranean, from Marseilles to Alexandria, for these were the years of the widest settlement of Greeks abroad since the ancient world. Many of the collections and smaller gifts were therefore formed in specific places in and out of Greece, which Svoronos duly recorded. Despite the international character of many of the cities in which the Greeks lived, such as Smyrna and Alexandria, their collections took on a local air. In the vast majority of cases, the collections were formed of bronzes found locally—in a broad sense—and not of the silver coinage that

---

5. I am indebted to Mando Caramessini-Oikonomidou, director of the collection, for her cordial help.
6. Cf. G. P. Oikonomos' remarks in *JIAN* 21, 1927, p. 11.

travels to international antiquities markets. In most cases we may take the collections as representative of what was available to the collector locally at reasonable prices.

One factor which cannot be readily assessed is the intent of the collectors, their preferences in coin buying. Some collections seem to be products of deliberate formation with the exclusion of all types save the chosen ones. But my reading of the catalogues of these collections persuades me that in general this was not the case; there was not a principle of exclusion, and coins from a wide variety of distant sources—wherever they may have been found—appear in collections of this type. What is crucial is the preponderance of coins; if 90 per cent of the coins in a collection come from the western and southern parts of Asia Minor, and the collector was a resident of Smyrna or Antalya, it is a fair supposition that his collection is both eclectic and local.

It is evident that in any individual case the absence or presence of a coin type may have many explanations. But if we have a number of collections from a given area, and all have markedly similar composition, it is only fair to conclude that these coins represent what is available in the region from which the bulk of the coins come.

Svoronos' accession books also contain a certain amount of excavation material lodged in the National Museum; use has been made of this information as well (which naturally pertains only to Greece proper). For the period from 1924 to the present, there are in most cases published reports of the principal acquisitions of the Collection, though only recently have these regained any systematic character.[7]

The information that I can offer here from all of these sources, for Greece and Asia Minor, cannot pretend to be final. Only a series of excavated and published sites in the areas in question will resolve the question with certainty and in detail. But the recent past and present do not encourage me to think that such information will be soon forthcoming, and it therefore seems to me worthwhile to give such information as I have gathered, in the hope that others will be spurred to contribute their knowledge also.

---

7. For long these reports appeared in the "Chronique" in *BCH*; in the last decade they are in *Arch. Delt.*

I. Syria

It does not appear that Ptolemy coined on any substantial scale in Syria during the years 301-286, before his acquisition of Tyre and Sidon from Demetrius at the end of that period. It seems, in fact, that the Jewish community of Palestine was allowed its own small coinage with the names of its magistrates.[8] It is with the reign of Ptolemy II that coinage in these territories becomes significant.

Five mints of the coast produced royal coinage of Ptolemy II. The most important of them was Tyre, from which came four series distinguished by Svoronos. The first of these, including gold, silver, and bronze, has among other issues a dated group with dates expressed by letters from Z on: Z, H, O, Π, and Σ appear. Calculated on the basis of a 283/2 accession of Philadelphos for the beginning of the series, these coins fall between 278/7 and 266/5.[9] A second dated series of silver tetradrachms gives dates of years 20-25 and 27-39, clearly now the regnal years of Philadelphos figured from 285/4 and expressed in normal Greek numerals, thus running from 266/5 to 247/6, the year of Ptolemy II's death.[10] Contemporary gold octadrachms of Arsinoe II are dated in years 34, 35, 38, and 39. It would appear, therefore, that a major shift occurred about 266/5, with the new dating of Philadelphos' reign taken into account. Bronze coinage after this time is not dated, but there are seven varieties in the later bronze coinage to attest its occurrence.

The other mints of the area issued similar series with their own mint symbols or letters and sometimes magistrate's monogram. They, too, sometimes had dates. For example, Sidon has a series of silver tetradrachms dated from years 25 to 39 and gold octa-

---

8. The sole example of this coin (found at Beth-Zur by O. R. Sellers, *The Citadel of Beth-Zur*, Philadelphia, 1933, p. 73) bears (according to Sellers' publication) the names Onias and Hezekiah, both elsewhere attested (the high-priest and a lesser high-priest) in literary sources. But subsequent study of the coin has shown Onias to be a misreading; certainty about the correct reading is not possible. Most recently, Sellers has proposed YHWD as the true form: *The 1957 Excavation at Beth-Zur* (Annual of the American Schools of Oriental Research 38, 1968), pp. 2-3, giving an account of the arguments of others.

9. Svoronos, *Die Münzen* II, pp. 94-97, nos. 626-649. On the dates of coins of Philadelphos, note 62 below. The dates are expressed not by ordinary numerals but by an A-Ω = 1-24 system.

10. Svoronos, *Die Münzen* II, pp. 98-102, nos. 650-700.

drachms in the last four years of the sequence.[11] Some bronzes may also belong to Sidon, but the attribution is uncertain.[12] Similar issues at Ptolemais are dated in years 25 and 29-38 (silver) and 35 (gold).[13] Joppa's silver is dated 25, 27, 29-39, its gold in year 23.[14] Both cities provided undated coins of various types as well, including bronzes.[15] Gaza followed a similar pattern.[16] Svoronos catalogued some other series of coins, mainly bronzes, that he thought belonged to cities of this region, without any specific and certain attribution being possible.

Ptolemy III, less rich in gold and silver than his father, issued far fewer coins from the mints of Syria and Phoenicia; what we have come from the first years of his reign. Tyre issued silver tetradrachms in years 2-5, Sidon in 1-6, Ptolemais in 2-5, Joppa in 2-6, and Gaza in year 2. In addition, all but Gaza produced Arsinoe II gold octadrachms at various points during the same six years, which coincide with heavy Ptolemaic activity in these areas during the Third Syrian War.[17] A group of bronzes, undated, was assigned to Syria and Phoenicia by Svoronos, with Ptolemais and Berytos fairly certain mints and others less so.[18]

Even fewer coins are attributed to the area under Ptolemy IV: silver and gold issues in small numbers come from Tyre, Sidon, Ptolemais, and Askalon.[19] His son, Ptolemy V, also issued silver tetradrachms in Tyre, Sidon, Ptolemais, and Berytos, during the few years that he possessed these provinces.[20] After him, only one enigmatic silver tetradrachm with the legend ΠΤΟΛΕΜΑΙΟΥ ΘΕΟΥ ΦΙΛΟΜΗΤΟΡΟΣ and the date ΛΓ (33) was issued in 𝕞, presumably Ptolemais; Svoronos dated it to 149/8, but the interpretation of this coin is problematical.[21]

11. Svoronos, *Die Münzen* II, pp. 105-111, nos. 712-757. The gold and silver series, mostly but not all dated, parallel the issues of Tyre.

12. Svoronos, *Die Münzen* II, pp. 111-112, nos. 758-762.

13. Svoronos, *Die Münzen* II, pp. 113-116, nos. 765-784.

14. Svoronos II, pp. 119-121, nos. 794-817.

15. Svoronos II, pp. 113-122, nos. 764, 785-793, 818-820.

16. Svoronos II, pp. 123-124, nos. 821-838.

17. Svoronos II, pp. 159 ff., nos. 1011-1045. The mints are the same and have much the same relative importance, as under Philadelphos.

18. Svoronos II, pp. 166-169, nos. 1046-1063.

19. Svoronos II, Taxis E; the coins bear the mark ΣΩ, monogram of Sosibios, minister of the king.

20. Svoronos II, pp. 213-215, nos. 1285-1301.

21. Svoronos II, nos. 1486-1488. Philometor's brief period of regained power in Phoenicia came in the last two years of his reign, and 149/8 may

The pattern of circulation of money in Syria and Phoenicia follows the Egyptian exclusivist direction; it was, indeed, probably on his knowledge of Syria that Rostovtzeff relied for his generalization, in the remark quoted at the beginning of this chapter. In general, for the Ptolemaic period we find Ptolemaic coins virtually exclusively in the third-century hoards and excavation finds, while even in the first half-century after the Seleucid conquest Ptolemaic coins continue to be found in hoards in the area formerly ruled by the Ptolemies.[22] Only a few examples need be cited in detail; for example, a hoard found in the excavation of Beth-Shan in Galilee yielded about twenty tetradrachms of Ptolemy II, from the mints of Tyre, Sidon, Ptolemais, and Joppa, with Tyre far outnumbering the other mints.[23] Another group deserving mention is the excavation coins from Samaria-Sebaste. Their publication rests in part on lists made at the excavation which did not record mints, so that indications can be only approximate.[24] It appears that Alexandria, Tyre, and Sidon were the principal sources of those which were later recorded, and that the other cities of Phoenicia may have been represented. For the third century, 92 Ptolemaic coins were found in all, against 2 Seleucid and little else. The homogeneous character of these finds is apparent.

The contrast to the situation north of the Eleutheros river, in Seleucid territory, is striking. Of some 62 hoards known from this region, only 3 have any Ptolemaic coins at all. Of these, two are

---

be a bit early for this activity. But another attribution does not seem possible.

22. In the *Inv. Coin Hoards*, all six hoards buried before 170 are Ptolemaic (1584-1589), while of 42 buried after 170, 5 have some Ptolemaic coins (1591, 1592, 1593, 1597, and 1601).

23. The date of burial must be at or near the end of Philadelphos' reign. The plate in G. M. FitzGerald, *Beth-Shan Excavations, 1921-1923*, Publ. of the Palestinian Section of the University Museum, Philadelphia, 1931, pl. xli, where only a brief description is given, is not clear enough to permit the identification of all the coins, but of the 20 illustrated, 6 are of Tyre (years 31, 35, 36, 37, and two unreadable years), 2 of Sidon (year 36 and one uncertain), 2 of Joppa (years 35 and 38) and 1 of Ptolemais (year 36). These come from the Πτολεμαίου Σωτῆρος series. Nine others, of Πτολεμαίου Βασιλέως types, are indistinctly pictured.

24. J. S. Kirkman, "The Evidence of Coins," in J. W. Crowfoot, G. M. Crowfoot, and K. M. Kenyon, *The Objects from Samaria (Samaria-Sebaste, Report . . . no. 3)*, 1957, pp. 43-70. Kirkman indicates that of the coins available to him most were minted in Alexandria or Tyre. The notes of his predecessors indicated only that Tyre and Sidon were known to them as mints of coins found.

from Seleukia-in-Pieria, a Ptolemaic base during the period when these hoards apparently were buried.[25] The third was buried in the early third century in the mainland area belonging to Arados.[26]

The coinage of Ptolemaic currency in Syria and Phoenicia provided the bulk of the needs of silver and gold in those provinces, and probably nearly all of the bronze, though our evidence for bronzes, which are rarely published thoroughly, is poorer. These mints also produced coins for the empire in general, just as those in Cyprus and Alexandria did. Neither precious metals nor bronze coinage from outside the Ptolemaic empire circulated inside Ptolemaic Syria, except by rare happenstance. Tyre and Sidon played a dominant role in providing currency for this part of the Ptolemaic kingdom; a less important part was filled by Ptolemais and Joppa. Beyond them was Askalon, which filled part of the needs of Palestine under Ptolemy IV, Gaza, long a small producer of money, and Berytos, from which issued bronze coinage. It is possible that some of the coins for which Svoronos could find no secure attribution will one day be assigned to another of the cities of the region, though the wide circulation of coins from different mints within the province makes it difficult for excavation finds to localize the mint with security.

2. CYRENE

The history of coinage in the Cyrenaica under the Ptolemies may be divided into three broad parts: the early Ptolemaic period, down to the revolt of Magas (322-ca. 280); the independent rule of Magas (ca. 280-250) and its aftermath; and the main period of restored Ptolemaic control (246-96).

When Ptolemy Soter assumed a dominant protectorate over Cyrene in 322, the city already had a long history of autonomous coinage during the fifth and fourth centuries. Ptolemy did not alter

25. *Inv. Coin Hoards*, 1526 and 1571. The first of these is a hoard found in excavations at Seleukia, containing coins of Ptolemies I, II, and III, with issues of Tyre, Sidon, Gaza, and Joppa: D. B. Waage, *Antioch-on-the-Orontes* IV, Princeton, 1952, pt. 2, p. 90. See the remarks of H. Seyrig, *Rev. num.* 6 ser. 1, 1958, p. 179, reviewing Waage's work. Seyrig consistently emphasized the importance of the Eleutheros river as a boundary; cf. *Rev. num.* 6 ser. 6, 1964, pp. 43-46.

26. *Inv. Coin Hoards* 1538; the date of burial is given as around 190, and the Ptolemaic coins are only part of the ensemble. This find does not affect the validity of the conclusions of H. Seyrig on the status of Arados (cf. n. 25).

this situation: an autonomous coinage in gold and silver continued in the first eight years of Ptolemaic alliance, with the mint magistrates Chairis and Polianthes represented.[27] The next few years were of critical importance, though we can understand their significance only partially. Two more magistrates, Pheidon and Theupheides, appear on autonomous gold coinage.[28] One of Theupheides' issues bears the legend ΚΥΡΑΝΑΙΟΝ ΠΤΟΛΕΜΑΙΩ; this coin, with its use of the Athena Alkidemos, is taken to be approximately contemporary with an issue of ΑΛΕΞΑΝΔΡΕΙΟΝ ΠΤΟΛΕΜΑΙΟΥ, dated to about 314-313.[29]

The Ptolemaic issue in Cyrene [30] was not the first royal coinage for which Ptolemy was responsible in that city. An Attic gold stater and half-stater of Alexander types are known, bearing both the device of the silphium plant (the symbol of Cyrene) and the Ptolemaic eagle. They are to be dated ca. 321-311, during the years in which Ptolemy was issuing Alexander gold coinage in Egypt.[31]

From a period following this, perhaps about the time of Ophellas' Carthaginian adventure, we have both gold and silver for the magistrate Polianthes (II) and Pheidon. They were also responsible for an issue with ΔΑΜΩ ΚΥΡΑΝΑΙΟΝ, seen sometimes as a retort to Ptolemy's ΚΥΡΑΝΑΙΟΝ ΠΤΟΛΕΜΑΙΩ of a few years before.[32]

After this series the situation becomes harder to assess and emissions almost impossible to date. Naville, working with the gold coinage, outlines five further periods of Cyrenaean civic gold

27. L. Naville, *Monnaies d'or de la Cyrénaïque de 450 à 250 av. J.C.*, Genève, 1951, pp. 40-53. Cf. E. S. G. Robinson, *BMC Cyrenaica*, pp. 29-30, 32, 33, 39-40.

28. Naville (n. 27), p. 56. On the date of the chronological groups I am not always in accord, but the groups themselves I accept.

29. Naville (note 27), p. 54. On the date of the ΑΛΕΞΑΝΔΡΕΙΟΝ ΠΤΟΛΕΜΑΙΟΥ issues (in which I take ΑΛΕΞΑΝΔΡΕΙΟΝ to mean a coin of the type of Alexander rather than a coin struck in Alexandria) see O. H. Zervos, *ANS Mus. Notes* 13, 1967, pp. 1-16. P. M. Fraser, *Ptol. Alex.* II, pp. 10-11, n. 26, follows the view that 'Αλεξανδρεῖον refers to the city, but admits the difficulties of that view and offers no plausible arguments for it; his bibliography of the question is very full.

30. I take ΚΥΡΑΝΑΙΟΝ to mean "Cyrenaean coin" (as in ΑΛΕΞΑΝΔΡΕΙΟΝ, "coin of Alexander") rather than the old genitive with *omicron* of ΚΥΡΑΝΑΙΟΙ.

31. Svoronos II, nos. 59-60; on the date of the comparable gold coinage in Alexandria, cf. the studies of Zervos and Jenkins (note 1, above).

32. *BMC Cyrenaica*, p. lxiv, no. 173b; Naville (note 27), p. 56. (I take Κυραναῖον [nominative neuter singular] δάμω [= δήμου, gen.] to mean 'Cyrenaean coin of the *demos*').

coinage,[33] now on the "Phoenician" standard for the most part, and thus later than 305.[34] The civic silver that accompanies these issues is mostly on the Rhodian standard, and is of a great variety and abundance.[35] Its date is uncertain; many of the mint magistrates whose monograms appear on the civic coinage also appear on apparently contemporary royal issues, but their dating, too, is uncertain.[36]

The period of the revolt of Magas is directly linked to the preceding one. Magas coined no coins in his own name, as is well-known, and it is possible that he tried to emphasize the legitimacy of his regime by continuing to produce coins of the type of his step-father Ptolemy Soter.[37] Robinson suggests that silver didrachms of Soter on the Phoenician standard and similar didrachms with the legend ΒΑΣΙΛΙΣΣΗΣ ΒΕΡΕΝΙΚΗΣ and the monogram $\mathcal{M}$, plus a related bronze issue, are issues of Magas after his revolt. The emphasis on his mother Berenike, the source of his position with his step-father, is understandable in this context. I do not share Naville's reluctance to see in these issues the monetary activity of Magas as independent king in the Cyrenaica.[38] To what extent civic issues continued with his must remain at present uncertain.

After the death of Magas a period of political confusion ensued for several years. A *koinon* of the Cyrenaica appears to have flourished briefly, and it issued a silver didrachm of Rhodian standard together with a series of bronzes. The only legend on these coins is KOINON except for one bearing a moneyer's monogram.[39] The issues of the Cyrenaic *koinon* are the last autonomous coins of Cyrene. For 75 years of rule by various members of the Ptolemaic dynasty it had maintained its civic coinage together

---

33. Naville (note 27), pp. 61-88. The magistrates' names are from this time on given on the coins only in abbreviated form.

34. I follow here the chronology of Zervos and Jenkins (note 1).

35. *BMC Cyrenaica*, pp. xcviii ff.

36. Robinson (note 34) thought the silver went down only to 277. G. Le Rider, *Monnaies Crétoises* (note 97, below), pp. 43-48, thinks the latest series goes down to 250.

37. *BMC Cyrenaica*, pp. cxlii-clvi.

38. Naville (note 27), pp. 83-84, is at a loss to explain $\mathcal{M}$, which must be resolved Μάγ(ας) or even Μάγας, and makes the improbable suggestion that he was a Cyrenaean magistrate. Robinson's arguments (pp. cxlvii ff.) on the subject seem to me sound.

39. *BMC Cyrenaica*, pp. cxxxiv-cxxxvii and 68-71.

with the royal coinage, a privilege notably lacking in Cyprus after the final Ptolemaic conquest and likewise missing in Syria and Phoenicia. With the coinage went a turbulent history of civic activism in political relations with the crown and repeated attempts to escape the power of Alexandria. It may be that Ptolemy III hoped to suppress the latter tendency together with the local coinage.

But the cessation of Cyrenaean local coinage was not compensated by major royal minting activity in Cyrene. Svoronos attributes no coins of Ptolemy III to Cyrene, and subsequent studies have not changed the situation. For Ptolemy IV, Svoronos assigned an issue of gold octadrachms and four series of bronzes to Cyrene, but only one bronze issue out of these bears the silphium plant and is thus certainly a product of the mint of Cyrene.[40] For the next reign, Svoronos assigned a group of gold, silver, and bronze issues to Cyrene on the basis of the technique of the coins.[41] Though not all of these issues are attributed with certainty, it is likely that at least some of them do belong to the mint of Cyrene.

It is not surprising that the reign of Ptolemy VI Philometor is not represented numismatically at Cyrene, for he never had effective control of that city. It is less certain whether Ptolemy VIII Euergetes II minted coins in Cyrene during the years when he ruled only the Cyrenaica, 163-145. A bronze series of his reign with the silphium plant emblem was placed by Svoronos after 145, when Euergetes had reunited the entire kingdom (Egypt, Cyprus, Cyrenaica) under his control; but K. Regling suggested that they could as well belong to the years 163-145.[42] They are in any case the only certain Cyrenaean issues of the reign of Ptolemy VIII.

One last bronze issue, bearing the head of Libya, is attributed to Cyrene by Svoronos; the king, he thought, was Ptolemy IX Soter II,[43] but he felt considerable misgivings about their date. Regling, too, thought the date entirely uncertain.[44] It would not be improbable that Ptolemy IX issued the coins, for he controlled the Cyrenaica for quite some time, but we must await further evidence.

---

40. Svoronos II, nos. 1039-1058; discussion, IV, col. 214. The head of "Libya" on the other bronzes makes them likely to be Cyrenaean issues. Silphium is on no. 1058.
41. Svoronos II, nos. 1254-1268; IV, cols. 264-266.
42. Svoronos II, nos. 1657-1658; IV, col. 319. K. Regling in IV, col. 498.
43. Svoronos II, no. 1725; IV, col. 337.
44. In Svoronos IV, col. 504.

It appears, then, that aside from occasional issues of small and large bronzes, the mint of Cyrene was not active after the end of civic coinage about 246. There was never any large-scale coinage there as elsewhere in the key Ptolemaic provinces. The coinage in circulation nonetheless appears to have been as exclusively Ptolemaic as in Syria and Phoenicia, except for the autonomous coins still in circulation. Little has been published of the coins found in the extensive Italian excavations at Cyrene or in the other cities of the Cyrenaica, but a small sampling from the British excavations at Cyrene showed several Ptolemaic bronzes, some earlier Cyrenaean coins, and no Hellenistic coins from elsewhere. The situation was therefore probably comparable to that in Syria and Cyprus.[45]

3. Cyprus

The detailed history of the coinage of the kingdoms of Cyprus before the coming of Alexander to the Levant cannot yet be written. It is known that certain important kings coined, but a host of other attributions remain uncertain, capable of being pushed like pawns from one city to another on the basis of a new attribution anywhere among them.[46] For the time of Alexander we can with confidence associate a coinage with the following kings: Nikokles of Paphos, Pasikrates and Eunostos of Soloi, Stasioikos II of Marion, Praxippos of Lapethos, Pumiathon of Kition, and Nikokreon of Salamis. In the case of Praxippos, only a bronze is known, which is undatable within the period.[47] Eunostos of Soloi also has but one coin attributed to him.[48] Stasioikos of Marion, on the other hand, had a very extensive coinage in gold, silver, and bronze, evidently terminated only by his deposition and the destruction of Marion by Ptolemy in 312.[49]

Pumiathon's coinage is dated as late as a forty-seventh year; he, too, was executed in 312. There is apparently a blank in his coinage from the years between ca. 333 and 323, probably the result

---

45. J. Healy in Alan Rowe, *Cyrenaean Expeditions 1955-7*, Manchester, 1959, pp. 29-32. *Inv. Coin Hoards* 1686, from Tripolis, is the only Hellenistic hoard from the area, and it is all Cyrenaean coins.

46. For example, see the article of A. J. Seltman, *Numismatic Chronicle* 7 ser. 4, 1964, pp. 75-82.

47. *BMC Cyprus*, pp. liii-lv.

48. *BMC Cyprus*, pp. cxiv-cxviii.

49. *BMC Cyprus*, pp. lv-lxii, 33-34.

of the disfavor with Alexander into which Pumiathon is said to have fallen.[50] Nikokles of Paphos, on the other hand, seems to be known only by a gold stater of Attic standard in Turin; a similar one in Florence is declared by G. F. Hill and others to be a forgery.[51]

Nikokreon of Salamis was responsible for three issues in gold and silver bearing the legends BA NI and BA $\neq$. No precise dating is possible for these.[52] After his death, Menelaos, brother of Ptolemy, continued to mint very similar coins with $\neq$ MEN, $\neq$ being the first syllable in Cypriot script of βασιλεύς. The issues can be placed with confidence in the years 310-306. This royal coinage is the only one to continue—to our knowledge—after the period 312-310, during which Ptolemy eliminated the kings of Cyprus, subordinating their cities first to Salamis, and then, on the death of Nikokreon, more directly to himself through his brother. But he had Menelaos retain the royal coinage of Salamis in his own name, and to Cypriots Menelaos legally may well have been as much king of Salamis in place of Nikokreon as a deputy of Ptolemy.

Ptolemy, like Alexander, permitted—perhaps even encouraged—the local coinages of the kings so long as they existed. But the petty royal issues appear to have been only by-products of the mints on the island, which were engaged primarily in producing standard Alexander-type currency. This fact was first demonstrated in 1915 by E. T. Newell, who showed that certain series of Alexander issues were to be attributed to Cyprus. Salamis was most prominent in this respect, having three series of Attic-weight tetradrachms of Alexander; Newell dated these series to (I) 332-320, (II) 320-317, and (III) 316-306. The third group indeed bears a $\maltese$ or NK mark on certain issues, but other magistrates' initials are also found in the same series, so it is perhaps wiser not to place too much emphasis on these two monograms.[53] Newell also distinguished a series of bronzes that probably accompanied series III of Salamis.[54] All

---

50. *BMC Cyprus*, pp. xxix-xliii.
51. *BMC Cyprus*, pp. lxxix-lxxx; pl. XXII, 10.
52. *BMC Cyprus*, pp. cxiii, 64.
53. E. T. Newell, *Numismatic Chronicle* 1915, pp. 306-316.
54. D. H. Cox, *Coins from Curium* (*Numismatic Notes and Monographs* 145), 1959, p. 92, took these bronzes with a shield device to be coinage of Demetrius, on the grounds that similar types were probably minted elsewhere in Asia (Tarsos, Sardis, Seleukia in Pieria, Priene) and Europe (Olynthos); cf. her remarks in H. Goldman, *Excavations at Gözlü Kule, Tarsus* I,

of this came to an end in 306, when Demetrius Poliorcetes conquered Cyprus from Ptolemy, but Demetrius himself coined in
Salamis—apparently his only mint in Cyprus—from which an
abundant and varied coinage was issued.[55]

Newell also identified two series of Alexander coins issued at
Paphos, both before 320; none were attributed to a later period.[56]
A further Alexander series, Cypriot but probably not Paphian, was
placed by Newell at Marion, albeit somewhat doubtfully.[57] The
Alexander issues thus form a second major part of the output of
Cypriot mints in the years 323-306, indeed probably the major
part of all coinage in precious metals.

There is a third element to Cypriot coinage in the first Ptolemaic
period, a series of bronze coins with the legend ΠΤΟΛΕΜΑΙΟΥ,
attributed to Cyprus by Svoronos and others.[58] Their attribution
to the island is universally accepted. It is uncertain which mint was
responsible for them; Svoronos did not determine this aspect.
D. H. Cox, commenting on the finding of a substantial number of
this issue at Kourion, suggested Paphos as more likely than Salamis,
but there is little evidence.[59] It is in any case certain that Menelaos
minted not only his own small coinage in precious metals at Salamis
but also a bronze coinage in the name of his brother and sovereign.

The coinage in Cyprus under Ptolemy Soter before 306 can
hardly be called a system. Ptolemy maintained the systems al-

Princeton, 1950, pp. 41-42. She cites E. T. Newell, *Coinage of Demetrius
Poliorcetes*, London, 1927, to support her position. But Newell (pp. 18-19)
is quite specific about the attribution to Ptolemy and the years 316-306.
Cox is thus driven to assert that Antigonus controlled the mint of Salamis
during these years, an unhistorical and impossible fantasy. It is perhaps
unwise to place too much reliance on stylistic resemblances during the period
before 305, when a considerable similarity of styles prevailed over the
successor kingdoms.

55. E. T. Newell (cited note 54), pp. 19-43, gives the series in detail;
p. 29 on the absence of issues from other Cypriot mints. It is interesting
that some of Demetrius' earlier series are almost continuous with the later
Ptolemaic ones, an exact line being hard to draw. Some mint officials appear
on both Ptolemaic and Antigonid coinage of Salamis, in fact. This similarity
underlines my argument (note 54) about difficulties of using stylistic criteria
to separate issues of Ptolemy and Demetrius.

56. *Numismatic Chronicle* 1915, pp. 316-320.

57. Newell (note 56), pp. 320-321.

58. Svoronos II, nos. 74-82; R. S. Poole, *BMC Ptolemies*, p. 7.

59. Kourion yielded 21 examples of Svoronos' types 74, 76, 78, and 80;
see D. H. Cox (note 54), nos. 31-35a. For the attribution to Paphos, Cox,
pp. 94-95.

ready in existence, even having Menelaos fit himself into the Salaminian royal line. He added his own bronze coinage to the pre-existing situation. All of this falls in the period when Ptolemy did not yet call himself king, when there was no Ptolemaic coinage or Ptolemaic monetary system as such to impose on the island.

After the resumption of Ptolemaic control over Cyprus in 294, there was probably a revival of royal minting at least of bronze currency, but only the publication of large-scale excavation finds will enable us to say which issues belong to Cyprus; one emission assigned by D. H. Cox to Paphos on the basis of an $\mathbb{A}$ monogram and finds at Kourion has recently been shown by G. Le Rider to share other monograms with coins that Miss Cox assigned to Alexandria.[60] The case is therefore still open.

It appears certain, however, that Ptolemy II minted gold, silver, and bronze in Cyprus, in several series with letter-dates from A to Y (1 to 20) though the series are by no means continuous.[61] The series ends with year 20, which must be year 20 of the reign of Philadelphos (old reckoning), or 264/3. The reason for its end is uncertain, but the fantasies of Svoronos and Cox about a capture of the island by Antigonus Gonatas have no basis in reality.[62]

For the reign of Ptolemy III, little can be cited but *Taxis* E in Svoronos, a series of six bronze issues presumed to have been issued in Cyprus: they bear the head of Ammon on the obverse, a statue of Aphrodite on the reverse, suggesting perhaps the

---

60. G. Le Rider, *Rev. num.* 6 ser. 11, 1969, pp. 28 ff.

61. Svoronos II, *Taxis* Z, series A-Γ (pp. 81-93, nos. 547-625). Their attribution to Cyprus has most recently been maintained by G. Le Rider (note 60).

62. Numismatists have traditionally preferred to reckon this series and Philadelphos' accession from 285/4, the beginning of his co-regency with his father; so Le Rider as late as 1969 (note 60). But Philadelphos in fact began his count of regnal years with 283/2, at his father's death, as has been established by A. E. Samuel, *Ptolemaic Chronology*, 1962, pp. 26-30 and P. W. Pestman, *Chronologie égyptienne d'après les documents démotiques*, Leiden, 1965, pp. 18 ff. Philadelphos retroactively began his reckoning with 285/4, two years before he became sole ruler, but this practice dates only to his seventeenth year, 267/6, which thus became his nineteenth. The coin series appears not to have been affected by this shift, for it recorded not so much regnal years as years since the start of the series, and continued to be numbered consecutively. Thus, while no documents with dates in years 17 and 18 are to be expected, in Svoronos *Taxis* Z, B (2), bronzes of type A were issued in a year P (17) as well as T and Y (19 and 20). On the theory of Antigonus Gonatas' capture of Cyprus, see Le Rider's convincing rebuttal (note 60, above).

sanctuary of Aphrodite at Paphos. For Ptolemy IV, not much more is certain. Svoronos assigned his *Taxis* Δ, bronzes, to a Cypriot mint. It should be pointed out that for the reigns of Ptolemy II, III, and IV the coinage of the Phoenician coastal mints is pre-eminent, while Cyprus plays a minor role.[63]

But Coele-Syria and Phoenicia were lost to the Ptolemies shortly after the death of Ptolemy IV, and it is from about this time that the great series of dated Cypriot coinage begins. Mint initials for ΚΙ(τιον), ΣΑ(λαμις), and ΠΑ(φος) appear on gold, silver, and bronze issues. The series are not continuous in time, and the mints' issues come in part in the same years, in part in different ones. Gold octadrachms were minted in Paphos under Epiphanes (according to Svoronos' catalogue) in five years, in Salamis twice, in Kition only once, all in different years. The aggregate silver series coined in the island, on the other hand, cover years 15 to 24 of Epiphanes' reign.[64] Dated bronzes, on the contrary, were issued only by Paphos and only in the fifteenth year. Svoronos suggested a fourth mint, at Amathous, on the basis of coins of years 1 and 2 with monograms that could represent that city's name, but in the absence of evidence for any other issues from such a mint, it is perhaps best to reserve judgment.[65] From Svoronos' lists it would seem that Paphos was more active in issuing gold and bronze than the other mints, but that both Kition and Salamis exceeded it in production of silver issues.

The dynastic chaos of the first fifteen years of the reign of Ptolemy VI makes the attribution of Cypriot coins of the first part

63. For Ptolemy IV, Svoronos also assigns his nos. 1189-1193 to Cyprus, with much hesitation and almost certainly incorrectly; R. Hazzard points out that the provenance of these coins is almost without exception Palestinian, citing G. K. Jenkins in *Proc. Int. Num. Congr. (Jerusalem)* 1967, p. 74, and unpublished hoards known to Hazzard. *Taxis* Δ (nos. 1160-1162) is assigned on the basis of vague indications of provenance rather than any mint symbols.

64. These figures are based on E. T. Newell's revision (*Standard Ptolemaic Silver*, New York, 1941) of Svoronos' catalogue of the issues of Paphos in *Die Münzen* II, nos. 1306-1322; of Salamis, 1323-1348; of Kition, 1349-1371. Svoronos also notes (nos. 1302-1305) silver tetradrachms with the letters ΠΟ, which he takes to be the beginning of the name of Polykrates, strategos of Cyprus ca. 203-197. Of these Newell accepts only nos. 1302-1305, 1339, 1340, 1342-1348, 1362-1371. Cf. now *Studii Clasice* 11, 1969, pp. 211-224 for a new issue.

65. Svoronos II, nos. 1372-1373. The monograms are Ⱥ and ℳ. Newell attributes these coins to Philometor.

of the reign difficult. It is uncertain, for example, whether one series with dates of years 2, 6, and 7 is to be taken as referring to the beginning of Philometor's reign in 180 or to the joint reign with Cleopatra II and Ptolemy Euergetes II from 170.[66] Whatever the case, it seems that Philometor was able to issue coins with his own regnal years in Cyprus from year 19 (163/2) to the end of his reign, with an almost continuous series of tetradrachms known from each of the three mints of Paphos, Salamis, and Kition.[67]

The main series of silver tetradrachms continued at all three mints under Ptolemy VIII, with dates of years 26 to 54, or 145/4 to 117/6; the series is without gaps at Kition only, though mere accident of preservation may account for this fact.[68] A bronze series with dates from years 26 to 41, but without a characteristic mint abbreviation, was assigned by Svoronos to Cyprus.[69]

With the death of Ptolemy VIII, dynastic strife broke out again. It is certain that ΠΑ on a coin can no longer at this time be taken to be a certain indication of Cypriot minting. Coins of Ptolemy X Alexander and his mother have double dates from 11/8 to 16/13, that is, from 107/6 to 102/1; they all bear the letters ΠΑ.[70] But Ptolemy IX Soter II controlled Cyprus from 106/5 on, and would not have minted money for his enemies. In view of this uncertainty it is hard to make any attributions. It seems that the mints of Kition and Salamis continued to produce in the first decade of the reign, under Ptolemy Alexander, but then were by and large shut down. Money ostensibly Paphian was minted in both Alexandria

66. Svoronos II, nos. 1388-1391 from Paphos, bear dates of years 6 and 7; nos. 1392-1393, Salamis, years 2 and 6. On a reckoning of Philometor's sole reign, year 2 would be 180/179, in his minority, and years 6 and 7, 176/5 and 175/4, immediately after his mother's death in 176. This dating is perhaps the more likely. A later date would yield 169/8, 165/4, and 164/3, which appear to me less likely, as we have dates of 13 (Salamis) and 14 (Kition) on tetradrachms certainly struck under Philometor alone, i.e. in 169/8, and 168/7 (Svoronos' nos. 1452 and 1470). These latter issues create a problem, however, coming as they do when the joint reign was in its early years and ought to have been observed. Place must also be found for the gold tetradrachms on the Attic standard issued by Antiochus IV at Salamis, perhaps in 168. The situation is therefore far from clear at present.

67. Again according to Newell, Svoronos II, nos. 1309-1314, 1317, 1318, 1322, 1324, 1326, 1327, 1329-1338, 1349-1351, etc. This period 163/2-146/5, corresponds exactly with the known limits of Philometor's effective sole reign in Egypt and Cyprus.

68. Svoronos II, nos. 1501-1620, with exceptions noted by Newell.

69. Svoronos II, nos. 1621-1632.

70. Svoronos II, nos. 1727-1731, assigned by Newell to Alexandria.

and Paphos, in all probability. Paphos seems to have continued to be Soter's mint during his island reign and even after his return to Egypt in 88.[71]

The cities of Cyprus were thus the major mints of the Ptolemaic kingdom from 200 to 80 B.C., as well as lesser centers of coinage in the nine decades preceding. As one might expect from this fact, the monetary circulation in Cyprus under the Ptolemies consisted largely of Ptolemaic currency. For example, the excavations at Kourion produced 290 Ptolemaic coins, but only about 17 Hellenistic coins from other sources.[72] There is little published hoard evidence from Hellenistic Cyprus, but one hoard contained bronzes of years 26 to 33 of Ptolemy VIII.[73] More recently, a very large hoard of 2484 uncirculated silver tetradrachms from the reigns of (probably) Ptolemies VI through X was excavated by K. Nicolaou at New Paphos; all three mints on the island are represented.[74] Though the published evidence for circulation is not extensive, the pattern is clear, and it is to be expected that publication of the coins from excavations now in progress on the island will confirm it.

It is worth pausing at this point to disengage the common characteristics of these three provinces, Syria, Cyrene, and Cyprus, mostly shared by them with Egypt. In each case coinage of various sorts was under way at the time of the beginning of Ptolemaic control, whether regal—Alexander or local rulers—or civic. In the initial phase, covering various parts of the reign of Ptolemy I, these diverse coinages were allowed, perhaps even encouraged, to continue, as a Ptolemaic coinage was developed side by side with the local. The date of the elimination of non-Ptolemaic coinage varies according to local circumstances. In Syria and Egypt, Ptolemy dropped the Alexander coinage when he came to have

---

71. A new study of the coinage of the period 116-80 is needed. I can in the absence of such a study refer only to the catalogue of Svoronos II, nos. 1659-1784; his explanations, IV, cols. 327-329; K. Regling's critical remarks in IV, cols. 501-502; and Newell's study cited above. Regling expresses a suspicion that some of these IIA issues might belong to Ptolemy XII Auletes, who did not rule Cyprus but used that mint mark.

72. D. H. Cox (see note 54).

73. *Inv. Coin Hoards* 1473-1477 are the only Ptolemaic ones from the island, and they are homogeneously Ptolemaic. No. 1476 is the hoard of bronzes of Ptolemy VIII.

74. Brief notice by K. Nicolaou in V. Karageorghis, *BCH* 89, 1965, pp. 292-293.

enough confidence and power; in Cyprus, Alexander issues and local issues continued until the gradual extinction of the Cypriot monarchies and were even preserved in form at Salamis by Ptolemy's brother until the loss of the island to Demetrius in 306. Cyrenaean municipal coinage enjoyed its existence right through the reign of Magas, thanks no doubt to that king's lack of a sufficient base of independent power to suppress it. When the crown in Alexandria once again got control of Cyrene, the coinage came to an end, never to be revived under the Ptolemies. Thus, while royal policy was flexible, it looked for opportunities to impose the uniformity of royal coinage.

The currency which replaced the local issues in the provinces was to a considerable extent locally coined by the royal mints. Ptolemaic coins found in each area tend to have been minted there. But this rule is no more than a tendency, for Ptolemaic currency circulated freely within these provinces, particularly the gold and silver; but even bronze seems to have had relatively wide circulation. Future excavations will help to make this picture more precise.[75]

However widely different issues of Ptolemaic coinage circulated, however, other currencies did not do the same. For these areas, finds of coins minted outside the kingdom are extremely rare. There are no hoards in Ptolemaic Egypt, Cyprus, Cyrene, or Syria, of gold, silver, or bronze coins of other monarchies or of independent cities, nor do excavations reveal any but scattered traces of outside coinage. These four territories formed a unified and isolated currency zone, within which the local currency circulated freely, but which did not import foreign money at all nor, in general, export its own. When we leave these territories the situation changes completely.

4. South Asia Minor

There is no evidence of any Ptolemaic minting activity in this area of the empire. It is true that Svoronos, cataloguing coins which he could not assign to any mint with confidence, suggested

---

75. For example, a hoard of Ptolemaic bronze coins recently found in Nubia included seven Ptolemy II coins generally agreed to have been minted in Cyprus: G. Le Rider, *Rev. num.* 6 ser. 11, 1969, p. 32, accepts the Cypriot provenance of these, though he challenges D. H. Cox's thesis that an earlier issue also belongs there.

that a silver tetradrachm with the monogram ⊠ might belong to Patara in Lycia, but he himself admitted that this guess rested on no evidence, and that the monogram might just as well represent a magistrate's name.[76] In the absence of other evidence we will be safe in assuming that no royal mints operated in the south coast of Asia Minor under the Ptolemies.

Autonomous coinage poses more complicated problems. In Samos the situation can be described in some detail, thanks to J. P. Barron's recent study of the silver coinage of the city.[77] Barron showed that a period of very active coinage ca. 310-300 was followed by a period of no coinage. In the time of Ptolemy II (Barron places the issues in 270-259), there is renewed minting, with three main issues. These are, in turn, separated by a gap from a fourth series, which Barron places after the renewal of Ptolemaic control in 246.[78] All of these issues are minted on "a slight reduction of the old Lydo-Milesian standard," in octobols and tetrobols. A hiatus in the later third century was followed by minting of Alexander type tetradrachms on the Attic standard, of whose date Barron is unsure, placing them either late under Ptolemaic rule or just after Samos was freed from it.[79] In short, Samos enjoyed the privilege of autonomous silver currency, though it may not have had the resources to take advantage of it more than occasionally. As to the standard on which the coins are struck, Barron, while seeing the coins as local change for Ptolemaic tetradrachms, evidently means this in a sense other than weight-standard, for he writes, "under the Ptolemies, Samos reverted to their favoured Lydo-Milesian standard." [80] In the thicket of coinciding and overlapping weight systems, it is best not to insist further on Ptolemaic influence on the choice of weight.

In Caria, of cities that came under Ptolemaic control, Mylasa, Myndos, Amyzon and (the future) Stratonikeia had no autonomous

---

76. Svoronos II, no. 910; IV, col. 138, he admits the possibility of a magistrate's mark, a more plausible solution for this and other marks for which he offers resolutions as mints.

77. J. P. Barron, *The Silver Coins of Samos*, London, 1966.

78. Barron (note 77), pp. 122-123; 141-145.

79. Barron (note 77), pp. 146-154. Barron suggests (p. 153) that the Rhodian Alexanders, closest in style to the Samian, appear exclusively in hoards of the period 200-190, and he takes this to support a 210-197 range as more likely than a 197-185 one.

80. Barron (note 78), p. 11.

issues until the second century B.C., and Iasos apparently did not begin until the mid-third century, perhaps after the end of Ptolemaic sovereignty.[81] Halikarnassos, a plentiful issuer of earlier coinage, is represented only by rare bronze coins, but it was hardly more prolific in the second century after the end of Ptolemaic control.[82] Knidos, for long inactive after a great archaic coinage, minted again in the third century on the Rhodian standard, including tetradrachms, drachms, hemidrachms, and tetrobols; its bronzes were also very extensive.[83] Kaunos, while never a prolific coiner, produced silver hemidrachms (on the Rhodian standard) and bronzes under Ptolemaic administration; it retained the same standard in the second century.[84] In the islands, both Kos and Kalymna coined autonomously in silver and bronze; indeed, this century was that of Kalymna's best and last coinage.[85]

For the coastal towns of Cilicia held by the Ptolemies as fortresses, we know of no autonomous coinage either preceding Ptolemaic control or contemporary with it. There can therefore be no question of any Ptolemaic effect on the local currency. In Pamphylia, the question is less straightforward. Aspendos coined silver fairly extensively before the Ptolemies came, from the fifth century to the third. But the dating of these issues is not sufficiently specific to establish a terminal date nor a relationship between Ptolemaic control and this event.[86] Side also had extensive early issues, but these seem to have ended in the fourth century and no resumption of silver coinage took place in the third century, though some bronzes are rather vaguely assigned to that century.[87]

81. Amyzon issued few coins before the Roman period; see a rare example in *SNG Von Aulock, Karien*, no. 2416. On Iasos, *BMC Caria*, pp. 124-126; it used the Persic standard in third century silver and also issued bronzes. On Mylasa see Aşkidil Akarca, *Les Monnaies grecques de Mylasa*, Paris, 1959.

82. *SNG Von Aulock, Karien*, pl. 8.

83. *BMC Caria*, pp. 1, 90-94; *SNG von Aulock, Karien*, pl. 6.

84. *BMC Caria*, p. 75; *SNG von Aulock, Karien*, pl. 6.

85. Svoronos II, nos. 16-17, assigned some satrapal coins of Ptolemy I to Kos on grounds of the use of a club as symbol, but K. Regling (in IV, col. 459) rightly found the decision "unglaubwürdig." A silver series of the early Hellenistic period issued by Kos was taken by Svoronos to represent Berenike I, and he catalogued them as nos. 83-90, but his suggestion has not been accepted (e.g. by *SNG von Aulock* and *SNG Copenhagen*). Kalymna issued Rhodian didrachms, drachmas, and hemidrachms as well as bronzes.

86. *BMC Pamphylia*, pp. 93-101; *SNG von Aulock, Pamphylia*, 4477-4578.

87. On Side's silver issues, see H. Seyrig, *Rev. num.* 6 ser. 5, 1963, pp. 57-64. For bronzes, *SNG Copenhagen Pamphylia*, 368-378. The bronzes, 379-389. Some bronzes are also assigned to this century at Sillyon.

More specific information about the monetary history of Pamphylia has been disengaged by Henri Seyrig in a recent study. Seyrig identifies four series of autonomous silver tetradrachms, three identified by mint initials (Phaselis, Sillyon, and Aspendos) and one without mark but suggested by Seyrig to be Perge.[88] These coins are dated by an unspecified era; issues of Phaselis and Perge run from years 1 to 33, Aspendos 1 to 31, and Sillyon 3 to 11. Seyrig takes it that these contemporary issues all refer to the same era, which must refer to the independence of these cities. Two lines of evidence lead to a conclusion: only in the period 221-188 can there be found a period of 33 years of autonomy; and the tetradrachms are found in hoards of Asia Minor together with pseudo-Alexanders of that period. Year 1, then, would have been 221/0.[89]

An era beginning in 221 can only refer to the end of Ptolemaic rule, which Seyrig therefore places in the immediate aftermath of the death of Ptolemy III in late 222. The assumption of independence was thus commemorated by the issue of tetradrachms and the dating of an era. It is hard not to conclude that the striking of tetradrachms had been forbidden to these cities by Ptolemy III. Seyrig proceeds from this base to consider another series of autonomous silver of Perge, bearing dates 1-13 on Attic-weight tetradrachms. Once again a period of freedom from Ptolemaic control is suggested: from the loss of Pamphylia in the Second Syrian War, perhaps somewhat before 253, to its recovery in the Third Syrian War; the outline of events depends on Theocritus, who claims Pamphylia as a possession of Philadelphos and on the Adoulis inscription, in which Euergetes considers the area his own conquest. If the assignment of the era to these years is correct, we have one further piece of evidence for the effect of Ptolemaic control on local coinage of tetradrachms. Aspendos seems to have issued staters on the Persic standard simultaneously.[90]

Lycia, like Cilicia, had no autonomous coinage under the Ptolemies. But here again there is no conclusion about royal action to be drawn, for no city in Lycia subject to the Ptolemies had issued its own coinage in earlier times. It is not until after 168 that local

88. H. Seyrig (note 87), pp. 38-51.
89. Seyrig notes that Achaeus seems to have found Pamphylia free in 218 during his campaign against Selge, and he suggests that any subsequent Seleucid domination was nominal.
90. H. Seyrig (note 87), pp. 52-56.

coinage became significant in Lycia, with various cities issuing money as members of the Lycian *koinon*. Some of Xanthos' bronze coinage probably antedates 168, and the same may be true at Telmessos and Pinara, but precision is again difficult.[91]

Turning from currency to circulation, we find a shortage of evidence. In Caria, there are two sources of interest. W. R. Paton, who lived in the area for 12 years and visited Myndos frequently, remarked that of the Greek coins he saw that came from the site of Myndos, 80 per cent were autonomous Myndian, and the remainder chiefly Ptolemaic, this in a sampling of several hundred coins.[92] L. Robert, citing Paton's information, mentions his own observations of Ptolemaic coins in Caria: four at Mylasa, one at Kildara.[93] No hoards in Caria are known to have contained Ptolemaic coins. While it will take much more observation and excavation before any pattern can be drawn with certainty, it appears that the circulation of Ptolemaic coins in the area was limited to Myndos, for which a particular explanation should be sought. Myndos was not a minting city at this time, so that the Ptolemaic coins may be taken to have been the overwhelming bulk of currency in use in Myndos during Ptolemaic domination. We will not be able to attain any certainty until excavations give us comparable information for other non-coining cities under Ptolemaic control in Caria.

Further east, we have no excavation material published for any significant site of the coast from Lycia to Cilicia. It is only by such excavation that we will find out what the currency in circulation in these areas was in the third century. The few indications that I have been able to gather give some idea of what might be found, but they are tentative in the extreme.

In the course of his travels in Lycia, Charles Fellows made an attempt to examine the coins found on the sites he visited and those brought to him by local residents, and for several ancient cities he recorded the results: at Telmessos, he saw coins of Rhodes, Side, Apamea in Phrygia, Koresia, various Lycian cities, and "several" Ptolemaic coins. At Pinara, besides local issues he saw coins of Rhodes, an Antiochus, two Ptolemies, and other Lycian cities. At Patara, Lycian, Seleucid, and Ptolemaic coins were found.

---

91. *BMC Lycia*, pp. 92 (Xanthos), 86 (Telmessos), and 84 (Pinara).
92. *JHS* 20, 1900, p. 80; I owe the reference to Thomas Drew-Bear.
93. L. Robert, *Villes d'Asie Mineure*², Paris, 1962, p. 21, n. 3.

All of these coins were bronze. At Xanthos and Tlos, on the other hand, no Ptolemaic coins appeared.[94]

The collection of the Direction of Public Instruction of Alanya, on the site of the ancient Korakesion (in eastern Pamphylia) is also of interest as a locally formed group. L. Robert has examined it and indicated that it contained more than 50 per cent coins of Side (20 of 38). The remainder were also Pamphylian (Selge 6, Aspendos 2, Perge 2, etc.) except for three Ptolemaic bronzes.[95] It is probable that these Ptolemaic coins come from Alanya itself or a nearby Pamphylian site.

These reports are the only ones known to me of Ptolemaic coins found in southern Asia Minor. A note of contrast is provided by a large collection formed by D. Mavromichali and given to the National Numismatic Museum in Athens.[96] Mavromichali was a man of wide experience and travel, but his collection was formed during his years as Greek consul in Antalya (ancient Attaleia) in the heart of Pamphylia. As such, it may in aggregate be taken to reflect what was available in the market of Antalya, drawn from its hinterland of southern Asia Minor. And in fact the contents of the collection confirm this view entirely: of 856 coins in the collection, 677 come from Lycia, Pamphylia, Pisidia, and Cilicia, and another 37 from Phrygia. But it does not seem that Mavromichali imposed artificial limits on the range of the coins he collected; four Seleucid coins appear in the collection. But not one Ptolemaic coin was in it. The evidence of this collection is confirmed in a general way by the collections reflecting Asia Minor more generally, which are discussed below in section 6. Ptolemaic coins, it would seem, are found in southern Asia Minor, but in small quantities. They are not in any sense the predominant currency of any period.

It is a curious situation that we have in the south coast of Asia Minor. Ptolemaic coins do not turn up in hoards and are found only very occasionally on the sites of the area, Myndos being the only one that has them in quantity. Nor is there any evidence that Ptolemaic coins were minted in the region. It would seem that there was little circulation of Ptolemaic currency in most of Caria, Lycia,

---

94. Charles Fellows, *An Account of Discoveries in Lycia*, London, 1841, pp. 280-283.

95. L. Robert, *Docs. Asie Min. mérid.*, p. 71, n. 2.

96. A catalogue is given by Svoronos in *JIAN* 6, 1903, pp. 1-92, but the entry in the museum's records comes in the next year (1904/5).

Pamphylia, and Cilicia. On the other hand, the cities of the area did not in general mint their own currency. In Pamphylia, in fact, it seems that the Ptolemies halted the coining of silver. A few cities had autonomous bronze coinages that may have been issued under the Ptolemies: Phaselis, Side, Sillyon, perhaps others. In effect, we have for the most part neither local coinage nor royal coinage.

For an explanation, I think we must turn to the lack of a tradition of coinage in these areas. Most of these cities had never coined their own money, not even small silver or bronze for small local transactions. The people of these cities probably did not use coins for everyday transactions. What they had of foreign coins of silver and gold, they might well hoard or use for larger transactions, but opportunities to use or to acquire such money must have been limited. The Ptolemies encountered in much of the region a vacuum; they felt no need to fill it. They did prevent the issue of autonomous silver in the few cities that had a tradition of tetradrachms, except for Samos and perhaps a few others, and those cities were to seize on the chance to resume coinage when Ptolemaic control disappeared. The Ptolemies probably paid their troops in their own currency; so one may at least explain the bronzes occasionally found on these garrisoned sites. But it does not appear that there was an active monetary policy in effect.

5. CRETE AND THE AEGEAN

In Crete also there was no royal coinage. Many Cretan cities had an extensive autonomous coinage in the Hellenistic period, and there is no evidence of any Ptolemaic attempt to curtail these emissions. At the same time, Ptolemaic bronzes are found in Crete with fair frequency: G. Le Rider saw 10 in Heraklion, 2 at Neapolis, 4 at Chania, and 30 in the Rethymnon museum, where they form the largest category of non-Rithymnian coins in the collection of that museum aside from coins of Athens. Le Rider also mentions seeing Ptolemaic coins at Gortyn, Hierapetra (ancient Hierapytna), Eleutherna, Polyrhenia, and Lisos.[97] Most of these places were not Ptolemaic possessions and, as Le Rider says, no official actions are to be sought as an explanation of their presence. These coins are

---

97. G. Le Rider, *Monnaies crétoises* (Études Crétoises 15), 1965, p. 244, n. 4; cf. p. 251.

the traces of individual careers and travels; one thinks particularly of Ptolemaic mercenaries, recruited in Crete in great numbers. At the same time, the Cretan evidence warns us that finds of small numbers of Ptolemaic coins do not indicate that that was the normal currency in circulation in an area. Only consistent evidence of excavated sites or, at the least, a pattern drawn from many hoards and surface finds, can establish such a conclusion. Our caution in using the few reported finds of Ptolemaic coins in south Asia Minor is thus justified by the evidence from Le Rider's Cretan studies.

It is worth pursuing the case of Rithymna somewhat further. We have discussed above the history of the city as G. Le Rider has outlined it from the coinage (p. 119): it was refounded as an Arsinoe, perhaps by Ptolemy IV, and it retained an autonomous bronze coinage, even using the same dies previously used for Rithymnian issues.[98] And yet it is here, in a city which certainly had an autonomous bronze coinage under Ptolemaic control, that we observe the largest concentration of Ptolemaic bronze coins in Crete. It is clear, then, that even in this case the Ptolemies did not seek to impose monetary uniformity on a possession. It would indeed have been difficult to exclude external sources of currency from a city surrounded by territory not under Ptolemaic control. One may suggest that the garrison of Rithymna was paid in Ptolemaic currency, and that this fact accounts in large part for the disproportionate number of Ptolemaic bronzes found in and near Rethymnon.

In Svoronos' catalogue three issues of tetradrachms of Ptolemy I are attributed to two mints of the Greek mainland, Corinth and Sikyon. The two issues attributed to Corinth were so placed because of a Pegasos symbol on them.[99] But recent study shows that these issues belong to the very early days of Ptolemaic coinage, ca. 322, and one of them is linked by an obverse die to a certainly Alexandrian emission.[100] The issue attributed to Sikyon, likewise, belongs to a well-defined series and may be dated to about 313 B.C.[101]

---

98. Cf. above, p. 119.

99. Svoronos II, nos. 93-94 (Corinth) and 95 (Sikyon).

100. O. H. Zervos (note 1), p. 4, n. 13, shows the die-linkage and adduces the presence of these "Pegasoi" in the Demanhur hoard, buried ca. 318, whereas the Ptolemaic presence in Corinth comes a decade later.

101. On Zervos' chart it is issue D XIV.

Svoronos' attribution of this issue, indeed, rested primarily on the fact that many of them had been found in the Peloponnesos.[102]

There is, however, one royal issue discovered since the time of Svoronos' catalogue that does appear to have been minted in Corinth, an issue of silver drachmas found in a hoard some 18 kilometers south of Corinth at Chiliomodi.[103] They bear the magistrates' initials Δ-Ο in the same characters and position as the same letters on some drachmas of Corinth also found in that hoard. Both groups were in mint condition. Also present in the hoard were some slightly worn tetradrachms of Ptolemy I on the reduced standard, thus after 310. It appears that the hoard must certainly date to the Ptolemaic occupation of Corinth in 308-306 and that the drachmas of Ptolemy I were minted in Corinth, perhaps for the purposes of his campaiging there.[104]

This special emission during a temporary occupation is the only royal coinage of the Ptolemies known to have been minted in the Greek mainland; none is attested for the islands, seat of Ptolemaic power in Greece. While Corinth clearly maintained autonomous coinage during the brief Ptolemaic control and more or less lent the mint to the king for special purposes, we cannot make any specific statements for the islands. Most of them issued bronze coinage in the Hellenistic period, a few silver. But these emissions are in general poorly known, inadequately studied, and only vaguely dated. It is, therefore, pointless to try to correlate developments in the coinage of the Greek islands with the relationship of the islands to the Ptolemies. In all probability some of the bronze autonomous issues belong to the Ptolemaic period. But most islands coined infrequently, and we are far from being able to make historical sense out of these isolated issues.

Most of the Ptolemaic coins found in Greece come from two areas, the Peloponnesos and Central Greece, especially Euboea. They have been discussed more than once; Eirene Varoucha-Christodoulopoulou drew attention to the pattern of distribution thirty years ago.[105] She found that silver coins were found only for

---

102. Svoronos IV, cols. 27-28.

103. O. Ravel, *Transactions of the International Numismatic Congress, 1936*, London, 1938, pp. 98-108.

104. The special character of the emission is underlined by the fact that Ptolemy was not issuing drachmas in Alexandria at this time.

105. E. Varoucha-Christodoulopoulou, 'Επιτύμβιον Τσούντα, Athens, 1941, pp. 668-679.

Ptolemies I and II, while bronzes of Ptolemy III, of a single type, were commonly found in the Peloponnesos. Tony Hackens has now taken the subject up again, with new material, in a pair of articles. For Euboea and Boeotia he finds that through the end of the third century Ptolemaic coins are found fairly commonly, though only bronze after Ptolemy II, but in the next century Ptolemaic coins are not found at all in hoards. Hackens, like Mme Varoucha, is inclined to see the answer to this situation largely in the Ptolemaic subsidies and gifts in the area in the third century,[106] though mercenaries returning home are also recognized as a possible source for some of the coins. Hackens documents Ptolemaic activity in Boeotia in detail.

His conclusions draw added force from his other study on circulation in the Peloponnesos, where he follows Mme Varoucha in thinking that the bronze issues of Ptolemy III come from gifts of diplomatic importance.[107] But where she suggested Aratos as the recipient, Hackens prefers a shorter period of time for this homogeneous issue, suggesting Sparta in the years 227-223. The gift of bronze is explicable by the severe shortage of silver in the Ptolemaic kingdom from the middle of Ptolemy III's reign on. For the silver of Ptolemies I and II, however, Hackens thinks commerce the most likely source, a conclusion that strikes me as implausible; the Ptolemies were not exporters of currency but of produce for which they received both goods and cash. It appears to me far more likely that returning mercenaries are responsible for most of the material found.

A third area in which Ptolemaic coins have been found has attracted much attention in the last decade: Attica. The finds have been enumerated by Eirene Varoucha-Christodoulopoulou;[108] since she wrote we have had a fuller publication of the Koroni material,[109] and now a bronze coin of Ptolemy II found at Rham-

---

106. T. Hackens, *BCH* 93, 1969, pp. 701-729. His full treatment of the material, taken with Mme Varoucha's work, makes it unnecessary to repeat here the detailed contents of the hoards and chance finds on which his work is based. I may add that G. Picard tells me that Ptolemaic coins have been found in the Swiss excavations of Eretria.

107. T. Hackens, *Antidoron Peremans* (Studia Hellenistica 16), 1968, pp. 67-95; the table on p. 78 shows the contents of the important hoards.

108. 'Αρχ. 'Εφ. 1953-1954 (1961), III, pp. 321-349, where the coins appear as part of the evidence on the Chremonidean War.

109. Bibliography and most recent discussion in J. R. McCredie, *Fortified Military Camps in Attica* (*Hesperia* Suppl. 11), 1966.

nous.[110] The coins belong to the reign of Ptolemy II for the most part, are predominantly bronzes, and include in particular a dated series of his reign generally thought to have been minted in Cyprus, for which dates range down to year Y in the alphabetic series, or to year 20, 264/3.[111] The coins are in general associated with what appear to be Ptolemaic military emplacements of a temporary sort at various sites in Attica and which, given the date of the coins, can hardly be other than from the Chremonidean War of the late 260's. The coins were therefore in all probability lost by Ptolemaic soldiers in Attica. It is worth remarking in this connection that one bronze coin from the same period was found on Keos, the only Ptolemaic coin known to me to have been discovered on that island.[112]

We have spent a great deal of space on the circulation of Ptolemaic currency in areas that the Ptolemies did not control. There is value in the exercise for the light it throws on the possible causes of Ptolemaic finds elsewhere. Tony Hackens linked the finds of central Greece and the Peloponnesos to the empire with the following statement: [113] "Jusqu'ici, les plus grands quantités de monnaies ptolémaiques ont été trouvées dans les zones géographiques où les relations humaines se doublaient de visées politiques et économiques des Lagides et qui, par surcroît, se trouvaient plus près de leur empire." Leaving aside the validity of the appeal to economic aims, what is most striking about the statement is that while Ptolemaic coins are found in the areas Hackens discusses, they are not in those areas of the Ptolemaic empire itself closest to these zones of circulation.

For only one island of the Ptolemaic Aegean possessions enumerated in Chapter VI have any finds of Ptolemaic coins ever been reported, so far as I know, and that is Delos. But it requires only

110. Published by Mando Caramessini-Oikonomidou in *Arch. Delt.* 22, 1967, B. 1, p. 11; it is Svoronos, *Die Münzen* II, no. 554 or 556.

111. McCredie (note 109), p. 10, regards some coins with a monogram Ⱥ and Ⱥ as being of year 21. But these elaborate symbols can hardly be dates, given the consistently simple style of the letter dates. They are monograms, rather, and the coins belong elsewhere, where Svoronos catalogued them, under nos. 551 and 553. On the date of this series cf. above, note 62.

112. 'Αρχ. 'Εφ. 1953-1954 (1961), III, pp. 321-349; the variety is Svoronos no. 617.

113. T. Hackens (note 107), p. 89, n. 2. Mme Varoucha (note 105), pp. 668-669, concluded similarly.

a brief look at the Delian material to see that it is unrelated to Ptolemaic control. In the recent publication of the Ilot des Comédiens at Delos, Tony Hackens provides a synopsis of the coins found in the area of this excavation, and compares the figures to some obtained from reports of coins found at Delos in the early part of this century and entered in the National Numismatic Collection in Athens.[114] In the recent finds, there were 8 Ptolemaic coins (all bronzes) found of a total of 509, of which 103 were foreign, i.e. neither Delian nor Athenian. In Svoronos' group, a total of 781 yielded 315 foreign, of which 26 were Ptolemaic. The discrepancy is no doubt to be explained by the fact that the Ilot des Comédiens is entirely residential and entirely of the second century B.C., while the earlier excavations included the sanctuary with its correspondingly wide range of time. All of the Ptolemaic bronzes found in the Ilot des Comédiens are dated after 166. The earlier finds are mostly third century, with a concentration in the reigns of Ptolemy III and Ptolemy IV and smaller amounts throughout the remainder of the dynasty.[115] If the presence of Ptolemaic coins reflected the influence of the empire, we should find a large and preponderant number of issues of Ptolemy II, who ruled the archipelago and for a time controlled the island.

For the rest of the Aegean islands there is silence. There are several factors that weaken somewhat the value of this silence as evidence. First, there have not been systematic excavations with publications of coins for any of the islands; Hiller von Gaertringen never mentions coin finds in his monumental work on Thera, and sites on most islands have not been excavated. Then too, the islands have not on the whole been plenteous sources of coin hoards and chance finds. But the silence is nonetheless somewhat impressive: no hoards containing Ptolemaic coins, no isolated finds in the Athens Museum register, no excavated coins. There was no gift to the National Numismatic Collection of any private accumulation formed in the islands. One must for the present assume that Ptolemaic currency did not as a rule circulate in the Aegean in

---

114. T. Hackens in P. Bruneau et al., *Exploration archéologique de Délos* XXVII, Paris, 1970, pp. 412 ff. Hackens gives references and a table for the finds of the earlier excavations, which were published by Svoronos in the *JIAN*, and promises an article on monetary circulation on Delos.

115. Of the coins assignable to reigns reported in the articles cited by Hackens, I count: Ptolemy I, 1; II, 2; III, 3; IV, 5; VI, 2; VIII, 1; IX, 1; Cleopatra VII, 2.

the league of the islanders. Nor, as we have seen, did the Ptolemies mint their own coins in this region. Nor, finally, is there any attested interference here by the king in local coinage. For the present the royal role in Aegean currency must be rated nil.

6. THE NORTH AEGEAN AND IONIA

Svoronos assigned Ptolemaic royal issues to the mints of two cities of the North Aegean, Ainos and Abdera. The former was given a group of tetradrachms of Πτολεμαίου Σωτῆρος and Πτολεμαίου βασιλέως types with the head of Ptolemy III.[116] The distinguishing characteristic of the issues was the representation of a cult idol of Hermes which Svoronos identified as a symbol of Ainos. The weakness of this type of reasoning is already apparent from the example of the Corinthian Pegasoi (section 5), and in this instance I can find no parallels in the coinage of Ainos itself sufficiently compelling to warrant acceptance of the assignment by Svoronos.

For Abdera, the reasons for assigning a tetradrachm are similar, namely the presence of a griffin on the coin.[117] But the griffin in fact bears little resemblance to the one on the autonomous Abderan coin that Svoronos cites as a parallel.[118] For this issue as for the one of Ainos it is best to avoid assignment to a mint not otherwise attested as a royal issuing agent in this period.

In Ionia, also, two royal mints come into question. Svoronos assigned a complex series of emissions to Ephesos. The major part of these are Ptolemaic issues taken by Svoronos to have been issued by the mint of a city Arsinoe, whose letters he disengaged from various monograms.[119] Ephesos had been called Arsinoe under Lysimachus for a time. Alternatively, the presence of the letters ΕΦ or a bee, or both, served to suggest Ephesos.[120] Already

---

116. Svoronos II, nos. 930-933.

117. Svoronos II, no. 928.

118. Svoronos II, no. 929.

119. Svoronos II, nos. 894-898 have monograms which suggested ΑΡΣΙ to Svoronos, together with monograms which he claimed to be dates Κ, ΚΑ, ΚΒ. There is no reason to see in these latter dates rather than minting officials. Svoronos also assigned his no. 893, a gold Arsinoe octadrachm, on the basis of the presence of a quiver as symbol. Since Ephesos' existence as Arsinoe fell under the reign of Lysimachus, the coins issued by Ephesos-Arsinoe do not, *pace* Svoronos, come into consideration here (nos. 875-892).

120. Svoronos II, nos. 901-904. I see no basis for his placing of nos. 899, 900, and 905, which have no marks of importance.

K. Regling doubted most of the attributions, accepting only those two issues with EΦ as certain, for the letters are placed and formed precisely as on Ephesian coins of the third century.[121] H. Seyrig has recently supported the position of Regling in the course of a study of the supposed Seleucid emissions of Ephesos, none of which he thinks certain.[122] Seyrig points out that Ephesos seems to have coined autonomous silver didrachms on the Rhodian standard during the third century, though the chronology of the issues is uncertain. Seyrig placed the Ptolemaic issues at Ephesos in the brief period before 258 when the Ptolemies controlled the city. G. Le Rider has recently suggested instead that the years after 244, under renewed Ptolemaic possession, are more probable. Le Rider also discerns an extensive Ephesian series of autonomous silver coins during this period. [123]

The second mint is that of Lebedos. As has been pointed out in Chapter VII, Lebedos was refounded by a Ptolemy and renamed Ptolemais; it is certain that the refounded city issued autonomous bronzes bearing the legend ΠΤΟ.[124] Svoronos attributed to it as well a series of royal tetradrachms.[125] His reasons were two: (1) the tetradrachms have a grape-leaf symbol found also on Lebedian bronzes of Ptolemais, and (2) they share an artist with the autonomous bronzes. As to the first argument, Svoronos' analogy is faulty, for the bronzes in question do not belong to the series which Waddington and Dieudonné were able to assign to Lebedos. Rather, they are part of Dieudonné's first series, of an entirely different type, about which Dieudonné himself felt great doubts and which

---

121. K. Regling in Svoronos IV, col. 475, doubts all but nos. 901 and 904.

122. H. Seyrig, *Rev. num.* 6 ser. 5, 1963, p. 35, n. 2; pp. 33-35 on the Seleucid issues usually given to Ephesos.

123. G. Le Rider, *Annuaire de l'École Pratique des Hautes Études*, IVe sec., 1972/1973, p. 246. This is a summary of his course of that year and does not have detailed argumentation or documentation. Le Rider considers the Ephesian coins of the period after 244 to have been struck on the Ptolemaic standard. He also (p. 253) cites an issue of Miletos on the same standard under the Ptolemies (as he thinks), which he places between 279/8 and 259 or after 244. He thinks the latter the more probable period, but the views of Holleaux quoted on pp. 174-5 about this period appear to me to suggest the contrary. A third city, Priene (p. 251) may have had analogous issues, but this is more dubious. Neither of the latter two cities is known to have been a Ptolemaic royal mint.

124. Cf. above, p. 169.

125. Svoronos II, nos. 912-917; his arguments are to be found in *JIAN* 5, 1902, pp. 61-70.

has generally been taken not to belong to Ptolemais-Lebedos.[126] Svoronos' second argument is more subjective, and K. Regling found it weak; I do not see that it can stand as the sole basis for the establishment of royal minting activity in Lebedos.[127] Lebedos issued autonomous bronzes as Ptolemais, but no silver, and we have no evidence that the crown minted in the city.

In the realm of autonomous coinage in the North Aegean, we have once again no chance of precision. For example, on Lesbos the *BMC* lists bronze issues of Antissa dated 300-167; bronzes of Eresos, third century or later; bronzes and small silver of Methymna, 330-240; small silver of Mytilene, 350-250.[128] With these wide timespans and the relatively small amount of local coinage known, it is not possible to relate the issues to periods of Ptolemaic control. Ainos issued some few Hellenistic bronzes, while Maroneia is far better represented in both bronze and silver.[129] Abdera has a few third century bronzes.[130] Samothrace, finally, had four main series of Hellenistic bronzes, but they yet await the study that might give them a more precise context.[131]

In Ionia, Miletos, never a royal mint, appears to have minted throughout the third century, though probably not continuously. It used the Rhodian standard down to the middle of the century and the Persic standard thereafter, but the Apollo/Lion types, the M monogram, and the presence of a magistrate's name remain constant.[132] Priene, as K. Regling's exhaustive study has shown, appears to have coined silver through most of the third century.[133] Chios, on the other hand, issued only bronzes in the third century.[134]

The question of Ptolemaic circulation in the North Aegean is

---

126. Cf. L. Robert, *BCH* 70, 1946, pp. 516-519.

127. K. Regling in Svoronos IV, col. 476.

128. *BMC Troas*, pp. 176-197.

129. Ainos, *BMC Thrace*, p. 81, and *SNG Copenhagen, Thrace*, pl. 8. Maroneia, *BMC Thrace*, pp. 128-130.

130. *SNG Copenhagen Thrace*, nos. 377-380.

131. Information from James R. McCredie, who remarks that it is likely that Samothrace issued during all parts of the Hellenistic period but probably not continuously.

132. *BMC Ionia*, pp. 191-193; *SNG Copenhagen, Ionia*, 978-980, 986-989. Cf. above, p. 207, for the issue of Miletos of a silver coin perhaps on the Ptolemaic standard.

133. K. Regling, *Die Münzen von Priene*, Berlin, 1927, pp. 25-31.

134. *BMC Ionia*, pp. xlv, 332; *SNG Copenhagen, Ionia*, pl. 35.

simple—there was none that is known; no finds of Ptolemaic coins are known to me in the area. We are fortunate here in having the evidence of Samothrace, where of some thousand to two thousand coins found, 90 per cent are Samothracian, most of the rest from the cities of Thrace and Greek imperial issues—and not one Ptolemaic coin.[135] It is a fair conclusion that Ptolemaic currency did not circulate in the North Aegean and that there was neither royal minting in this area nor interference with the autonomous emissions of the subject cities. This conclusion is of particular interest in view of the regulation of the Samothracian wheat trade that is attested in the inscription for Hippomedon; it does not appear that currency was a part of the scheme of control.

There is no evidence of Ptolemaic coins circulating in the Ionian area, and some evidence that they did not. Regling's publication of the coins found at Priene showed no Ptolemaic coins among the 304 non-Prienian Greek coins discovered.[136] Nor are Ptolemaic coins common in the collections found in Smyrnaean gifts, though one might expect that a port of Smyrna's importance would have attracted finds from a wide area. A collection given to the Athens Museum in 1891-2 contained 2 Ptolemaic coins out of a total of 703, mostly of Anatolia; the collection was formed in Smyrna. Another collection from Smyrna received the same year had 482 coins, none Ptolemaic.[137] In 1919, a collection of 1,962 Greek coins, formed in Smyrna, had 13 Ptolemaic bronzes, compared to 81 coins of Syria and the Seleucids, and 1460 coins of Asia Minor.[138] The Waddington collection of more than 7000 coins included only 5 Ptolemaic bronzes, but an element of planning may be in large part responsible for the composition of his collection.[139] But Waddington had wide experience in Asia Minor, and the fact that he nowhere mentions being shown Ptolemaic coins in Anatolia is at least suggestive that these coins have not commonly been found

---

135. Information from James R. McCredie.

136. K. Regling (note 133), pp. 179-183. Almost all of the coins in this group came from cities in Ionia, Caria, and the offshore islands.

137. National Numismatic Collection, *Accessions Record* II, 1891-2, p. 79, nos. 672 and 673, silver and bronze.

138. NNC *Accessions Record* 1919, pp. 59 ff. Another 87 came from Thrace, 86 from Macedonia.

139. E. Babelon, *Inventaire sommaire de la collection Waddington*, Paris, 1898.

there.[140] Within the limits of this negative evidence, then, we are entitled to conclude that Ptolemaic currency was not circulated in the Ionian area.

7. SUMMARY

It would be unreasonable to expect an entity with so varied and eventful a history and composition as the Ptolemaic empire to present a single pattern of treatment in the realm of coinage. But some conclusions emerge, I think, from the mass of data we have observed. (1) There is a distinction to be drawn between two groups of possessions, Cyrene, Cyprus, and Syria on the one hand, Asia Minor, Greece, and the Aegean on the other. The former group shares its characteristics with Egypt. These areas have in general royal mints of varying degrees of activity, do not have autonomous coinage, and use only the royal coinage in all metals, though coins minted in one area may circulate in another. Foreign currency is probably prohibited throughout and in any case is imported not at all or in insignificant quantities. There are many local variants, and the cessation of local currencies and the creation of the system did not come all at once, though for the most part the pattern was complete by the start of the reign of Ptolemy III and indeed is largely the work of Ptolemy I, though his son may have been responsible for the somewhat systematic aspect under which we see it.

(2) The areas outside the Ptolemaic monetary zone are a less homogeneous group. In general, cities that had in the past issued coins were not prevented from doing so, if they had the resources. Bronze local coinage is quite common and was probably widespread even in the islands, which mostly lacked the resources to issue silver. In the wealthier cities—Samos, Miletos, Ephesos, Knidos, Kalymna, Kos, Kaunos, and others—coinage of small silver denominations is of frequent occurrence, and the weight standard used seems in general to be a matter of local option and convenience, with the Rhodian standard prevalent in an area whose commerce was increasingly dominated by Rhodes. There are cases where a city that had coined before, that would coin again, that was prosperous, did not do so: Halikarnassos seems to be one

---

140. W. H. Waddington, *Voyage en Asie Mineure au point de vue numismatique*, Paris, 1853, which is of somewhat more importance for Caria and South Asia Minor than for Ionia.

example, Aspendos another and perhaps the most striking. It is difficult to know the reasons for these differences in treatment.

(3) Royal mints appear only twice outside the monetary zone, in Corinth about 308 and in Ephesos around 240. In both cases there were few issues, probably for a pressing local and temporary use in wars. In both cases local issues parallel the royal ones; in Corinth an almost identical local emission is precisely contemporary. These were temporary creations of a crisis, not normal parts of a functioning system of royal mints.

(4) Ptolemaic coinage circulated outside the monetary zone very little. Some was brought back by mercenaries in Ptolemaic service, who must have been paid largely in Ptolemaic bronze currency, especially after the middle of Euergetes' reign and his shortage of silver. It is in this way that the Ptolemaic bronzes in Crete and Asia Minor are mostly to be explained. For two cases, however— Myndos and Rithymna—the proportion of Ptolemaic coins in local finds far exceeds that heretofore discovered at other sites controlled by the Ptolemies. This situation may reflect the presence of a Ptolemaic garrison in these two cities. It is not impossible that this situation obtained elsewhere and that future excavations will give us other such garrisons. When Ptolemy VI granted some revenues of lands in Thera to soldiers in the garrison there, the sum is stated in Ptolemaic drachmas, a sign both that this was not a normal currency in Thera and at the same time that it would have been in use in the Ptolemaic establishment there.[141]

(5) A not insignificant part of the empire, largely coastal cities of southern Asia Minor, probably used neither royal coinage nor local; for the rare large deal in cash, any currency would do, while for local trade in small transactions, coinage had never been used anyway. Coinage came late to much of this area, and there would hardly have been profit in a close royal regulation of the small use of coins here. There is no sign that the Ptolemies attempted to introduce the use of coined money or to develop the economy here to the point of demanding it.

(6) The many variants and differences noted, especially the cleavage between the monetary zone and the other possessions, must to a large extent reflect the realities of Ptolemaic power and its limits. Two questions surely governed the royal decision about

---

141. Cf. Chapter VI, note 55.

treatment of a subject area or city: was it desirable (that is, profitable to the crown) to impose a monetary zone of isolation; and was it possible to do so. The amount of autonomy a city had in its coinage no doubt reflected the power or weakness of the crown at various times and the power of the city itself to get favorable terms from the king.[142]

---

142. I have omitted discussion of the so-called "alliance coinage" of Arsinoe dekadrachms of similar weight and type to some Roman coins (refs. at E. Will, *Histoire politique* I, p. 175, n. 2) because although H. Mattingly thinks them intended for circulation in south Italy, he presents no evidence that they did so or that they were minted there (*Numismatic Chronicle* 6 ser. 6, 1946, pp. 63-67). See the lucid discussion of P. M. Fraser, *Ptol. Alex.* II, pp. 268-269, n. 185, rejecting the Mattingly thesis. Fraser also discusses (I, p. 153, and II, p. 266, n. 173) connections between Syracusan and Ptolemaic coinage.

CHAPTER NINE

PATTERNS OF ADMINISTRATION

A. INSTITUTIONS

The form of this collection and evaluation of the evidence for the administration of the various parts of the Ptolemaic empire has heretofore been a survey by region. In it I have tried to disengage what can be known of the means the Ptolemies employed in each area. The result has been the exposition of a great variety of systems and methods, to all of which no single province can have been subject. Particular emphasis has been placed on the relationship of each bureaucrat to his fellows in his province. Only in this geographical survey, I think, could the diversity of the Ptolemaic empire be fully appreciated and the problems raised by the individual documents adequately considered.

This demonstration and explanation of diversity is not, however, the end of the inquiry. The question remains: is there any sense to be made of the evidence? Two lines of discussion will provide what answers I can suggest. There is first the study of offices and aspects: the various bureaucrats, diplomatic relations, and local institutions. It is here that we encounter most previous studies on the subject, those of Cohen, Bengtson, Peremans and Van 't Dack. The second path is more general: the patterns of administration of the empire. An attempt will be made to provide an accounting for similarities and differences among the provinces and to assess the extent to which these patterns developed or were static.

1. *The Provincial Governors*

It is natural that we begin with the highest-ranking officials of the empire. There are a number of persons attested holding high command over various regions under the control of the king during the fourth century, in the first quarter-century of the attempt to secure possessions aside from Egypt. These men are with one exception attested primarily by literary sources; the late fourth century is a period from which we have few inscriptions but a considerable amount of historical writing in Diodorus, Arrian, and Plutarch. The result of our dependence on literary materials is an inability to be sure of the official title of any of these men. Ophellas was Ptolemy Soter's subordinate general responsible for the Cyrenaica, but we cannot give him a title with any certainty. His eventual successor, Magas, was in the same situation until the time of his break with Ptolemy II, when he took the title of king. We do not know what position he held as representative of the crown before this time. Both men were put in their commands to exert military control over the Cyrenaica and to prevent renewed revolts by a citizenry obviously not pleased with control by the king (see above, pp. 25-6).

The situation in Cyprus is similar. Nikokreon and Menelaos have generally been taken to be *strategoi*, because the literary sources call them that. But Cohen, though he accepted these men as *strategoi*, emphasized that he could not rely on the literary sources: "nam ad magistratuum titulos bene discernendos scriptores usui nobis non sunt." [1] This position, logically pursued, demands that we withhold acceptance of Menelaos and Nikokreon into a list of *strategoi*, as I have argued in detail (pp. 38-42). Both men were kings of Salamis, it would seem, but their authority came from being subordinate commanders to Ptolemy. Their positions

---

1. Cohen, *De Magistratibus*, p. 1. Cohen argued that the extant evidence allowed *strategoi* to be certainly discerned only in Thrace and Cyprus, but (p. 8) prudently remarked that he had no doubt that others would come to light. He doubted not the presence of *strategoi* but rather the specific instances alleged by other scholars. It is unfair to the nature and intentions of ancient writers to use them for technical terminology, even in the case of reputable historians like Polybius, for they did not use technical terms with any consistency, and without corroborating evidence it is impossible to tell instances when they do use technical terms from those where they are merely descriptive. For example, Polybius calls Philammon λιβυάρχης τῶν κατὰ Κυρήνην τόπων (cf. pp. 33-34 and 219). On the basis of τῶν . . . τόπων Bengtson has erected the theory that Philammon was responsible only for the *chora*, not for the cities. But Polybius (5.34.7-8), in speaking of Philopator's holdings, says he held lands up to the Hellespont καὶ τῶν κατὰ Λυσιμαχείαν τόπων. Both phrases are surely periphrases and hence descriptive rather than technical language. The same is true in Polybius' discussions of Syria: see p. 14.

In this passage (5.34.10-11) Polybius contrasts Philopator's neglect of foreign affairs with the care of his predecessors. In reality, nothing except Pamphylia seems to have been lost to the Ptolemies during his reign, and the evidence cited in Chapters II-VII gives the impression of, if not strength, at least activity. See the remarks on Philopator by C. B. Welles, *Alexander and the Hellenistic World*, Toronto, 1970, pp. 103-106.

probably did not differ materially—aside from the kingship—from that of Leonidas, Soter's commander in Greece in 308.

A similar situation prevailed in Caria, where we have documentary evidence of the first importance in the Iasian inscription discussed in detail on pp. 89-91. Two men, Aristoboulos and Asklepiodotos, swear oaths to the Iasians about the status of the city with respect to the king: that the city be a free and autonomous ally and master of its own revenues, paying to the king a contribution toward defense, the amount of which the king is to decide. I have argued that these men are probably successive regional governors appointed by the king. We know little of Ptolemaic control in Caria at this time (probably the end of the fourth century) or of the extent of these men's power in the region. It is clear that they exercised general powers over the city even in the realm of finance, although one important decision is referred to the king.

In this quarter-century, then, the pattern of appointing governors seems to have been one of placing subordinate generals over the military operations in a region. These generals no doubt exercised broad powers in various situations, dealing with problems as they arose and acting in the place of the king in most matters. It must be remembered that this period was one of almost incessant warfare and that we are dealing with military commanders, not bureaucrats. It is not likely that their appointments followed any system or that their actions were governed by any legalistic conception of the position of a royal general. That these men were called *strategoi*, generals, is very probable; that they controlled roughly or closely defined regions is also likely. But we have no evidence that these appointments were seen as provincial governorships at this time or that the notion of designating a man as *strategos* of a region was yet current. The fluidity of the situation in these early years should be sufficient deterrent against postulating systematic arrangements for them in the absence of documentary evidence that supports doing so.

The next half-century also forms a natural unit; it is Ptolemy I's more secure and powerful period coupled with the reign of Philadelphos. Cyrene was independent under Magas during the latter part of this period, and his governorship of it in the first part no doubt followed the lines indicated above. For Cyprus and Syria, we have a virtual blank. But in Caria our evidence points out a major development: the broad *ad hoc* competence of Aristoboulos' time has been crystallized into the provincial *strategia*.[2] Already in 278, soon after Philadelphos' conquest, the *strategos* Margos is found. A Samian inscription of the decade 270-260 honors Aristolaos son of Ameinias, στρατηγὸς ἐπὶ Καρίας. It is clear from the title that it is now attached to the area governed. Other than that Aristolaos benefited Samos, however, we learn little more than this bare fact from the inscription (cf. pp. 83, 101). The Zenon papyrus concerning Kalynda, however, tells us more. Motes is named as *strategos*; he and the *oikonomos* serve as a board to pass on complaints against the city government in matters of finance. The *strategos* therefore enjoyed a wide competence in civil affairs at this time (pp. 99-100). It is likely that he visited each city in his province from time to time to adjudicate disputes, advise the cities, review garrisons, and perform the other duties of his office. The earliest *strategos*, Margos, was honored by Amyzon in an unpublished decree (p. 93). We do not know if he had a permanent place of residence, a "provincial capital", as it were. It should hardly be a surprise that the reign of Philadelphos, in which so many aspects of the rule and exploitation of Egypt were systematized and rationalized, saw the same phenomenon abroad in the *strategia*. The spread of this system to other areas is not attested until succeeding reigns, but it is not at all unlikely that it in some cases goes back to the reign of Philadelphos.

A second breed of provincial officials appears in the period as well: their titles incorporate the name of the region with the suffix -archos. The nesiarch is the better known of these and is discussed at length on pages 156-157. He was a royal appointee who served as chief executive of the Ptolemaic-dominated league of the islanders, exercising his powers also through sending judges to settle internal strife on islands. In military matters he is overshadowed in the inscriptions by the powerful figure of Philokles king of Sidon, but Bacchon at least had nonetheless a military role, for Zenon, the commander of undecked ships honored by Ios, is called a subordinate of the nesiarch Bacchon. It is therefore likely

---

2. H. Bengtson, *Die Strategie* III, p. 175, takes the remark of Polybius that Kaunos was sold to Rhodes by the generals of Ptolemy to mean by the *strategos* of Ptolemy, thus by the provincial governor, acting on orders from Alexandria. (The plural for singular he considers stylistic, citing the phrase τῶν διοικητῶν [27.13] for the *dioiketes* of Alexandria; but there it could mean a succession of *dioiketai* over several years.) I take it rather that the local garrison commander sold out for his own profit, not the crown's.

that the nesiarch, even if he did not control a war fleet had at least substantial local forces at his disposal to enforce his decisions. He collected contributions from individual islands toward sums voted by the league. It would seem that his governorship of the islands was broader than a presidency of the league, even though that may have been an important conceptual part of his position. As I argue in Chapter VI, I do not take the nesiarch to be a "paper tiger" subordinated in practice to an admiral.

His position was, however, not that of a *strategos* of an area. The differences in practice were important, I suspect, primarily in that the nesiarch did not have, so far as we know, resident subordinates in most of the islands which were members of the league. The nesiarch's position also no doubt reflects the fact that the league antedates Ptolemaic control of it, and it was easier to take over and exploit a pre-existent structure than to impose a military governor of a more autocratic type on a group of island cities no doubt jealous of their relative autonomy. It may also be noted that the nesiarch's office antedates our evidence for that of a provincial *strategos* by some years. It is a remnant of the wars of the successors, not an aspect of systematic royal administration.

An office similar in name and perhaps in content is attested for Pamphylia in the inscription of Termessos recently published by Louis Robert, though the word Παμφυλι[άρχης] is partly restored (p. 111). We know almost nothing about his role in this command, however. His nationality (Macedonian) fits well with the phrase ὑπὸ βασιλέως Πτολεμ[αίου] κατασταθείς. He was a royal appointee like Bacchon, and his date is contemporary with Bacchon —278. Beyond this we can only speculate on the reasons for his title. It may be that this first period of Ptolemaic domination in Pamphylia (ca. 280-259) was marked by a league under royal control, perhaps created for the purpose. It may be also that such a situation would reveal a royal attempt to win over Pamphylia (which apparently never liked Ptolemaic rule) without seeming too oppressive. But we do not know. Beloch suggested that the later office of Lykiarch in Lycia might go back to Ptolemaic times;[3] the appearance of the Pamphyliarch suggests that a Lykiarch

---

3. K. J. Beloch, *Griechische Geschichte*[2] IV 1, Berlin-Leipzig, 1925, p. 396; the Lykiarch was president of the Lycian league. On this league see above, chapter V, n. 111, and J. A. O. Larsen, *Greek Federal States*, Oxford, 1967, pp. 240-263 (251-252 on the Lykiarch).

might yet be found in an analogous role. But for Lycia we have no evidence yet of governors in any period.

As the remainder of the third century passes, we find *strategoi* in several other provinces. We do not know to what extent the present state of our evidence reflects the ancient reality; I suspect that future finds may have many surprises in store. But I may suggest that it was under Euergetes that the nome *strategoi* in Egypt expanded their competence most extensively and that we might well have the same phenomenon abroad. It is to this reign that the inscription from Thera honoring - - - -opaphil[os] is generally dated. He is called [naua]rch and *strategos* of the city by the Theraeans, but I have argued that the latter term reveals an egocentric view on the part of the Theraeans similar to that which led Itanos to call Patroklos "*strategos* sent to Crete." - - -opaphil[os] was, I think, admiral of the Ptolemaic fleet and *strategos* of the Aegean possessions then left (Thera, Methana, Keos, Itanos, and perhaps others), who was resident in Thera. His role in his inscription is in the area of defense, protecting the island from pirates. The necessity of his commanding the fleet and defending widely-scattered fortresses probably made his position in fact predominantly a military one.[4] (Cf. p. 133).

Some of Euergetes' new conquests of the Third Syrian War also received *strategoi*. Best known is Hippomedon, *strategos* of Thrace and the Hellespont.[5] The inscription from Samothrace honoring him shows him active both in defense and in economic affairs, for it is to him that the Samothracians appeal alike for soldiers, funds, and exemption from import restrictions and duties on wheat. The competence is that of Motes in Caria: the *strategos* had a key role to play in controlling financial affairs in his province (see pp. 164-165). It is possible also that Antiochos, left by Euergetes to govern Cilicia at the end of the Third Syrian War, was a strategos; it would certainly be the most likely title for such a governor.[6]

4. Contra, D. Cohen, *De Magistratibus*, p. 8, who takes - - -opaphilos to be a visitor honored by the Theraeans with the title *strategos*.

5. H. Bengtson, *Die Strategie* III, p. 182, suggests that the Aphrodisios of *P. Teb.* 8 could be a successor of Hippomedon. But the unpublished second column of this papyrus contained a letter to or from Hippomedon himself; the suggestion is therefore not probable. I discuss this problem at greater length in *JEA* 61, 1975, 168-180.

6. D. Cohen, *De Magistratibus*, p. 8, disbelieves Hieronymus' use of *strategos* for Antiochos and prefers to call him a *hegemon*. This rank is rather too low for the duties given to Antiochos, however.

In Cyprus, it is not until the next reign that a *strategos* is attested in an inscription. The earliest inscription in which Pelops son of Pelops bears the title *strategos* comes from the years 217-209 (Cf. Appendix A); although Cypriot inscriptions of the third century are not rare, none before this time gives us a name that is certainly that of a governor of the island. It is admittedly difficult to imagine that there was no governor, but we are not entitled on present evidence to extend the *strategia* back from Pelops. It may well be the case that Cyprus occupied a less important place in the estimation of the kings of the third century, when other foreign possessions were numerous, than in that of the later Ptolemies, whose empire was diminished by losses of the decade 205-195.

It is at about the same time that we have our first evidence of a governor for Syria and Phoenicia. Theodotos the Aetolian, who went over to Antiochus III, is often considered a likely *strategos*. After the battle of Raphia in 217, Ptolemy IV left Andromachos of Aspendos as *strategos* of the area, according to Polybius. We have only literary evidence for these two men.[7] Very few Hellenistic inscriptions are known from the area that the Ptolemies controlled, although recent discoveries make it certain that the Seleucid *strategos* and high priest governed the area from the year of the conquest by Antiochus. It may yet be that there will appear documents to enlighten us on the title and role of the putative governors of this province for the Ptolemies.

There is thus a good likelihood that all of the main areas of the empire were governed by *strategoi* by the reign of Philopator—with one exception. We know nothing of the rule of Cyrene between its return to the crown with the marriage of Berenike to Ptolemy III and the death of Philopator. After Ptolemy IV's death, Agathokles sent Philammon to Cyrene, says Polybius, as λιβυάρχης τῶν κατὰ Κυρήνην τόπων. I argue above (p. 214, n. 1) that this title probably is not technical terminology but refers to a governorship of the entire region, cities and *chora* alike. The question of the real title of Philammon is for the present insoluble. It is not until 185-180 that the *strategia* is attested for Cyrene, in the person of Philon son of Kastor (p. 34).

That every step of the development outlined here corresponds

---

7. D. Cohen (note 6), pp. 99-100, is nonetheless inclined to accept both men as *strategoi* of the entire area.

not only to the present documentation but also to historical reality
is rather doubtful; but we have no way of knowing at present what
modifications future discoveries will bring. As to the powers and
duties of the *strategoi*, enough has been said here and in earlier
chapters to show the breadth of military, civil, and economic affairs
dealt with by the *strategoi*. It is not likely that the competence of
the *strategos* was legalistically defined [8] or that his duties were
outlined to him in a manual. It was a job for a man of flexible
temper and with the ability to improvise to protect the royal
interests in the many and varied problems that might arise.

2. *Garrisons and their Commanders*

The placing of garrisons in cities under the control of the Hellenistic kings was an almost universal practice. In general the
garrisons were made up of mercenaries whose only tie to the crown
was their paymaster. They were often enough accompanied by a
retinue of their families, slaves, and possessions. The Ptolemies
were like the other kings in this regard. In a few instances from the
early Ptolemaic period we encounter cities not garrisoned, whether
through the unimportance of the place, the weakness of the royal
power in the area, or the king's desire not to antagonize a city
in the early stages of making it a dependency. At the time of its
first contact with Ptolemy Soter, for example, Iasos was guaranteed
freedom from a garrison; Ptolemy was indeed freeing it from a
garrison of mercenaries placed there by another. And most of the
Aegean islands never had Ptolemaic garrisons, so far as we can see.
There are many cities for which we do not yet have evidence of a
garrison in parts of Asia Minor, but new finds will no doubt eventually provide this evidence.

In addition to garrisons, Ptolemaic cities often had the burden
of quartering less permanent bodies of men. Abuse of this custom
was a serious issue between city and king, as the letter of a Ptolemy
to Soloi in Cilicia shows (p. 115). The *oikonomos* (no doubt in
collaboration with the *strategos*) seems to have had major responsibility for looking after quartering, but much of the detailed work

---

8. The attempt of Alfred Heuss, *Stadt und Herrscher*, Leipzig, 1937, pp.
18-22, to define the relationship among king, *strategos*, and city in closely
legal terms therefore seems to me fundamentally misguided and untrue to the
nature of the historical situation.

rested on the city government, which did the specific allotting of places and exemptions.

The primary function of the garrison was to protect the royal control over the city from assault by external or internal enemies. This military role was not a narrowly circumscribed one, for the commandant of Maroneia responded to a request to help protect the mainland possessions of Samothrace (p. 160). This aspect does not require discussion here, nor do other matters; organization, rank, ethnic and social background, milieu of the men, recruiting. These are treated in detail by M. Launey and by J. Lesquier.[9] The role of the commander of the garrison, however, goes beyond military affairs to the realm of administration; it is, indeed, one of the stock problems of the administration of the Ptolemaic empire.

As the problem is generally posed, it concerns the relationship between the post of φρούραρχος, "garrison-commander," and ὁ ἐπὶ τῆς πόλεως, "the one set over the city." [10] It is widely accepted that the latter position follows the former in the history of the Ptolemaic possessions; Mitford, one of the most enthusiastic proponents of this chronological division, places the dividing line at ca. 200 B.C.[11] Mitford seemingly bases his remarks solely on the Cypriot evidence. Beyond this question, however, is a more important one, that of the difference between the two and the reason for any difference. Mitford has suggested that the difference was one of title only and that the change probably was aimed at appeasing Cypriot sentiment by making the realities of Ptolemaic power less overt. Bengtson, on the other hand, followed by Peremans and Van 't Dack, saw in the change a reflection of a gradually increasing civil competence of the commandant, a process he felt to be analogous to that of the development of the *strategia*.

The title *phrourarchos* is not frequently attested in the Ptolemaic possessions. One is known from Kition, in the reign of Ptolemy I; a second was in Xanthos under his son. Two more are known from

---

9. M. Launey, *Armées hellénistiques*; J. Lesquier, *Les institutions militaires de l'Égypte sous les Lagides*, Paris, 1911.

10. A summary of the history of the question may be found in the study of W. Peremans and E. Van 't Dack, in *Antidoron Martino David* (Papyrologica Lugduno-Batav. 17), 1968, pp. 81-99. I need not repeat their work here. See now also P. M. Fraser, *Ptol. Alex.* II, p. 194, n. 101, who thinks the ἐπὶ τῆς πόλεως had wider powers.

11. Cf. for example, *I. Kourion*, pp. 76-77, and references there.

Itanos, one of Philopator's reign, another from that of Epiphanes. The latter has the court rank "first friend" and also the military rank of chiliarch. In all of these cases the word φρούραρχος stands without modification and by itself. In a late third century text from an unknown Cypriot city, however, we find the phrase ὁ ἐπὶ τῆς [πόλεως] γενόμενος φρούραρχος, and Mitford has restored (wrongly, I think), an inscription of Kourion (which he dates ca. 235) [ὁ γενόμενος ἐπ]ὶ τῆς πόλεως [φρούραρχος]. The wording of these texts is noteworthy, and we will return to them.

The ἐπὶ τῆς πόλεως is known under many names, for the title was, to anyone outside the city in question, ἐπὶ plus the name of the city: ἐπὶ Σαλαμῖνος, ἐπὶ Μαρωνείας, and so forth. In the second century the phrase ἐπὶ τῆς πόλεως or ἐπὶ plus the city name generally formed a complete unit of titulature, but this was not always the case. I have already cited the third-century Cypriot example where *phrourarchos* is added. There are other instances of note: at Kition (probably under Euergetes II) a τὸν γενόμενον ἐπὶ τῆς πόλεως ἡγεμόνα καὶ ἱππάρχην ἐπ' ἀνδρῶν; at Charadros in Rough Cilicia (Ptolemy III), ἡγεμόνα τὸν τεταγμένον ἐπὶ Χαράδρου. There is, therefore, some variation in titulature. From the assemblage it is clear that in all of these cases the group of titles forms one phrase: one should translate the phrase at Kition, for example, "the *hegemon* and hipparch over troops, formerly in command of the city." As Cohen recognized many years ago, it is not possible to separate the military rank and the position over the city chronologically.[12] At the same time, Mitford's chronological scheme is embarrassed in Cyprus by the combined titles of *phrourarchos* and ἐπὶ τῆς πόλεως in one inscription and still further by the appearance in the third century of an ἐπὶ Μαρωνείας and the ἡγεμόνα τὸν τεταγμένον ἐπὶ Χαράδρου, for these men are ἐπὶ τῆς πόλεως. Similarly, the phrourarch at Itanos after 200 ruins the other side of the division.

It would seem, then, that the realities of history do not fit the schemes proposed. It is true that the titles with ἐπὶ start later and continue later than the *phrourarchoi*, but there is a period of about half a century during which both titles and a combination of them all appear. Only one explanation seems to me to provide any

---

12. D. Cohen, *De Magistratibus*, pp. 41-42 (against the view of Dittenberger that the rank of *hegemon* represented a step up for Melankomas).

reasonable means of understanding the seeming lack of order: *phrourarchos*, like *hegemon*, hipparch, and chiliarch, is a military rank, not an office. A man was named a *phrourarchos* as he might be named to any other rank of the army or bureaucracy. The position of ἐπί a city, on the other hand, was a position to be filled by one person. The rank of the person who filled it might vary according to the importance of the garrison and the availability of high-ranking manpower to fill positions. If there were insufficient *phrourarchoi* to command all of the minor garrisons of Rough Cilicia, a *hegemon* could be used. Being commandant did not automatically entail promotion to *phrourarchos*. The phenomenon is therefore analogous to that of bureaucratic rank: if there was not a nomarch available, a toparch might perform the duties of the bureau for the whole nome without having to be promoted in rank for the office.[13]

It is worth noting that in the documents concerning *phrourarchoi* this title is used alone only in dedications placed by the *phrourarchoi* themselves.[14] The phrases with ἐπί are, in the third century at least, restricted to use by others honoring the person, usually his own city or another that he has helped. It is therefore a question of the relationship of the man to a city that is of importance to those honoring him; this is to be expected. Whether a commandant might be without military rank is uncertain. It is this emphasis on the office and not the military rank that becomes characteristic of second century dedications. The court rank of that time was more impressive than the rank of *phrourarchos*, and the Cypriot cities chose to emphasize court rank and office. It is significant, in this respect, that the sole dedication concerning a second century commandant that mentions a military rank is that of Melankomas, which was a statue placed not by the city of Kition but by a member of his family (his daughter-in-law).

This interpretation therefore allows for the local vagaries and nuances of titulature that we have observed. It also suggests that the process of change was irregular and that only over the long run can we look for an empire-wide change in the competence of the commandant. I am inclined to think that Bengtson is at least

---

13. This salient fact emerges from A. E. Samuel's study of the nomarch's bureau in *Essays Welles*, pp. 213-229, especially pp. 228-229.

14. I exclude of necessity the unpublished document from Xanthos from consideration here.

partly right, that civil—and civic—duties came to be more important. It was not the crown but the cities that recognized this
development in the changing modes of reference to their commandants.

A word about the *epistates* is needed here to complete the study
of commandants. Only two such men are definitely attested as
holding office in the Ptolemaic empire.[15] Both were sent to Aegean
islands by Patroklos during the Chremonidean War, one to Thera,
one to Arsinoe (Koresia) on Keos. For details of their missions,
see pages 124 and 141-143. It is often asserted that they were
temporary officials like foreign judges, differing from them in not
being private citizens but rather royal officers.[16] I argue above
that the case of Hieron, *epistates* in Arsinoe, seems best explained
by taking him to be a more long-resident official; but I do not
see that certainty is possible, despite the flat assertions to that
effect by many scholars.

3. *Economic Administration*

It is generally agreed that the chief financial official of a province
was usually called the *oikonomos*, the term used in Egypt for that
position in each nome. We have evidence of *oikonomoi* of Cyprus,
the Aegean islands, Caria, and the hyparchies of Syria, all under
Philadelphos. An *oikonomos* of Crete, Methana, and Thera is also
attested in the reign of Philometor. Only Syria seems to have
diverged from the pattern in which the *oikonomos* was the head of
the financial system, for it had its own *dioiketes* to whom the
oikonomoi of the hyparchies reported. It is also generally agreed
that the *dioiketes* of Syria and the *oikonomoi* of the provinces were
directly subordinate and responsible to the *dioiketes* in Alexandria.[17]

The manner in which the *oikonomos* shared his duties with the
strategos and the relationship between these two officials and
between the *strategos* and the *dioiketes* in Alexandria are far less

15. Mitford restores [ἐπιστάτ]ην in a Cypriot inscription honoring (seemingly) a commandant of a Neapolis the location of which is unknown (above,
p. 115), but this restoration is too uncertain to permit use of it here. And
Archagathos, *epistates* of Libya, whom I shall discuss elsewhere, is too
peculiar a case to be helpful.
16. The assumption goes back a long way; cf. D. Cohen, *De Magistratibus*
p. 83, and the remarks by Peremans and Van 't Dack (note 10, above),
pp. 93-98; also those of P. M. Fraser, *BSA Alex.* 41, 1956, p. 52.
17. For example, D. Cohen, *De Magistratibus*, pp. 51-54, and M. Rostovtzeff, *SEHHW*, pp. 338-339.

clear and by no means the subject of a common opinion. Bengtson, for example, suggests that the *strategos*, although in general independent of the *dioiketes'* bureau and responsible directly to the king, probably in most cases followed the instructions of the *dioiketes* in financial affairs.[18] Préaux apparently sees the control as more direct.[19] Both point to the actions of Polykrates and Ptolemaios Makron as illustrative of the situation. It was in defiance of the wishes of the *dioiketai* (Polyb. 27.13) that Ptolemaios Makron withheld revenues from Cyprus in order to accumulate them for the king's *anakleteria*, and Polykrates may have done the same. Since it seems that disobedience to the *dioiketes* is a remarkable thing, it is concluded that subordination was the usual pattern. Some support might be thought to be given to this thesis by the fact that Theopropos of Kalynda (pp. 99-100) asks Apollonios to write to the *strategos*, *oikonomos*, and city about money owing him.

Our information about the relationship of the ἐπὶ τῆς πόλεως and the *oikonomos* is somewhat conflicting. On one hand one may consider the letter of Philometor to the commandant of Thera, telling him that the king would have the *dioiketes* write to the *oikonomos* about the revenue from lands confiscated to the crown by the *oikonomos*. The commandant has an interest in the affair, but the channels of action for such things are clearly marked: financial affairs are to be handled through financial officials. But the letter of Ptolemy IX Soter II to the cities of the Cyrenaica informs them that the king was circulating to all commandants his decree limiting the procedural actions of the ἐπὶ χρείαις in matters of confiscating the property of defendants; it is, it would seem, to be the responsibility of the commandant to enforce obedience to the edict by these financial officials.

A reflection of the curious chains of communication in the Ptolemaic administration is to be found in the differing responses to *P. Teb.* 8 among scholars. There is a letter about revenues in Thrace and Lesbos addressed to one Aphrodisios. Rostovtzeff took this man to be an *oikonomos*.[20] Bengtson, on the other hand, suggests that it is at least as likely that Aphrodisios was a *strategos*, perhaps the successor of Hippomedon.[21] Since Hippomedon appears

---

18. *Die Strategie* III, p. 149.
19. *Économie royale*, p. 423.
20. *SEHHW*, p. 335.
21. *Die Strategie* III, p. 182.

as sender or addressee of a letter in the second (unpublished) column of *P. Teb.* 8, it is unlikely that Bengtson's suggestion is right. The appearance of Hippomedon in the next column, however, indicates that the *strategos* might be expected to occur in this correspondence along with the *oikonomos*.

Another area of joint action between the *oikonomos* and the *strategos* and commandants was the supplying of the military forces. Eirenaios, the *oikonomos* of Thera, Itanos, and Methana, was also secretary of the armed forces in those places, thus having in military affairs as well as economic rather a superior position to his colleague Aristippos, commandant of Thera (who was also of lower court rank). His role is paralleled by that of Diodotos and Apollodotos in Caria a century before. Apollodotos, whose role is financial in all his documents, had the care of supplying loan funds for the maintenance of a royal ship in *P. Cair. Zen.* 59036. Diodotos, *oikonomos* in 248/7, also was involved with the military: a Kalyndian asks Zenon to get Apollonios to write to Diodotos and to his city in order to get his late father's exemption from quartering and supplying soldiers passed on to him (p. 100). Zenon found the request reasonable enough that he drafted a letter on the subject to Apollonios. It is impossible to know exactly what part the *oikonomos* played and what part the city government, but each obviously had a say. We do not, unfortunately, know what official received the Ptolemaic royal letter of which a copy was published by the Cilician city of Soloi; it reprimanded the official for allowing abuses (p. 115).

Most financial affairs were the responsibility of the *oikonomos*, even those financial matters concerning the support of the military. The royal government adhered to the routine of proper channels in its operations. The *oikonomoi* were certainly subordinates of the *dioiketes*, although they were not necessarily appointed by him. The *strategos*, appointed by the king and responsible directly to him, was probably not formally subordinated to the *dioiketes*. The degree to which actual relationships followed any particular organizational model no doubt depended more on the personal influence of the various men than on any scheme of organization. If the *dioiketes* had the confidence of the king, if he had the practically vice-regal powers that Apollonios seems to have had, the *strategoi* were no doubt entirely cooperative with him. A weak minister might easily be trampled under by a *strategos* of Cyprus with the ear of the king or regent. If Apollonios is asked to write to the *strategos* of Caria about a financial matter, it is because he is Apollonios, not merely because he holds the position he does. It must be understood that the Ptolemaic court and bureaucracy were run at least as much through personal ties and influence as through theoretical rules. Any attempt to find a principle of organization to fit all behavior in Ptolemaic Egypt is bound to failure for this reason. This was an empire of men, not of bureaucratic positions.

Financial officials existed primarily to ensure and maximize the king's revenue. The sources of these revenues are known rather fragmentarily. An attempt seems to have been made to establish monopolies on key industrial products as they existed in Egypt: in the reign of Ptolemy IX an ἐπὶ τῶν μετάλλων is attested in Cyprus, and it can hardly be doubted that a close supervision of mines was at all times a key part of royal policy.[22] We learn from *P. Teb.* 8 that the purple manufacture in Lycia was farmed out for a substantial sum; the farmers no doubt had a monopoly.

Taxes levied on the empire were undoubtedly of importance, but it is hard to describe any system of taxation. Customs duties were important; they figure prominently in the Phoenician cities in various letters from the Zenon papyri (pp. 19-20), and a letter draft in *P. Teb.* 8 notes a shortfall in the farming of the διαπύλιον in Lycia by over two talents. Wine formed an important part of this, for it is records concerning wine that the writer requests. Iasos was granted the right to have control over its own harbor and other revenues in the late fourth century in return for a lump sum payment to the king each year; the concession shows how prevalent the opposite practice was. In general the Ptolemies seem to have kept control of all customs revenues and import permission in their subject cities, farming out the contracts as usual to ensure full collection of the taxes.

Beyond these levies on trade, the Ptolemies received substantial sums from lump payments by the cities, like the one negotiated by Iasos in lieu of direct taxation (pp. 90-91). Sometimes these were

22. *OGIS* 165; the person in question was Paphian and had served as gymnasiarch of his native city (cf. *OGIS* 164). Rostovtzeff, *SEHHW*, p. 339, treats the existence of an *antistrategos* in charge of the mines as the customary situation; it is surely rather the extraordinary circumstances of Soter II's Cypriot rule that one sees here.

officially voluntary, "crowns" given to the king by a city decree; the islanders did this, as did some individual islands and Halikarnassos (p. 95). We have no definite evidence yet of lump sums levied by royal command as taxes, although Préaux has suggested that the φόροι in money, grain, and other goods from Lesbos and Thrace mentioned in *P. Teb.* 8 were part of this kind of taxation.[23] Ptolemy I and Ptolemy II may have levied an εἰσφορά on the league of the islanders, but this, too, is uncertain.[24]

The question of direct royal taxation inside the provinces— beyond the customs barrier—is much controverted. Rostovtzeff remarked that new direct royal taxes were an addition to city taxes and formed a considerable burden on the populace;[25] Préaux on the other hand inclines to think that royal direct taxation did not generally go much beyond customs duties.[26] Syria, which resembled Egypt in so many respects, was certainly taxed directly, with contracts auctioned in Alexandria to local capitalists; individual members of a consortium might underwrite as small a unit as a village. The census of livestock suggests taxes on them like those in Egypt. The *oikonomoi* and komarchs were also responsible to the *dioiketes* of Syria and Phoenicia for the revenues. About Cyrene, on the other hand, we know nothing of this domain. Cyprus is scarcely better known, for it is uncertain what we are to make of the man who calls himself a tithe-collector; we have noted that some landholdings in Cyprus were managed like those in Asia Minor. A fragment from Arsinoe (Marion) mentions the *apomoira* and has language that suggests that some elements of the taxation system of Egypt were also in use on the island. The *apomoira*, which was a tax on private lands rather than a rent, shows that at least some private land was in production.

The *apomoira*, levied on wheat, beans, millet, and other crops, recurs at Telmessos in the system of taxation that existed when

---

23. C. Préaux, *Économie royale*, pp. 416-417. The argument is based on the fact that this letter speaks only of "revenues" rather than the specific ones mentioned in other letters. But the letter might have been meant to have more general application, and the argument seems to me weak.

24. They are thanked in *Syll.*[3] 390 for κουφίσας the εἰσφορά; the word can mean lighten or remove, and debate on the meaning has continued for many years. Cf. I. L. Merker, *Historia* 19, 1970, p. 151, n. 46. Préaux, *Économie royale*, p. 416, ignores the controversy to state baldly that the lightening of the payment proves its existence under the Ptolemies.

25. *SEHHW*, p. 335.

26. *Économie royale*, pp. 416-419.

Ptolemy son of Lysimachus received his *dynasteia*, but its exact nature is not certain. Ptolemy changed the payment to the tenth familiar in Asia Minor.[27] Other taxes at Telmessos were levied on orchard crops and the use of pasture land, taxes again typical of Ptolemaic practices in Egypt. The money taxes, which do not figure in this list, nonetheless existed in Lycia, for their farming is mentioned in *P. Teb.* 8. What these money taxes were we do not know. They probably also existed in Caria. I take the *iatrika* of *P. Cair. Zen.* 59036 to have been a royal tax on the Halikarnassians, and the trouble of Danaos in the same city may well have concerned the farming of an important money tax.[28]

It is difficult to form an over-all picture of Ptolemaic fiscal policy in the empire. We have particularly little about the three provinces in which royal mints operated and in which only royal currency circulated, Cyrene, Cyprus, and Syria. It is therefore not possible to make a significant distinction between the character of Ptolemaic financial administration in these provinces and that in cities which could coin money. Syria, with its *oikonomoi*, komarchs, *telonai*, and lessees of village taxes, and Cyrene, with the ἐπὶ χρείαις, were clearly administered directly by royal officials and under-writers. This is perhaps not the case in Lycia and Caria, where the civic governments played a more important role. Time and again it is with the civic officials that royal bureaucrats deal or are asked to deal. But the royal bureaucrats acted as a supervisory board over the civic government, not being content simply to receive revenues, but insisting on proper management of civic affairs. And it can scarcely be doubted that there was royal land in the areas of many cities, like the land confiscated on Thera.

4. *Diplomacy*

A wide range of activity is subsumed under this classification. A large part of Ptolemaic activities outside Egypt was carried out by means other than resident bureaucrats in the places in question. A first fundamental division is in this movement of persons which

---

27. I do not see why Rostovtzeff (*SEHHW*, p. 337) takes the *apomoira* to have been a fixed sum payment here, when it manifestly was not so in Egypt (where it was a sixth on vineyards).

28. Préaux contends that the *iatrikon* was a city tax, *Économie royale*, p. 421 (cf. her bibliography on p. 421, n. 5). See above, Chapter V, n. 60, and E. Boswinkel, *Eos* 48.1, 1956, pp. 181-190.

we have encountered with some frequency in preceding chapters: on the one hand activity initiated by the cities, or envoys sent to the crown for a specific purpose, and on the other, activity begun at the behest of the king or his officials. I believe that three divisions can be seen in the uses of diplomatic interchange: (1) settling problems in states directly governed by Ptolemaic officials and the furthering of relations between such cities and the crown; (2) indirect administration of areas under Ptolemaic control but not directly governed by Ptolemaic magistrates; and (3) expansion and maintenance of Ptolemaic influence in areas not under the king's control but either friendly to him or neutral and of importance to Ptolemaic interests. I shall try to explain these categories through examples from previous chapters.

(1) The story of Joseph (pp. 20-21) makes it clear that the contracts for underwriting the collection of taxes in the provinces were auctioned each year in Alexandria; it also suggests (and the woes of Danaos of Halikarnassos may confirm) that local capitalists, who would have known the situation and the potential revenues very well, took a major part in these auctions. This financial world must have accounted for a large flow of men and money between the provinces and the government. It can hardly be doubted that much business aside from the auctions was transacted during these visits to Alexandria.

A major source of visits to Alexandria was also the fulfilling of various religious missions. For example, Boulagoras of Samos (p. 81) served as his city's *theoros* to the court shortly after the island returned to Ptolemaic control in the first years of the reign of Ptolemy III. The league of the islanders sent a group of *theoroi* to the Ptolemaia early in Philadelphos' reign. When Theopropos and Diophantos of Kalynda served as *theoroi* [29] to Alexandria in 248, the former used the opportunity of his presence there to try to secure the intervention of Apollonios on his behalf in one of his financial problems in Kalynda.

Ptolemaic-controlled cities also sent embassies to Alexandria—and to officials in their region but not in their city—to ask for concessions, clarification, or redress of problems. There are several examples. Iasos sent to Aristoboulos and later to Asklepiodotos,

---

29. The many vases found in cemeteries near Alexandria with the names of foreigners who came as *theoroi* attest that the traffic of such men was a large one.

whom I regard as Ptolemaic governors in Caria, to ask a clarification of its financial status and a reaffirmation of the oath to protect the city and its autonomy. Samothrace asked the *strategos* Hippomedon and the commandant of Maroneia, Epinikos, for help against attack; later the city sent another embassy to the *strategos* about exemption from export restrictions and taxes. Halikarnassos sought permission from the king for the financing of a new gymnasium. Soloi in Cilicia complained to the king about abuses of quartering soldiers. Thera too sent ambassadors to the king, but we are not told their reasons for making the journey.[30]

All of this is activity involving cities ruled by the Ptolemies. In certain cases it is not sure that there were any Ptolemaic officials resident in the city, notably at Iasos and Samothrace. But in general these cities had resident officials. It is clear that such diplomatic relations played an important role in making the relationship between king and city work smoothly; religious honors were paid, business transacted, actions of bureaucrats appealed. Perhaps most important, a constant interchange of travellers enabled the cities to keep in touch with the center of power and to maintain informal contacts that could be of great value in keeping the city on good terms with the administration. Influence, we have seen, played as large a part as formal bureaucracy in getting things done, and diplomacy to Alexandria played an important role in keeping influence.

The traffic in return, of royal officials temporarily visiting cities abroad, is not so well documented in the cities where there was a resident bureaucracy. The honors given to Straton by Samos (pp. 85-87) could be an instance, but we do not have any firm evidence for resident Ptolemaic officials on Samos at this time. It would seem that if there was such movement of officials, it was not of enough significance to find its way into our sources. It is true that agents of Apollonios the businessman, in his private rather than official capacity, appear in the Zenon documents travelling and trading in Cyprus, the Levant, and South Asia Minor; it can hardly be disputed that Alexandrian businessmen were active

---

30. It is worth mentioning here the embassy of a citizen of Eresos, Damon son of Polyarchos, to a king Ptolemy, about φιλία, κρίσις, and ἐπιστατεία (pp. 161, 163). The text is too laconic to tell just what was at stake, but it was clearly of importance.

throughout the Mediterranean. But of visiting officials we hear virtually nothing.

(2) In marked contrast to this situation, there is a very large diplomatic traffic between Alexandria and a number of provinces that seemingly had little or no resident bureaucracy. In these cases the flow went in both directions, but we find a large preponderance of royal emissaries. In this class may be placed, first, the *dikastai*, the foreign judges sent to bring order to the internal affairs of the cities. These judges appear primarily among the islands, such as Samos, Kalymna, Karthaia (on Keos), Ios, Thera, and Naxos. In Keos and Thera, they were sent seemingly at the beginning of Ptolemaic control and were accompanied by *epistatai* whom I regard as marking the start of resident garrisons and officials.[31] But in Kalymna, Ios, Naxos, and perhaps Samos, the judges left on the completion of their duties and seemingly were not succeeded by a garrison. Foreign judges are, of course, a widely known Hellenistic institution.[32] Their presence in the Ptolemaic empire differs from the practice among autonomous cities in the role of the king: whether the city or the king (or one of his officers) takes the initiative, it is Ptolemy who sends for the judges—usually from a city in subjection or alliance with him (for example, Myndos, Halikarnassos, Ioulis in the first category, Athens and Kos in the second). And the *dikastai* operated according to instructions given them by the king. The royal intervention on these two points makes the *dikastai* to a certain extent agents of the royal power: they are a form of royal administration not involving permanent resident officials in the cities.

Other Ptolemaic officials also visited the islands.[33] Many of these were simply military commanders passing through and taking the opportunity to regulate affairs where necessary. Philokles king of Sidon often operated in this way; Zenon, the commander of undecked ships honored by Ios, may also be cited. Some Ptolemaic courtiers honored by Samos under Philadelphos may also have

---

31. The garrison on Keos was in Arsinoe (Koresia), however, and not in Karthaia; it seems that Karthaia itself had no resident commandant (p. 143).

32. See the general introduction to this subject by L. Robert, *Xenion, Festschrift für Pan J. Zepos*, Athens, 1973, pp. 765-782.

33. A list of these various visiting officials and some discussion of them may be found in the article of Peremans and Van 't Dack cited above, note 10.

fallen into this category. Others were sent on financial missions, like Philotheros son of Antiphanes, who visited Karthaia on an errand of collecting money.

It would seem that this sort of diplomatic administration, carried on in the absence of resident bureaucrats, is limited to the early Ptolemaic period, the reigns of Ptolemies I, II, and perhaps III, and is found only in the Aegean islands. These island cities maintained the exchange from their end; Siphnos had an envoy in Alexandria who returned to announce the progress of the current war (p. 146). What this diplomacy means as a pattern of administration I will discuss later.

(3) The Ptolemies maintained diplomatic relations with a great many cities that they never controlled. On the whole, these fall outside the scope of an inquiry into administration. In some cases, however, influence exerted through diplomacy must have bordered on the type of control through visitors outlined above. An example is the Ptolemaic role in Crete.[34] The sovereigns were widely honored in Crete in cities for which we have no reason to postulate Ptolemaic control, such as Lappa, Eleutherna, and Phalasarna. They were also allies of Gortyn and that city's choice as arbitrator in a dispute with Knossos; the ambassador sent by Ptolemy VI helped effect a settlement. In this strife some "gunboat diplomacy" was also used: Ptolemaic troops were sent to aid Gortyn. A similar intervention on the side of Itanos against Hierapytna occurred during Philometor's reign, with troops and diplomats complementing one another. What we have here, I suspect, is Ptolemaic action to preserve a situation to the best interests of the king without involving royal bureaucrats in the process more than necessary. Philometor's reign was no time for the expansion of direct administration in the Aegean, but that king was active in maintaining a Ptolemaic presence and making his will felt. This kind of activity extended the Ptolemaic sphere of influence beyond the area of actual control. It is not always easy to find the line that divides the one from the other, and in actual practice there were no doubt ill-defined areas.

---

34. An interesting if not always convincing attempt to fit the Ptolemaic role into the larger currents of Cretan politics has recently appeared, *Ptolemaic Itanos and Hellenistic Crete*, by Stylianos Spyridakis. For some reservations on his methods, see my review in *Phoenix* 25, 1971, pp. 405-406.

5. Dynasts

Under the category of *dynasteiai* Rostovtzeff [35] included the domain of Ptolemy son of Lysimachus around Telmessos and the independent or quasi-independent rule of other members of the Ptolemaic royal family in Cyprus and the Cyrenaica; he calls the latter "a kind of appendage to Egypt, ruled by a member of the Ptolemaic dynasty." This classification appears to me to rest on nothing. Cyrene was separated from the control of the king in Alexandria on several occasions, none of which appears to fit the label of *dynasteia*. Magas was simply governor for his step-father and then probably for his half-brother until the time of his revolt from the latter, after which he called himself king. Cyrene was thus either under direct royal control through a governor or independent under its own king in the time of Magas. No member of the Ptolemaic family ruled Cyrene after Magas until it became the independent kingdom of Euergetes II. Here again there was no state of "appendage." Ptolemy Apion, finally, styled himself king, not governor or dynast. Rostovtzeff's statement is thus at variance with the evidence.

In Cyprus, again, Ptolemy IX Soter II and Ptolemy X Alexander each served for a time as *strategos* of the island, being in no way independent. Each in turn later was independent king of the island in opposition to the government in Alexandria. Ptolemy the bastard was also (80-58) an independent king. Cyprus, therefore, is no more the scene of a quasi-independent *dynasteia* than is Cyrene. [36]

We are therefore left with Telmessos and Ptolemy son of Lysimachus. Although he apparently held a grant of land in the area under Philadelphos, it was Euergetes who transformed this land-grant into a wider control of the area. The Telmessians used παραλαβών to refer to Ptolemy's receipt of the area from the king. None of our inscriptions ever assigns Ptolemy son of Lysimachus or his descendants a title; nor does any make it clear just what the relationship of the dynast to Alexandria was. The king's authority was recognized in 240 (the date is by the reign of Ptolemy III), but by 193 the authority of Antiochus III was paramount and Ptolemy

---

35. *SEHHW*, pp. 333, 336.
36. Still more peculiar is the distinction of P. M. Fraser, *Ptol. Alex.* II, p. 189, n. 81, about Cyprus "which was an integral part of the realm and not a dependency." One is hard-pressed to see a difference in this regard between Cyprus and the Cyrenaica.

(grandson of the first dynast) was a prominent subject of the Seleucid. It is impossible to provide any theoretical or organizational framework for these relationships in the state of our knowledge; it may always be so. It should not surprise us that an informal relationship based on personal ties and power should be found here, for this is a Ptolemaic characteristic.

6. *Civic Institutions*

In a sense, everything in this study pertains to the life of the cities of the empire, for the Ptolemaic empire was in the main an empire grouping Greek cities. The royal component of the relationship between king and city has already been discussed at some length, and I need not take it up here. The patterns of the relationship as a whole and the administration will be discussed in the next part of this chapter. But there remains the question of the local institutions themselves. A comprehensive study of local institutions for the cities of the empire would be a work of its own and cannot be attempted here.[37] Nor would it be a fruitful task from the point of view of the scope of this study of Ptolemaic administration. Instead, I want to examine here a few aspects of civic life under the Ptolemies that may have contributed something of interest and importance to the relationship between crown and *polis*. The fact that only a few such areas of inquiry stand out is itself an indication of the normality and integrity of the political systems of cities under the Ptolemies. We find relatively few items that would surprise us in an independent city.

a. It is a negative characteristic that is most salient: we have almost no examples of the penetration of Ptolemaic personnel into the ranks of city officials. Civic offices are held by local citizens. The one important exception is Ptolemy Soter's holding office as a perpetual member of the college of *strategoi* at Cyrene, but the early date makes it impossible to extrapolate from the constitution to later periods or other areas. It appears that the king did not extend to other possessions this pattern of involving himself directly in civic government. We do not even know if the custom

---

37. If I have attempted such a collection for the cities of Cyprus, two aspects of the situation there differentiate that island from other areas and seem to me to require it: the relative paucity of the material, coupled with its wide dispersal; and the fact that the organization of Cyprus into *poleis* had been denied by Rostovtzeff.

was long maintained at Cyrene. The divorce was not so complete in cultural institutions, as we will see below, but in matters of government the city and crown were separate entities operating in cooperation but without any interchange of personnel so far as we can tell.

Coupled with this fact is another negative one: the civic institutions of Ptolemaic cities show no remarkable features that would suggest adaptation of normal political methods to suit a subordinate position before the king. No special offices are attested for carrying on relationships with the crown; no modifications of existing forms of government are known. The real test of this tendency is the Cypriot experience, for there it can only have been under Ptolemaic rule that many of these institutions developed. Cypriot cities, long under monarchies, were not the less Hellenic for that fact, but their democratic political life was probably somewhat retarded. Under Ptolemaic rule there was a rapid development of regular Greek institutions; certainly by the middle of the third century Kourion—hardly one of the most important or prosperous cities—had the apparatus of civic self-government. The kings therefore not only did not interfere with democratic institutions; it would seem that they encouraged their development.[38]

b. It is hardly to be expected, however, that long years of Ptolemaic control, especially in Cyprus, Cyrene, and Syria, would not produce some interplay of civic and royal government. Obviously there was a great deal. It rarely resulted in situations where one person was active in both areas. Onesandros, the prominent Paphiot (and holder of many civic offices) who rose to become director of the Alexandrian library and probably eponymous priest under Soter II, was an exceptional man in unusual times. The same may be said of the Paphiot gymnasiarch Potamon, who served the same king as *antistrategos* and head of the mines. Soter, largely isolated for two decades from the Alexandrians who provided much of any

---

38. One might conclude that the Ptolemies favored oligarchic city governments if one followed Mitford's argument that both Kourion and Paphos had such regimes under the Ptolemies (*I. Kourion*, pp. 78-79). But the evidence he cites is slight and does not seem to me to point in the direction he thinks. Cf. my arguments on the subject in *Chronique d'Égypte* 49, 1974, p. 181. The somewhat oligarchic character of the constitution of Cyrene probably reflects (1) the previous form of government, and (2) the fact that in this dispute it was a group of wealthy exiles who afforded Ptolemy I a chance to intervene in Cyrene.

king's retinue, and entirely dependent for survival on the safety of his Cypriot base, made capable use of the manpower he could tap on Cyprus. It was a remarkable period for the island.[39]

These men held unusually high positions, but the elevation of a Cypriot to royal office was not without precedent. It is of interest to see that in the mid-second century a Salaminian, Dionysios son of Aigibios, had the court rank τῶν φίλων and was at the same time a royal judge and former city *strategos*. He therefore held both civic and royal office; both soldiers and local villagers united to honor him. The royal judge was in this instance a local man appointed to a royal office. A similar situation obtained in the Macedonian institutions of Dura-Europos, where most of the characteristic institutions of the Greek city are lacking. It may well be that we have yet to learn much about the cities of Cyprus; perhaps the Macedonian heritage of the Ptolemies was of more importance than present evidence allows us to say.

c. A second area of interpenetration was the gymnasium. There is evidence from Cyprus and Thera of contributions by Ptolemaic soldiers to the upkeep of the gymnasia, generally through funds for the purchase of oil. Launey devoted a long chapter of his great work to Ptolemaic gymnasia, mostly in Egypt, where they were, he concluded, a means of soldiers' preserving their families' Hellenic culture in the face of an overwhelmingly present native one.[40] Thus even to late Ptolemaic times no natives took part in the gymnastic and military education of the gymnasia of Egypt. In the foreign possessions we are in a somewhat different situation, one to which Launey did not give any special attention. Thera and Cyprus were both Hellenic lands already possessing Greek institutions such as the gymnasium.

T. B. Mitford, however, has applied to Cyprus the conclusions that Launey drew for Egypt: [41] "There would seem, then, little doubt that these anonymous 'members of the gymnasium' were predominantly military." This statement appears to me to go beyond the evidence. The garrison took part in the support of the gymnasia of the cities where they were stationed; there can be no doubt that their sons were trained in the gymnasia that they

39. T. B. Mitford has promised a special study of Soter's Cypriot reign, *JHS* 79, 1959, pp. 128-129.

40. *Armées hellénistiques*, pp. 813-879.

41. *I. Kourion*, pp. 101-102.

supported. But the alumni of the gymnasia were not therefore only or primarily members of the Ptolemaic garrison.[42] These organizations, I suspect, provided a common ground for soldier and citizen to share religious and educational traditions.

d. The Ptolemies founded or refounded a number of cities which received dynastic names, mostly Arsinoe or Ptolemais. Outside of Egypt, Cyprus, Syria, and the Cyrenaica, these cities were all refoundations, none of which retained the dynastic name for long after the end of Ptolemaic control. Most of these were of minor importance and we know little of them except notices in the geographers. Of the more important ones, we know too little about their institutions under Ptolemaic domination. Two at least coined, Ptolemais (Lebedos) and Arsinoe (Rithymna); their issues indicate a degree of civic autonomy like that of other cities. We are probably justified in thinking that refoundation did not alter civic institutions significantly.

In the core regions of the empire, the cities retained dynastic names in later times, a clear demonstration of the deeper roots Ptolemaic rule had there: Ptolemais in Phoenicia, Ptolemais in the Cyrenaica (along with Berenike), Arsinoe in Cyprus, all remained as testimony to Ptolemaic control. Arsinoe (Marion) had, so far as we can see, Greek political forms, but we know little about local institutions in the others. So far as one can tell, they shared the lot of other cities in their regions, differing from them not at all as a result of the dynastic foundation.

7. *The* Chora

In Egypt, the bulk of the country was ruled directly by royal bureaucrats; it had no connection to any Greek city, for only small tracts around Ptolemais, Naukratis, and Alexandria belonged to the cities. The officials of the nomes had nothing to do, officially, with the governing of cities. In Syria and Phoenicia, we have seen,

---

42. Mitford remarks correctly that the gymnasium was a center of dynastic loyalty (more precisely, of the dynastic cult). His only other argument for making the ἀπὸ γυμνασίου members of the garrison is that they are not found after the end of Philometor's reign, after Euergetes II withdrew many small garrisons from the island and replaced settlers with mercenaries. Yet Mitford himself admits that there was a connection between the military, "both mercenaries and settlers" and the gymnasium and in the large cities from which our evidence comes, the garrisons remained under Euergetes. There seems to be no logic in his argument that this shows a royal military character in the ἀπὸ γυμνασίου.

a similar situation obtained: the Phoenician cities of the coast, though ruled by the king, retained local institutions of self-government, while the territories inland, devoid of cities, were directly subjected to the crown officials who ruled the hyparchies, the administrative districts. We know little about the governors of Syria, but in all probability they governed both the cities and the country. The same can be said of Egypt only with respect to the king himself, for we know little of the relationship of the *dioiketes* to the cities. In other external possessions, our discussions have shown the *strategoi* to be governors of both cities and their lands in their provinces.

For one province, however, it has been argued by Bengtson that this is not the case, that is, that there was a governor who ruled only the *chora*: Philammon in the Cyrenaica. Polybius gives him the title "libyarch τῶν κατὰ Κυρήνην τόπων" (see pp. 33-34). We know that there were tribes living in the interior of the Cyrenaica, in the *chora*, and Bengtson sees Philammon as governor only of these.[43] The argument rests on the word τόποι; Bengtson cites its usage in other Hellenistic kingdoms, where he takes it to mean the lands (but not cities) of a satrapy, which are subject to its governor.[44] One may doubt Bengtson's interpretation of the Seleucid and Attalid record; and one may hesitate to state flatly that a term must mean the same thing in different kingdoms (for there are examples where this is not true). But more importantly, there is Ptolemaic evidence to contradict the hypothesis: the title of Hippomedon, *strategos* of the *topoi* in Thrace and the Hellespont. Hippomedon was incontestably governor over Samothrace, with discretion to grant or refuse its requests in matters of customs barriers, and the word τόποι cannot, therefore, be used to demonstrate the limitation of Philammon's competence to the *chora*.[45]

B. PATTERNS

In the first part of this chapter we have followed the evolution and nature of certain key institutions in the Ptolemaic empire. It has been possible to discern patterns of action and attitude in the approach successive kings took to these problems. But a more

---

43. *Die Strategie* III, p. 157.
44. He cites his *Die Strategie* II, pp. 211 ff. Cf. pp. 246-247 on this problem.
45. In discussing Hippomedon, Bengtson does not allude to this problem.

fundamental question must be asked: is it possible to see and formulate any overall system of administration for the empire as a whole, for the entire Ptolemaic period? And if so, is this the work of planning on the part of the Ptolemies or their officials—or did it simply happen? The answer to the first question is, I suggest, a qualified yes, which needs amplification. The second is more difficult, and I will reserve it until after the nature of the system I will delineate is clearer.

It must be evident by now that a rather fundamental distinction is to be made between the central core of the empire—Cyprus, Cyrenaica, Syria and Phoenicia, in addition to Egypt—and the other possessions. This first group shares a cluster of important characteristics: all are near Egypt and capable of good communications with it; all are vital to the security of Egypt's frontiers, for a power controlling these three need not, in antiquity, fear any overland or naval attack on Egypt itself. They formed a closed currency zone in which only Ptolemaic coins were issued and circulated, and little of that money went out of this zone. All had, at least by the second century (and probably earlier) one dominant royal governor, a *strategos*. In all the principal cities and at many subordinate points there were royal garrisons stationed. It is likely that all of them had, like Egypt, a system of cleruchic military settlement. All had a large number of bureaucrats from the central government and no doubt visiting agents of the *dioiketes* who furthered the exploitation of the areas—for all of these areas were rich in natural and productive economic assets, many of which filled Egypt's deficiencies. Taxation was probably carried out directly by crown officials, with the tax farmers underwriting the results in all of these provinces.

There were no doubt a great many variations on this pattern; and it certainly took many years for it to emerge fully developed in all areas. But the main features are clearly recognizable as those of the Ptolemaic organization and exploitation of Egypt, as many scholars have already pointed out. What we have here is the closest thing one can find in the Ptolemaic kingdom to a standard form of administration, a "Ptolemaic norm." It is these provinces that led Claire Préaux to remark that the Ptolemies had a tendency to unify the fiscal systems of the parts of their empire.[46] What dif-

---

46. *Economie royale*, pp. 422-423.

ferences we can see among these provinces come largely from different degrees of urbanization and relationship between cities and country that existed in them. The Direct administration probably played a proportionately more important role as the amount of *chora* not directly attributed to the cities was larger. In Syria and Palestine this land was less extensive than in Egypt, in Cyrenaica less extensive than in Syria, and in Cyprus less than in Cyrenaica. The difference was largely dependent on the extent to which the cities could be used as an efficient administrative vehicle, and the Ptolemies showed no reluctance to delegate tasks to cities as much as possible. In this situation, the distinction made by Rostovtzeff [47] between Hellenic and Oriental provinces does not seem to be helpful, for all of the provinces in the core group were administered in much the same way, regardless of the degree of development of city life, the only differences being ones of degree.[48] What is important is that these areas formed the core of Ptolemaic power, wealth, and security and were accordingly administered in a generally uniform manner—although this developed over the years, and was not imposed all at once.

The remainder of the empire may be characterized in the first instance by the negative attribute of not belonging to the first group, or of not being a part of the core of the empire. Held mostly for shorter periods of time, these places had neither the military importance nor the economic primacy for the survival of the monarchy in Egypt that the core did. Not that their gain or loss was unimportant, but the empire did not rise or fall by them as it did by the core. The outer provinces all in common lack certain characteristics of the first group: Ptolemaic currency was in general neither minted nor circulated; direct taxation was no doubt a less important part of the total tax burden on the citizens of the cities; direct administration of the countryside by royal officials is largely lacking, as they act through city governments in most instances.

So much the areas have in common. The next task is to find any principles of differentiation among them. A fundamental division may be made first between those cities and areas having resident officials and garrisons and those lacking them. We take the former

---

47. *SEHHW*, p. 339.
48. Mitford, too, seems to accept the distinction, though he disagrees with Rostovtzeff over which category Cyprus belongs to: *Aegyptus* 33, 1953, p. 80, and *I. Kourion*, p. 76.

group first. It contains most of the Ptolemaic empire outside the
"core": all of south Asia Minor, Caria, Ionia, Thrace, and the
Hellespont, and a number of insular bases: Samos, Thera, Koresia,
Itanos, Lesbos (?) and Methana. The positive characteristics that
these share with the core are numerous: regional governors (*strategoi*); garrisons and their commandants; royal financial officials;
some direct taxation; royal monopolies; a tendency to act through
the cities. Their diplomatic activity is, as we have seen above,
characterized by a steady stream of visitors to Alexandria from
the cities, as they attempted to settle formally or informally
problems that the resident officials could not or would not solve.
They thus bore a considerable resemblance in overall pattern to
the core areas of the empire, differing chiefly in the lack of a close
fiscal assimilation to them.

Within this group another distinction may be observed, between
those regions in which the Ptolemies controlled many or most of
the cities and much of the territory, and those where—even though
a Ptolemaic governor might exist—the province consisted of no
more than isolated cities held as military or naval bases. It is not,
however, always clear in which division an area is to be placed.
As regionally controlled areas one may identify Cilicia Trachea,
Lycia, Pamphylia, Caria, and perhaps Thrace. In the category of
bases I would list Samos, Itanos, Thera, Koresia, Methana, and
the cities of Ionia. The situation of the islands in the period of the
league of the islanders was of course somewhat different, but for
the most part the islands I have named were truly isolated bases in
the naval network. Ionia and Thrace both remain somewhat uncertain, for we know of only a few cities in each area that were
definitely under Ptolemaic rule at any time. Future finds may yet
alter our perspective on these areas drastically. Ionia, for example,
is claimed by Euergetes as his conquest, in contrast to the evidence
known until a few years ago; but only recently, with the finds of
L. Robert, have such places as Kolophon (with Klaros) been added
to our list of cities for which Ptolemaic domination under Euergetes
is known. These divisions do not, however, affect the nature of the
administration very much; they mattered primarily in the degree
of economic exploitation that they allowed.

The third major group of dominions includes those of the Aegean
islands that were not bases but under Ptolemaic control: the
Cyclades, Chios, Samothrace, and probably Kos and Kalymna.

This is the group in which diplomatic activity of the second type discussed above is predominant: visiting Ptolemaic officials play a major role in maintaining internal order to the king's satisfaction, but no garrisons or resident bureaucrats are attested. The plentitude of evidence for diplomacy makes it unlikely that mere lack of sources has distorted the picture with respect to resident officials. It would appear that a nesiarch and *oikonomos* governed the area of the Cyclades without the aid of the multiple subordinates that we encounter in Caria, for example. They probably also did not interfere as much or as directly in internal affairs. Ptolemaic control in this area was not the less real while it lasted, and the kings were more than "powerful allies" [49] to the islanders. But the lack of resident forces and officials meant that Ptolemaic influence rested only on military superiority in the region and vanished quickly and with few traces when this waned. In the islands there are few of the signs of Ptolemaic occupation that lingered after them in other places (except, of course, for buildings on Samothrace, but these are of religious origin and purpose). And these cities probably paid no direct taxes, although they may have paid lump-sum tribute to the king and have even been subjected to a number of financial controls, as in the case of Samothrace. The measure of civic autonomy is greater in this group than in any other.

Such is the observed pattern; now it remains to explain it. A first point of note is chronological. The third group is mostly a creation of the reigns of Soter and Philadelphos, and it was extinct by the end of the third century. The regional groupings of the second type of province were also lost by the early second century. What remained was thus the core of the empire (less Syria and Phoenicia) and a few outlying bases that differed from the core only in fiscality. Even in financial matters the differences were probably small in the second century, except of course for coinage. In other words, the less closely administered parts of the empire were lost by the mid-point in the career of that empire. This date coincides with the end of the Ptolemaic dynasty as a major force in the Greek world, the dismemberment of the empire by Antiochus III and Philip V. The looser forms of administration thus belong to a period in which the range of Ptolemaic influence was great and in which different ends might be met by different means.

---

49. Rostovtzeff, *SEHHW*, p. 333.

This impression is confirmed by the growing systematization of administration among remaining provinces, especially in the core. It is no coincidence, I am sure, that what we have established as the classic, normal lines of Ptolemaic administration appear mainly after the middle of Philadelphos' reign, when a diminution in Ptolemaic sea power restricted the king's range of options. The standardization appears to have accelerated in the second century after the loss of the bulk of the empire took away even more latitude of action. The contrast between the relative uniformity of Cypriot inscriptions of the second century and the diversity of those of the third is striking and illustrative of the tendency. The air of formality is further heightened, as time goes by, in the use of court rank and the much fuller enumeration of titles in inscriptions. It would seem that along with flexibility in foreign affairs the Ptolemies lost much of the variety and flexibility of provincial administration. It was worth keeping many options open and lines of communication informal at a time when Ptolemaic influence was widely exerted in many different ways. The collapse under Epiphanes brought some rigidity and formality to the administration.

Pragmatic adaptation to circumstances is the characteristic that best describes the development of administrative structures. Rostovtzeff put it this way: [50]

> There was no *one* system of provincial administration at the court of the Ptolemies. The systems were adapted to local conditions and may have been changed very often according to circumstances. We have no right to postulate such a uniform organization for the Ptolemaic epoch, individual and informal as it was; a regular system of provincial administration first grew up in the Roman world state. The process of its formation was slow and in its beginnings it was very similar to the Ptolemaic system or rather to the Ptolemaic lack of system.

He thus emphasized the flexible and pragmatic character of Ptolemaic rule. It is significant that these words come from *A Large Estate*, a book that deals with the third century. Rostovtzeff goes too far, however, in emphasizing the variability of administration, even in the third century—and much more so for the second. Pragmatic adaptation does not exclude the existence of a system or attitudes that are adapted. These tendencies, which evolved

---

50. *Large Estate*, pp. 26-27, n. 36.

from the experience of the third century, included the territorial governorship, with the various forms tried for it, the widening competence of the city commandant, and the various aspects of the economic exploitation of the provinces. It was the reign of Philadelphos that served to crystallize these forms and forward the development that matured in the second century. The reign of Ptolemy I appears largely as a time of experimentation in administration, when problems were first faced. Soter was until near the end of his reign constantly involved in the acquisition of the empire. Philadelphos and Euergetes both experienced fluctuations, but their work was more important in the area of organization and systematization.

One further principle of administration that runs through the evidence is the dependence of officials on one another and the king. Our evidence for royal appointment of commandants is limited to the case of Epinikos at Maroneia, who according to the people of Samothrace was appointed by the king. Royal relations with these commandants could, however, proceed directly: thus Philometor wrote to the commandant of Thera, and Soter II promised to do so to commandants in the Cyrenaica. And Epinikos acted ostensibly on his own in aiding Samothrace, even though we know that the *strategos* of the area, Hippomedon, did so at the same time. Samothrace was concerned to thank Epinikos by a separate decree. In contrast, we have no attested instance of a *strategos* ordering a commandant to do something. This is not to say that commandants were not in theory and practice subordinates of the *strategoi*; but clearly their mandate and appointment—and often orders—came from the king. They were thus of consequence and not creatures of the *strategos*.

The *oikonomos* was evidently the colleague of the *strategos*, not his subordinate; so much one can gather from Diodotos' position on a tribunal with Motes in Caria under Philadelphos. And the *oikonomos* was at least the equal if not somewhat higher in rank than the commandant. We cannot be certain that the *oikonomos* was appointed directly by the king, however; this may have been the responsibility of the *dioiketes*. But the financial branch had its own channels of communication: Philometor says he will have the *dioiketes* write to the *oikonomos* on Thera; the king does not write himself. The commandant thus had closer access to the king than did the *oikonomos*.

The purpose of the division of authority and the royal appointments at the local level was probably to prevent the accumulation
of excessive power in the hands of any one man, especially that
of the *strategos*, whose power was difficult to curb. Two attempts
to betray Cyprus reveal the dangers of leaving the *strategos* in too
strong a position. The principle is not new; it was used by Alexander,
and it was not new to him either. As Ernst Badian remarks, "royal
appointees in hierarchically subordinate posts are a traditional
Achaemenid feature: like garrison commanders, tax-collectors and
other high officials may always have been thus appointed by the
king."[51] One may suspect that this idea of division of power through
royal control of lower levels did not always work. In Egypt the
strategoi gradually gathered more and more power into their hands,
rendering the other nome officials impotent. It is not unlikely that
such a process operated in the empire as well. And yet what second-
century evidence we have points to a continuation of the tradition
of division.

C. COMPARISONS

It may be hazardous to conclude with an attempt to place the
administration of the Ptolemaic empire in perspective against
Hellenistic administration as a whole; for only on the Ptolemaic
side can the comparison be based on my detailed study of the
evidence. But it is nonetheless a task worth trying in brief compass.
I have taken Bengtson as the most authoritative modern student
of the entire scene, for his exhaustive analysis of ancient sources
and detailed criticism of modern views have given his interpretations
a pervading influence on our conceptions of Hellenistic administration.

We may begin with his conception of a division between the
general imperial administration (*Reichsverwaltung*) and the territorial administration. The latter consisted, in the Seleucid empire,
of the lands subject to the governor of each satrapy, while the
former embraced also the cities in that area which depended
directly on the king.[52] The satrapal territories were under the
Seleucids called the *topoi*; as the king would call them in writing
to their governor (satrap or *strategos*), οἱ ὑπὸ σὲ τόποι. Bengtson

---

51. *Greece and Rome*, 2 ser. 12, 1965, p. 173.
52. Bengtson, *Die Strategie* II, pp. 9-12.

traces the similar use of τόποι in the Attalid kingdom,[53] and asserts also that the same distinction can be observed in the Ptolemaic empire.[54] We have already seen that this assertion is unfounded so far as the Ptolemaic kingdom goes; and under the Attalids, too, one may be doubtful, for Bengtson himself stresses the authority of provincial governors over cities in their provinces in the Attalid empire of the second century.[55] If we reject the distinction for Pergamon and the Ptolemies, are we to accept it for the Seleucids? Bengtson, while rejecting legalistic attempts to define narrowly the status of the cities in the Seleucid kingdom, argues that *strategoi* of those monarchs intervened in civic affairs only to carry out direct royal orders, never of their own will and discretion.[56] If this is true, it represents a marked difference between Seleucid and Ptolemaic practices with regard to cities. But the dividing line may be finally illusory in specific instances, when the king was distant and the *strategos* near.

A second area of interest is the structure of authority within provincial administrations. We have seen that while Ptolemaic governors held the supreme power in their provinces and acted in economic affairs as it seemed best to them, their authority was shared with a financial official, usually an *oikonomos*, who was a colleague rather than a subordinate and who answered to the king through the *dioiketes* and not through the *strategos* or his equivalent. The situation in the Seleucid empire as outlined by Bengtson is somewhat different. The early provincial governors, called satraps, united all of the governing power in their hands within their provinces; all functionaries were therefore responsible to the king through the satrap. The only exception came in certain satrapies where a native was satrap and a Macedonian *strategos* was left to command the garrison troops. The independent-mindedness of the major eastern satraps at times shows that most of them had complete military control of their provinces. Apart from the administration stood royal managers (*oikonomoi*) over royal estates; these were not a part of the royal administration but rather stewards over the king's personal—and directly managed—lands.[57]

53. Bengtson II, pp. 211 ff.
54. See note 52.
55. Bengtson II, pp. 215 ff., 225.
56. Bengtson II, p. 139; cf. his remarks, pp. 8-9, on the theories of Biker-mann and Heuss.
57. Bengtson II, pp. 48-56.

When Asia Minor, usually ruled by a *strategos* in Sardis and perhaps his subordinates, was added to the Seleucid empire, similar principles were followed there.[58] This system was maintained until the reign of Antiochus III, when Bengtson places a major change in the administration of the kingdom. In this reorganization, the financial branch of the administration was separated from the military-civil, which was now represented by *strategoi* in all provinces (except vassal states); an official called ὁ ἐπὶ τῶν προσόδων supervised economic affairs in each satrapy, reporting directly to the central government. This scheme is much like the Ptolemaic, and Bengtson goes so far as to see in it a deliberate imitation.[59] But the new system did not hold up for long under the successors of Antiochus III, for the title satrap re-emerged and with it, in all likelihood, the vice-regal powers long associated with the title. Bengtson is surely right to see in this the gradual disintegration of the centralist system that Antiochus created into the semi-autonomous arrangement of regions frequently characteristic of the Seleucids and of the Achaemenids before them.

When Bengtson discusses the Attalid kingdom, however, he isolates a similarity between it and the Ptolemaic empire that rather contradicts what he has said in considering the Seleucids: Attalid financial officials were dependent on the *strategoi*, and Bengtson supposes this to be the system in Cyprus.[60] It is true that the Ptolemaic *strategoi* had competence in some financial matters, but the *oikonomoi* were, it seems, their colleagues and not their subordinates; we are far from being able to delineate the separation of powers between these two positions, if formal separation there was. It would seem, therefore, that the true resemblance of the Attalid system was to the earlier Seleucids, not to the practices of the Ptolemies.

The area in which the Seleucids took some pains to provide separation of powers was the distinction between military and civil authorities. *Strategoi* would sometimes be in charge of the troops of a satrapy but not its administration, and the mobilization of military settlers in time of war was also the function of *strategoi*,

---

58. Bengtson II, pp. 125 ff.
59. Cf. note 58 and Bengtson II, p. 147.
60. Bengtson II, pp. 223-224. He is discussing only second-century Attalid administration here, having concluded (p. 210) that no firm statements can be made for the period before the peace of Apamea.

not of satraps.[61] Whether individual garrison commanders were also appointed directly by the crown, as in the Ptolemaic empire, we do not know. The Ptolemies themselves may have experimented in the early period with a separation of military and civil powers, for example in the division between nesiarch and admiral, for the latter was the military chief. But it would be unwise to push this suggestion very far, for we know that Bacchon had naval forces at his disposal. The early Attalids also separated the military establishment from the civil, in an even more complete division, so that the early *strategoi* in the Attalid kingdom are purely military commanders.[62] The Seleucids did not pursue this policy consistently—as the many satrapal rebellions show—and it took a centralist and strong king like Antiochus III to combat satraps' attempts to gather in all power in their provinces to themselves. Antiochus, indeed, reversed the trend by giving the civil powers to the military commanders, thereby following what had long been the Ptolemaic custom.

One other aspect of Seleucid administration marks the royal attempt to keep power in the hands of the king and not of the satraps, the *"Oberkommando"* of a larger area than one satrapy. Both in the "upper satrapies" and in Asia Minor there was at several points a *strategos* with authority over several satrapies.[63] The Ptolemaic empire had nothing comparable, although the *strategos* of the Thebaid occupied a structurally similar post. Each governor of a Ptolemaic province reported directly to the king without intermediary and received his orders in the same way.

The Ptolemaic system of administration in the empire, as in Egypt, rested on a carefully constructed set of checks and balances. The military security of each province was provided for by the concentration of military and civil authority in the hands of the individual governors. The *strategoi* faced any opponents confident in full power over their provinces. Their power was further bolstered by the fact that they were accountable to the king and to no other superior. On the whole, the system seems to have been fairly successful in providing for defense; it was only the simultaneous assault of Philip and Antiochus in the minority of Ptolemy V that was able seriously to dismember the extremities of the empire, at

---

61. Bengtson II, pp. 67-78.
62. Bengtson II, p. 205.
63. Bengtson II, pp. 78-89 (upper satrapies), 90-114 (Asia Minor).

a time when the generals could look to less than strong leadership in Alexandria.[64]

It was not enough to provide strong governors: their ability to defend their provinces was not to be allowed to make them strong enough to defy the king. Several checks were placed on them. First, most financial affairs and the direction of the logistical branch of the armed forces fell to the lot of the *oikonomos*, who reported not to the *strategos* but to the *dioiketes* in Alexandria. A strong *strategos* might overshadow his *oikonomos*, but his power to act independently of the king's wishes was effectively curbed by his having to share control of the funds on which he depended. Secondly, the commanders of garrisons were appointed directly by the king, so that a *strategos* could not (except by illegal force) eliminate a commander who might oppose his designs. And thirdly, no one was allowed to accumulate power over multiple provinces. Even a successful revolt, therefore, could inflict only limited damage.

These precautions seem to have been fairly successful. Magas revolted only with the support of Philadelphos' foe Antiochus I; Ptolemy the son also went over to the Seleucids during a war, but his damage, too, was limited to his own area. Theodotos the Aetolian, again a defection to the Seleucid side, did not have a lasting effect even on his own province of Syria. Of the governors of Cyprus who defected, Ptolemaios Makron did so in the crisis of the early 160's (and also had no lasting effect), while Archias was detected and committed suicide. It is a fairly good record for an empire that was scattered all around the eastern Mediterranean.

The Seleucids faced similar problems, but still more severe ones. Separatism was also a problem for them. But the response from most of the Seleucid kings was very different from the Ptolemaic one. The initial and usual pattern was that of a satrap uniting all powers in his person. This system achieved the goal of defense against attack, but left the satrap in too independent a position. The further he was from the king, the more serious this problem. The first response was therefore to separate military power from civil; the second was to impose super-commanders over large regions. The first of these was inherently dangerous to the defense

---

64. The weakness of Epiphanes' government should not, however, be overemphasized. The ministers evidently mounted an expedition to recapture Samos (successfully) as well as carrying on long campaigns in Syria in 202-198.

of the provinces, however, while the second simply moved the level of danger to the regional—as Antiochus Hierax and Achaeus demonstrated quite clearly. A third check was the limit on the satrap or *strategos* in dealing with the cities of his province; but this, too, tended to undermine his authority rather than to keep him subject to the king. Where the Seleucid response to the problem of governing a vast empire diverged from the Ptolemaic it was generally less successful in providing a centralizing force. Antiochus III recognized this and tried to counteract it, but weaker kings after him undid his work.

The characteristic that set Ptolemaic rule apart from other Hellenistic administrations, especially from the Seleucids, was described by Bengtson as uniformity: "haben die ersten Ptolemäer der ptolemäischen Reichsverwaltung eine gewisse Uniformität gegeben, die ihn erhalten geblieben ist, solange es überhaupt einen ptolemäischen Staat gegeben hat." [65] In contrast to this *"Einheitlichkeit"* he places the East-West dichotomy in the Seleucid empire. We have seen clearly that on the local level this uniformity is a mirage created by titles, and that the administrative treatment of different areas might be greatly divergent. What is remarkable about the administration of the Ptolemaic empire is the very substantial success with which the Ptolemies were able to combine the delegation of a large measure of authority to their officials with the maintenance of a strict control over their actions by the central government—in the last analysis, by the king.

---

65. *Actes VII Congr. Papyr., Museum Helveticum* 10, 1953, p. 174

STRATEGOI OF CYPRUS FROM 217 TO 40

1. PELOPS SON OF PELOPS [1]

The first *strategos* of Cyprus attested in the epigraphical evidence is Pelops son of Pelops son of Alexandros, Macedonian. His father had been a commander of Ptolemaic forces on or visiting Samos under Ptolemy II and was eponymous priest of Alexander and the Theoi Adelphoi in 264/3.[2] The son married Myrsine, daughter evidently of that Hyperbassas also honored on Samos in the reign of Ptolemy II, and sister to a canephore of Arsinoe in 243/2. His career began with positions in other areas, it seems: he was honored by the Cyrenaeans during the reign of Euergetes, but the inscription is mutilated and the description of Pelops' post, if any, lost.[3]

Pelops' first inscription on Cyprus is a dedication of a statue of Ptolemy IV in Salamis.[4] In it the king is lacking the cult title Philopator, and no mention of Arsinoe III is made. The latter circumstance does not prove an early date, since the text is a statue base rather than a motive-formula, but the omission of Philopator suggests a date before 217. Pelops seemingly has no title (there is no space at right and no trace of it below), so that his position during the years before 217 is not certain.

The title of *strategos* appears for the first time in Cypriot epigraphy in two inscriptions to be placed in the period 217-209. One is a statue of Pelops' wife Myrsine set up by the city of Paphos to honor her husband, στρατηγὸς τῆς νήσου, for his *eunoia* toward the city and the king and queen.[5] The second text is a similar statue of Myrsine erected at Salamis by members of the garrison, with an identical motive formula.[6] This formula places both dedications after Philopator's marriage in 217, but before the birth of Ptolemy V

---

1. *Pros. Ptol.* 15064.
2. See pp. 83-84; about 270-260.
3. Pelops in Cyrene: p. 36.
4. *OGIS* 75.
5. *I. Hell. Paphos* 39 (*OGIS* 84).
6. *JEA* 46, 1960, p. 110, no. 3; this brief note by Mitford is the best recent discussion of Pelops.

in 209. A third inscription, found at Lindos in Rhodes, but originally set up in Cyprus and moved in mediaeval or modern times, is a statue base for Pelops' son Ptolemaios (on Mitford's rereading) set up by the alumni of the gymnasium (of Paphos) in which the motive formula includes Epiphanes; the date is therefore 209-204.[7]

Pelops left Cyprus in 204/3, when Agathokles sent him to Antiochus III.[8] After this mission Pelops, by now probably an old man, is not mentioned again in our sources.

Pelops was probably on Cyprus in some position, perhaps as governor, before 217, but he seemingly did not use whatever title he had in a dedication before that date. Sometime probably after 217, perhaps not long after, but before 209, he was *strategos* and retained that post until 204.

2. POLYKRATES OF ARGOS [9]

The next *strategos*, Polykrates son of Mnasiadas of Argos, a famous wrestler, was a first-generation immigrant into Ptolemaic service, who had come to Egypt a few years before Raphia, helped train part of the army, and commanded cavalry at the battle in 217.[10] From that time until 203 we see nothing of him. But he had evidently risen in position very considerably, for his female relatives appear prominently in Polybius' account of the aftermath of the death of Philopator and Arsinoe; they appear to have been on at best guarded terms with Agathokles' family.[11] It is not impossible that Polykrates' appointment as *strategos* of Cyprus was not made until after the death of Agathokles.

---

7. *JEA* 46, 1960, p. 110, where the original publication of *I. Lindos* is corrected. The suggestion that *I. Lindos* 139 was a *pierre errante* was made by Kinch and approved by J. and L. Robert, *Bull. épigr.* 1942, 176. P. M. Fraser, *Ptol. Alex.* I, p. 104, asserts that Pelops' son Ptolemaios "was honoured by the Rhodians for his services to the city, no doubt as a Ptolemaic envoy," thus apparently missing the point of the note of Mitford in the *JEA*, which he cites as his evidence for his assertion. It should be mentioned here that T. B. Mitford has suggested that the man honored in *I. Kourion* 41 was a *strategos* and probably Pelops, but there is no real evidence for this suggestion.

8. See M. Holleaux, *Rome, la Grèce et les monarchies hellénistiques*, Paris, 1921, pp. 70 f.; H. Schmitt, *Untersuchungen zur Geschichte Antiochos' des Grossen*, Wiesbaden, 1964, p. 233, n. 2 and p. 236; Polyb. 15.25.13.

9. *Pros. Ptol.* 2172 and 15065.

10. Polyb. 5.64.4, 6; 5.65.5; 5.82.3; 5.84.8.

11. Polyb. 15.29.10 tells the story of how Polykrates' relatives tried to console Oenanthe, but being rebuffed cursed her heartily.

In any case, Polykrates was, according to Polybius, an energetic and careful governor of Cyprus, and when he returned to Alexandria in 197/6 for the trial of Skopas and the *anakleteria* of Epiphanes, he brought his master a large accumulation of revenues gáthered during a difficult period for the dynasty.[12] A number of inscriptions also attest his *strategia*. A group of Paphian inscriptions reveals the existence of a large family group of statues of Polykrates and his family erected by the city of Paphos: his wife, father, and children all apparently figured in it.[13] Paphos was also the location of a dedication by an Alexandrian woman, Stratonike daughter of Nikias, to Polykrates' wife Zeuxo of Cyrene,[14] and a dedication by part of the garrison to Polykrates and his family.[15] There is, finally, a statue of Epiphanes set up by Polykrates himself; Mitford suggests that it was erected shortly before the end of Polykrates' term on the island.[16] In all cases where his titulature is preserved, Polykrates is called *strategos* and *archiereus*, high-priest.

Polykrates' career did not end with his *strategia;* we find him again fighting rebellious Egyptians in 185/4.[17] Polybius also remarks that Polykrates spent much of his later life in licentious behavior and dissipated his good name (though not, it seems, the fortune he had amassed for himself while serving the royal interests in Cyprus).[18]

His family continued to be prominent: his sons Polykrates and Ptolemaios both served in Cyprus after the end of their father's *strategia*.[19] Various members of the family entered and won several

---

12. Polyb. 18.54.1; 18.55.4.

13. *I. Hell. Paphos* 43-45, with brief commentary. Cf. also M. Mitsos, *Revue des études grecques* 59-60, 1946-1947, p. 175 (identification of inscriptions of two daughters of Polykrates), and J. and L. Robert, *Bull. épig.* 1949, 202.

14. *I. Hell. Paphos* 41.

15. *I. Hell. Paphos* 42.

16. *I. Hell. Paphos* 40.

17. Polyb. 22.17.3, 7. Polybius relates that the ἀδικοδοξία of Polykrates kept Epiphanes from participating in the war. Büttner-Wobst (followed by Paton in the Loeb) put these events in 186/5, where Niese (*Gesch. Griech. u. Maked. Staat.* III, Gotha, 1903, p. 87) also put them. But if Epiphanes was born in October 209, he would have been 25 years old (as Polybius says he was at this time) in 184/3; if born in 210 (less likely), in 185/4. For a parallel in Polybius' reckoning of ages, see 3.11.5 and 15.19.3 with Walbank's comments *ad loc.*

18. Polyb. 18.55.7; cf. Suda (ed. Adler) IV, p. 165.

19. *I. Hell. Paphos* 46 for his son Ptolemy; *Mnemosyne* 6, 1938, p. 118 for his son Polykrates (at Lapethos).

Panathenaic contests in 190/189 and the years following.[20] A Hermione daughter of Polykrates was athlophore in 170/169, in the next reign, daughter more likely of the second Polykrates (who was a "first friend" under Epiphanes) than of the first, who would have been rather old by the time of Hermione's birth.[21]

3. PTOLEMAIOS OF MEGALOPOLIS [22]

Ptolemaios son of Agesarchos, Megalopolitan, followed Polykrates as *strategos* of Cyprus. His name indicates that his father was probably already in Ptolemaic service, and IJsewijn has suggested a possible candidate in the person of an eponymous military commander of the latter years of Euergetes' reign.[23] Ptolemaios was evidently a young man under Philopator, and he later wrote a scandalous history of that king's reign.[24] This did not, however, prevent his daughter Eirene from being eponymous priestess (probably for life) of Arsinoe Philopator at least from 199 to 171, and probably from the inception of the office in 203.[25] At about the same time Ptolemaios himself was sent by Agathokles to Rome as an ambassador.[26]

On Polykrates' return to Alexandria in 197/6, Ptolemaios was sent to replace him as *strategos* of Cyprus. Only one inscription attests his term on the island, a dedication of a statue of his daughter Eirene by her son Andromachos, at Kition.[27] Another inscription, from Kourion, is a dedication from the last few years of Epiphanes' reign of a statue of And[romachos] (cf. below) son of N[   ], who bears the rank of "first friend", by the city of Kourion.[28] It is possible, as Mitford argues, that this is the same Andromachos as the son of Ptolemaios' daughter Eirene.

---

20. References in *Pros. Ptol.*: 17211 (Polykrates' wife Zeuxo); 17210, 17209, and 17212 (daughters Eukrateia, Hermione, and Zeuxo).

21. IJsewijn, *De Sacerdotibus*, pp. 103-105, no. 117, leans toward the younger Polykrates, rightly I think.

22. *Pros. Ptol.* 15068 and 16944.

23. *De Sacerdotibus*, no. 88. Agesarchos: *Pros. Ptol.* 1825, ca. 225/4.

24. Jacoby, *FGrH* 161.

25. *Pros. Ptol.* 5104 and IJsewijn (note 23).

26. Polyb. 15.25.14.

27. First published by Mitford in *Archiv* 13, 1938, pp. 24-28, no. 12; its restoration (still highly dubious) and interpretation are defended by the editor in *Studi Calderini-Paribeni* II, pp. 163-176, where the author is identified as the grandson of the Megalopolitan, who is distinguished from Ptolemaios Makron.

28. *I. Kourion* 44.

It is probable, though our evidence is not conclusive, that Ptolemaios kept his post until the end of Epiphanes' reign in 180. Polybius mentions that the latter part of his life—like that of Polykrates—was full of licentiousness, but we have no means of placing this period chronologically.[29] We may tentatively assign Ptolemaios the entire period from 196 to 180. His title, like that of his predecessor, is *strategos* and *archiereus*.

4. PTOLEMAIOS MAKRON

The evidence for the *strategia* of Ptolemaios son of Ptolemaios son of Makron has been collected and discussed in detail by T. B. Mitford in an article whose main points and conclusions I set forth here.[30] From Polybius we know that a governor named Ptolemaios ruled Cyprus in Philometor's minority and turned over to him a large sum of money on his coming of age in 170/169, much in the way Polykrates had acted for Philometor's father. II Maccabees mentions a Ptolemaios called Makron who went over from Ptolemaic service to Seleucid but later killed himself in 163 on being accused of treason. Further, an inscription of Athens from the period honors a Ptolemaios *strategos* of Cyprus;[31] a Gortynian inscription honors a Ptolemaios son of Ptolemaios, brother of Ptolemaios the *strategos* of Cyprus.[32] Mitford further reads the erased name of a *strategos* in a Cypriot text as Ptolemaios son of Ptolemaios, Alexandrian.[33] From there a link is logically drawn to the appearance in the Delphic proxeny list of 188/7 of a Ptolemaios son of Makron and his sons, one of whom is a Ptolemaios, all Alexandrians.[34] From this assemblage of evidence, Mitford shows that Ptolemaios Makron was in fact Ptolemaios son of Ptolemaios son of Makron, Alexandrian, *strategos* of Cyprus from 180 to 168 (the only logical time after 169, Philometor's *anakleteria*, for a defection to Antiochus IV), a Seleucid official then for five years before his suicide. In his *strategia* seems to have been added the title "kinsman" of the king,

---

29. The Kourion inscription was communicated to the editors of *Pros. Ptol.* (note 22). On Ptolemaios' later life, Polyb. 18.55.8.

30. Mitford, note 27, above. I do not repeat all of his references, which will easily be found there.

31. *OGIS* 117 and 118, honoring him and a prominent Salaminian, were apparently passed on the same day.

32. *I. Cret.* IV 208.

33. *OGIS* 105; Mitford's text: note 27, p. 182.

34. *Syll.*³ 585.

which Ptolemaios bears in *OGIS* 105 along with those of *strategos* and *archiereus*. That text falls in the years 175 to 170, but the addition of "kinsman" may go back some years.

5. ARCHIAS [35]

For the troubled years 168 to 163, we do not know the name of any *strategos* of Cyprus. But in 163, it appears that Archias, the full name of whom is not preserved, took over the crucial post. He had accompanied Philometor to Rome in 164, and probably received the governorship on his return.[36] His titles are restored in his one known inscription, a dedication to him by the island garrison, placed at Old Paphos.[37] The restoration of his titles—the same as Makron's—is, however, very likely. Some years later he was detected trying to sell Cyprus to Demetrius I for 500 talents and thereupon hanged himself.[38] The date of his death is not certain; Otto suggested 158/7, Hill 155, and Bouché-Leclercq 154.

6. XENOPHON AND ANDROMACHOS

From the death of Archias to that of Ptolemy VI we have no certainly attested *strategoi*. There is, however, some difficult evidence to consider. An inscription of old Paphos is a dedication to Xenophon as *strategos* and *archiereus* (and presumably kinsman) by his wife and son An[dromachos]. The dating of the text is uncertain. The absence (and impossibility of restoring) of *nauarchos* in Xenophon's titles led Mitford to the conclusion that Xenophon must fall either before 142, when that title was given to Seleukos son of Bithys, or at some time thereafter when the *nauarchia* was not a possession of the *strategos*.[39] There are, however, no known gaps in the list of *strategoi* after 145 until some forty years later Soter seems to have abolished the office for the duration of his own reign in Cyprus. There are, however, two gaps earlier, 168-163 and ca. 157-152. The last years of Philometor are not possible, Mitford argues, because Xenophon's inscription is not defaced, whereas all those of Philometor's last *strategos* are (see below).

---

35. *Pros. Ptol.* 15037.
36. Diod. 31.18.1; Polyb. 33.5.
37. *I. Hell. Paphos* 52.
38. Polyb. 33.5. Mitford gives bibliography on the date in commenting on Archias' inscription (note 37).
39. *I. Hell. Paphos* 60. The *nauarchia*, Mitford, *Seleucus*, pp. 147-148.

On the other hand, An[dromachos] Xenophon's son seems to bear the title [τῶν ὁμοτίμων] τοῖς συγγενέ[σι], which is not otherwise attested before 124.[40] One must in all justice echo Mitford's statement that the problems this inscription raises cannot yet be solved.

For the years 152-145 a similarly complicated situation presents itself. A man named Andromachos served as an ambassador to Rome for Philometor in 154; an Andromachos was also tutor to Ptolemy Eupator.[41] It is not unreasonable to suppose (as Mitford has suggested) that these are the same. It is also possible that Eupator's tutor was the *strategos* who dedicated statues of Philometor and Eupator at Kourion [42] and Paphos [43] during the years 152-150, and another statue of Eupator at Paphos in the same years.[44] From the Kourion statues and the statue of Eupator at Paphos three and four lines of text have been erased, obviously carrying the name of the dedicant. It is obvious that *damnatio memoriae* after the death of Philometor is responsible for the erasure, and almost equally certain that someone of this importance and frequency of appearance on Cyprus can be none other than the *strategos*. That the *strategos* who honored Eupator was that prince's tutor is possible, though by no means assured.

It is in no case certain that this Andromachos is to be identified with either the An[dromachos] son of Xenophon or the son of N[   ] or with the son of Eirene, grandson of Ptolemaios son of Agesarchos (who may be the same as the son of N[   ]), though the last at least would have been of mature age at this time and an experienced courtier and official.[45]

7. SELEUKOS SON OF BITHYS

Seleukos son of Bithys, who bore the dual citizenship of Rhodes and Alexandria,[46] and his two successors have been discussed in

40. Mitford, *Helenus*, p. 107, n. 40.
41. The ambassador, Polyb. 33.11.4; the tutor, *Anthol. Palat.* VIII 241.
42. *OGIS* 123 and 125.
43. *I. Hell. Paphos* 56.
44. *I. Hell. Paphos* 57.
45. Mitford's restoration of *I. Kourion* 44, on which part of his reconstruction of careers is based, is weak and not founded on certain association of fragments; cf. my remarks on the inscription, *Phoenix* 27, 1973, p. 216.
46. P. M. Fraser, *Ptol. Alex.* II, p. 167, n. 333, thinks Rhodian was an honorary citizenship.

detail by Mitford, and only a summary need be given here.[47]
Seleukos was honored by Delphi in 157/6 for his help to a Delphic
mission to a king who can only be Philometor. Yet shortly after
that king's death 12 years later, Seleukos appears as "kinsman"
of his former master's rival brother Euergetes II, *strategos* of Cyprus,
honored by officers of his garrison on the island through his son
Theodoros, whose statue is thus erected (144-142). In 142, not long
before Euergetes' marriage to Cleopatra III, the title of *nauarchos*,
admiral, was added to Seleukos' designation, and he bore it in
some ten inscriptions of the years 142-131. By 131 he must have
been nearly 70, and his disappearance from the scene needs no
special explanation. His children and grandchildren were still
prominent in Alexandria in 105 (cf. below under Theodoros).

8. KROKOS

For Krokos, successor of Seleukos, we have three inscriptions,
two of them from the years in which Euergetes was at war with
Cleopatra II. These may be dated to 131-124. A third must fall in
or just after 124, when Euergetes had been reconciled with Cleopatra
II. Krokos' titulature is of considerable interest. In the earliest
inscription he is "kinsman", *strategos, nauarchos, archiereus*, and
epistates. But *nauarchos* is given first, evidently because of the
extraordinary situation at the moment, while *epistates* is unparalleled
on Cyprus. Mitford takes it to refer to his control over the capital,
Paphos, for which a commandant is never otherwise attested, a
control it was well to make explicit during these years. In the next
inscription the same titles remain, except that Krokos' title of
strategos is now qualified with *autokrator*, evidently a strengthening
of his hand for the crisis. By 124, Krokos is no longer *epistates*,
but he has added the epithet *hypermachos*, champion (of the king).[48]

9. THEODOROS

According to Mitford's chronology, Theodoros succeeded Krokos
about 123 and used a normal titulature of kinsman, *strategos*,

---

47. Mitford, *Seleucus*. References here are in general given only to this
article, where previous bibliography and in general the most convenient
editions of these texts are to be found. The many problems of this article do
not significantly affect its usefulness to us here.

48. Mitford, *Seleucus*, pp. 156-163, presents the inscriptions of Krokos
and a detailed interpretation.

nauarch, and *archiereus*, except that his first inscription has the
title *strategos autokrator*, evidently a carry-over from Krokos' term
of office.[49] In all of his inscriptions where a motive formula is
present, the sovereigns are Euergetes and both Cleopatras. It has
recently been claimed, on the basis of a new inscription, that
Theodoros' *strategia* fell before rather than after that of Krokos, or
before 131 rather than after 124.[50] The inscription, published by
P. Roesch, gives the normal titulature for Theodoros except that
by their genitive case the words τοῦ συγγενοῦς must modify Theodoros' father Seleukos, not Theodoros himself. Theodoros is thus left
without any court rank at all, an anomalous situation. Koenen
has pointed out the oddity of this feature and remarked that if
we do not know Theodoros' court rank in this text it will not do
to reconstruct his career on the basis of an assumption about it,
as Roesch has done.[51] Koenen suggests the possibility of an error
of the lapicide whereby the accusative has become genitive under
the influence of the neighboring Σελεύκου, and there is great plausibility in the suggestion.

The end of Theodoros' *strategia* depends on the dates of Helenos'
period of office, to which we must now turn. Theodoros himself,
once thought to have died about 118, is now known to have been
alive in 105/4, when he is attested as priest for life of Cleopatra III
in the prescript of a papyrus.[52]

10. HELENOS

For Helenos, also, we have a study by Mitford, whose conclusions
I follow.[53] He was present in Cyprus during Theodoros' *strategia*,
honoring now a son of Theodoros, now perhaps Theodoros himself.[54] In the first of these inscriptions Helenos has the rank τῶν
ἰσοτίμων τοῖς πρώτοις φίλοις, in the second τῶν ὁμοτίμων τοῖς συγ-

49. *Seleucus*, p. 139, no. 16.
50. P. Roesch, *Rev. arch.* 1967, pp. 225-238.
51. Roesch assumed that Theodoros was a first friend, since he is not
called kinsman, and that this inscription must therefore be Theodoros' first
as *strategos*, and his appearance as *strategos autokrator* therefore his last.
L. Koenen, *ZPE* 5, 1970, pp. 79-80, n. 29, has effectively criticized this
construction.
52. Published by L. Koenen, *ZPE* 5, 1970, pp. 61-84.
53. Mitford, *Helenus*; there is here, too, much uncertainty of restoration
in many texts.
54. *Helenus* 1 and 2.

γενέοι. Shortly afterward, Helenos himself became *strategos*, though perhaps not for long (ca. 118-117, Mitford suggests). He was honored by the priests of Paphian Aphrodite as kinsman, *strategos*, *archiereus*, and *archikynegos*, chief huntsman. He was not, however, nauarch.[55] He himself erected a statue of Ptolemy son of king Ptolemy, who can only be Soter.[56] Soter himself, however, was promoted to being *strategos* not long before his father's death. When he returned to Egypt, Helenos remained behind. Soter, like Helenos, had held the title chief huntsman.[57]

For the first two years of Soter's joint reign with Cleopatra III, Helenos remained on Cyprus as tutor of Ptolemy Alexander, who was the *strategos*. When Alexander declared himself king in 114, however, Helenos once again became *strategos*.[58] From the period 114-107 he is honored in three inscriptions as kinsman, *tropheus* of the king, *strategos*, and *archiereus*.[59] In 107/6, triumphant in his *strategia* and restored to an island from which Soter had been expelled, he added the title nauarch, and appears as a priest of Cleopatra III.[60] After this year, however, he disappears from view.

For the years 124-106, then, the following approximate sequence may be taken as established: Theodoros, 123-118; Helenos, 118-117; Ptolemy Soter, 117/6; Ptolemy Alexander, 116-114; Helenos, 114-106.

II. THE STRATEGIA AFTER 105

We know of no holders of the position of *strategos* of Cyprus during the 17 years Ptolemy IX ruled in that island before returning to Egypt to expel his brother. Indeed, an *antistrategos* Potamon son of Aigyptos is attested for these years, being also overseer of the mines.[61] The admiralty was vested, at least for the first few years, in Stolos of Athens.[62] When in 88 Ptolemy Alexander, expelled from Egypt, tried to capture Cyprus, he was defeated by Soter's admiral Chaereas; it is possible that the *nauarchia* and *strategia*

---

55. *Helenus* 3 and 4.
56. *Helenus* 4.
57. Mitford, *Seleucus* 29.
58. *Helenus* 5.
59. *Helenus* 6-8.
60. *Helenus* 9, where the analogous Brussels papyrus is also discussed.
61. *OGIS* 165.
62. "Stolos the Admiral," *Phoenix* 26, 1972, pp. 358-368.

had once again been united in a governor when the king was no longer resident on the island.[63]

On the death of Ptolemy IX in 80, Cyprus passed to his bastard son Ptolemy, who was in turn dispossessed by the Romans in 58. From before 43 B.C., however, we have evidence that the island was at least nominally returned to Ptolemaic rule by Antony. Appian names a Serapion who ruled Cyprus for Cleopatra VII in 43, and Dio mentions a Demetrios serving under Antony in 39.[64] Most recently, an inscription discovered at Salamis has given us a dedication of a statue of Stasikrates son of Stasikrates, who had served as gymnasiarch of Salamis during the fourteenth year, erected by Diogenes son of Noumenios, ὁ συ[γ]γεγὴς τῶν βασιλέων and *strategos* of the island and Cilicia. The date is year 15, Hathyr 19, or 19 November 40.[65] The old administrative system had been restored in form if not in spirit in the last days of the dynasty.

---

63. Porphyry, *FGrH* III, p. 721, F 7.3.

64. Serapion: Appian, *B.C.* 4.61; Demetrios: Dio 48.40.6.

65. Published by J. Pouilloux in Πρακτικὰ τοῦ πρώτου διεθνοῦς Κυπρολογικοῦ Συνεδρίου I, Nicosia, 1972, pp. 141-150, with a detailed study of this period in the history of Cyprus. Pouilloux concludes that in fact Ptolemaic control of Cyprus and parts of Cilicia goes back before 43, perhaps as far as 48.

THE GARRISON OF CYPRUS:
THE RANK AND FILE

For convenience of reference I provide here a list of non-Cypriots known from inscriptions of Cyprus in the Hellenistic period and generally presumed to be either rank and file members of the military forces on the island or their dependants. It is not certain that all were soldiers, but the probabilities overall are high: the Ptolemies maintained a large garrison on Cyprus for many years, and there is no alternative to explain a substantial number of foreigners buried in Cyprus without further explanation. Two recent publications make it possible for me to refer solely to them for the inscriptions in which these people appear, save in cases where I have had to add a critical note to correct errors or add supplemental information. Each person who appears in the *Pros. Ptol.* is given his number there, and each one appearing in Ino Nicolaou's study of the ethnics in Hellenistic Cyprus (part one, Κυπριακαὶ Σπουδαί 31, 1967) is given the number which she assigns (abbreviated by *N*). The list is subdivided by chronological groups, but more specific information about date is provided, particularly where there is some disagreement in the publications. An asterisk after a date in "N" indicates that a photograph is given in Nicolaou's article.

Name and patronymic	Pr. Pt.	Nic.	ethnic	provenance	date
			IV/III Centuries		
Ἀγαθοκλῆς Μάκρωνος	15279	35	Πέρσης	Kition	IV/III P, III N
Νικογένης	15581	7	Καλύμνιος	Amathous	IV/III P, III N
Σύμμαχος Ἀρχεσιλάου	15635	10	Ἄνδριος	Soloi	late IV P, N *
Ἀπελλῆς	15417	see note 1			
			III Century		
Στράταγος Ἀντέου	15628	1	Ἀρκας	Kition	III N *
Διονύσιος	15414	17	Καρδιανός	nr. Salamis	III P, N *
Εὔμηλος Κιλλέους	15458	29	Ἀστένδιος	Amathous	III P, N *
Εὔφράνωρ	15467	40	Κυρηναῖος	Kition	III P, N *
Μέλαν(θ)ος	15553	12	Κρῆς	Amathous?	III P, N *
Νίκων Θευγένους	15581a	15	Βυζάντιος	Soloi	III P, N *
Μελαινεὺς Κυδρογ[ένους]	15552		Ἀστένδιος	Pal. Paphos	ca. 250 P
Κλεαινέτη Τιμοσθένους				nr. Salamis	see note 2
Ἀριστόλαος Παυσανίου	15341	4	Θεσσαλος	Akanthou	III N [3]
no name given		6	Νάξιος	Amathous	III N
Ἀπολλᾶς Φιλότου		9	Ἀμφιπολίτης	Salamis	III N *
Καλλίστιον Ὀνομακλέους	15317a	14	see note 4	Akanthou	III N *
Βίων		16	Ἀντάνδριος	Kition	III N
Σμώρνος		24	Ξάνθιος	Kition	III early N
Θεύδωρος Ζήνωνος		27	Ἀράδιος	Kition	III N
Ἀγαθοκλῆς Μίκκου [5]	15785	33, 37	Ἀλεξανδρεύς	Soloi	300-250 P, III N *
Θευδαίσιος		39	Εὐεσπερίτης	Amathous	III N
			224/3		
Ἀντίοχος Φίλωνος	15311		Μυτιληναῖος	Pal. Paphos	224/3: a group
Διόδοτος Ζηνοδότου	15404		Καλυανδεὺς	Pal. Paphos	of contributors
Διονύσιος Νικάνορος	15413		Λιμυρεύς	Pal. Paphos	to the oil supply
[Εὐέπ]ης Εὐέπου	15456		Μυρεύς	Pal. Paphos	of the gymnasium

Εὐπόλεμος Εὐπολέμου	15462	Παταρεύς	Pal. Paphos	224/3
Καλλιπίδης Καλλιπίδου	15517	Παταρεύς	Pal. Paphos	224/3
Λύσανδρος Λυσάνδρου	15549	Ξάνθιος	Pal. Paphos	224/3
Τεισέας Φι[λάνο]ρος	15646	Τλωεύς	Pal. Paphos	224/3

Late III/Early II

Ἀγαθοκλῆς	28	15280	[Ἀσπ]ένδιος	Kition	III end P, III/II N
Ἀγέμαχ[ος]	5	15282	Θέσσαλος	Kition	same
[Κά]λλιππος	2	15518	Καρύστιος	Kition	same
[Τέ]ρπνος	19	15647	Θραῖξ	Kition	same
Ἐράτων		15441	note 6	Crete	ca. 220-200 P
Ἡλιόδωρος Ἀθηνοδώρου	32	15477	Σιδώνιος	Amathous	III/II P, N
Κλέων Διονυσίου	32	15533	Σιδώνιος	Amathous	III/II P, N
Σωγένης Σωκράτους		15638	[ ]ιτεύς	Soloi	III or II, P
Ἀπολλώνιος	3			Amathous	III/II N (guess)
Εὐφράτις Διασθένους	11		note 7	Amathous	III/II N (guess)
Τελεσσὼ Ἱεροφατίδου	31		note 8	Amathous	III/II ? N

1. This man never existed, but his unqualified appearance in *Pros. Ptol.* has given him a specious hold on life. The first publication of the stone by Ino Nicolaou in *BCH* 84, 1960, p. 261, gave the text as an epitaph for the Aeolian woman Myrto, from Elaie (ἀπ' Ἐλαίης Αἰολίδος). She dated it to the second-third centuries A.D., a date revised by J. and L. Robert in *Bull. épig.* 1961, 827, to the third century B.C. In 1961 also appeared Mitford's independent and first (as he thought) publication of the text, reading Apelles' name where ἀπ' Ἐλαίης had been before (*AJA* 65, 1961, p. 138). The Roberts, reporting on the inscription again in *Bull. épig.* 1962, 342, maintained the first text, and the published photographs vindicate that reading. Apelles is therefore to be deleted from *Pros. Ptol.*

2. A Chalkidian woman, perhaps a military dependant. Published in *RDAC* 1968, p. 82, no. 16, where the date is given as early third century.

3. I place this man here with hesitation, on the basis of Mrs. Nicolaou's dating; but I do not see her reasons for so dating a stone apparently now lost and published without photograph.

4. A Byzantine woman, also perhaps a dependant.

5. Mrs. Nicolaou gives the patronymic as Μιχίχου, but the Roberts (*Bull. épig.* 1969, 603) read Μίχχου on the photograph.

6. A Cretan who remained on Cyprus after serving in armed forces there: *I. Cret.* II 5.19.2, 5; cf. M. Launey, *Armées hellénistiques*, pp. 679-680.

7. Euphratis was a Cretan woman.

8. Telesso was an Aspendian woman. On the correct form of her patronymic, *Bull. épig.* 1969, 603.

Name and patronymic	Pr. Pt.	Nic.	ethnic	provenance	date
Κοσμία Ἀριστάρχου	15392	34	note 9	Amathous	III/II ? N
missing	15692	36	Βαβυλώνιος	Amathous	III/II ? N
Νίκων		41	Λίβυς	Amathous	III/II ? N
II Century					
Δημήτριος Δημητρίου		18	Λυσιμαχεύς	unknown	II N
------ Μενίππου		21	Ἰλλύριος	Soloi?	ca. 150 P, II N*
missing		23	Μιλήσιος	Kition?	II N
Ἀπολλώνιος Λέοντος	15328	26	Στρατονικεύς	Lapethos	note 10
------ Δημάρχου	15689	30	Ἀσπένδιος	Amathous	II N
Μενέδημος Ζωίλου	15559		Ἀσπένδιος	nr. Salamis	ca. 190-170 P
Μενέδημος Μενεδήμου	15560		Ἀσπένδιος	nr. Salamis	ca. 190-170 P
Δίων Φαι[	15249		Κ[	Nea Paphos	ca. 150
Οἰνέας Ἑρμωνος	15583			Nea Paphos	ca. 150
Διόδωρος Διονυσίου	15406			Nea Paphos	ca. 150
Ἀντίφιλος Νεοπτολέμου	15313			Nea Paphos	ca. 150
Δημήτριος Δημητρίου	15391			Nea Paphos	ca. 150
Ἀρτεμίδωρος Μενελάου	15353			Nea Paphos	ca. 150
Ἐπιγένης Ἀρτεμιδώρου	15433			Nea Paphos	ca. 150
Ἀλέξανδρος Ἀσκλητ[ιοδόρου]	15293			Nea Paphos	ca. 150
Ἀρτεμίδωρος Μενεκράτους	15352			Nea Paphos	ca. 150
Εὔνομος Κλεάνορος	15460			Nea Paphos	ca. 150
Μενέστρατος Πτολεμαίου	15562			Nea Paphos	ca. 150
Πτολεμαῖος Τιμοχρέοντος			Ἀθηναῖος	Salamis	II N[11]
Τιμοχρέων Τιμοχρέοντος			Ἀθηναῖος	Salamis	II N[11]
------ς	15708		Ταρσεύς	Salamis	116-81?
------ς	15709		Ἀντιοχεύς	Salamis	116-81?
--]εαγένους	15691		Ἐφέσιος	Salamis	116-81?
--ς Ἀριστομένους	15686		Μαγνής	Salamis	116-81?
------ Πλουτάδου	15699		Ὑπαιπηνός	Salamis	116-81?
------ Δι]ονυσίου	15690		Ἀντιοχεύς	Salamis	116-81?
--]υσ Εὐβίοτος Εὐβιότου	15433		unknown	Salamis	116-81?

9. An Arabian woman.

ADDENDA

General: Throughout this book I have used the chronology proposed by A. E. Samuel and P. W. Pestman for the reign of Ptolemy II. This still seems to me a reasonable procedure, since no systematic alternative has been offered. But recent work, in particular an unpublished paper by Richard Hazzard of Toronto, indicates that Philadelphos' retroactive dating of his reign may have come at the end of his first year, so that 283/2 was year 1 but 282/1 was year 4. If this is so, dates up to year 16 of this reign would need to be altered from those given in this book to two years later.

P. 106: Dr. Michael Wörrle (Munich) has kindly informed me that an inscription which he is to publish contains a letter of Ptolemy II to Telmessos written in his year 4 (279/8 on Samuel's system, 282/1 if this is incorrect [see above], i.e. shortly after his accession). This and the inscription mentioned below provide considerably greater antiquity for Ptolemaic control in these cities, in accord with the evidence of Lissa.

P. 108: Dr. Wörrle also will publish a decree of Limyra from year 36 of Ptolemy I (288/7) honoring two Ptolemaic functionaries.

P. 193: A new study of the IIA coins from Alexandria by O. Mørkholm appears in *ANS Mus. Notes* 20, 1975, pp. 7-24, written as part of the preparations for publishing the large Paphos hoard. Several important chronological conclusions are argued.

INDEX OF GREEK WORDS

Except for some titles beginning with ἐπί, proper nouns are indexed principally in the Index of Subjects.

INDEX OF SUBJECTS

This index is selective and does not duplicate information given in the table of contents, which should be used as the primary guide to the discussion of principal subjects, especially places. Greek words used in transliteration are indexed here, but their occurrences in Greek characters are indexed in the Index of Greek Words.

INDEX OF DOCUMENTS AND AUTHORS CITED

I. ANCIENT AUTHORS

II. INSCRIPTIONS

III. Papyri

I5